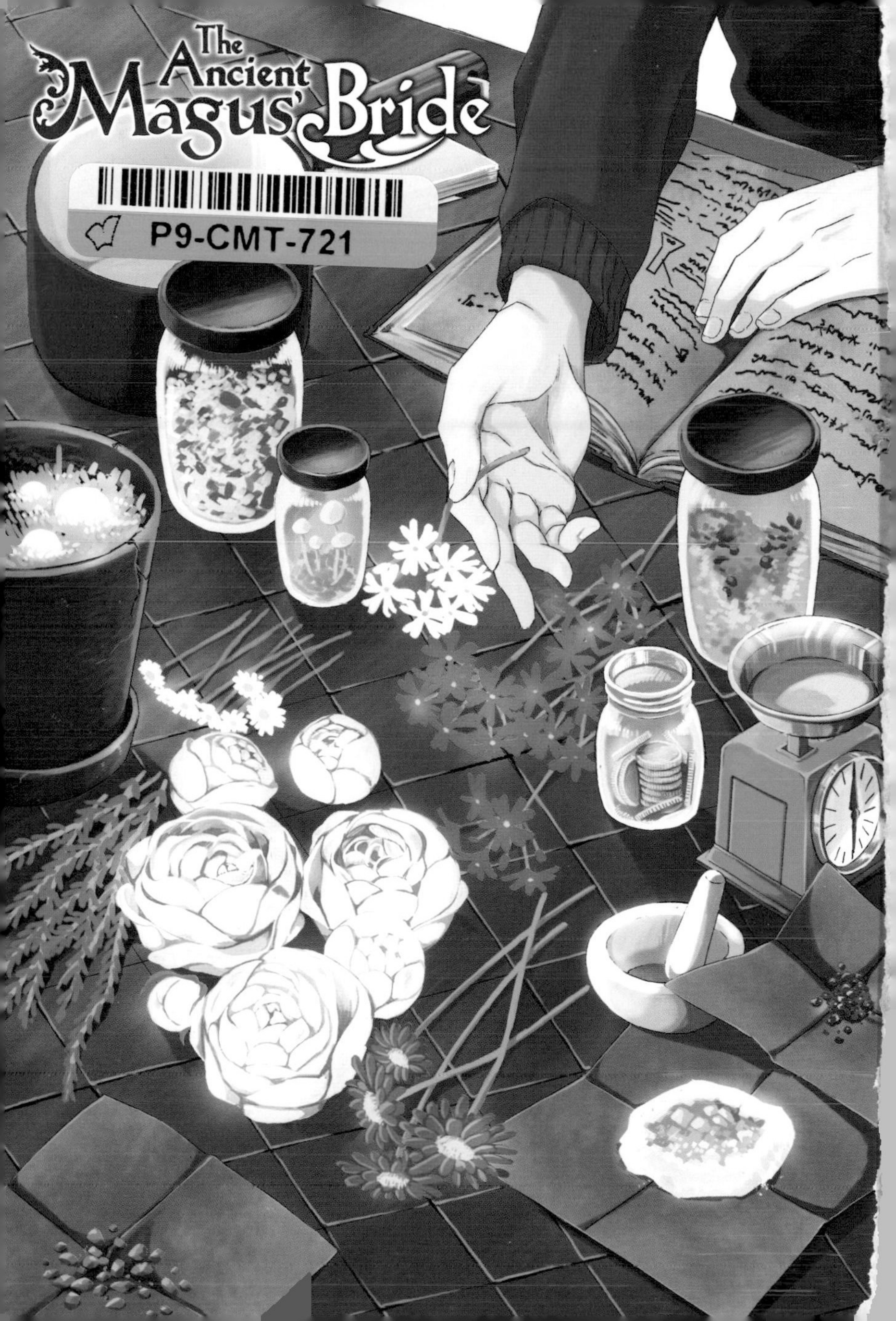
The Ancient Magus' Bride

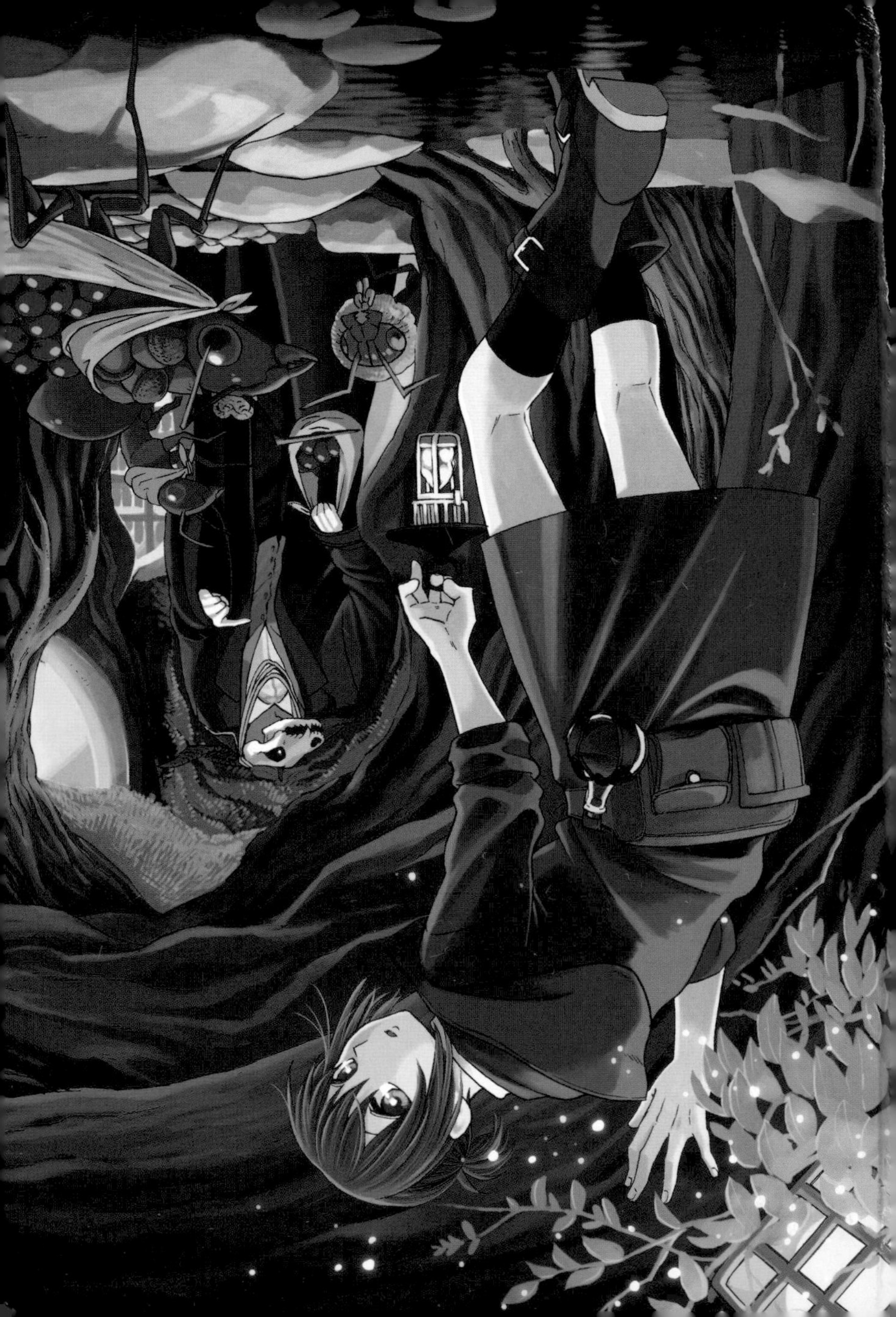

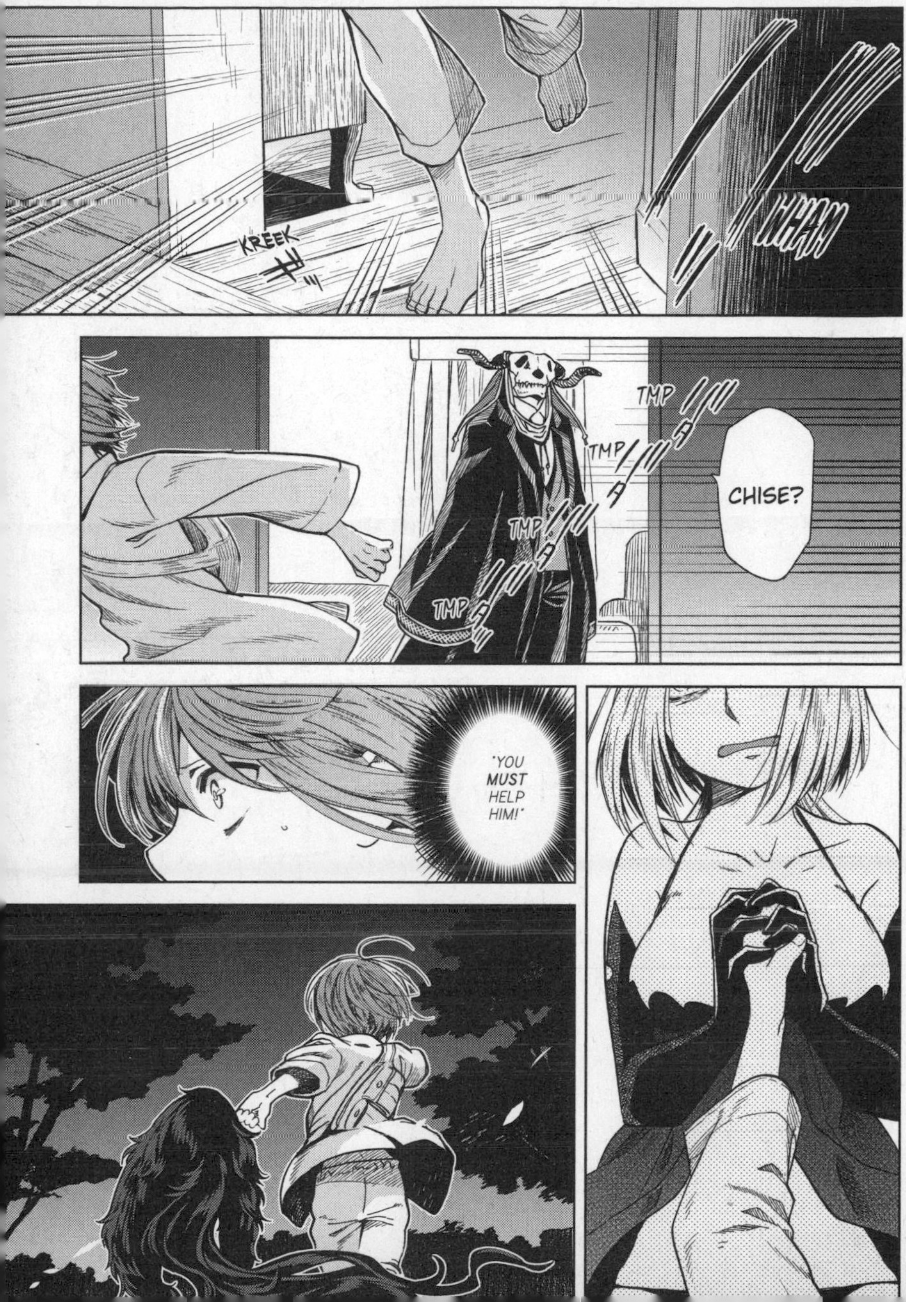
KREEK
CHISE?
TMP
TMP
TMP
TMP
"YOU MUST HELP HIM!"

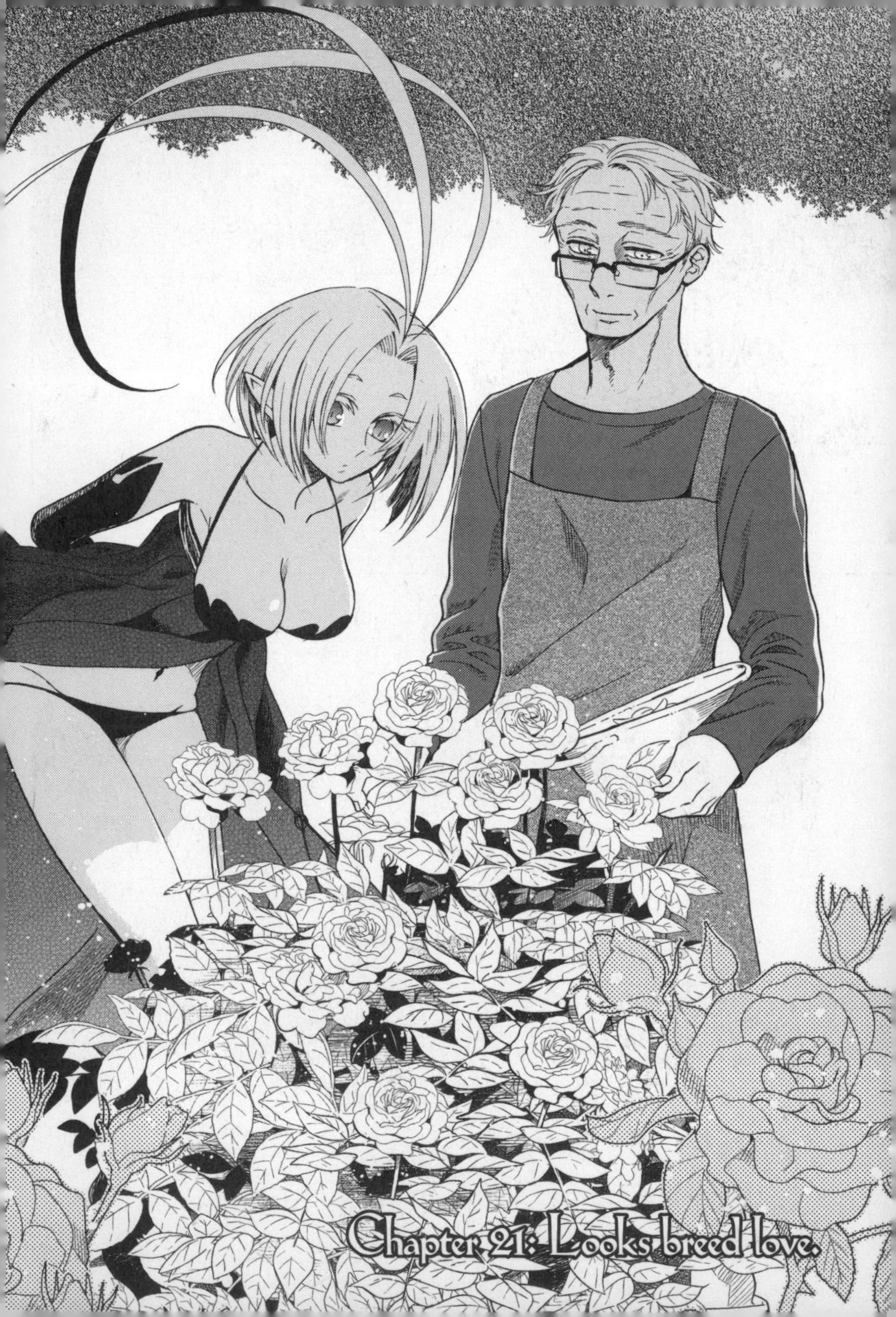
Chapter 21: Looks breed love.

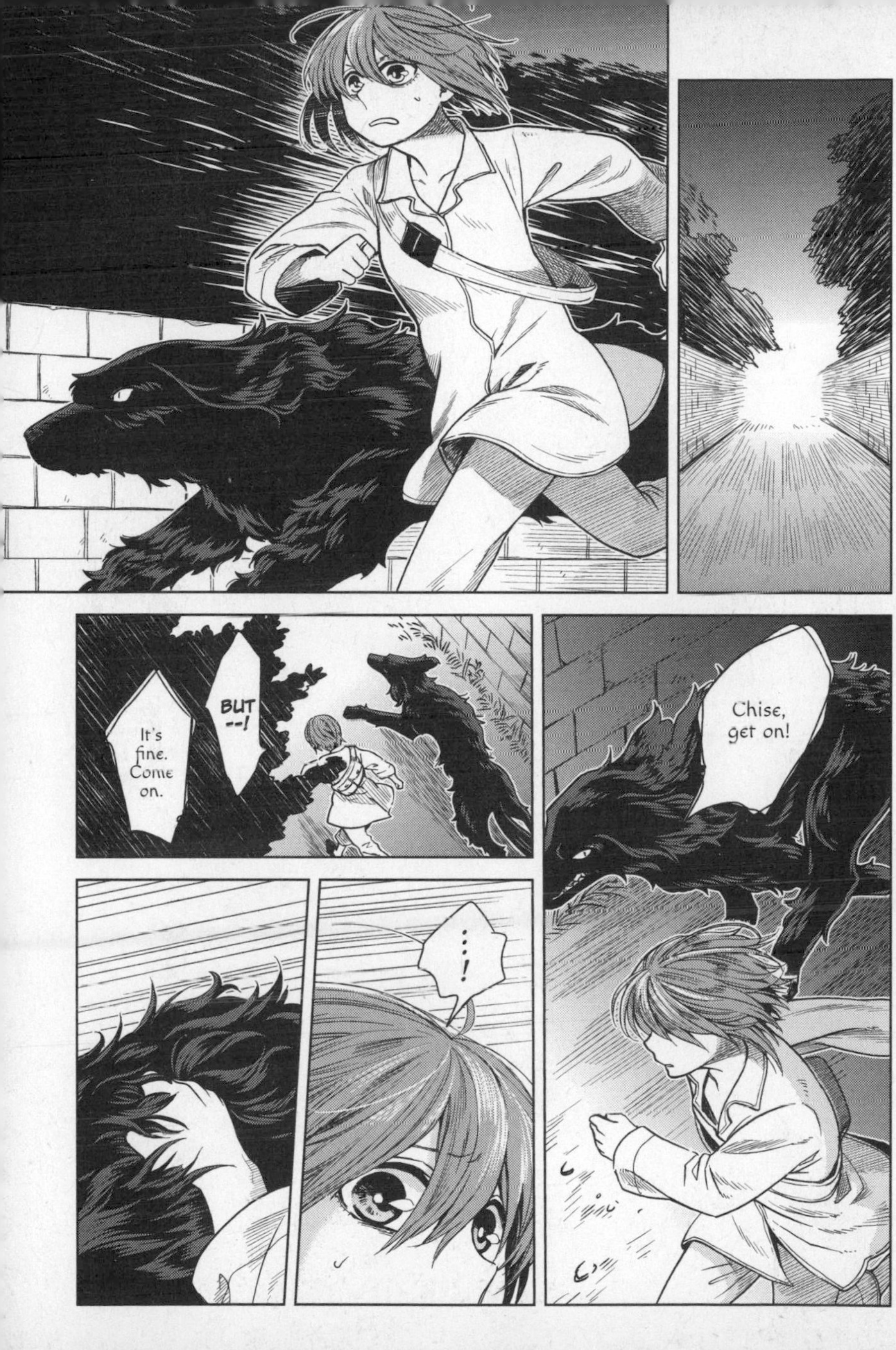
Chise, get on!
BUT --!
It's fine. Come on.
...!

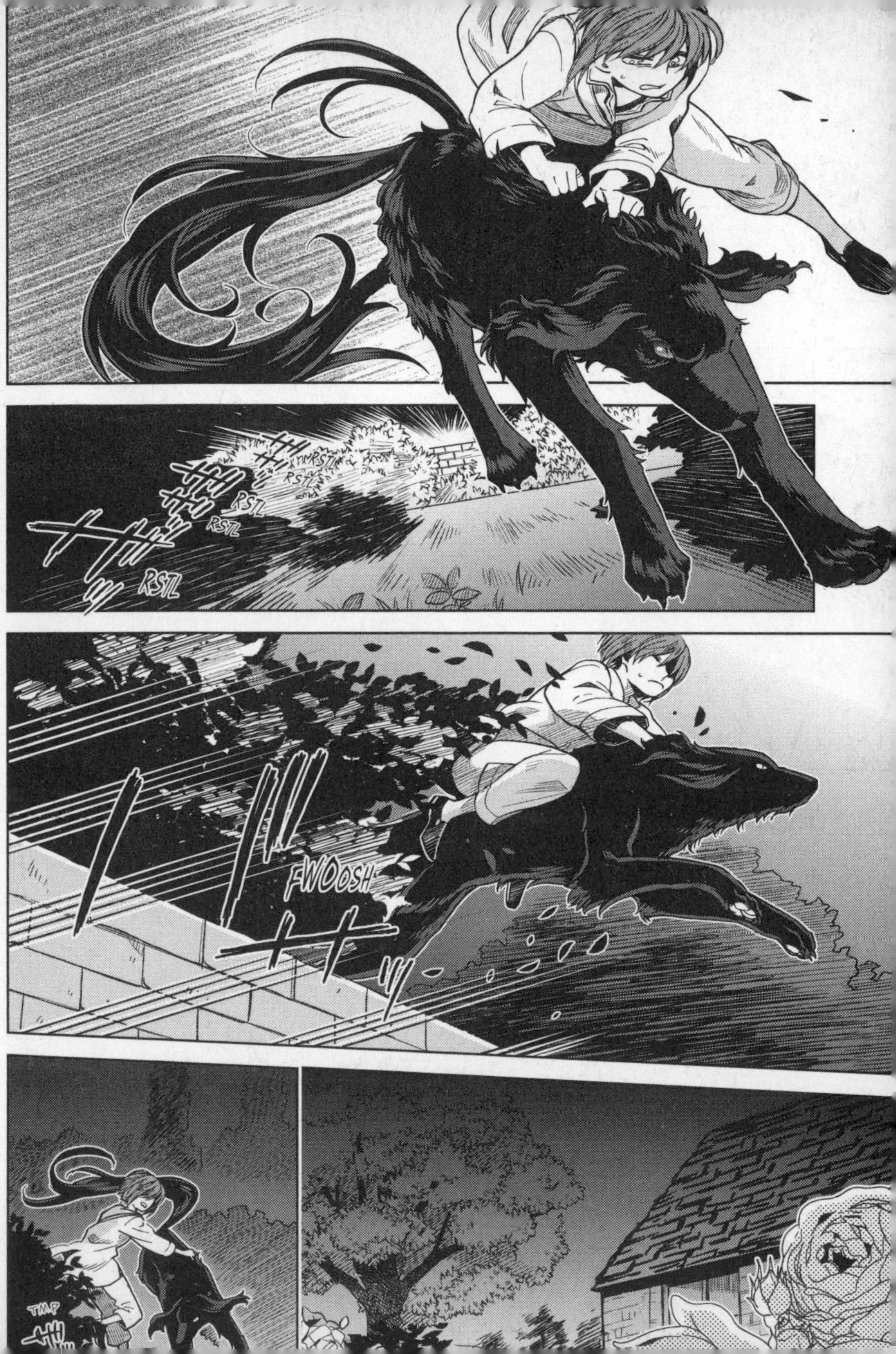
RSTL
RSTL
RSTL
RSTL
RSTL
FWOOSH
TMP

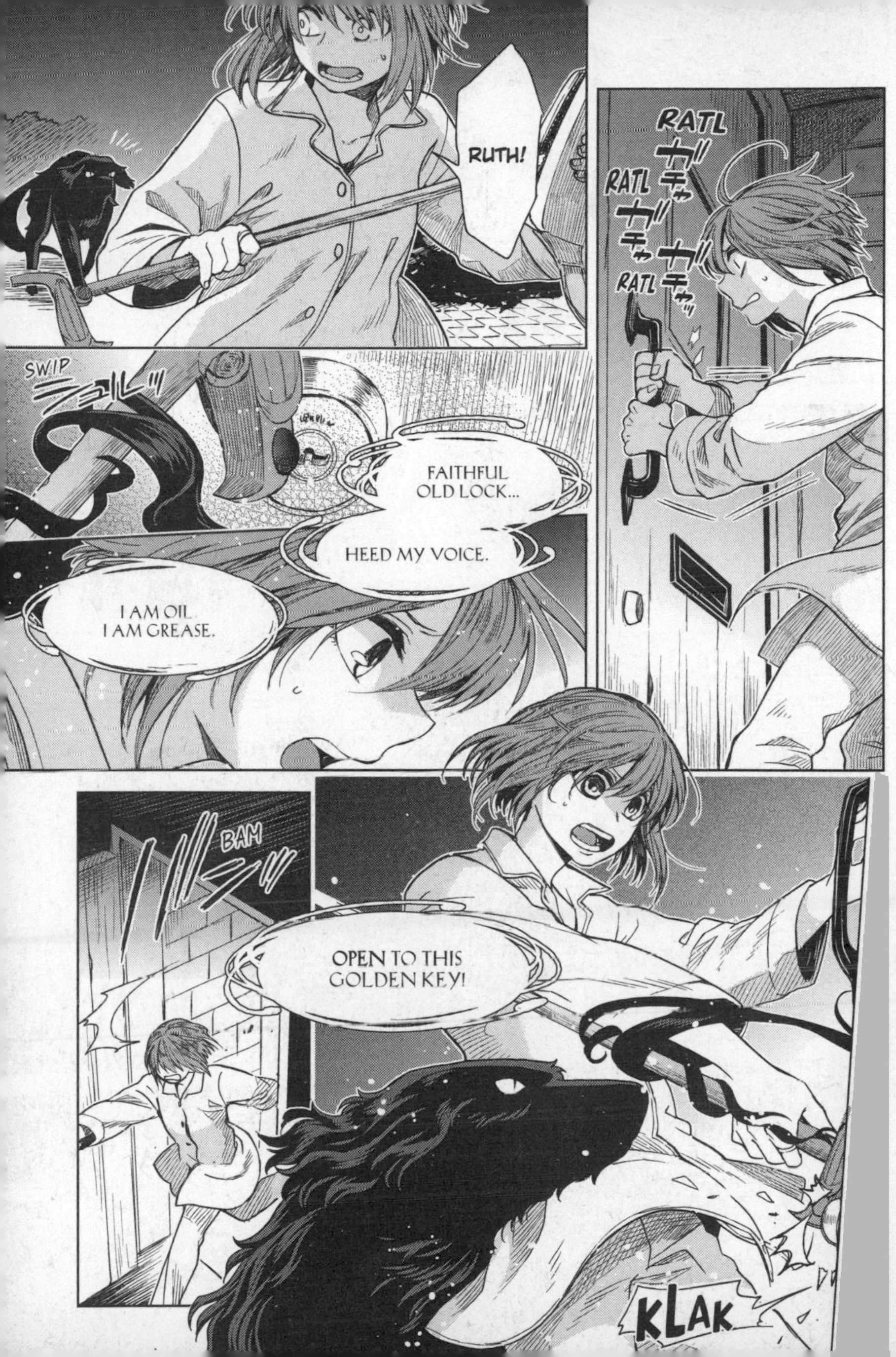
RATL
ガチャ
RATL
ガチャ
RATL
ガチャ
RUTH!
SWIP
FAITHFUL OLD LOCK...
HEED MY VOICE.
I AM OIL. I AM GREASE.
OPEN TO THIS GOLDEN KEY!
BAM
KLAK

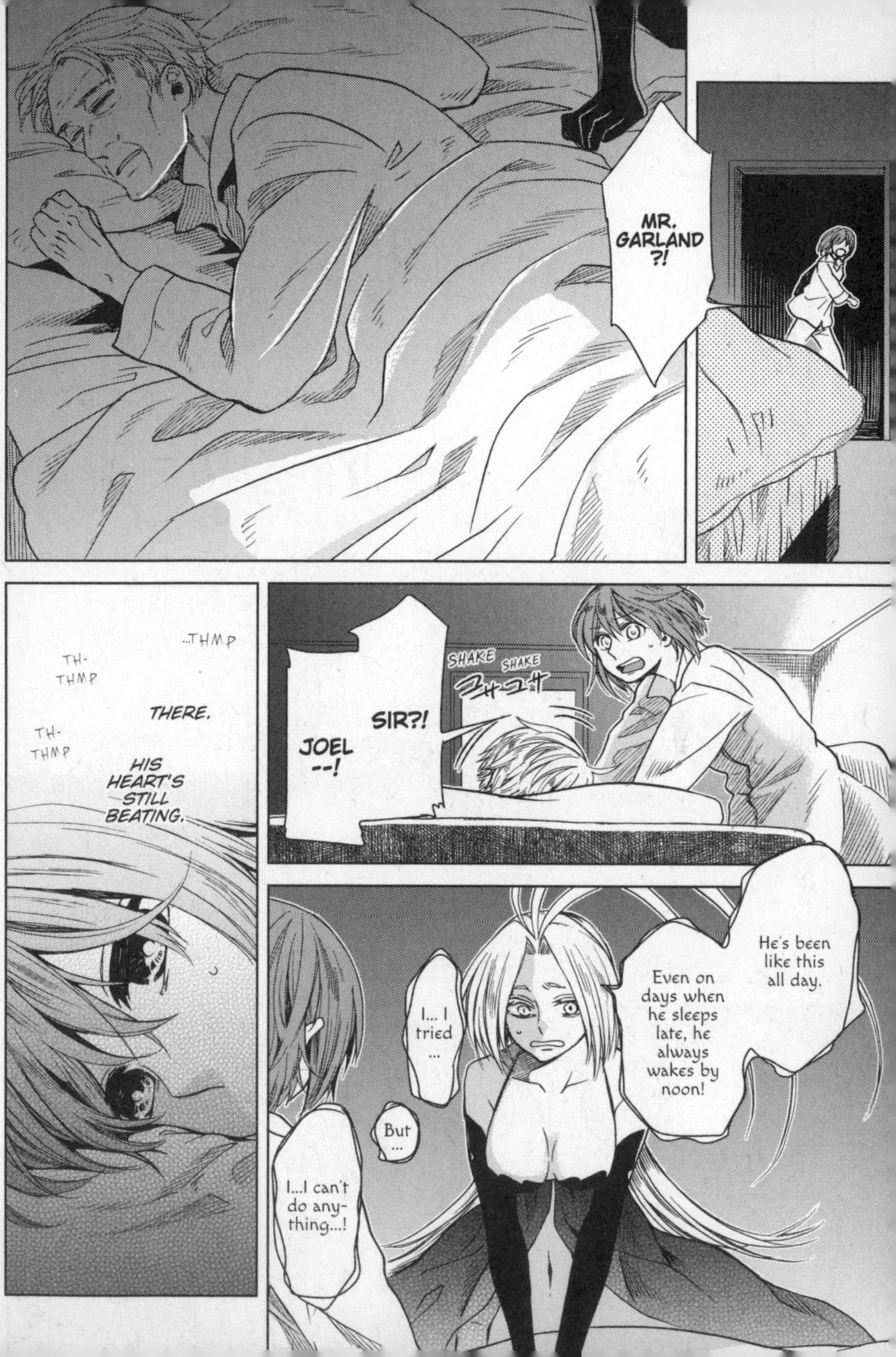
MR. GARLAND ?!
SHAKE SHAKE
SIR?!
JOEL --!
He's been like this all day.
Even on days when he sleeps late, he always wakes by noon!
I... I tried ...
But ...
I...I can't do any-thing...!
...THMP
TH-THMP
THERE.
TH-THMP
HIS HEART'S STILL BEATING.

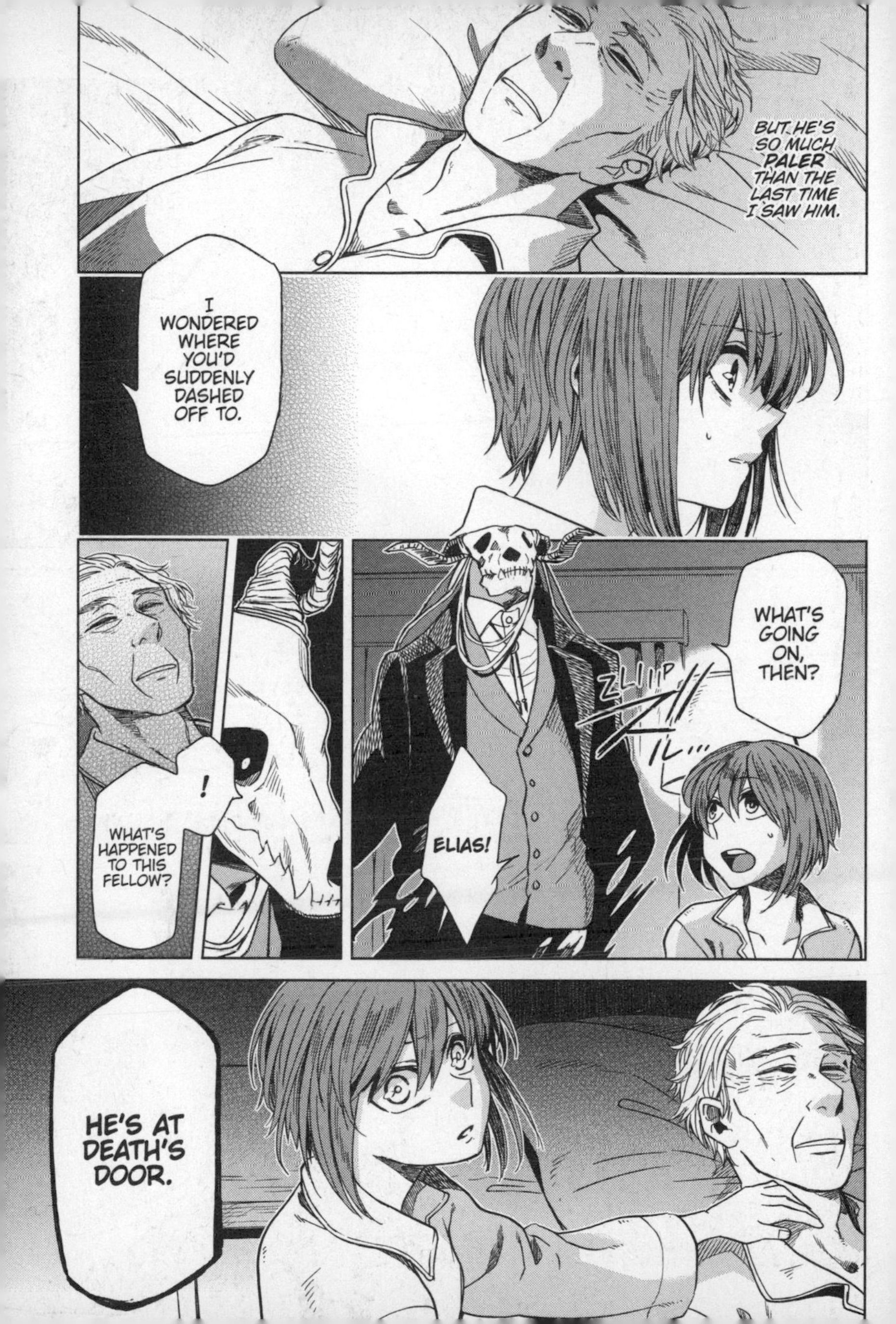
BUT HE'S SO MUCH PALER THAN THE LAST TIME I SAW HIM.
I WONDERED WHERE YOU'D SUDDENLY DASHED OFF TO.
WHAT'S GOING ON, THEN?
ZLIIIP
ル…
ELIAS!
!
WHAT'S HAPPENED TO THIS FELLOW?
HE'S AT DEATH'S DOOR.

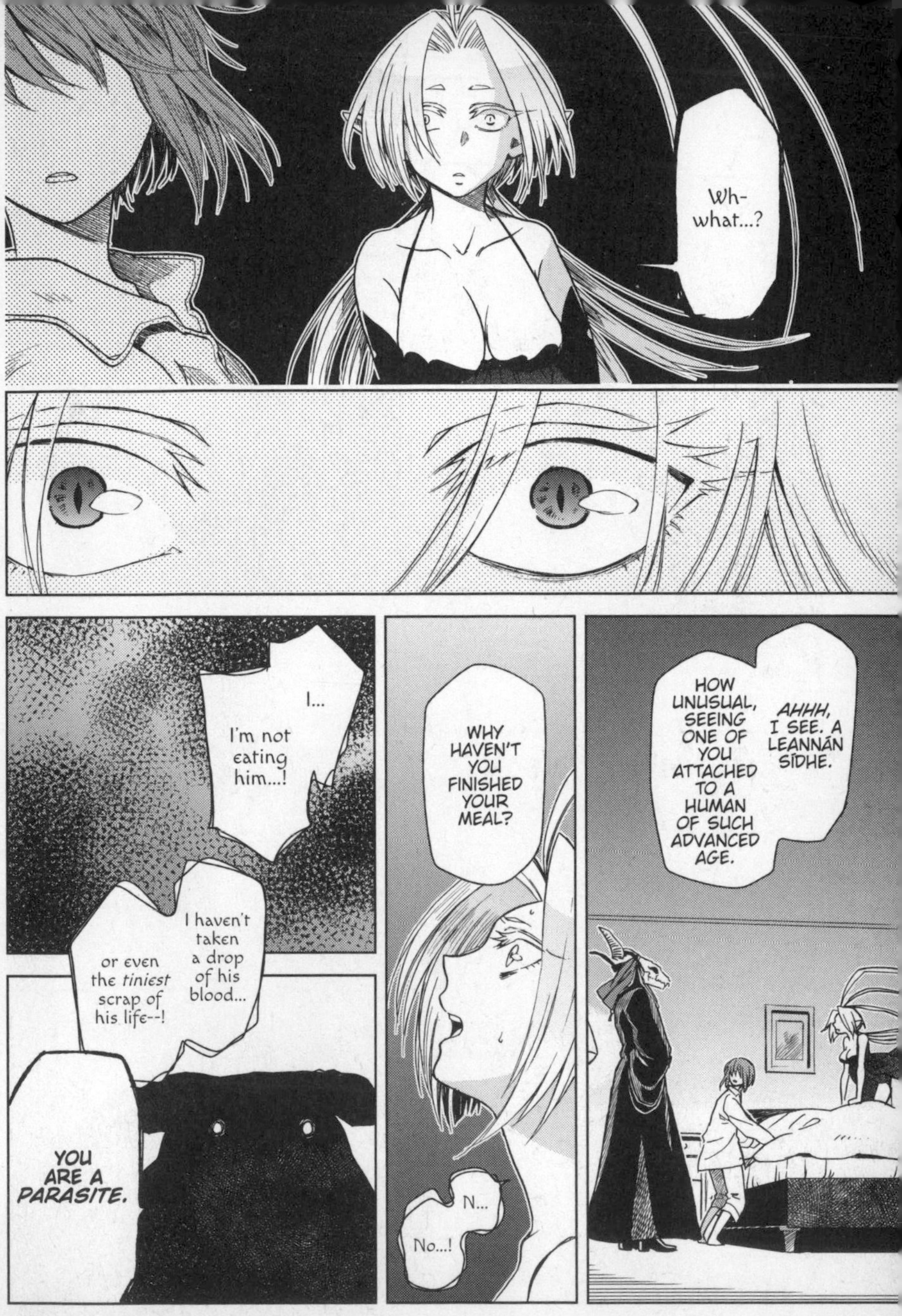
Wh-what...?
AHHH, I SEE. A LEANNÁN SÍDHE.
HOW UNUSUAL, SEEING ONE OF YOU ATTACHED TO A HUMAN OF SUCH ADVANCED AGE.
WHY HAVEN'T YOU FINISHED YOUR MEAL?
N...
No...!
I...
I'm not eating him...!
I haven't taken a drop of his blood...
or even the *tiniest* scrap of his life--!
YOU ARE A PARASITE.

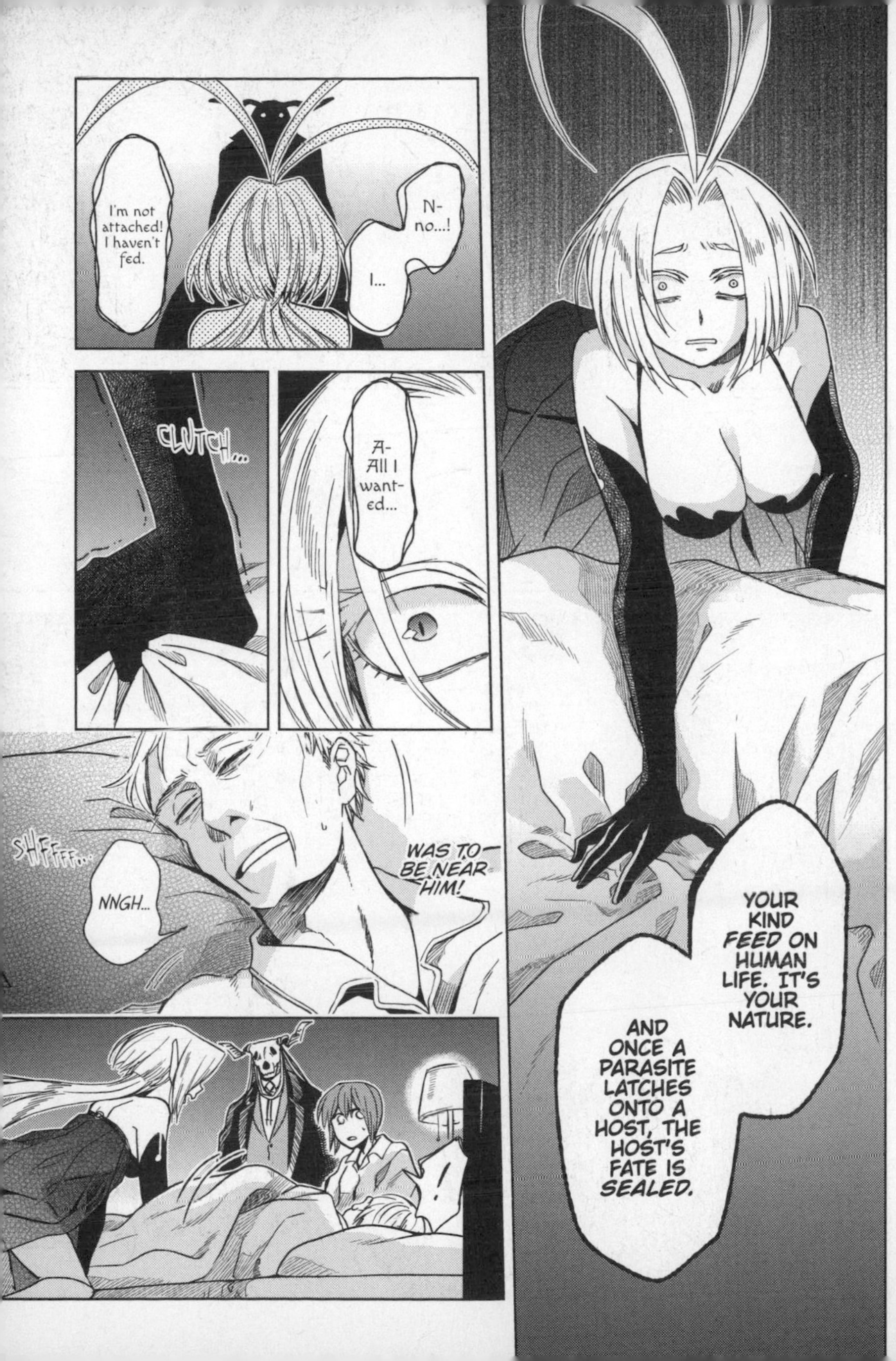
YOUR KIND FEED ON HUMAN LIFE. IT'S YOUR NATURE.
AND ONCE A PARASITE LATCHES ONTO A HOST, THE HOST'S FATE IS SEALED.
N- no...!
I...
I'm not attached! I haven't fed.
A- All I wanted...
CLUTCH...
WAS TO BE NEAR HIM!
NNGH...
SHFFFF...

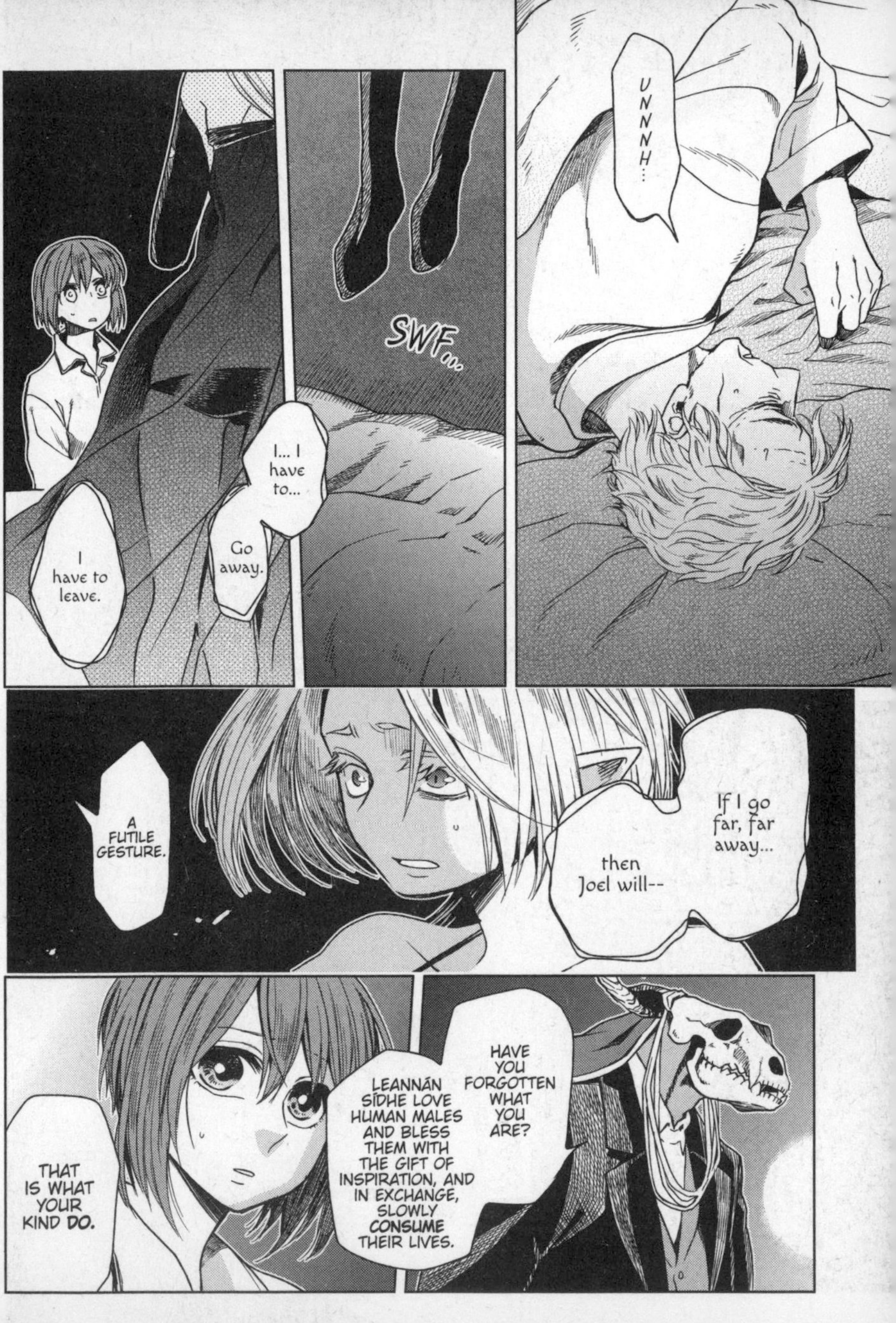
UNNNH...
SWF...
I... I have to...
Go away.
I have to leave.
If I go far, far away...
then Joel will--
A FUTILE GESTURE.
HAVE YOU FORGOTTEN WHAT YOU ARE?
LEANNÁN SÍDHE LOVE HUMAN MALES AND BLESS THEM WITH THE GIFT OF INSPIRATION, AND IN EXCHANGE, SLOWLY CONSUME THEIR LIVES.
THAT IS WHAT YOUR KIND DO.

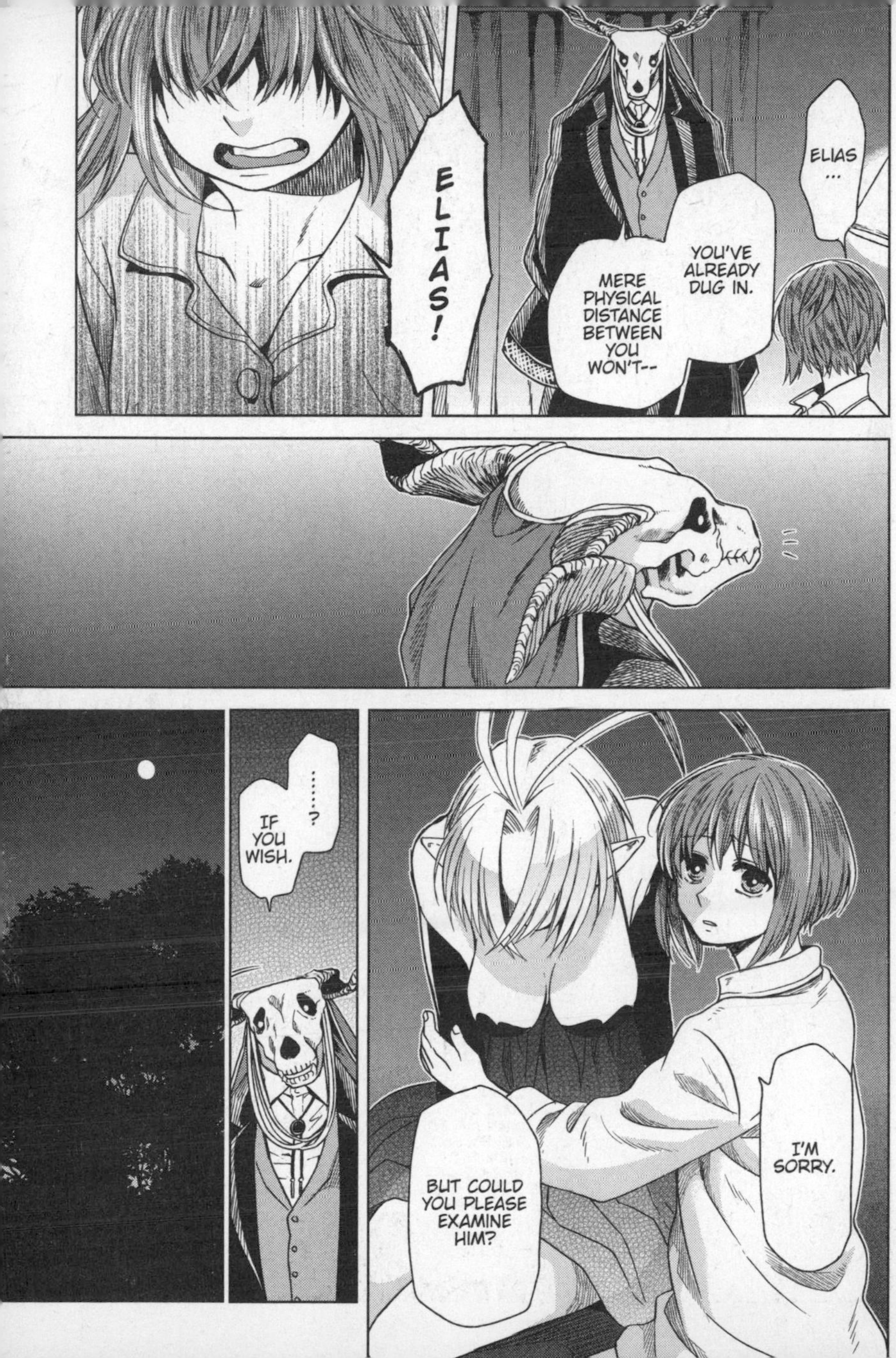
ELIAS...
YOU'VE ALREADY DUG IN.
MERE PHYSICAL DISTANCE BETWEEN YOU WON'T--
ELIAS!
I'M SORRY.
BUT COULD YOU PLEASE EXAMINE HIM?
......?
IF YOU WISH.

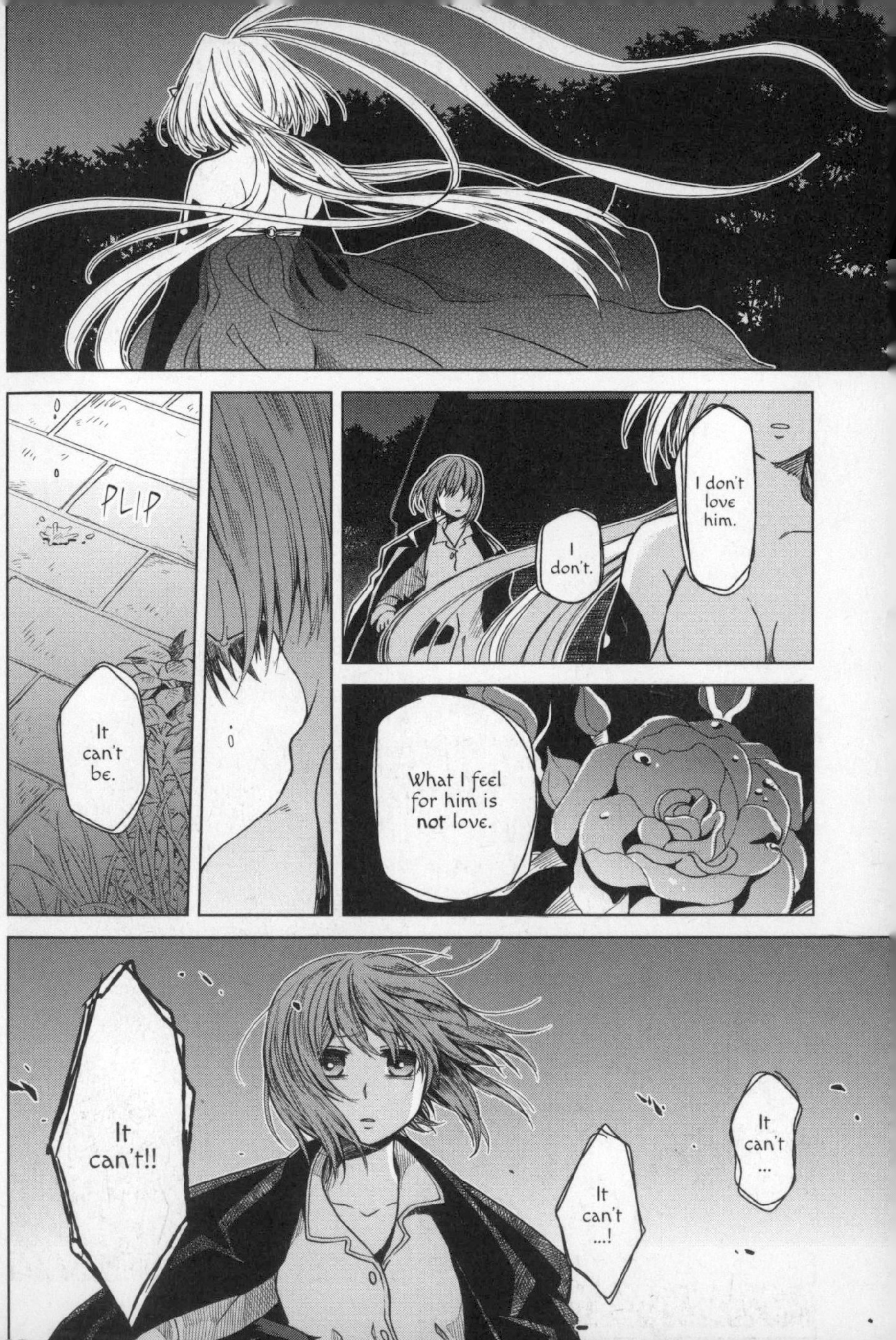
I don't love him.
I don't.
What I feel for him is **not** love.
PLIP
It can't be.
It can't ...
It can't ...!
It can't!!

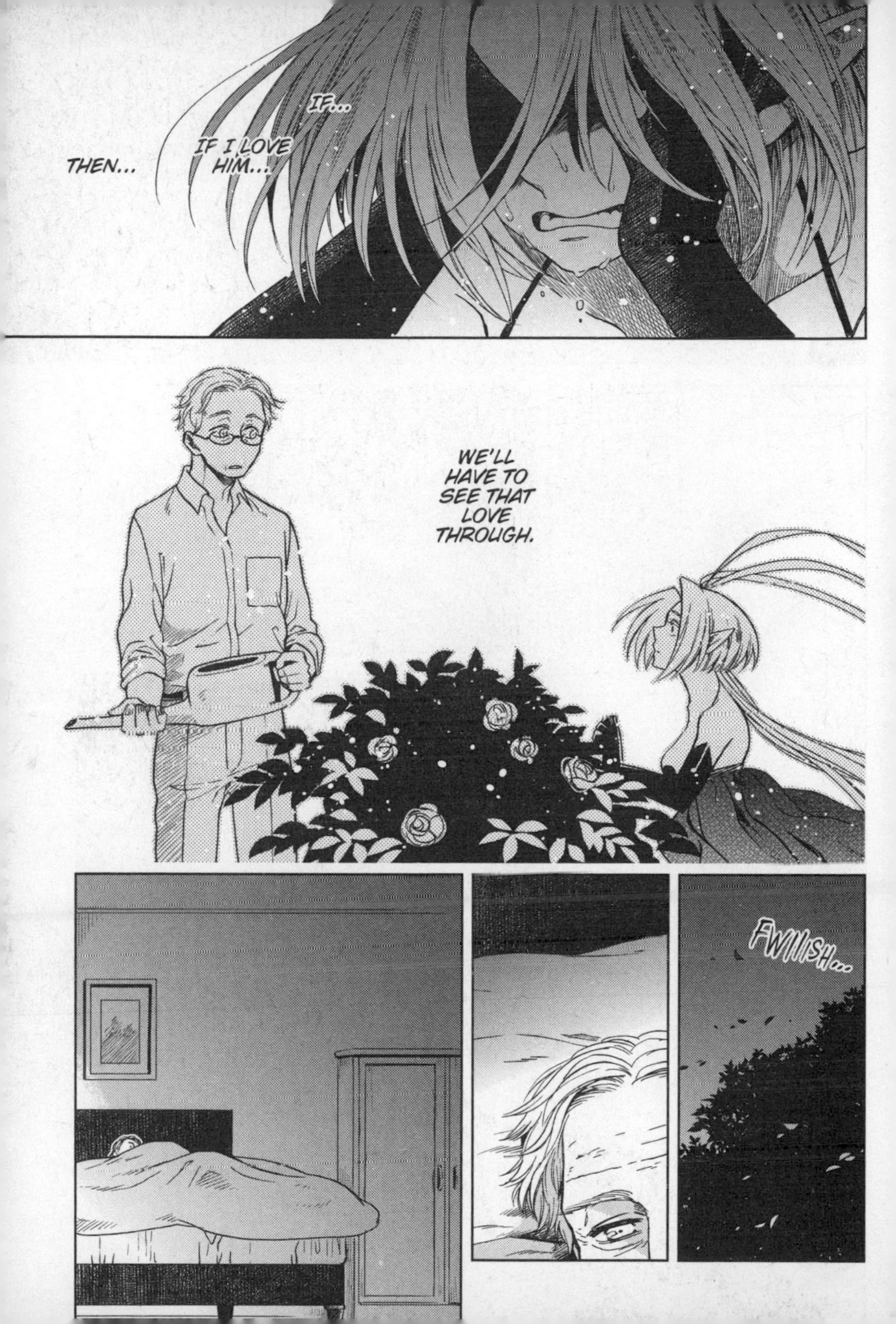
IF...
IF I LOVE HIM...
THEN...
WE'LL HAVE TO SEE THAT LOVE THROUGH.
FWIISH...

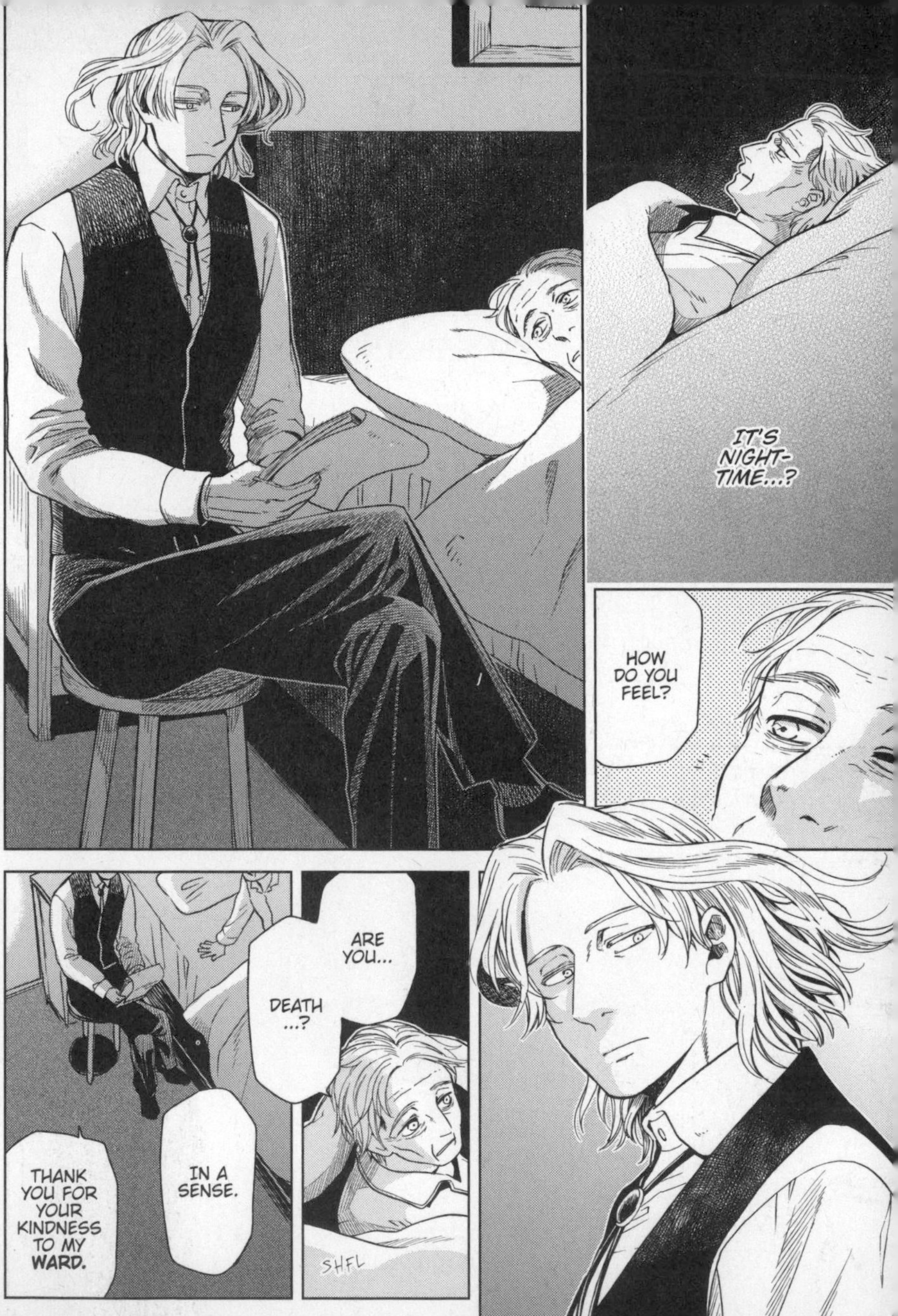
IT'S NIGHT-TIME...?
HOW DO YOU FEEL?
ARE YOU...
DEATH ...?
SHFL
IN A SENSE.
THANK YOU FOR YOUR KINDNESS TO MY WARD.

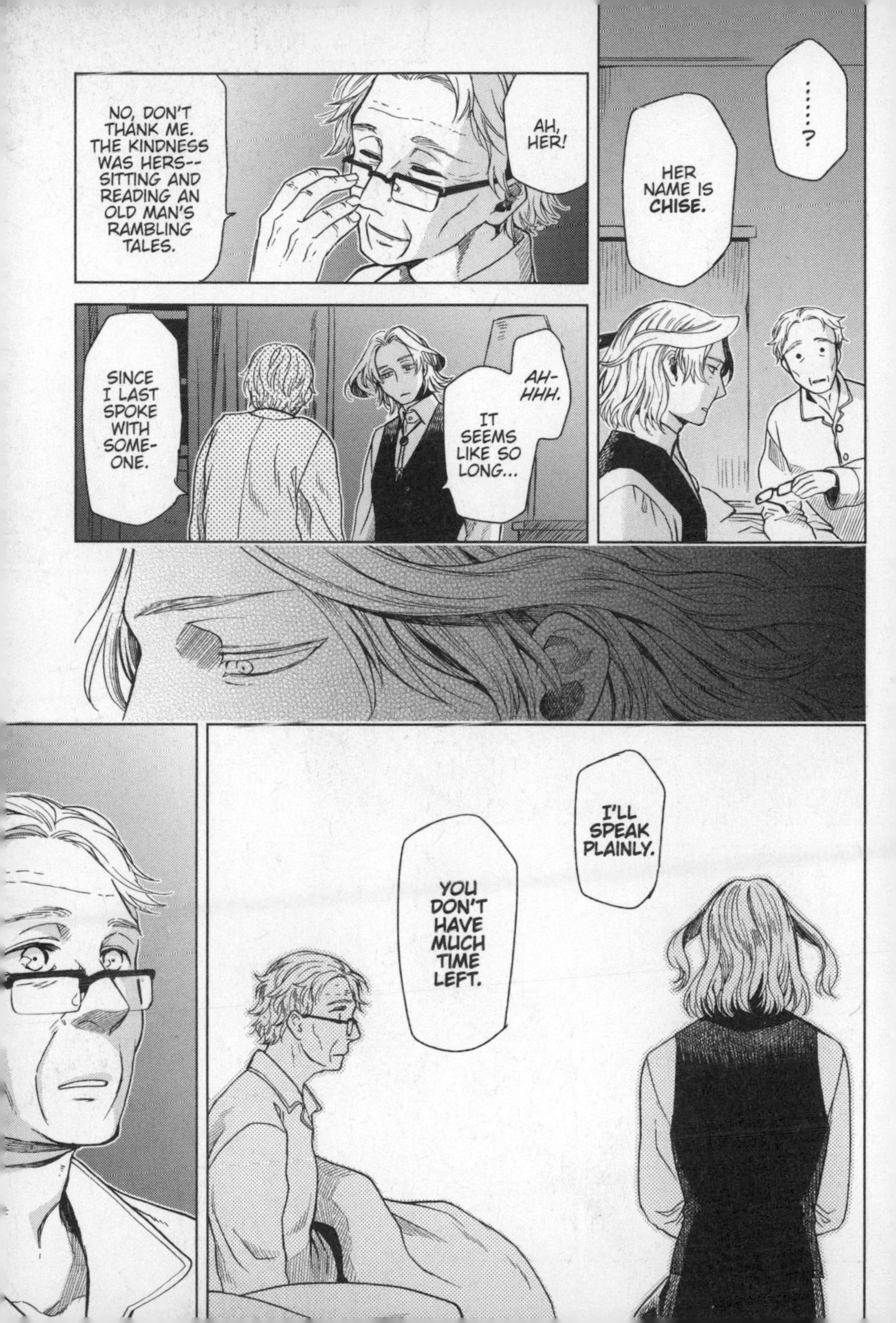
......?
HER NAME IS CHISE.
AH, HER!
NO, DON'T THANK ME. THE KINDNESS WAS HERS--SITTING AND READING AN OLD MAN'S RAMBLING TALES.
AH-HHH.
IT SEEMS LIKE SO LONG...
SINCE I LAST SPOKE WITH SOME-ONE.
I'LL SPEAK PLAINLY.
YOU DON'T HAVE MUCH TIME LEFT.

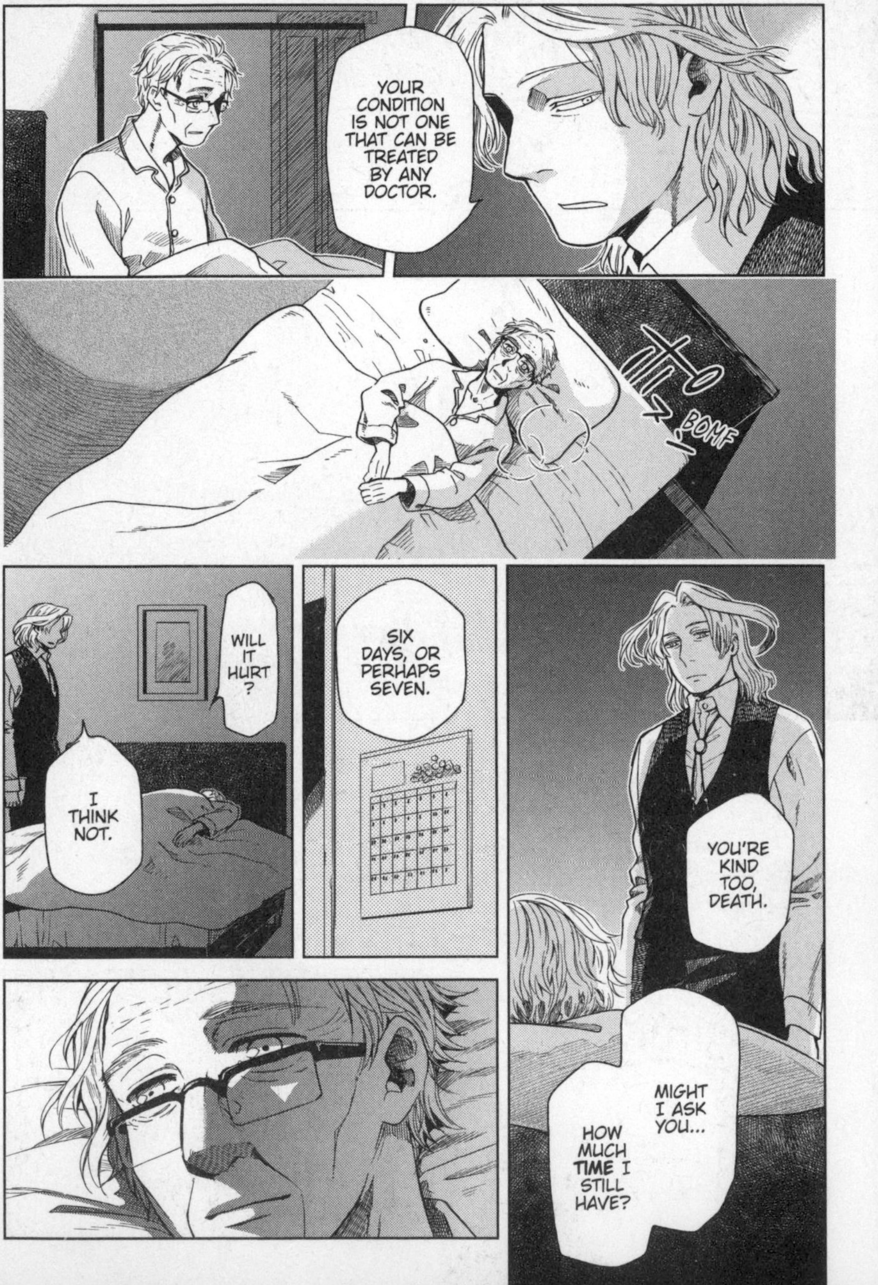
YOUR CONDITION IS NOT ONE THAT CAN BE TREATED BY ANY DOCTOR.
BOMF
YOU'RE KIND TOO, DEATH.
MIGHT I ASK YOU...
HOW MUCH TIME I STILL HAVE?
SIX DAYS, OR PERHAPS SEVEN.
WILL IT HURT?
I THINK NOT.

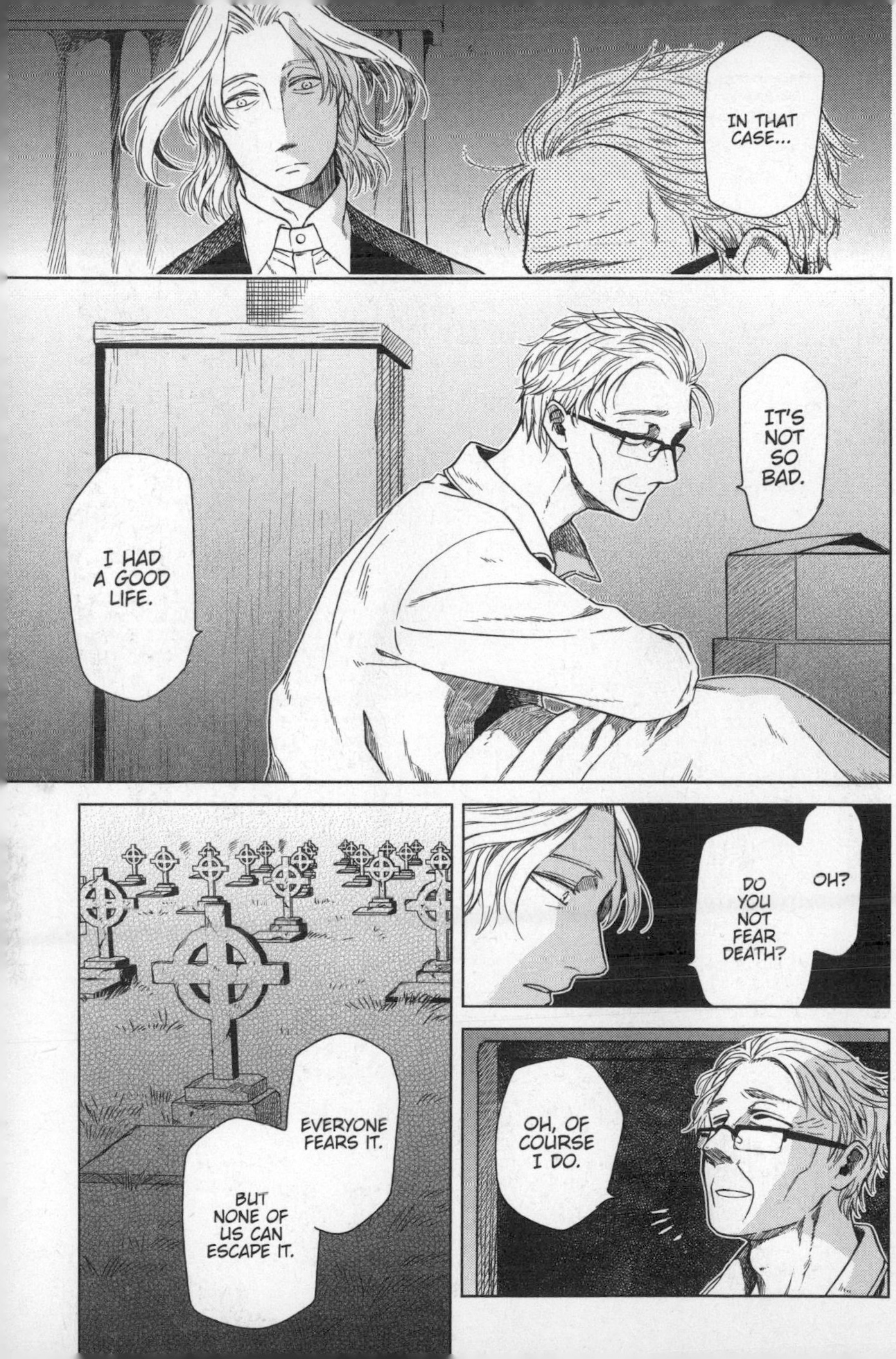
IN THAT CASE...
IT'S NOT SO BAD.
I HAD A GOOD LIFE.
OH?
DO YOU NOT FEAR DEATH?
OH, OF COURSE I DO.
EVERYONE FEARS IT.
BUT NONE OF US CAN ESCAPE IT.

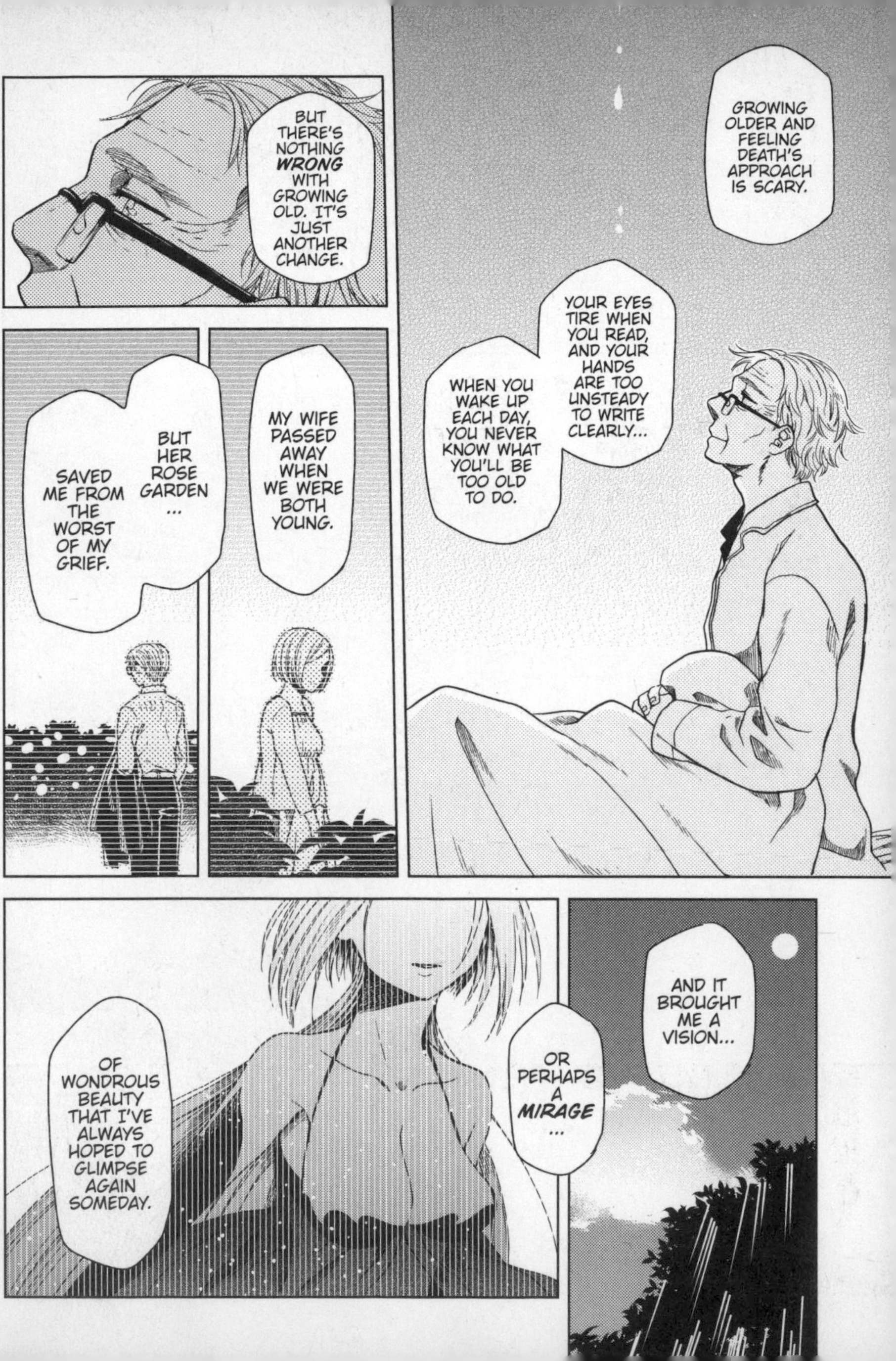
GROWING OLDER AND FEELING DEATH'S APPROACH IS SCARY.
YOUR EYES TIRE WHEN YOU READ, AND YOUR HANDS ARE TOO UNSTEADY TO WRITE CLEARLY...
WHEN YOU WAKE UP EACH DAY, YOU NEVER KNOW WHAT YOU'LL BE TOO OLD TO DO.
BUT THERE'S NOTHING WRONG WITH GROWING OLD. IT'S JUST ANOTHER CHANGE.
MY WIFE PASSED AWAY WHEN WE WERE BOTH YOUNG.
BUT HER ROSE GARDEN ...
SAVED ME FROM THE WORST OF MY GRIEF.
AND IT BROUGHT ME A VISION...
OR PERHAPS A MIRAGE ...
OF WONDROUS BEAUTY THAT I'VE ALWAYS HOPED TO GLIMPSE AGAIN SOMEDAY.

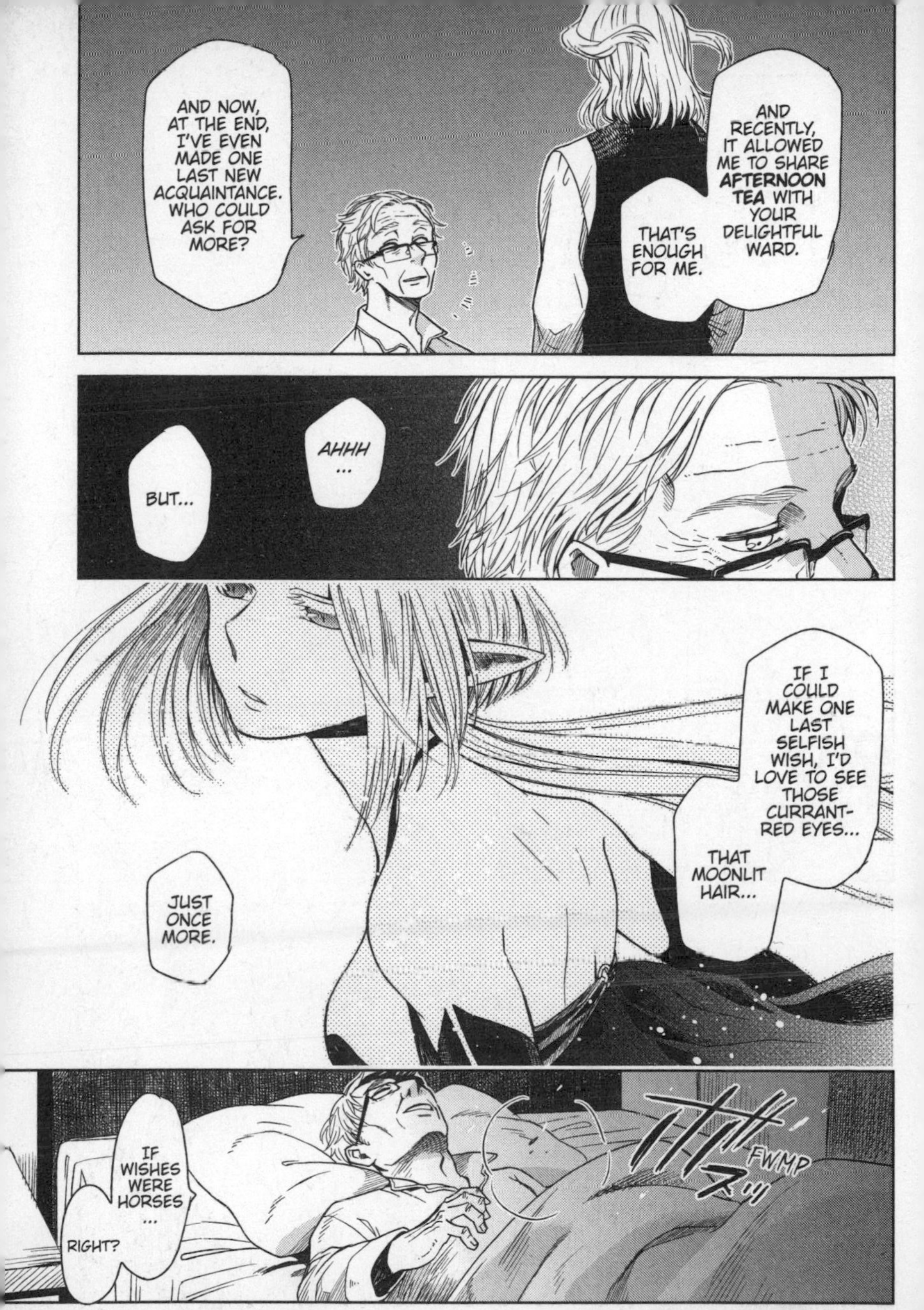
AND RECENTLY, IT ALLOWED ME TO SHARE **AFTERNOON TEA** WITH YOUR DELIGHTFUL WARD.
THAT'S ENOUGH FOR ME.
AND NOW, AT THE END, I'VE EVEN MADE ONE LAST NEW ACQUAINTANCE. WHO COULD ASK FOR MORE?
...
AHHH ...
BUT...
IF I COULD MAKE ONE LAST SELFISH WISH, I'D LOVE TO SEE THOSE CURRANT-RED EYES...
THAT MOONLIT HAIR...
JUST ONCE MORE.
FWMP
IF WISHES WERE HORSES ...
RIGHT?

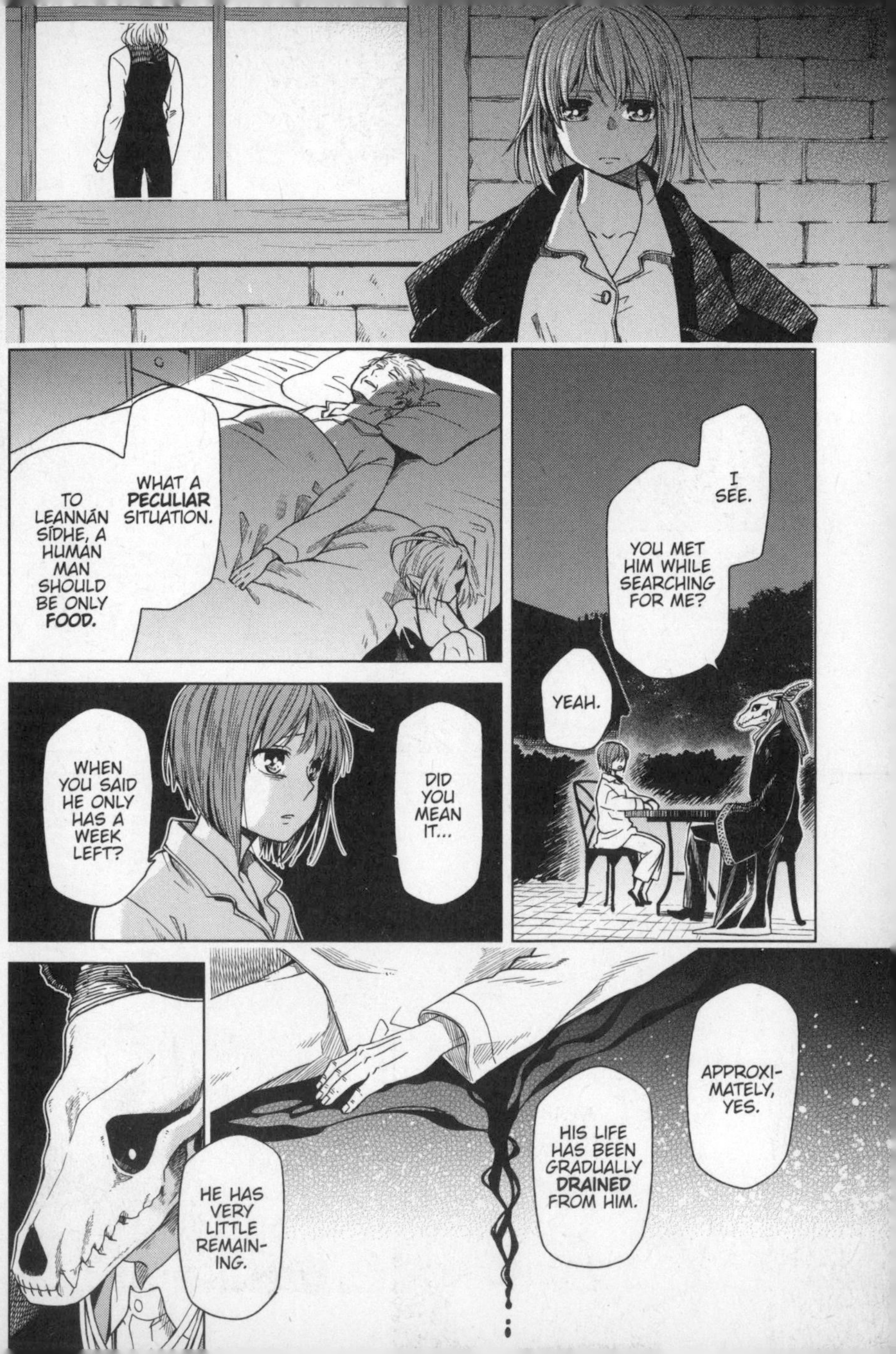
I SEE.
YOU MET HIM WHILE SEARCHING FOR ME?
YEAH.
WHAT A PECULIAR SITUATION.
TO LEANNÁN SÍDHE, A HUMAN MAN SHOULD BE ONLY FOOD.
DID YOU MEAN IT...
WHEN YOU SAID HE ONLY HAS A WEEK LEFT?
APPROXI-MATELY, YES.
HIS LIFE HAS BEEN GRADUALLY DRAINED FROM HIM.
HE HAS VERY LITTLE REMAIN-ING.

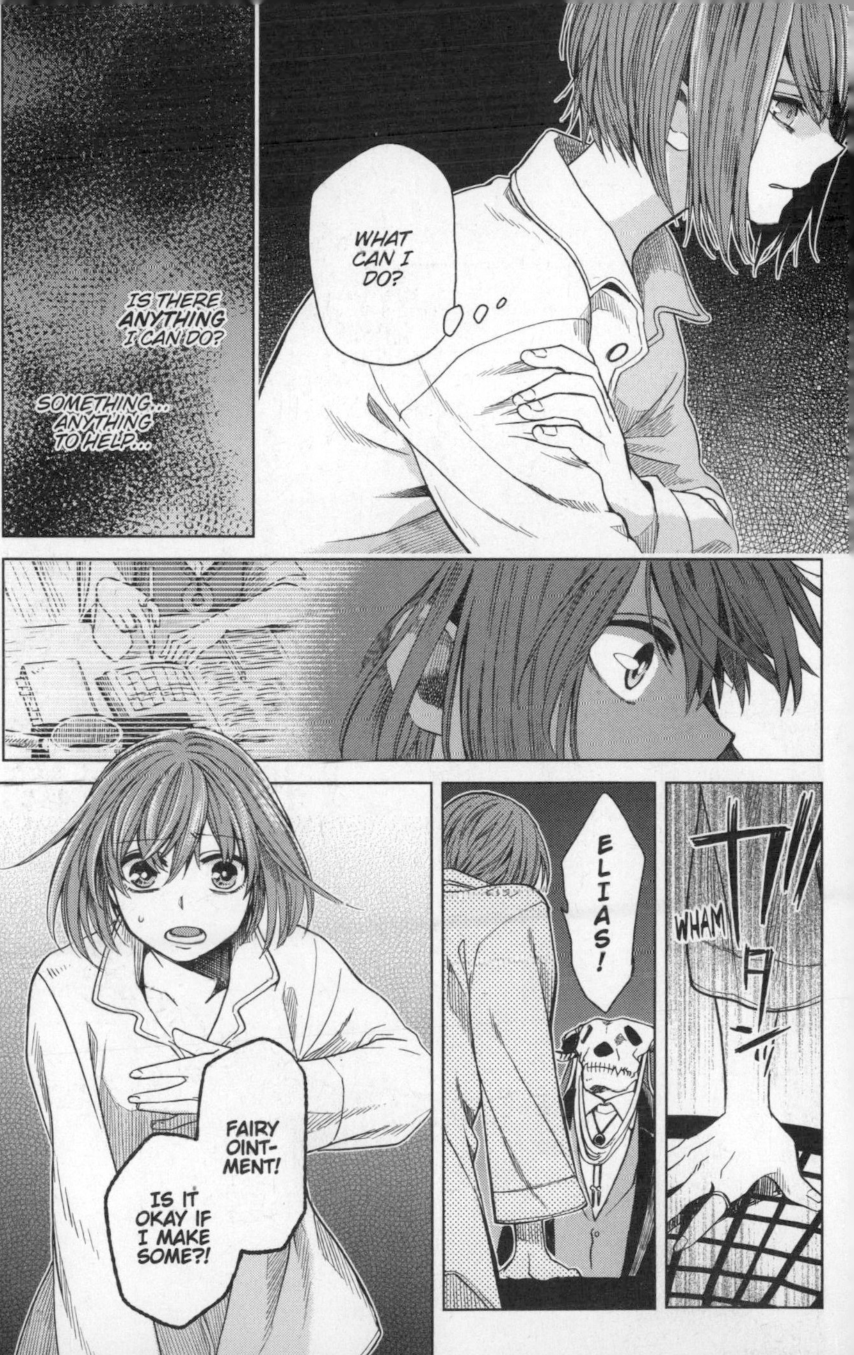
WHAT CAN I DO?
IS THERE ANYTHING I CAN DO?
SOMETHING... ANYTHING TO HELP...
WHAM
ELIAS!
FAIRY OINTMENT!
IS IT OKAY IF I MAKE SOME?!

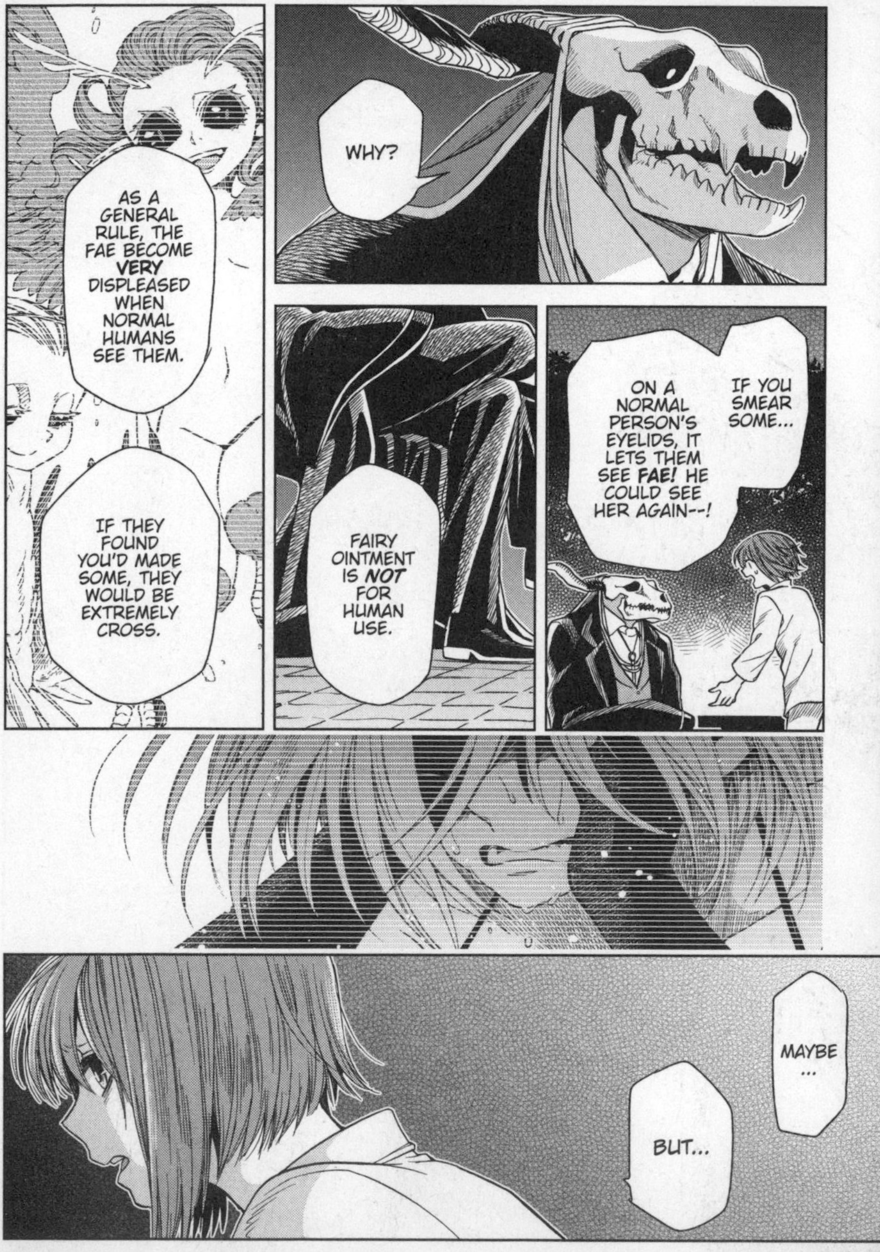
WHY?
IF YOU SMEAR SOME...
ON A NORMAL PERSON'S EYELIDS, IT LETS THEM SEE FAE! HE COULD SEE HER AGAIN--!
FAIRY OINTMENT IS NOT FOR HUMAN USE.
AS A GENERAL RULE, THE FAE BECOME VERY DISPLEASED WHEN NORMAL HUMANS SEE THEM.
IF THEY FOUND YOU'D MADE SOME, THEY WOULD BE EXTREMELY CROSS.
MAYBE ...
BUT...

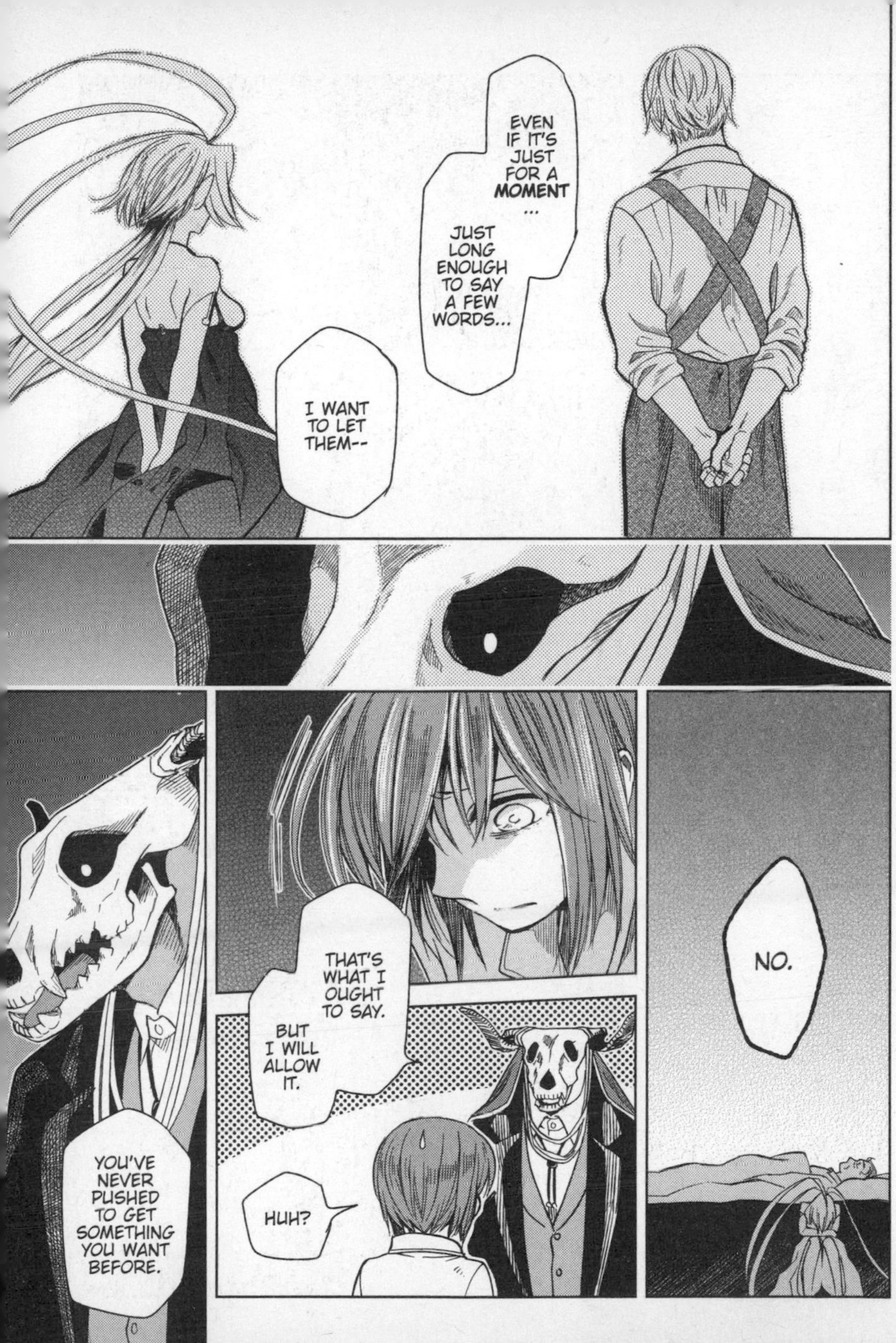
EVEN IF IT'S JUST FOR A **MOMENT**...
JUST LONG ENOUGH TO SAY A FEW WORDS...
I WANT TO LET THEM--
NO.
THAT'S WHAT I OUGHT TO SAY.
BUT I WILL ALLOW IT.
HUH?
YOU'VE NEVER PUSHED TO GET SOMETHING YOU WANT BEFORE.

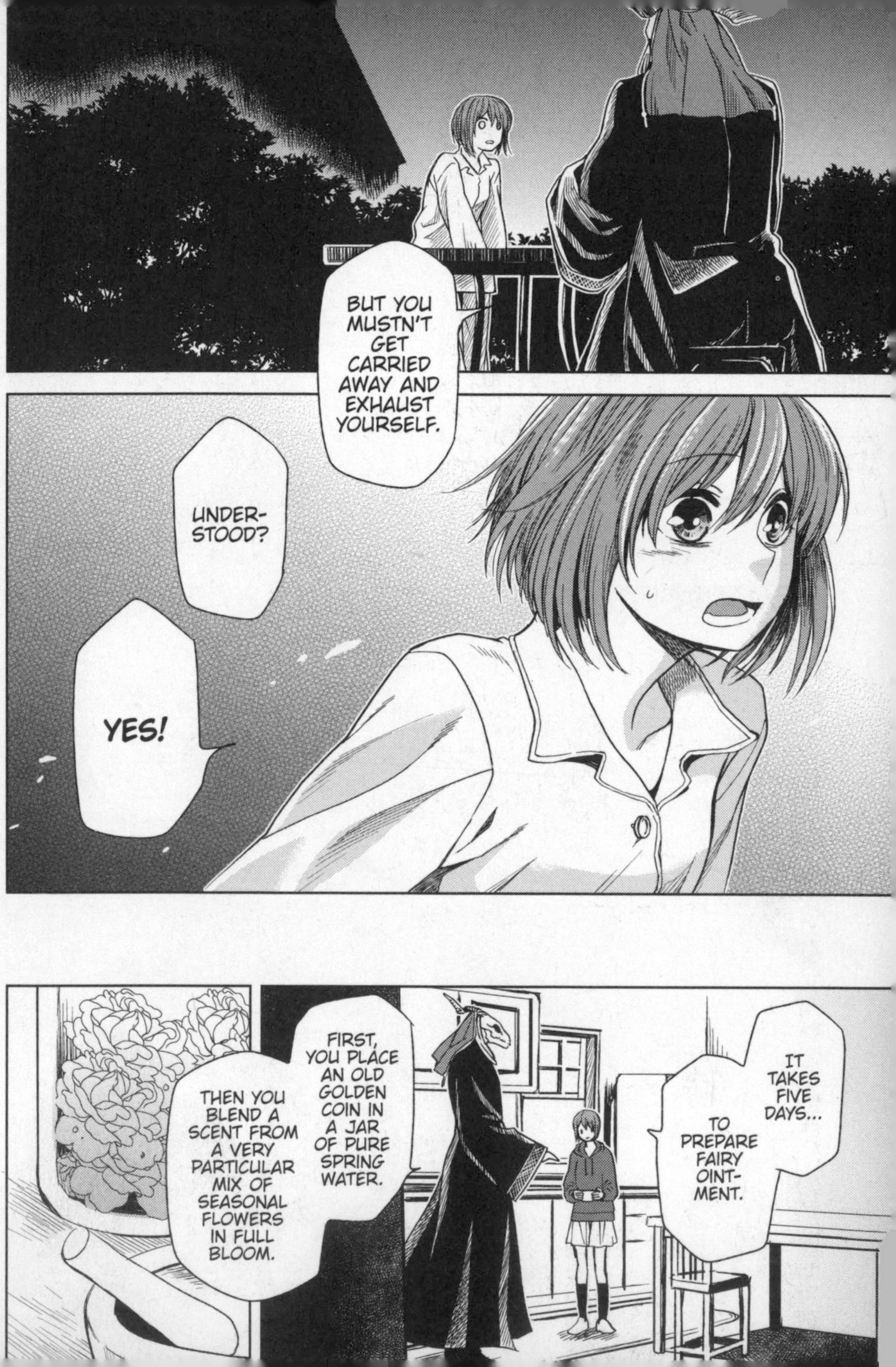
BUT YOU MUSTN'T GET CARRIED AWAY AND EXHAUST YOURSELF.
UNDER-STOOD?
YES!
IT TAKES FIVE DAYS...
TO PREPARE FAIRY OINT-MENT.
FIRST, YOU PLACE AN OLD GOLDEN COIN IN A JAR OF PURE SPRING WATER.
THEN YOU BLEND A SCENT FROM A VERY PARTICULAR MIX OF SEASONAL FLOWERS IN FULL BLOOM.

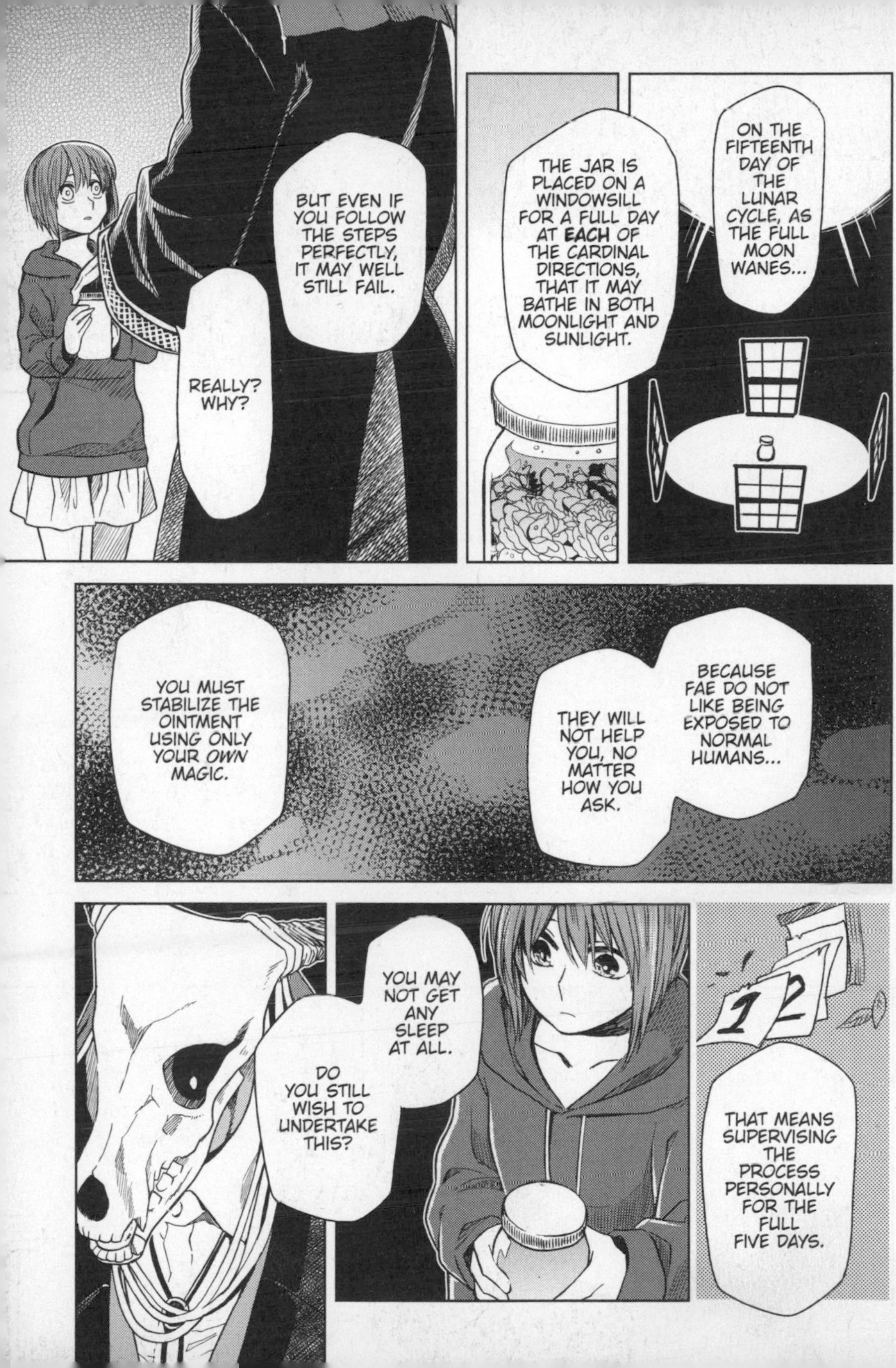
ON THE FIFTEENTH DAY OF THE LUNAR CYCLE, AS THE FULL MOON WANES...
THE JAR IS PLACED ON A WINDOWSILL FOR A FULL DAY AT **EACH** OF THE CARDINAL DIRECTIONS, THAT IT MAY BATHE IN BOTH MOONLIGHT AND SUNLIGHT.
BUT EVEN IF YOU FOLLOW THE STEPS PERFECTLY, IT MAY WELL STILL FAIL.
REALLY? WHY?
BECAUSE FAE DO NOT LIKE BEING EXPOSED TO NORMAL HUMANS...
THEY WILL NOT HELP YOU, NO MATTER HOW YOU ASK.
YOU MUST STABILIZE THE OINTMENT USING ONLY YOUR *OWN* MAGIC.
THAT MEANS SUPERVISING THE PROCESS PERSONALLY FOR THE FULL FIVE DAYS.
YOU MAY NOT GET ANY SLEEP AT ALL.
DO YOU STILL WISH TO UNDERTAKE THIS?

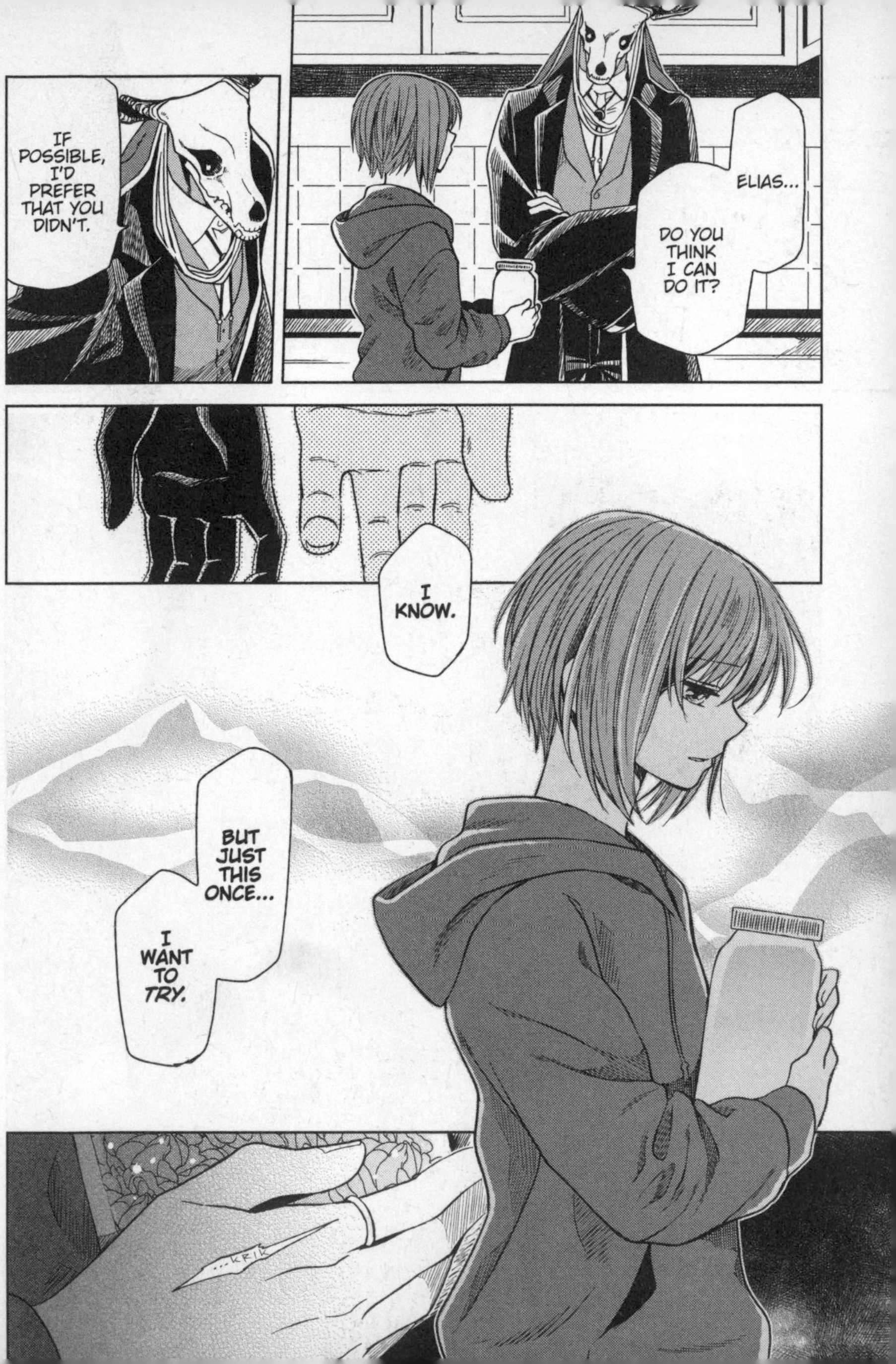
ELIAS...
DO YOU THINK I CAN DO IT?
IF POSSIBLE, I'D PREFER THAT YOU DIDN'T.
I KNOW.
BUT JUST THIS ONCE...
I WANT TO *TRY.*
...KRIK

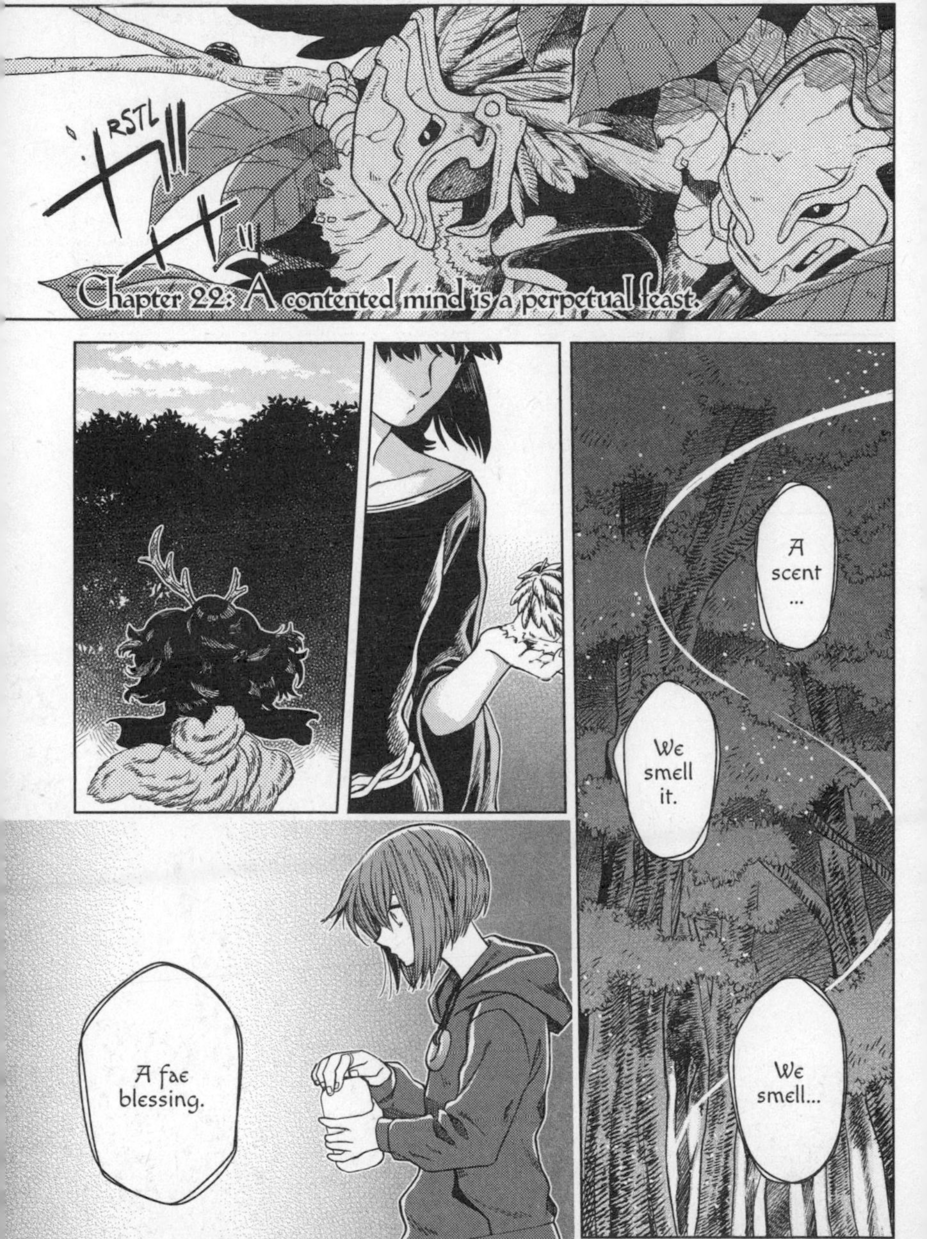
RSTL
Chapter 22: A contented mind is a perpetual feast.
A scent...
We smell it.
We smell...
A fae blessing.

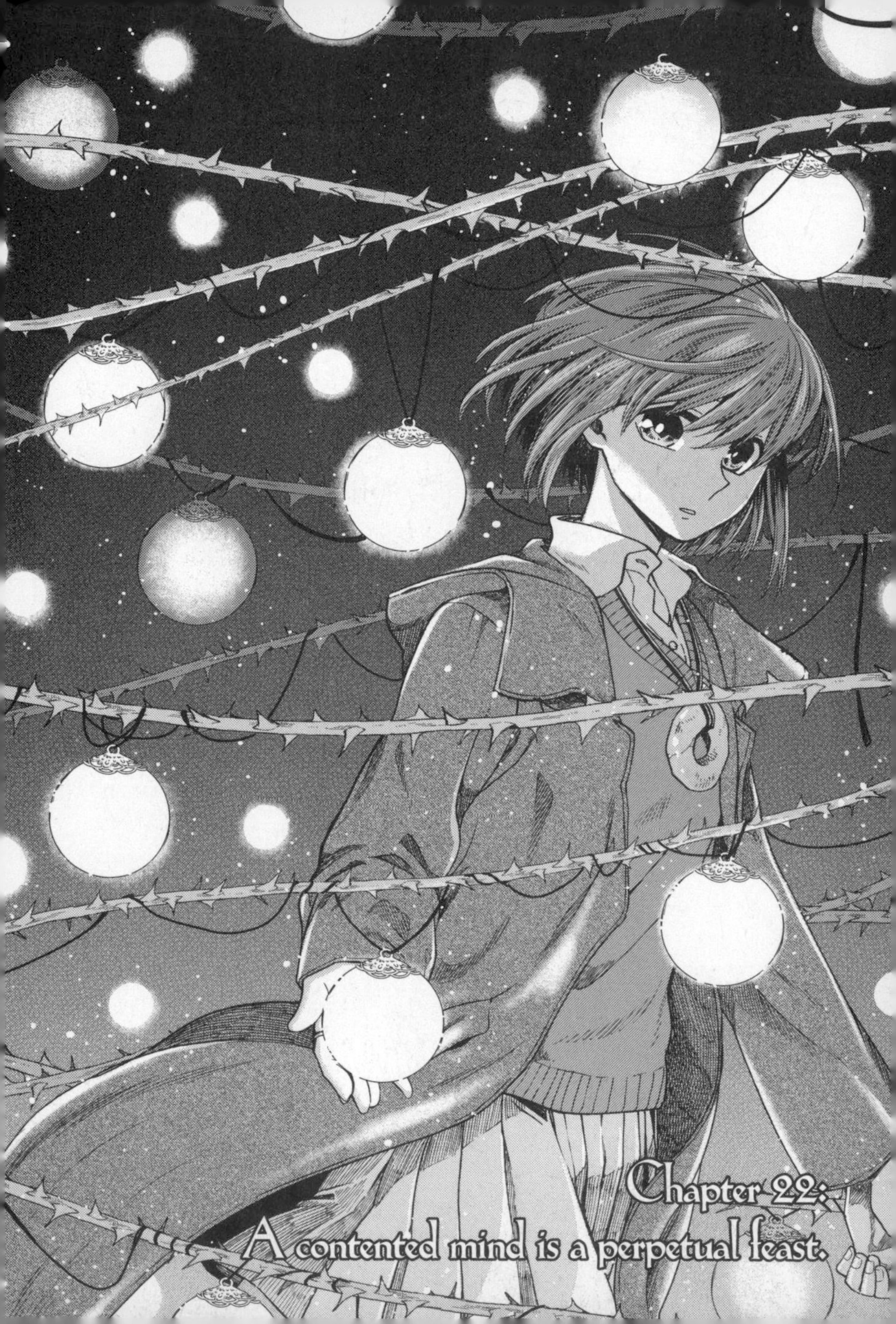
Chapter 22:
A contented mind is a perpetual feast.

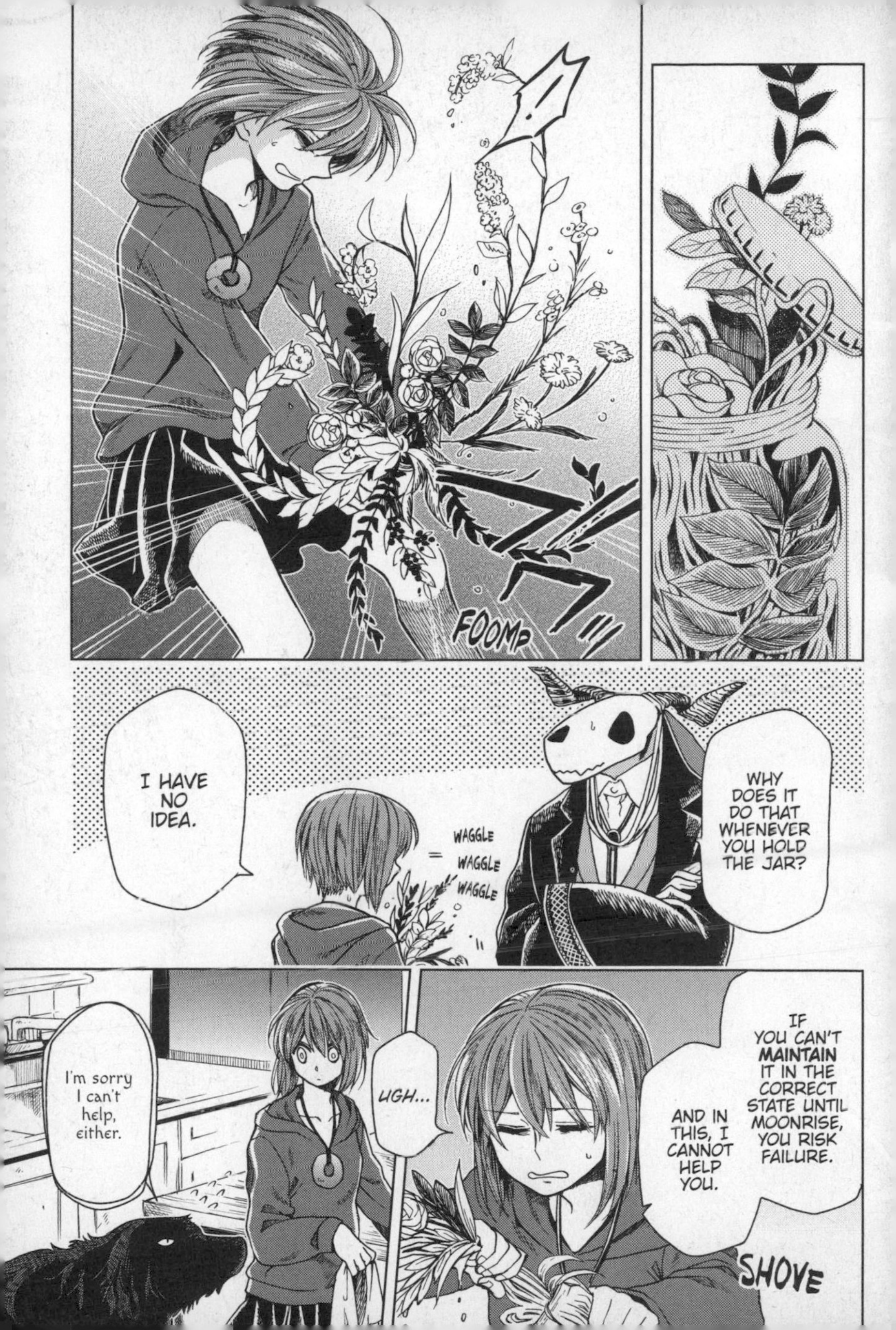
FOOMP
WHY DOES IT DO THAT WHENEVER YOU HOLD THE JAR?
WAGGLE WAGGLE WAGGLE
I HAVE NO IDEA.
IF YOU CAN'T MAINTAIN IT IN THE CORRECT STATE UNTIL MOONRISE, YOU RISK FAILURE.
AND IN THIS, I CANNOT HELP YOU.
SHOVE
UGH...
I'm sorry I can't help, either.

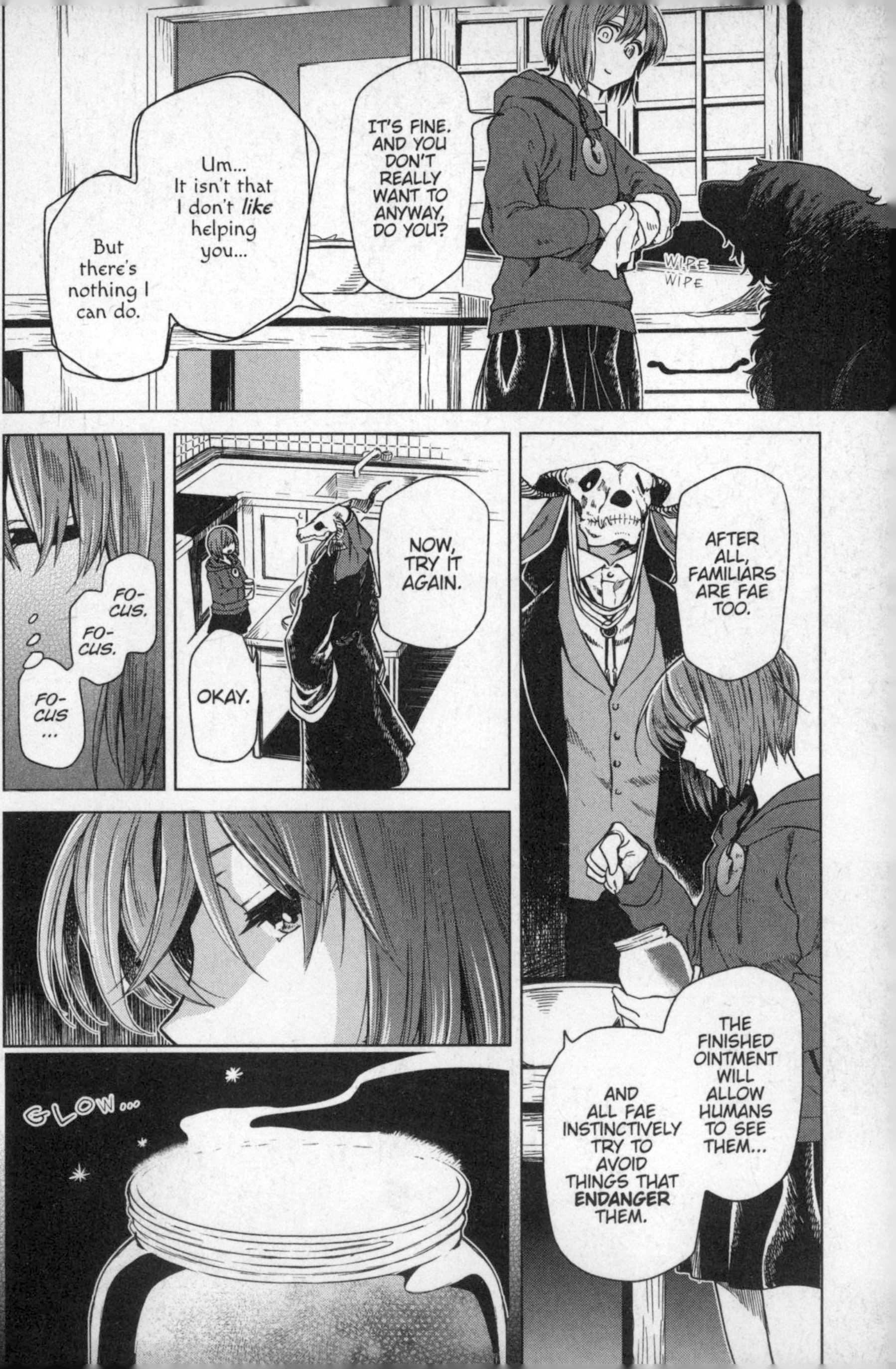
IT'S FINE. AND YOU DON'T REALLY WANT TO ANYWAY, DO YOU?
WIPE WIPE
Um... It isn't that I don't *like* helping you...
But there's nothing I can do.
AFTER ALL, FAMILIARS ARE FAE TOO.
THE FINISHED OINTMENT WILL ALLOW HUMANS TO SEE THEM...
AND ALL FAE INSTINCTIVELY TRY TO AVOID THINGS THAT **ENDANGER** THEM.
NOW, TRY IT AGAIN.
OKAY.
FO-CUS.
FO-CUS.
FO-CUS...
GLOW...

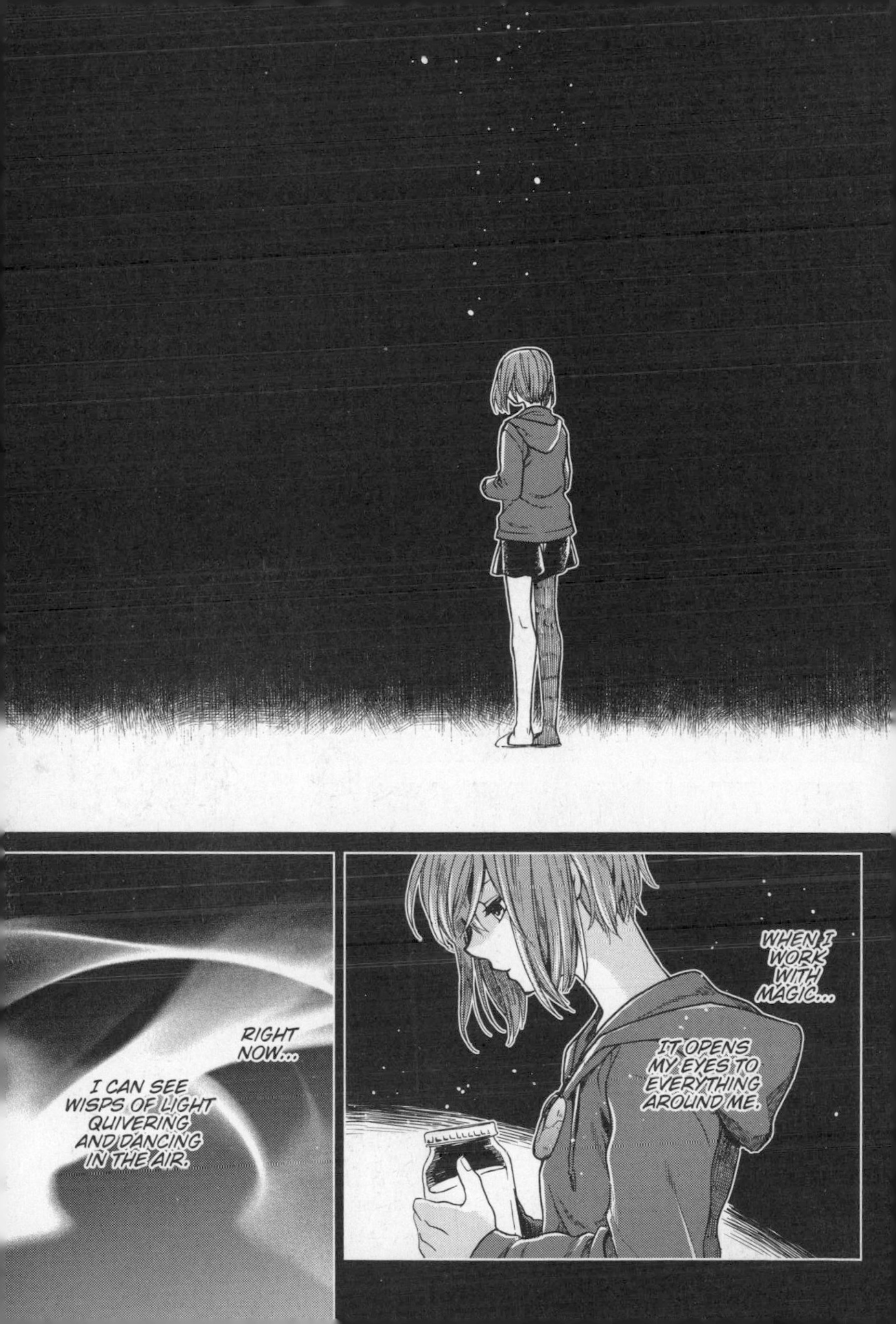
WHEN I WORK WITH MAGIC...
IT OPENS MY EYES TO EVERYTHING AROUND ME.
RIGHT NOW...
I CAN SEE WISPS OF LIGHT QUIVERING AND DANCING IN THE AIR.

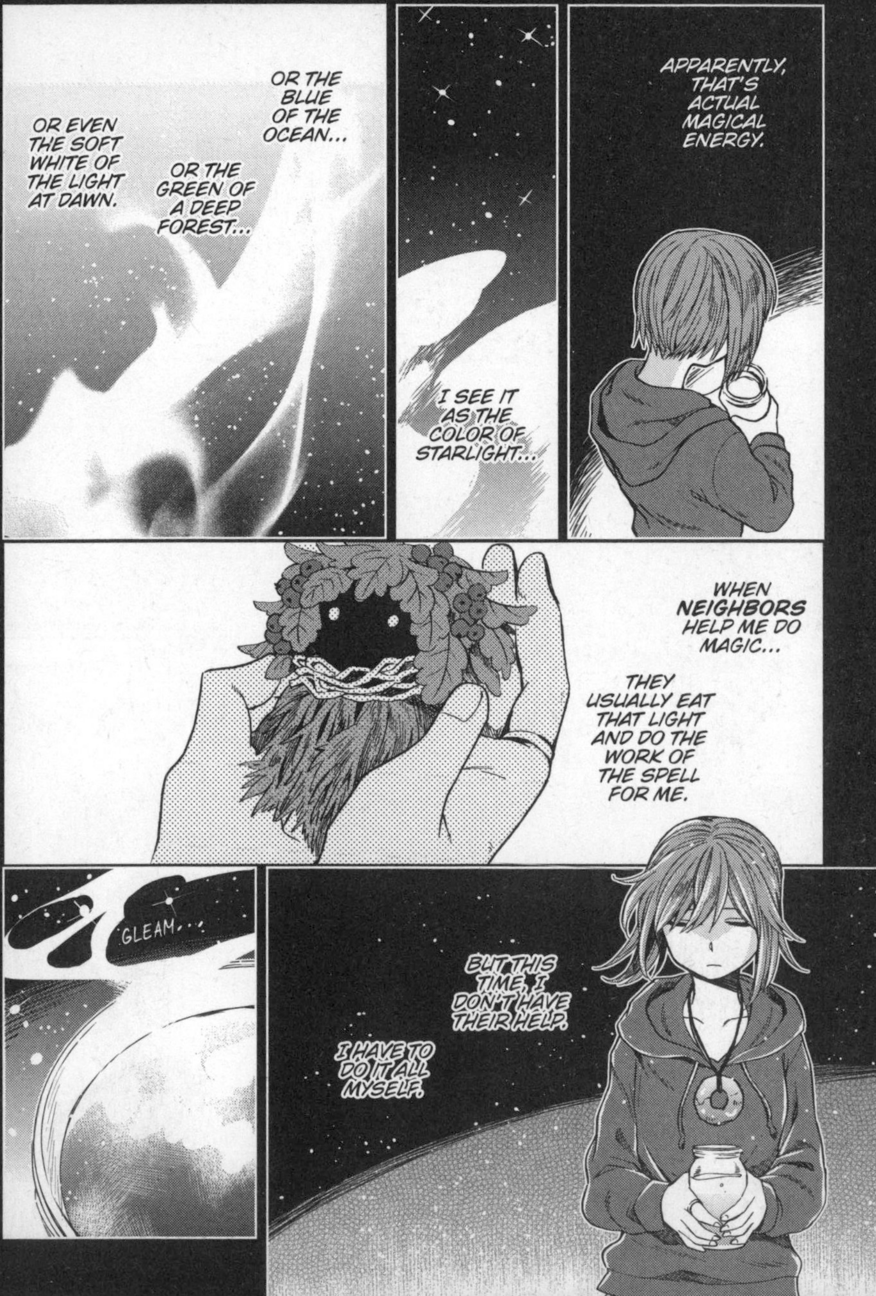
APPARENTLY, THAT'S ACTUAL MAGICAL ENERGY.
I SEE IT AS THE COLOR OF STARLIGHT...
OR THE BLUE OF THE OCEAN...
OR THE GREEN OF A DEEP FOREST...
OR EVEN THE SOFT WHITE OF THE LIGHT AT DAWN.
WHEN NEIGHBORS HELP ME DO MAGIC...
THEY USUALLY EAT THAT LIGHT AND DO THE WORK OF THE SPELL FOR ME.
BUT THIS TIME, I DON'T HAVE THEIR HELP.
I HAVE TO DO IT ALL MYSELF.
GLEAM...

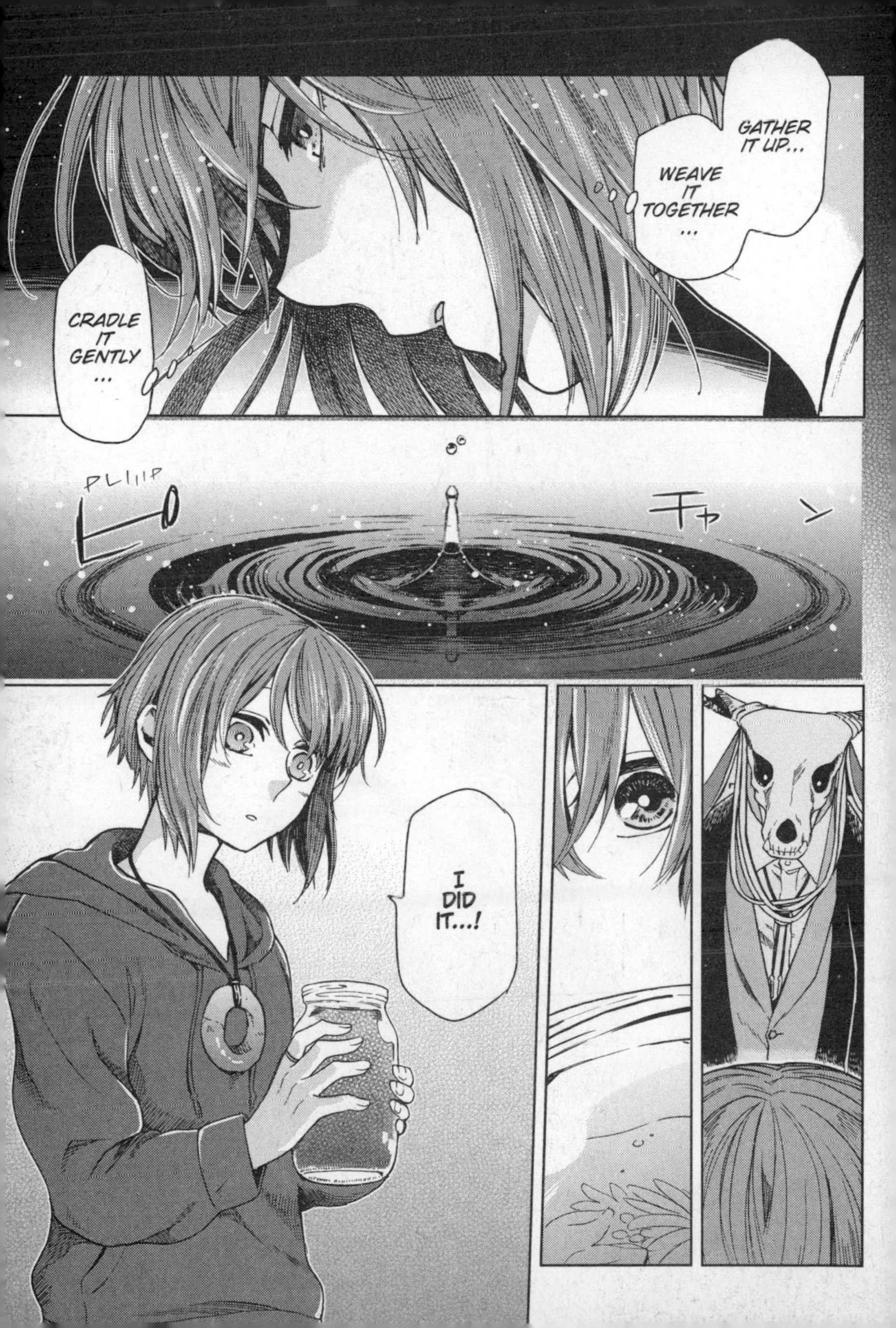
GATHER IT UP...
WEAVE IT TOGETHER...
CRADLE IT GENTLY...
チャン
ピロ
PLIIIP
I DID IT...!

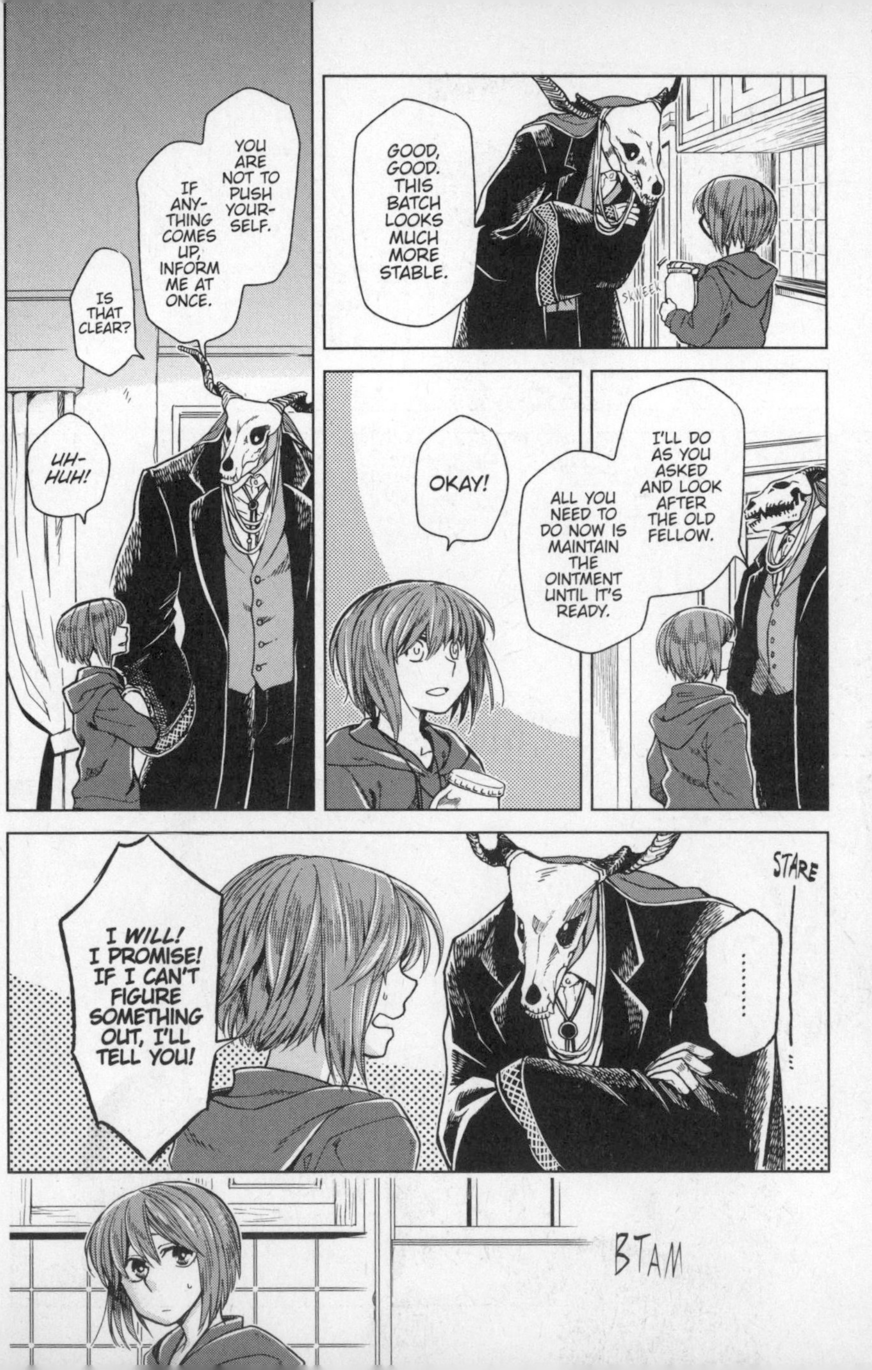
GOOD, GOOD. THIS BATCH LOOKS MUCH MORE STABLE.
SKWEEK
I'LL DO AS YOU ASKED AND LOOK AFTER THE OLD FELLOW.
ALL YOU NEED TO DO NOW IS MAINTAIN THE OINTMENT UNTIL IT'S READY.
OKAY!
YOU ARE NOT TO PUSH YOURSELF.
IF ANYTHING COMES UP, INFORM ME AT ONCE.
IS THAT CLEAR?
UH-HUH!
STARE
......
I WILL! I PROMISE! IF I CAN'T FIGURE SOMETHING OUT, I'LL TELL YOU!
BTAM

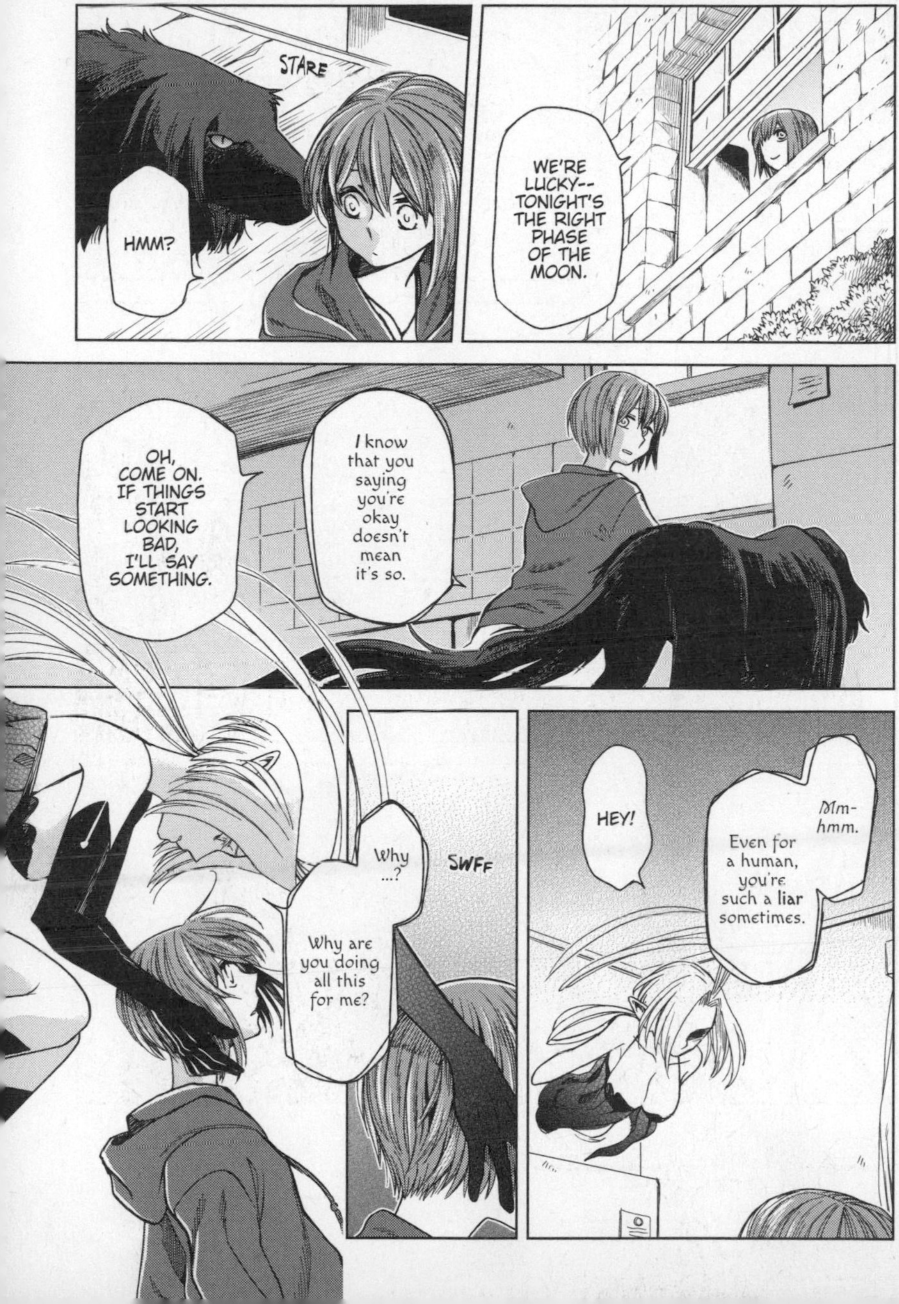
WE'RE LUCKY-- TONIGHT'S THE RIGHT PHASE OF THE MOON.
STARE
HMM?
I know that you saying you're okay doesn't mean it's so.
OH, COME ON. IF THINGS START LOOKING BAD, I'LL SAY SOMETHING.
Mm-hmm. Even for a human, you're such a liar sometimes.
HEY!
SWFF
Why ...?
Why are you doing all this for me?

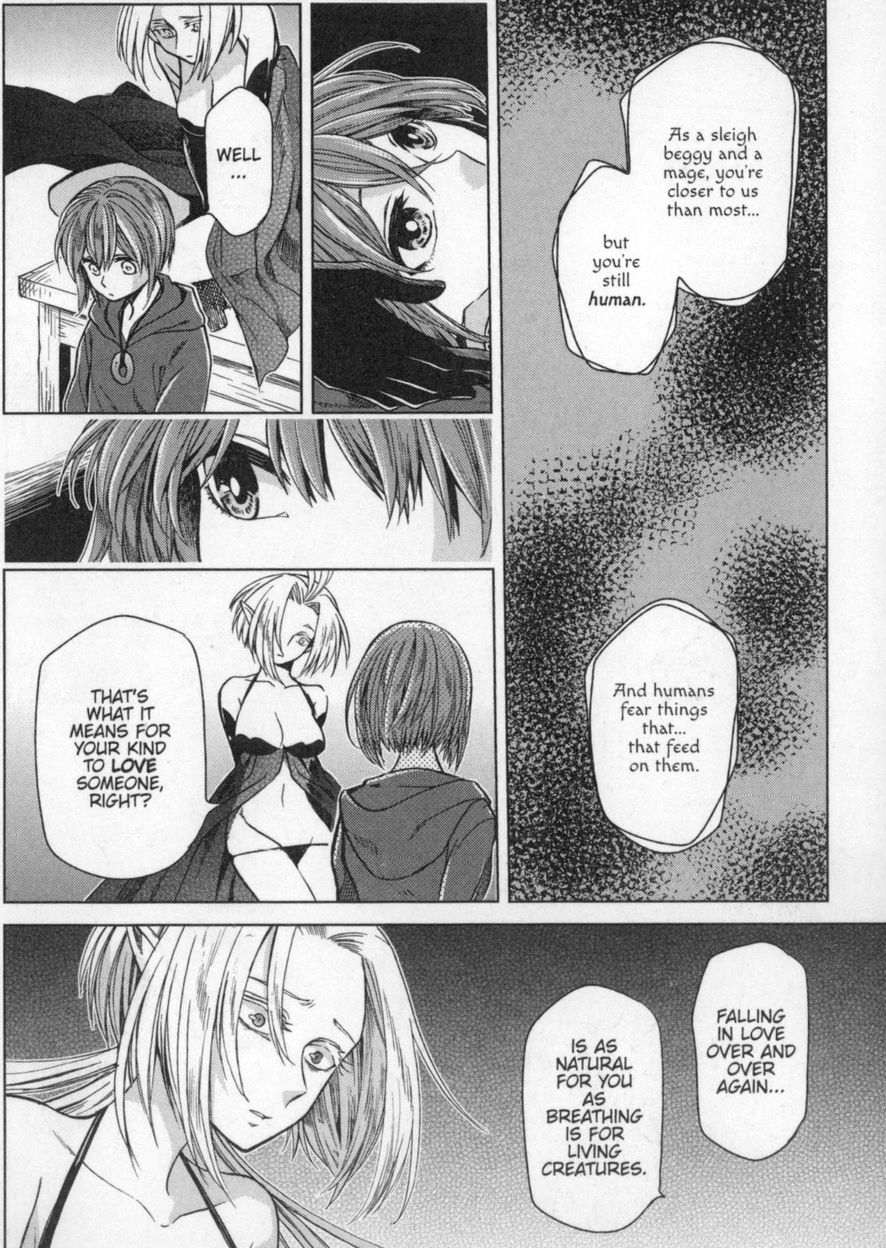
As a sleigh beggy and a mage, you're closer to us than most...
but you're still **human.**
And humans fear things that... that feed on them.
WELL ...
THAT'S WHAT IT MEANS FOR YOUR KIND TO **LOVE** SOMEONE, RIGHT?
FALLING IN LOVE OVER AND OVER AGAIN...
IS AS NATURAL FOR YOU AS BREATHING IS FOR LIVING CREATURES.

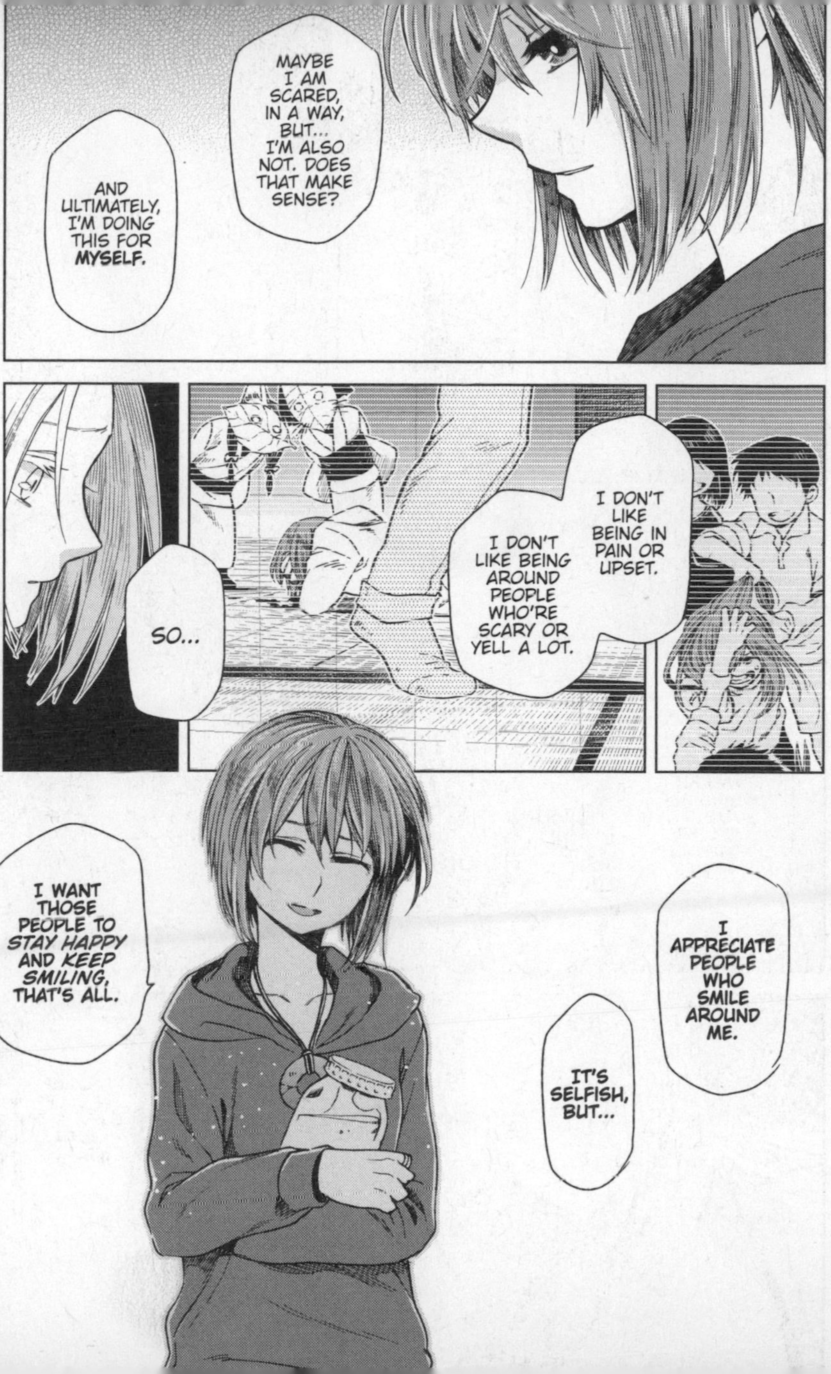
MAYBE I AM SCARED, IN A WAY, BUT... I'M ALSO NOT. DOES THAT MAKE SENSE?
AND ULTIMATELY, I'M DOING THIS FOR MYSELF.
I DON'T LIKE BEING IN PAIN OR UPSET.
I DON'T LIKE BEING AROUND PEOPLE WHO'RE SCARY OR YELL A LOT.
SO...
I APPRECIATE PEOPLE WHO SMILE AROUND ME.
IT'S SELFISH, BUT...
I WANT THOSE PEOPLE TO STAY HAPPY AND KEEP SMILING, THAT'S ALL.

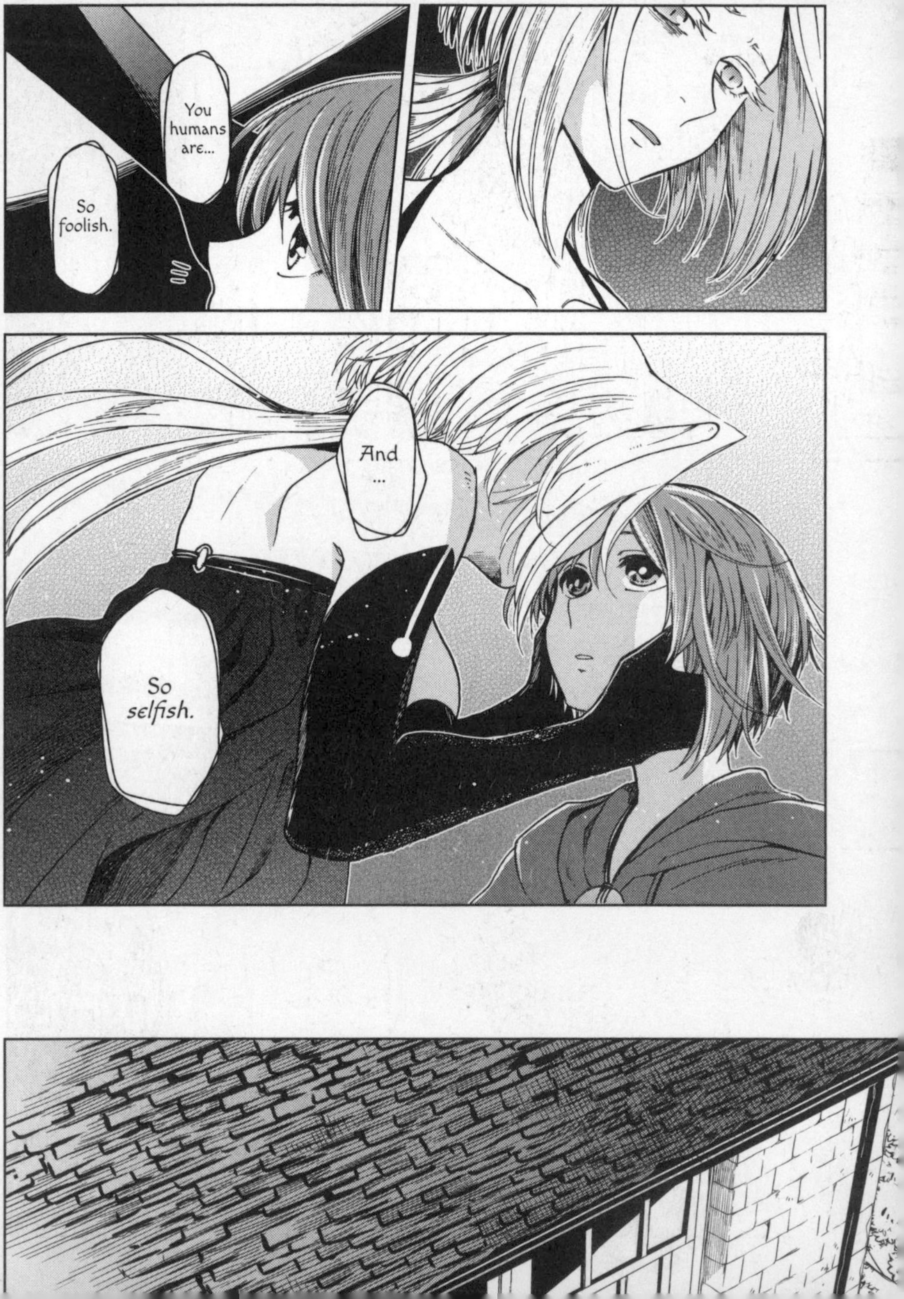
You humans are...
So foolish.
And ...
So selfish.

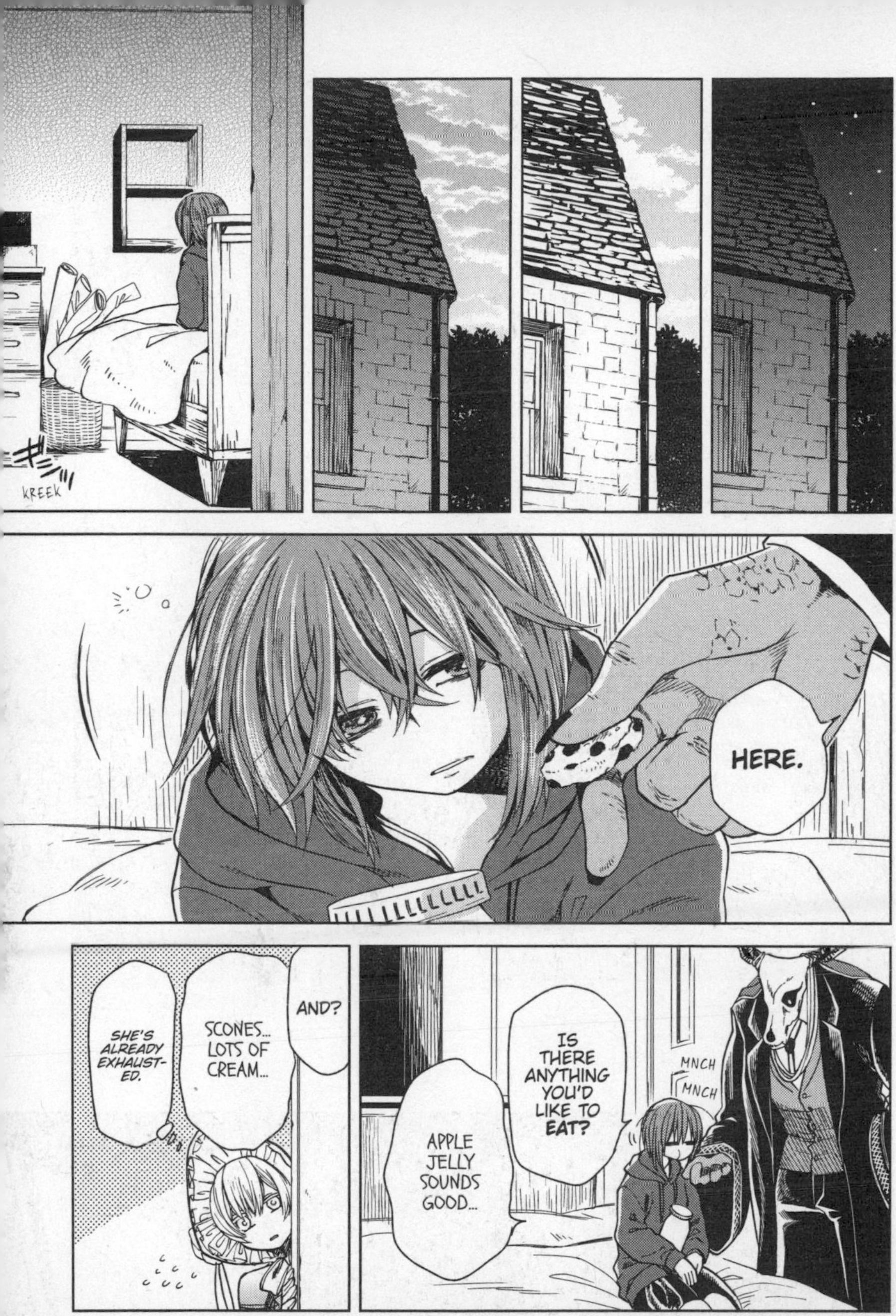
KREEK
HERE.
IS THERE ANYTHING YOU'D LIKE TO EAT?
MNCH
MNCH
APPLE JELLY SOUNDS GOOD...
AND?
SCONES... LOTS OF CREAM...
SHE'S ALREADY EXHAUST-ED.

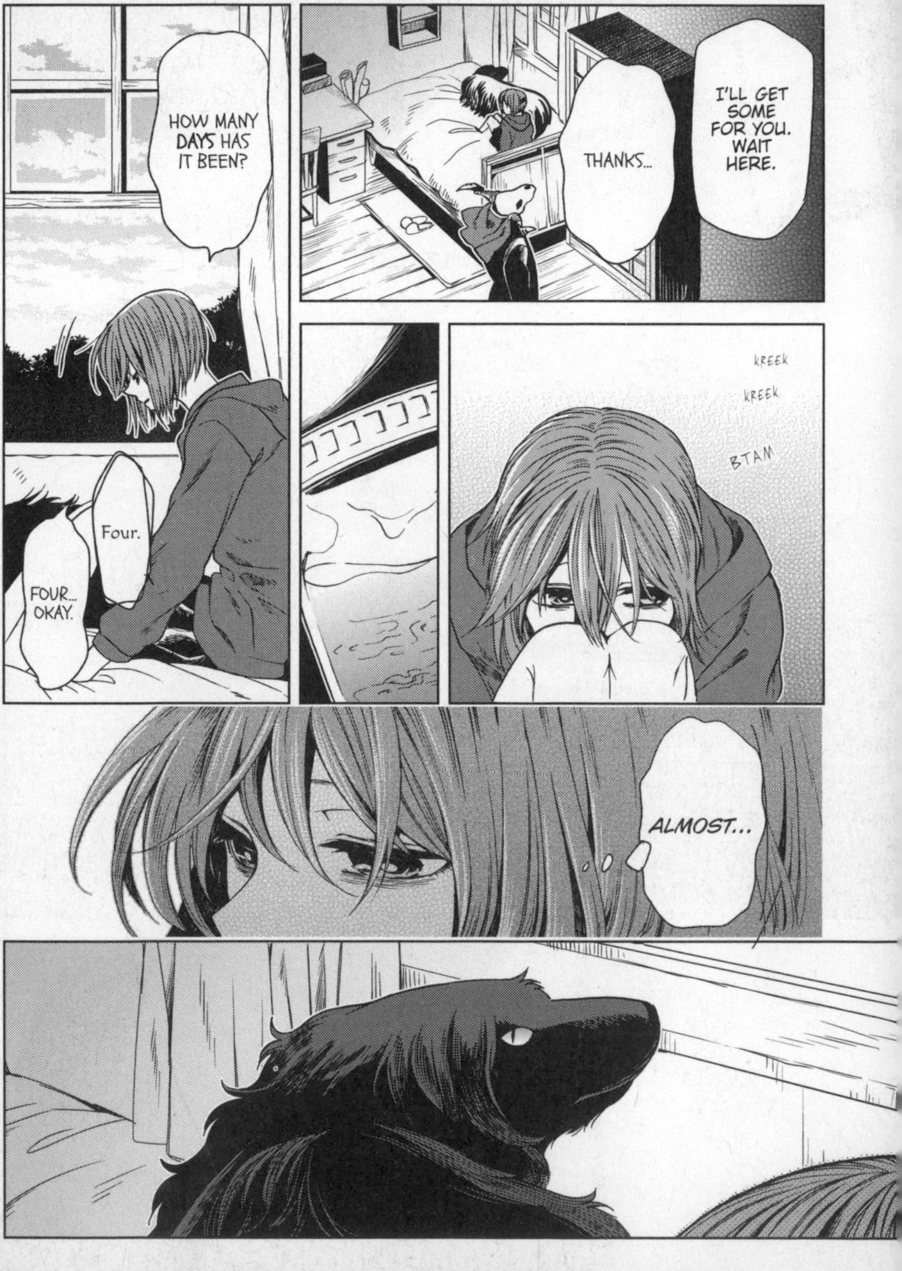
I'LL GET SOME FOR YOU. WAIT HERE.
THANKS...
KREEK
KREEK
BTAM
HOW MANY DAYS HAS IT BEEN?
Four.
FOUR... OKAY.
ALMOST...

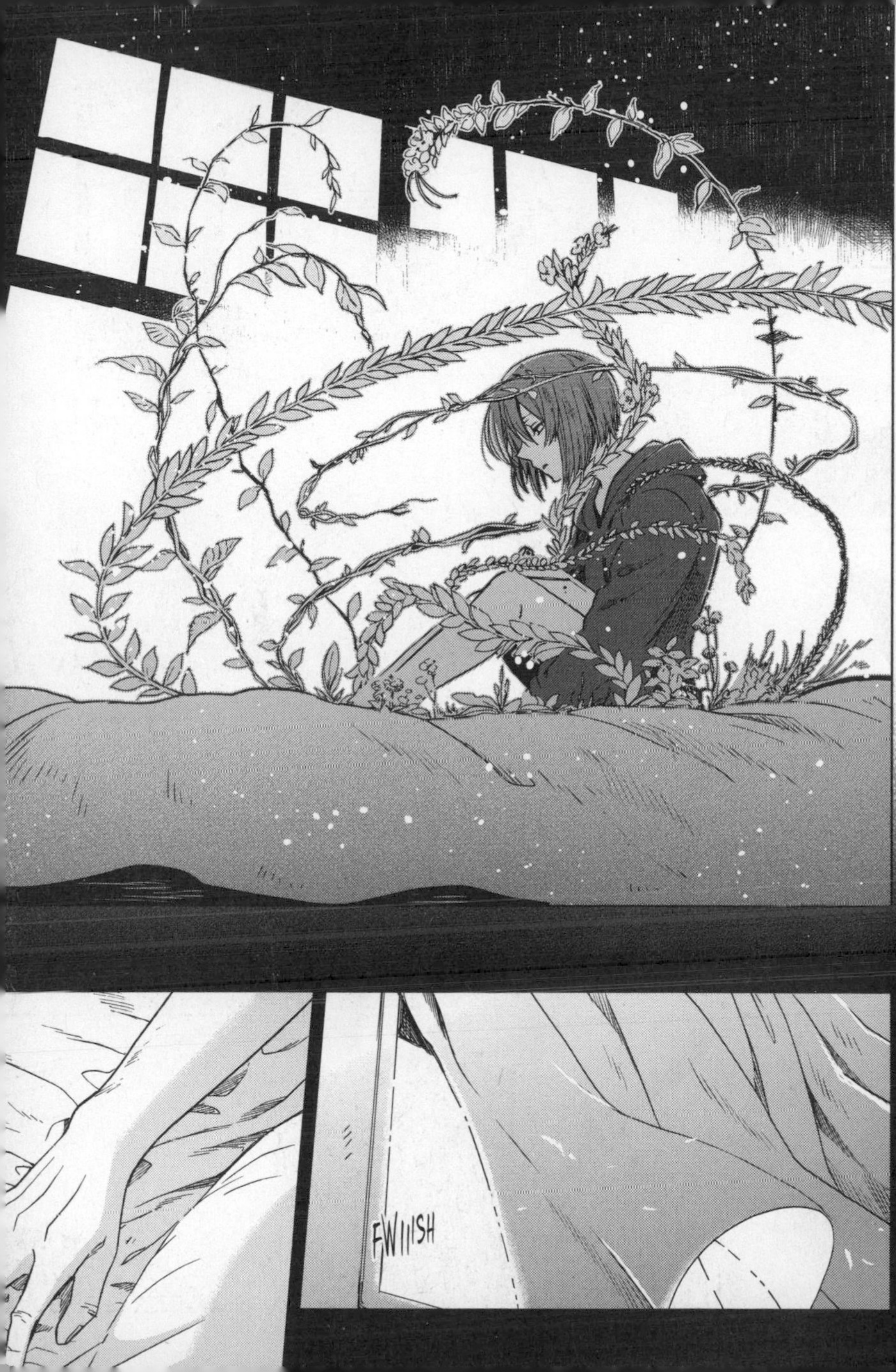
FWIIISH

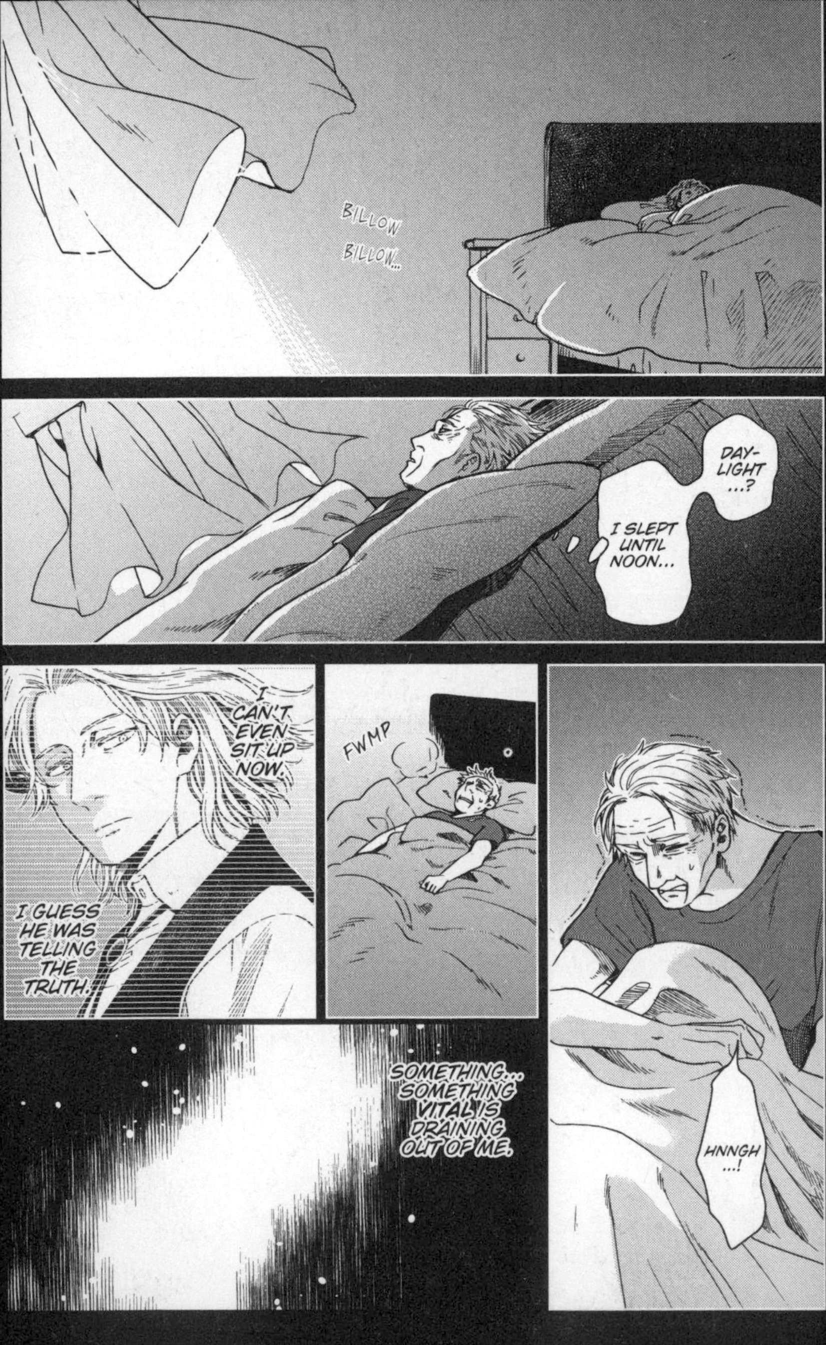
BILLOW
BILLOW...
DAY-LIGHT...?
I SLEPT UNTIL NOON...
HNNGH...!
FWMP
I CAN'T EVEN SIT UP NOW.
I GUESS HE WAS TELLING THE TRUTH.
SOMETHING... SOMETHING VITAL IS DRAINING OUT OF ME.

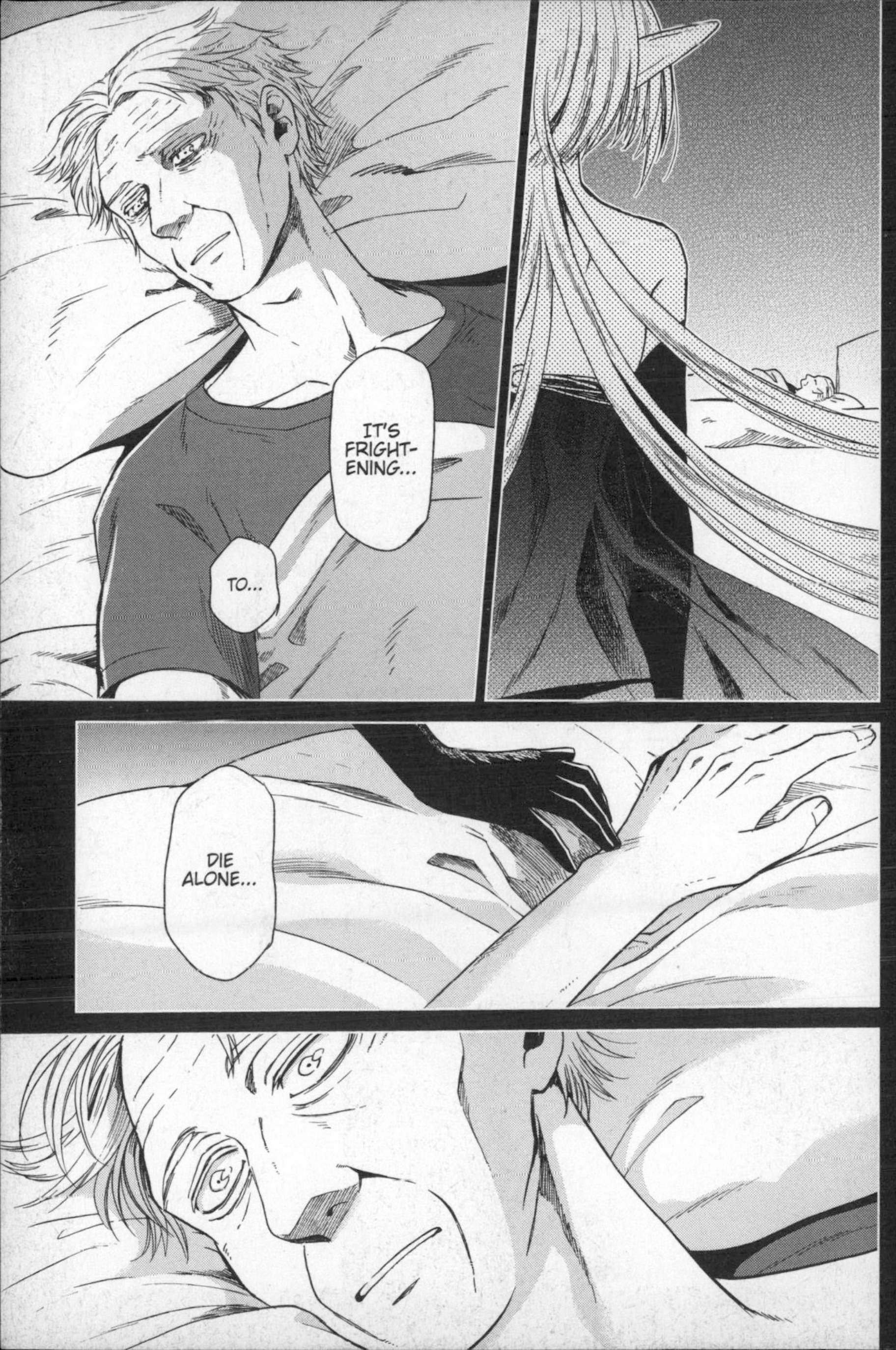
IT'S FRIGHT-ENING...
TO...
DIE ALONE...

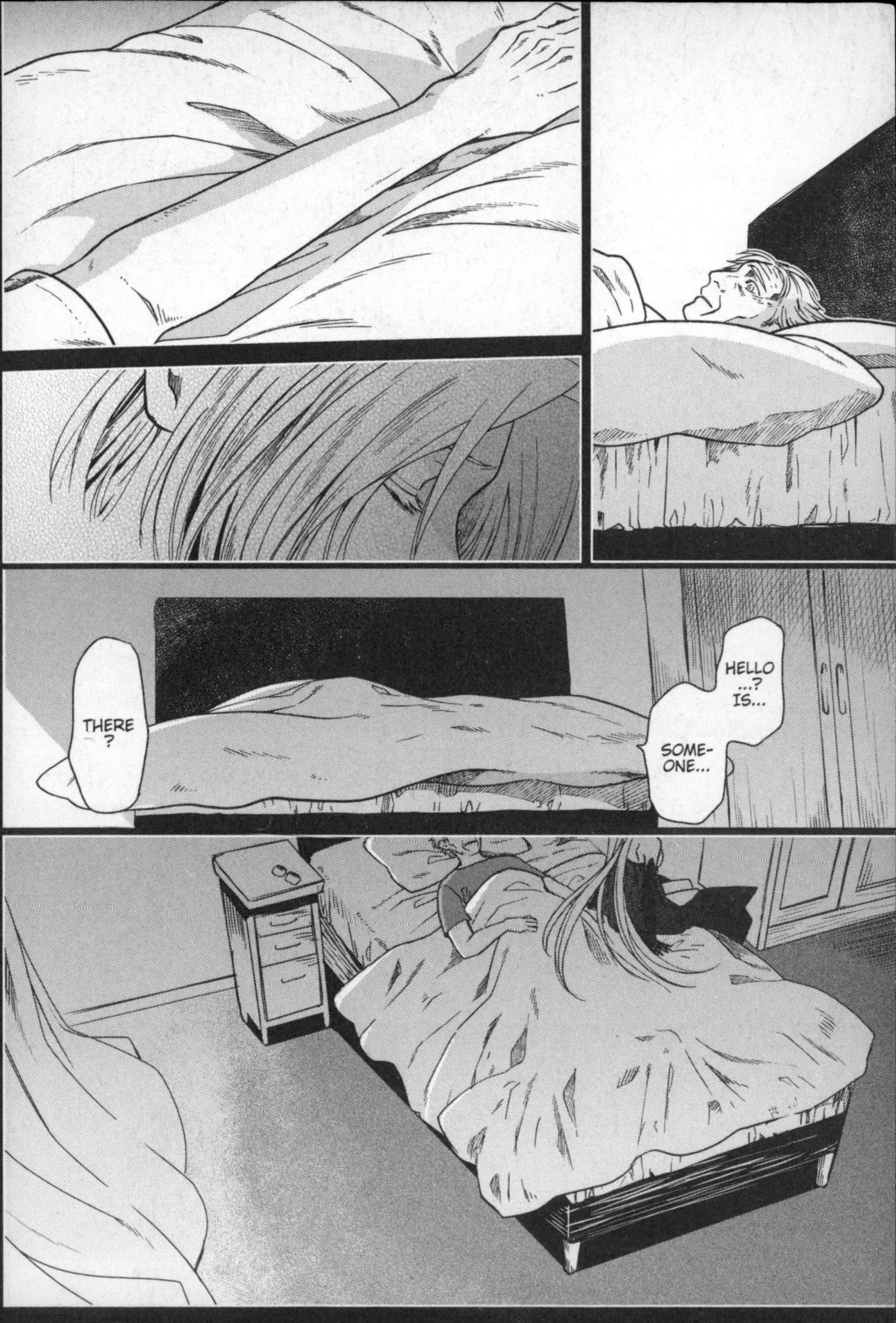
HELLO ...? IS... SOME-ONE...
THERE ?

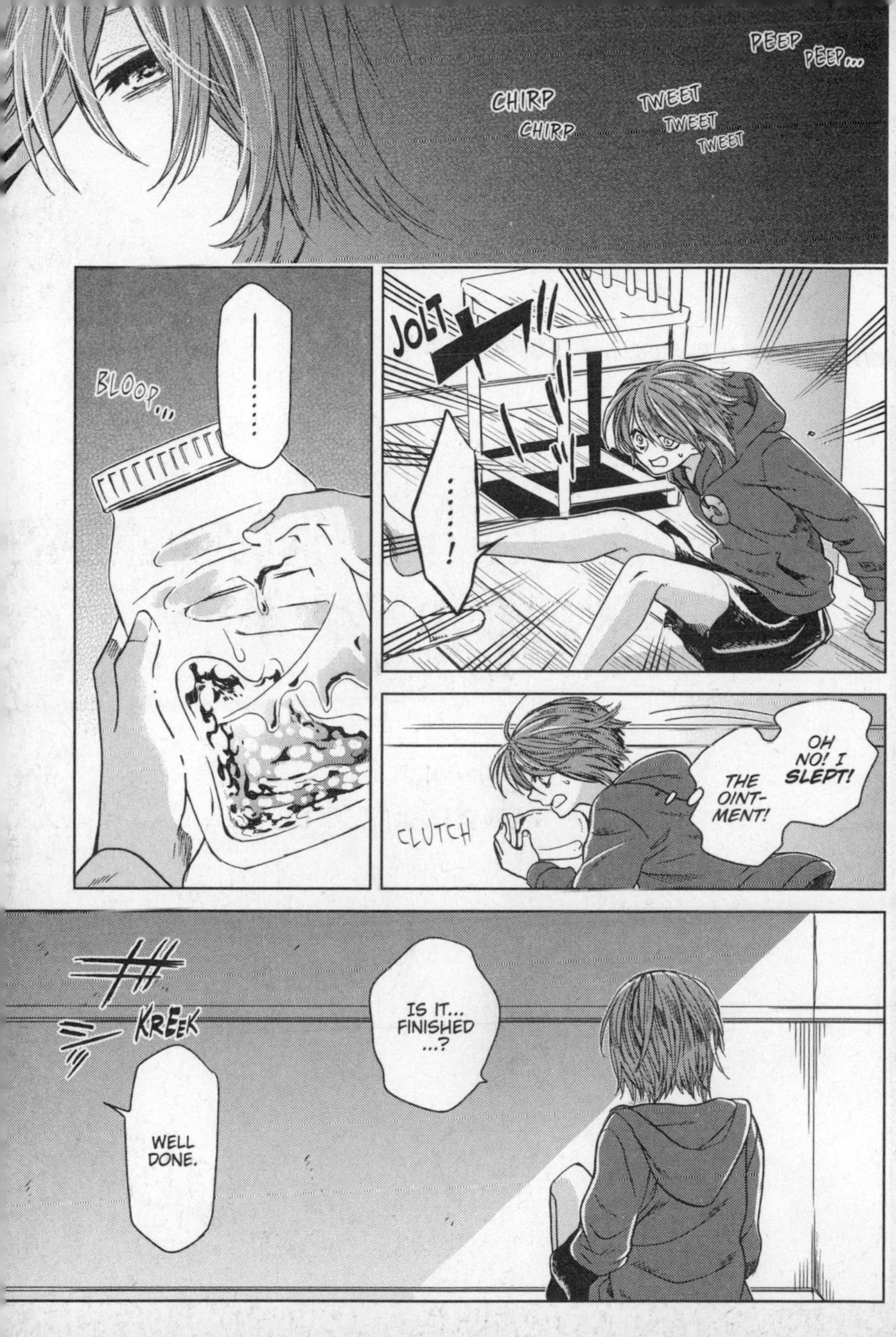
PEEP PEEP...
TWEET TWEET TWEET
CHIRP CHIRP
JOLT
......!
OH NO! I SLEPT!
THE OINTMENT!
CLUTCH
......
BLOOP...
IS IT... FINISHED ...?
KREEK
WELL DONE.

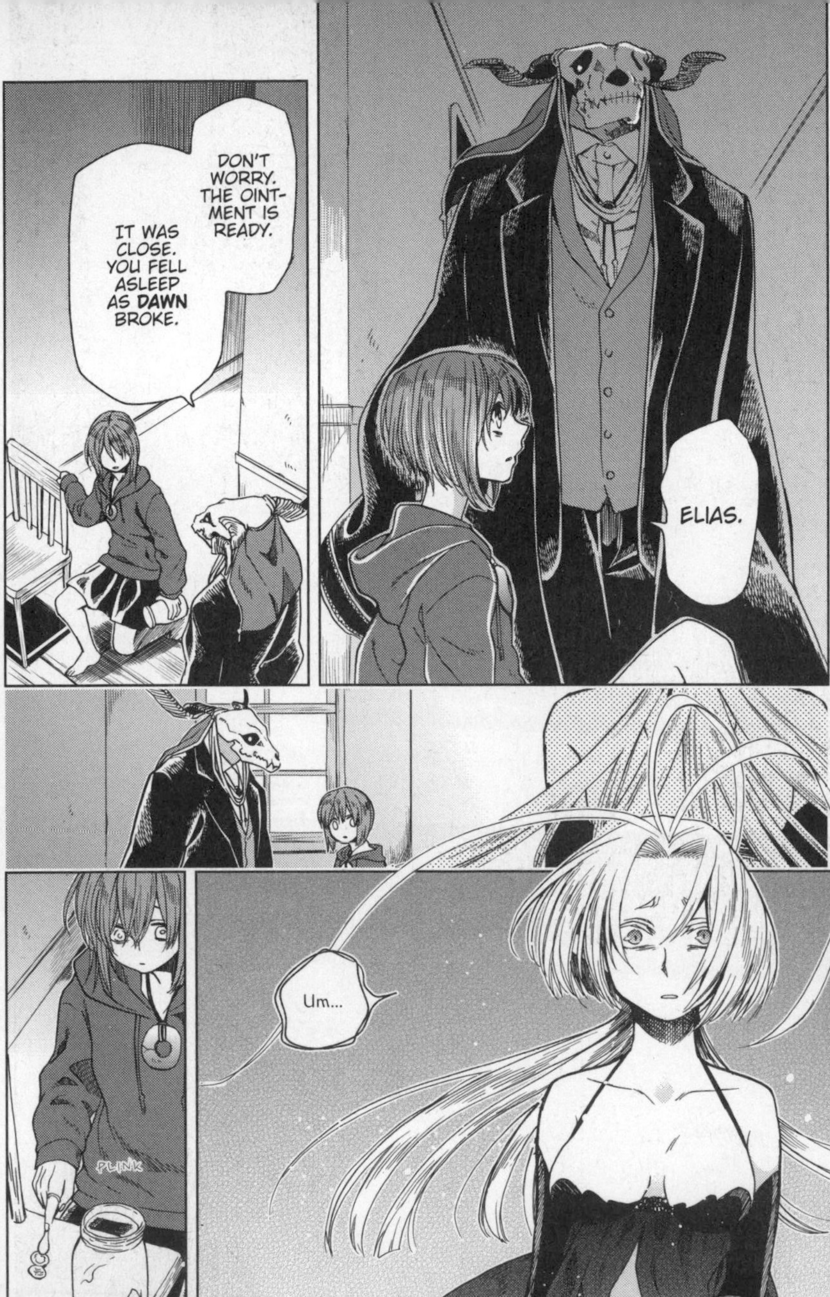
ELIAS.
DON'T WORRY. THE OINT-MENT IS READY.
IT WAS CLOSE. YOU FELL ASLEEP AS **DAWN** BROKE.
Um...
PLINK

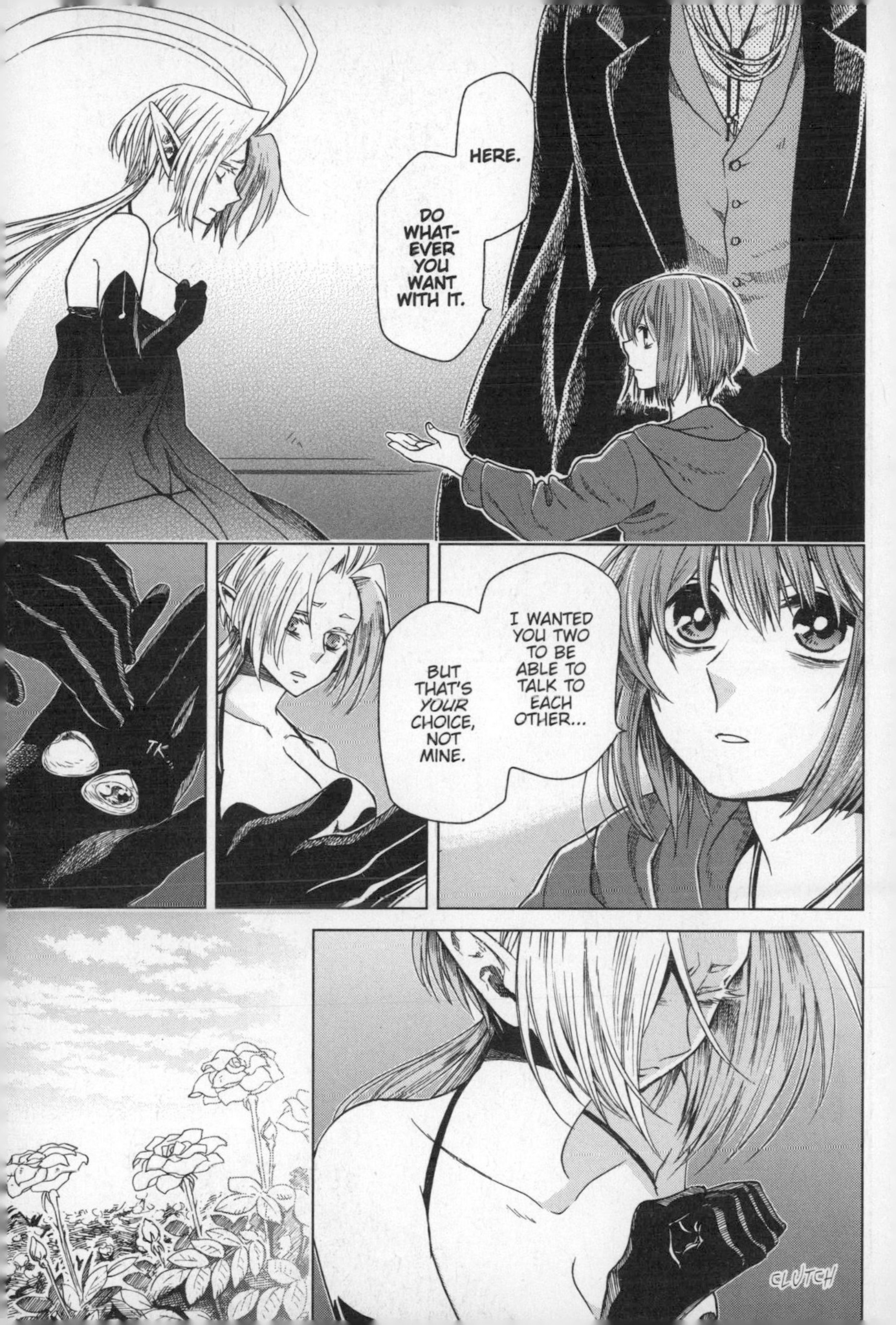
HERE.
DO WHAT-EVER YOU WANT WITH IT.
I WANTED YOU TWO TO BE ABLE TO TALK TO EACH OTHER...
BUT THAT'S *YOUR* CHOICE, NOT MINE.
TK
CLUTCH

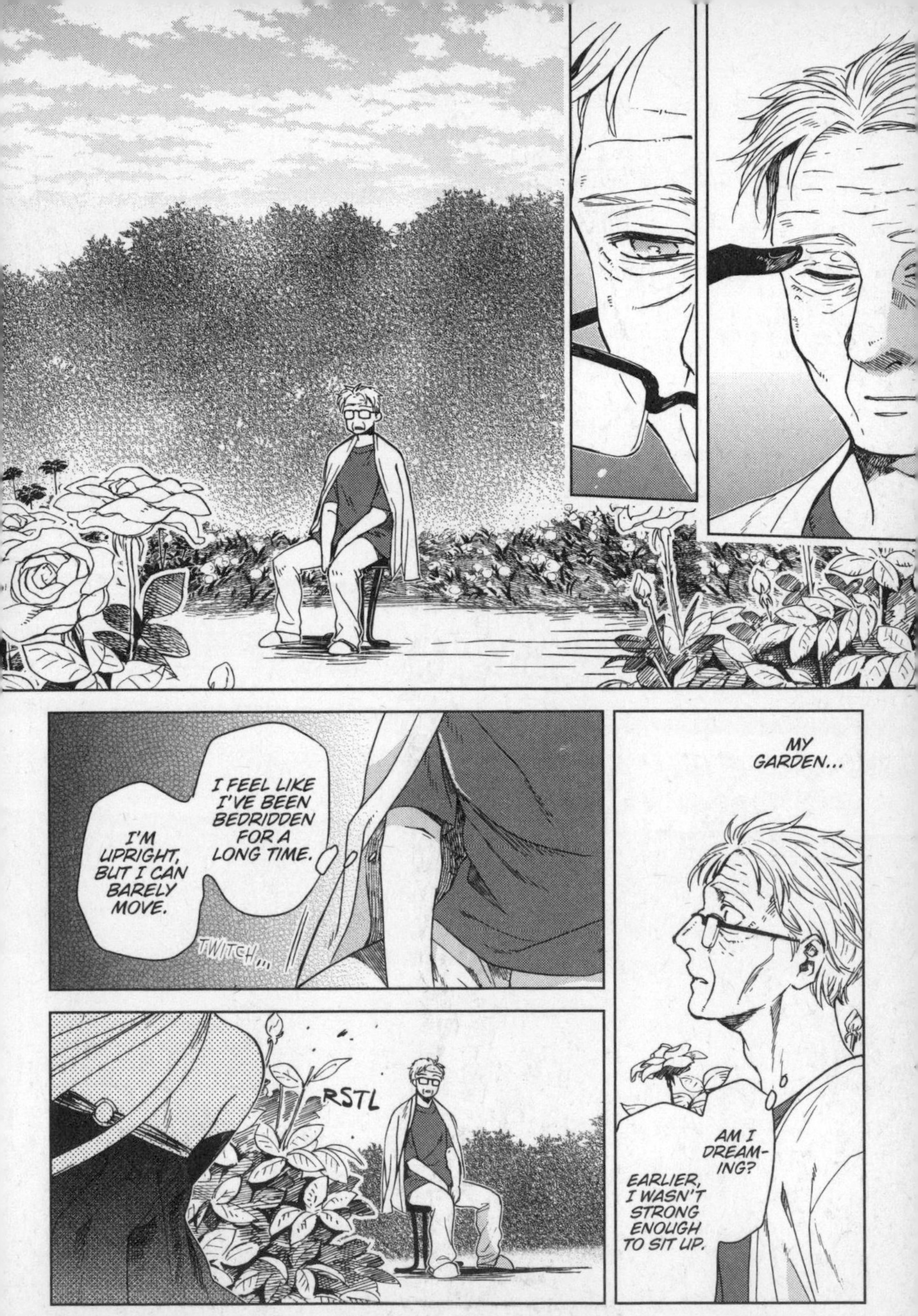
MY GARDEN...
AM I DREAMING?
EARLIER, I WASN'T STRONG ENOUGH TO SIT UP.
I FEEL LIKE I'VE BEEN BEDRIDDEN FOR A LONG TIME.
I'M UPRIGHT, BUT I CAN BARELY MOVE.
TWITCH...
RSTL

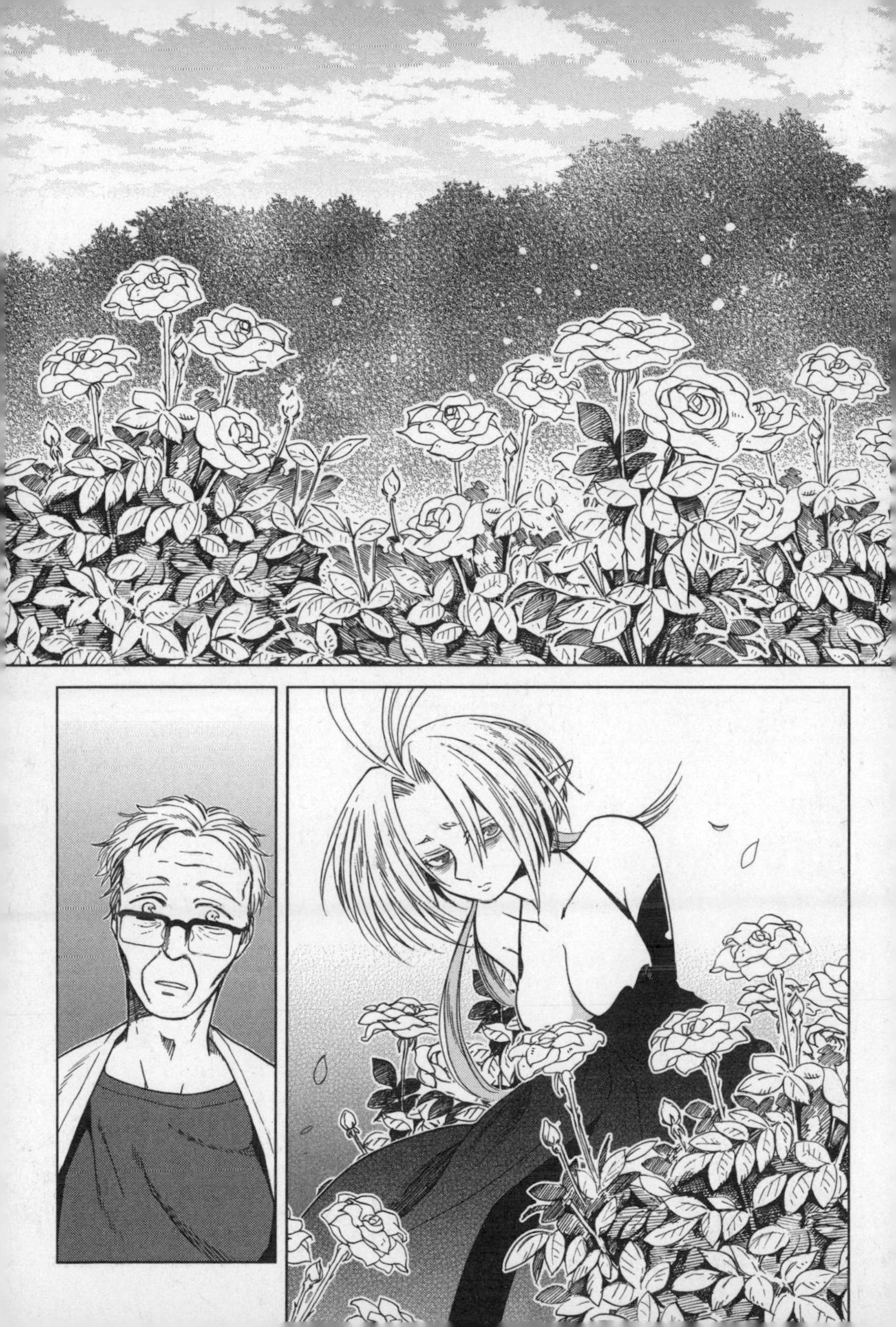

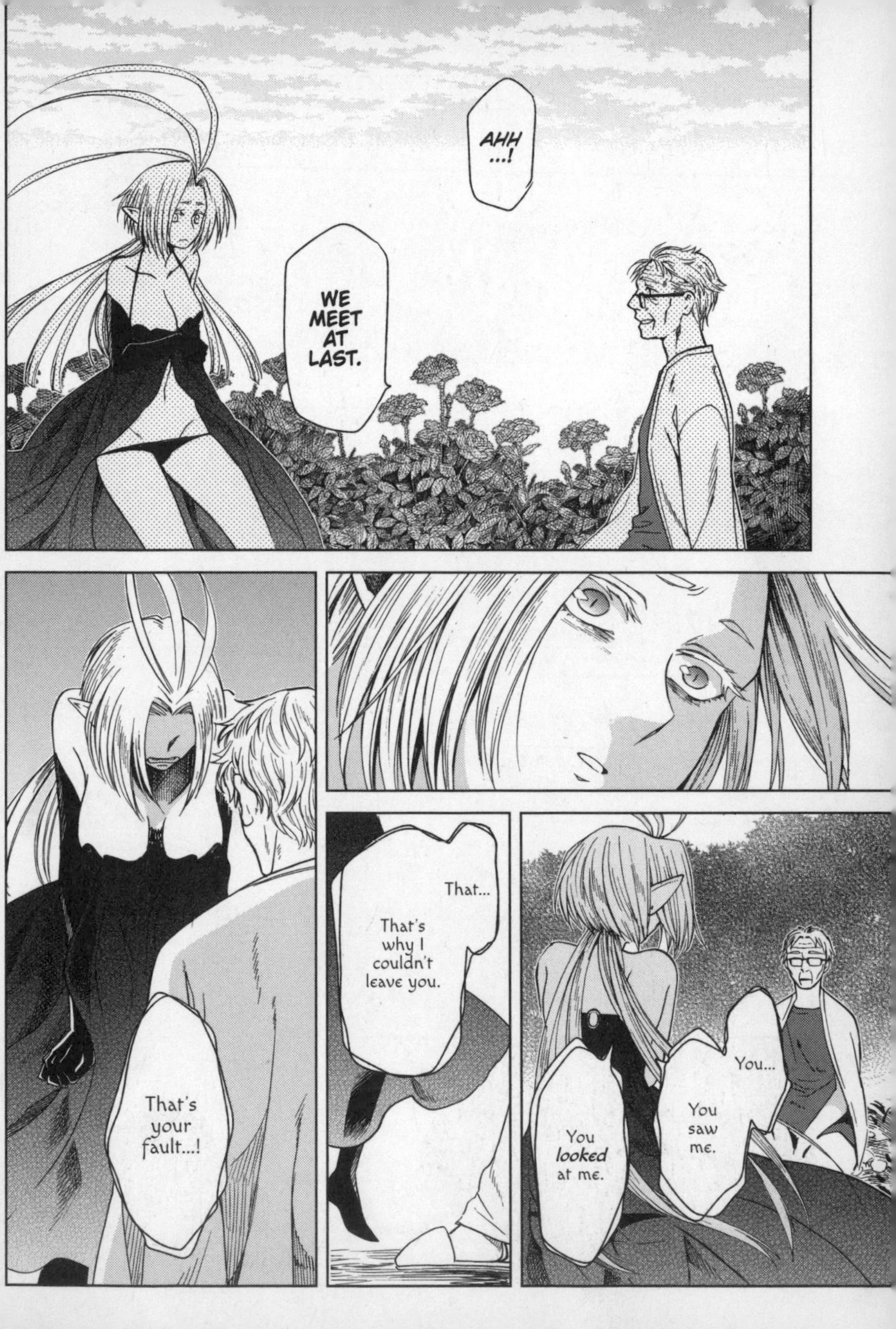
AHH ...!
WE MEET AT LAST.
You...
You saw me.
You *looked* at me.
That...
That's why I couldn't leave you.
That's your fault...!

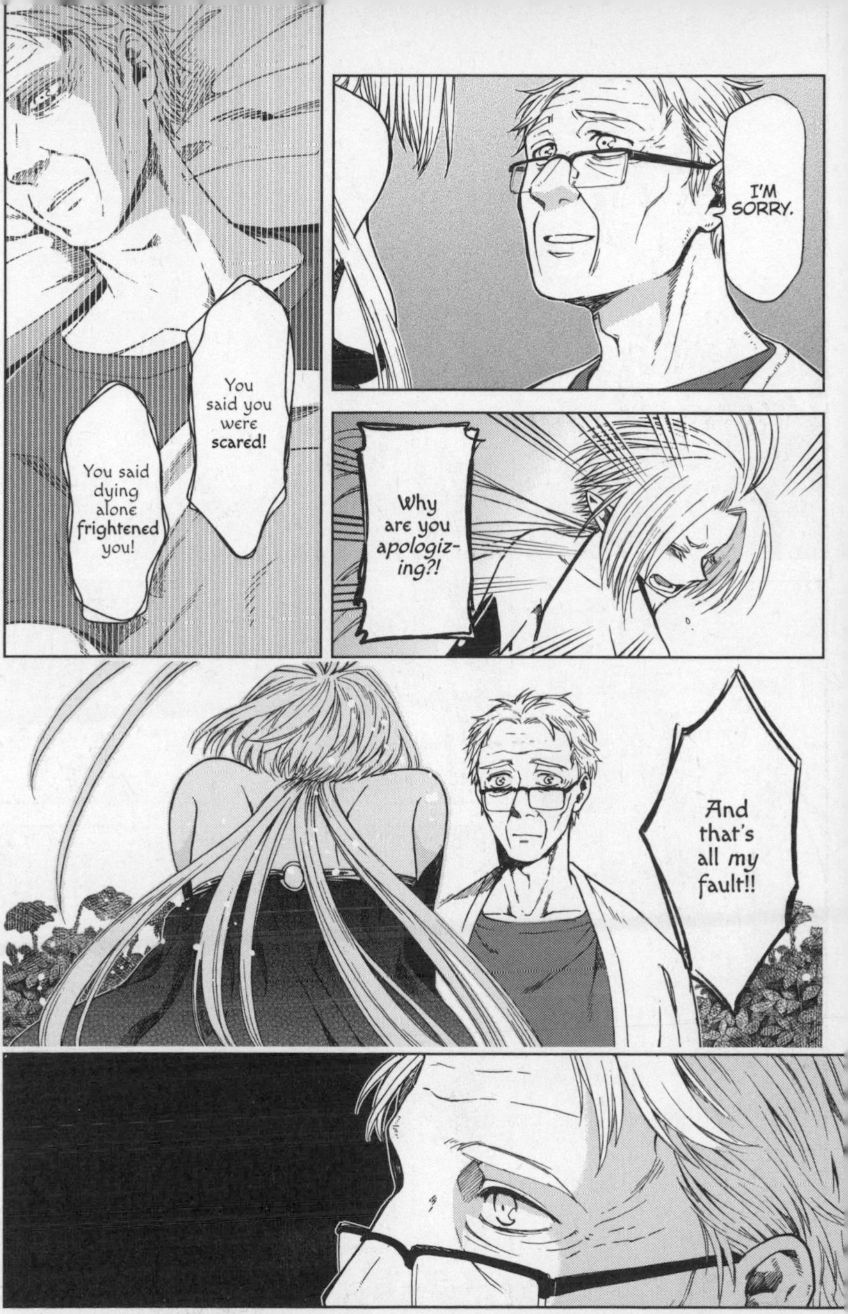
I'M SORRY.
Why are you apologizing?!
You said you were scared!
You said dying alone frightened you!
And that's all my fault!!

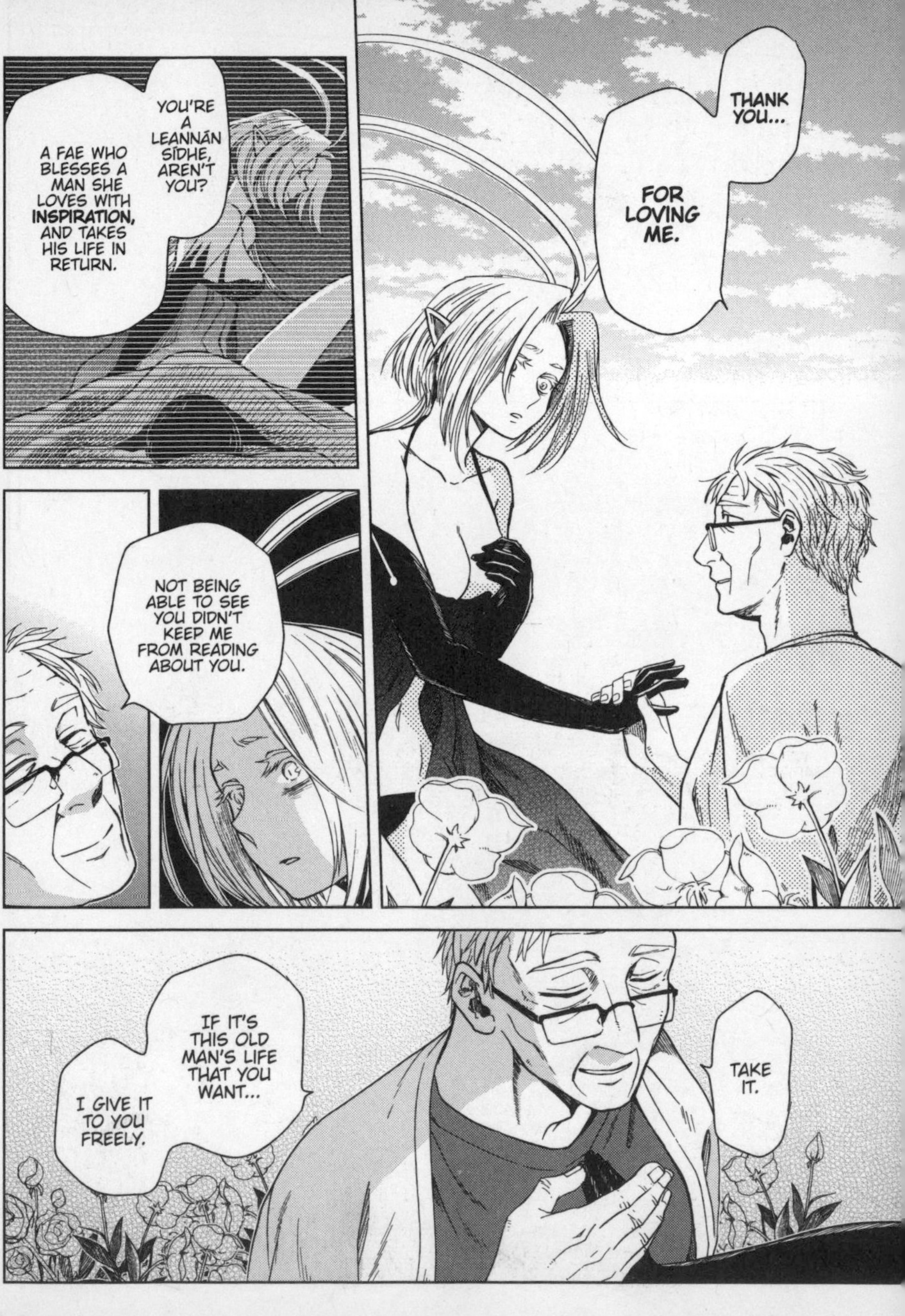
THANK YOU...
FOR LOVING ME.
YOU'RE A LEANNÁN SÍDHE, AREN'T YOU?
A FAE WHO BLESSES A MAN SHE LOVES WITH **INSPIRATION**, AND TAKES HIS LIFE IN RETURN.
NOT BEING ABLE TO SEE YOU DIDN'T KEEP ME FROM READING ABOUT YOU.
TAKE IT.
IF IT'S THIS OLD MAN'S LIFE THAT YOU WANT...
I GIVE IT TO YOU FREELY.

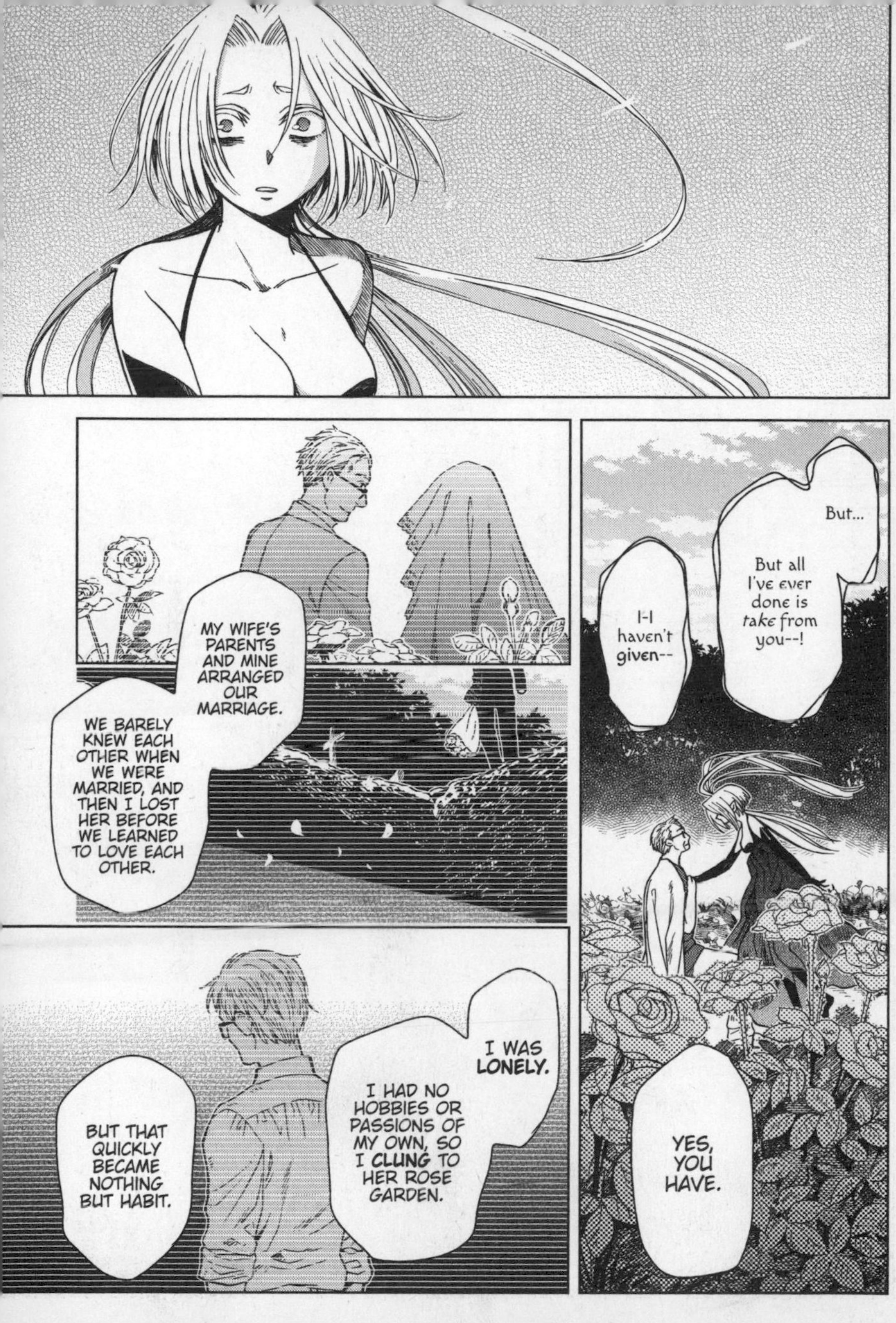
But...
But all I've ever done is *take* from you--!
I-I haven't given--
YES, YOU HAVE.
MY WIFE'S PARENTS AND MINE ARRANGED OUR MARRIAGE.
WE BARELY KNEW EACH OTHER WHEN WE WERE MARRIED, AND THEN I LOST HER BEFORE WE LEARNED TO LOVE EACH OTHER.
I WAS **LONELY.**
I HAD NO HOBBIES OR PASSIONS OF MY OWN, SO I **CLUNG** TO HER ROSE GARDEN.
BUT THAT QUICKLY BECAME NOTHING BUT HABIT.

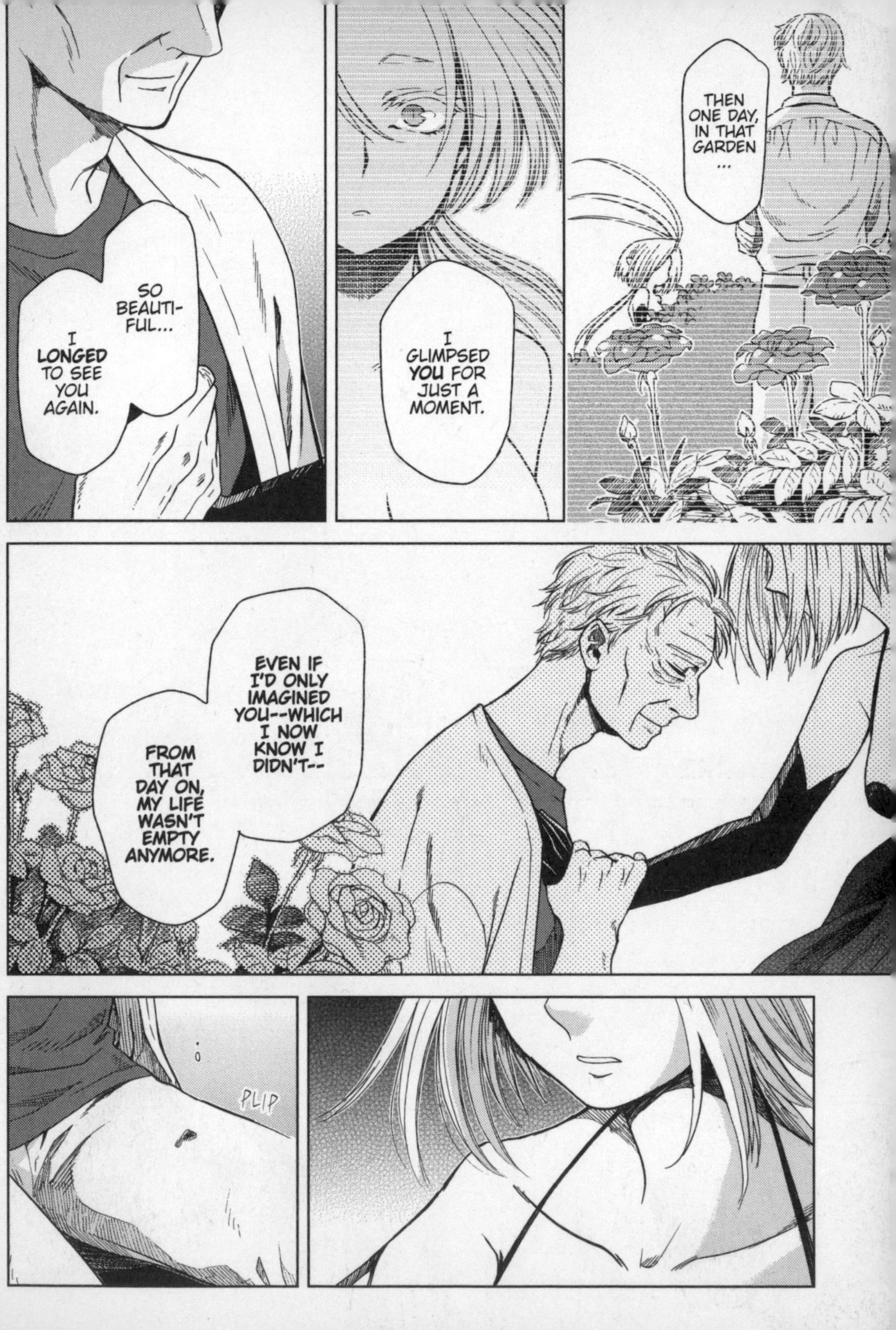
THEN ONE DAY, IN THAT GARDEN ...
I GLIMPSED YOU FOR JUST A MOMENT.
SO BEAUTIFUL...
I LONGED TO SEE YOU AGAIN.
EVEN IF I'D ONLY IMAGINED YOU--WHICH I NOW KNOW I DIDN'T--
FROM THAT DAY ON, MY LIFE WASN'T EMPTY ANYMORE.
PLIP

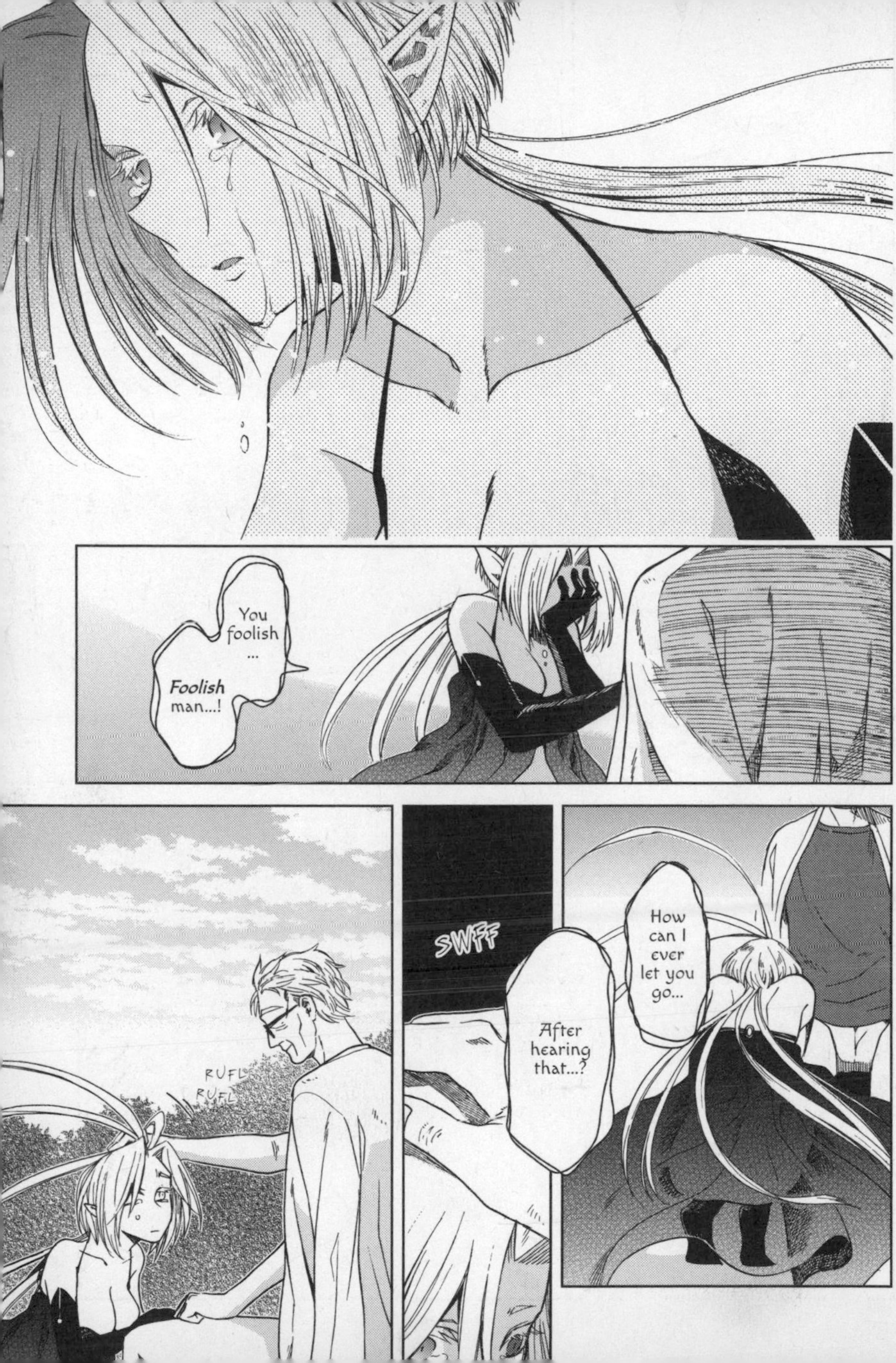
You foolish ...
Foolish man...!
How can I ever let you go...
After hearing that...?
SWFF
RUFL RUFL

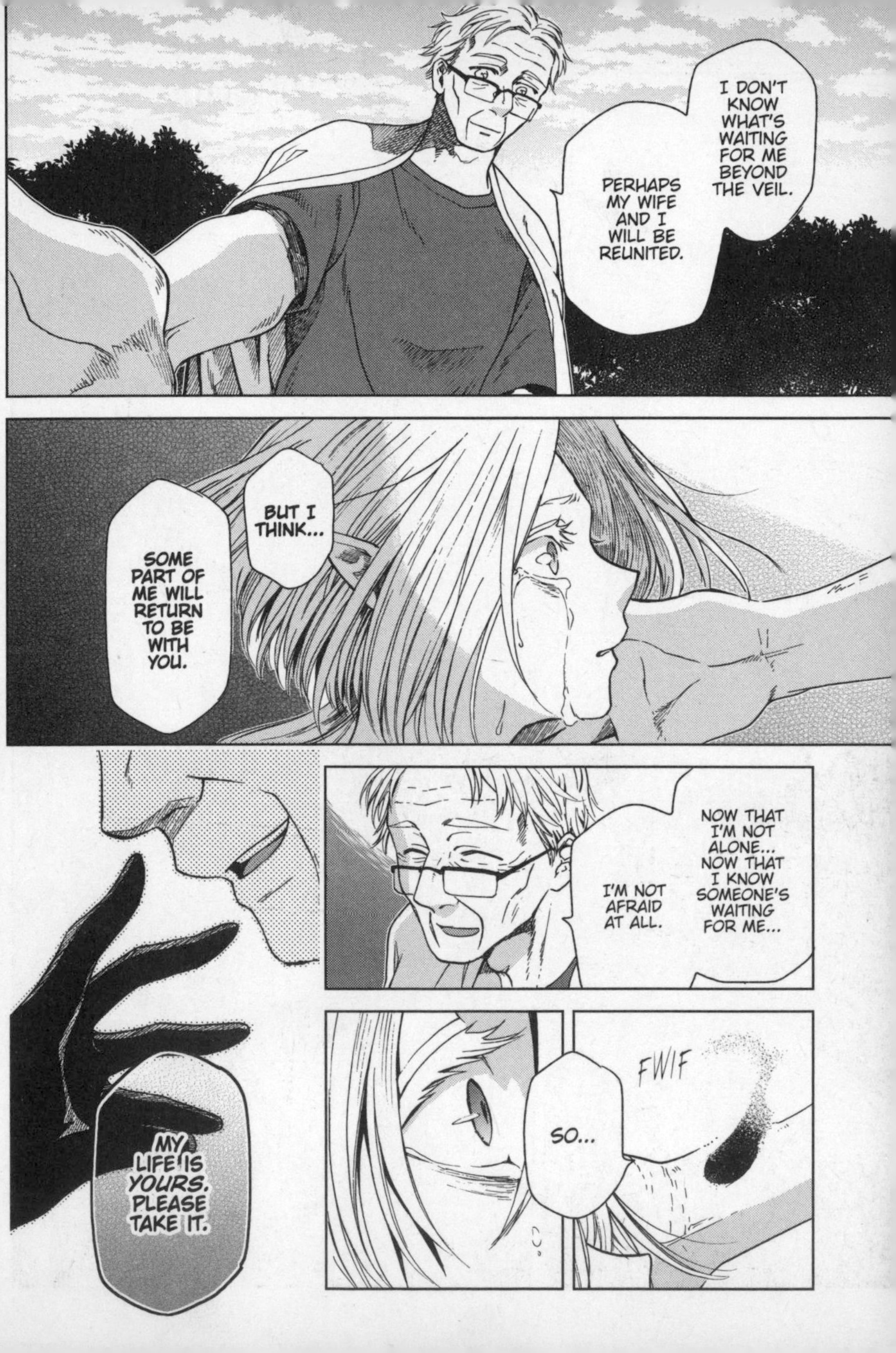
I DON'T KNOW WHAT'S WAITING FOR ME BEYOND THE VEIL.
PERHAPS MY WIFE AND I WILL BE REUNITED.
BUT I THINK...
SOME PART OF ME WILL RETURN TO BE WITH YOU.
NOW THAT I'M NOT ALONE... NOW THAT I KNOW SOMEONE'S WAITING FOR ME...
I'M NOT AFRAID AT ALL.
FWIF
SO...
MY LIFE IS YOURS. PLEASE TAKE IT.

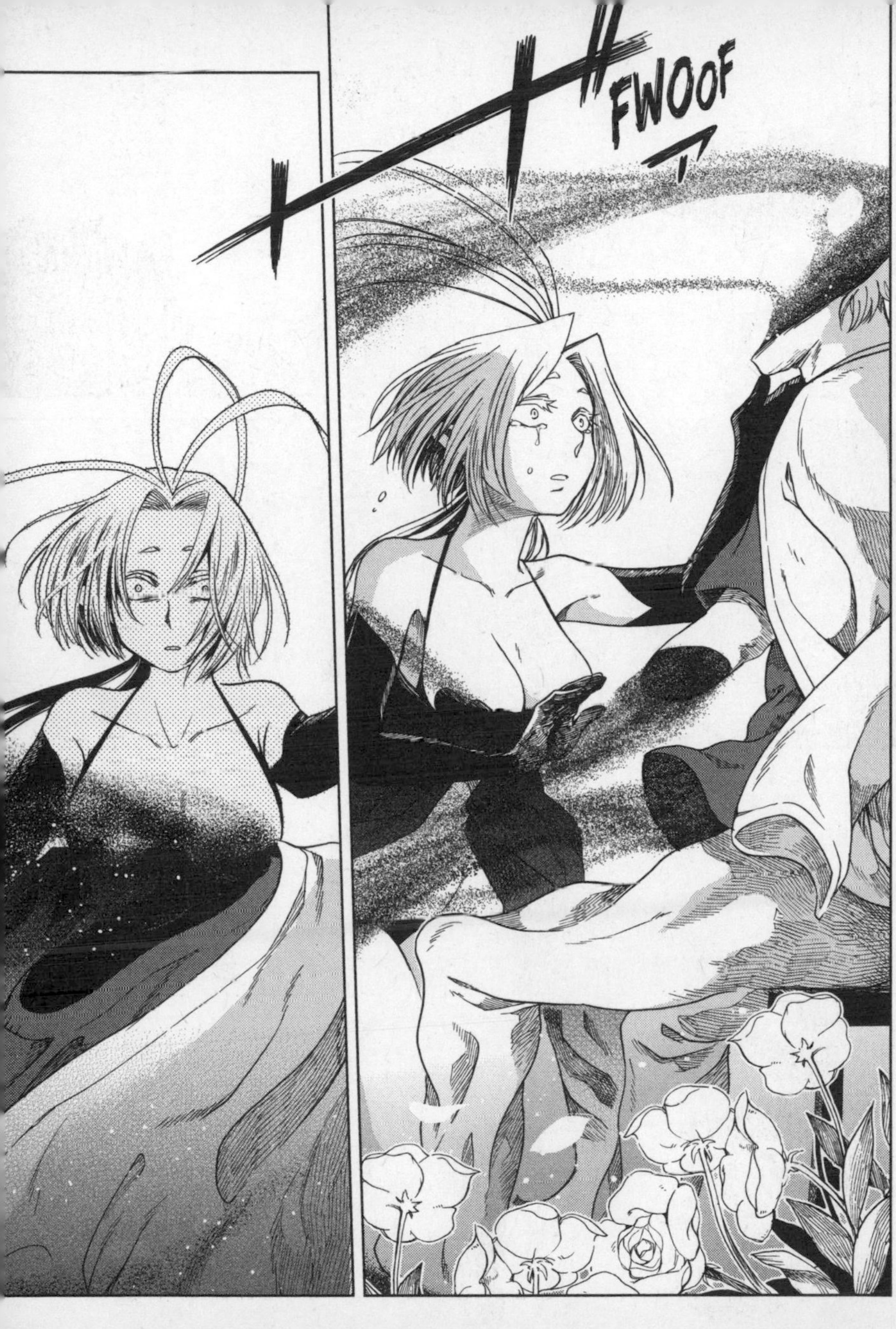
FWOOF

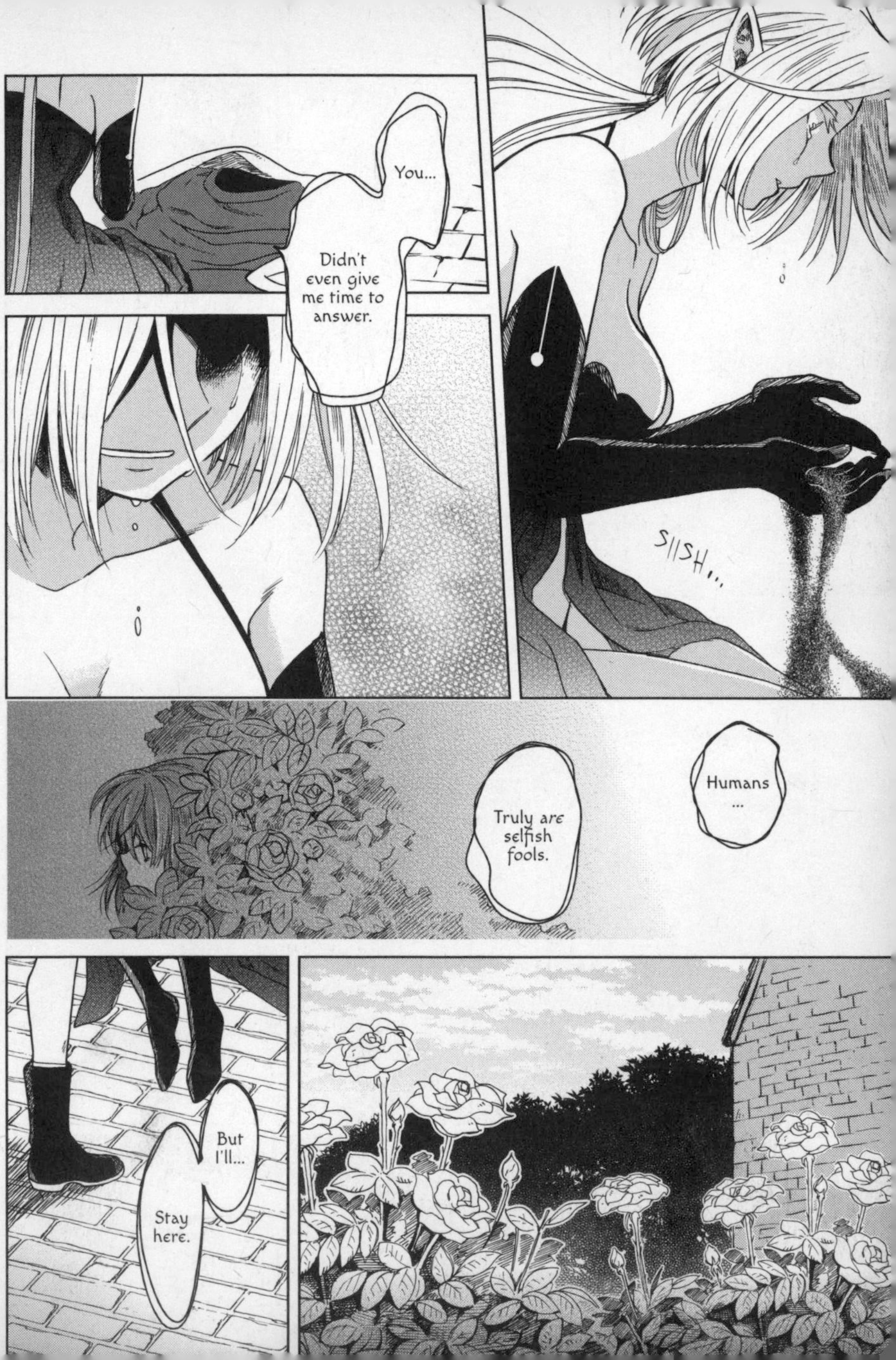
SIISH...
You...
Didn't even give me time to answer.
Humans...
Truly are selfish fools.
But I'll...
Stay here.

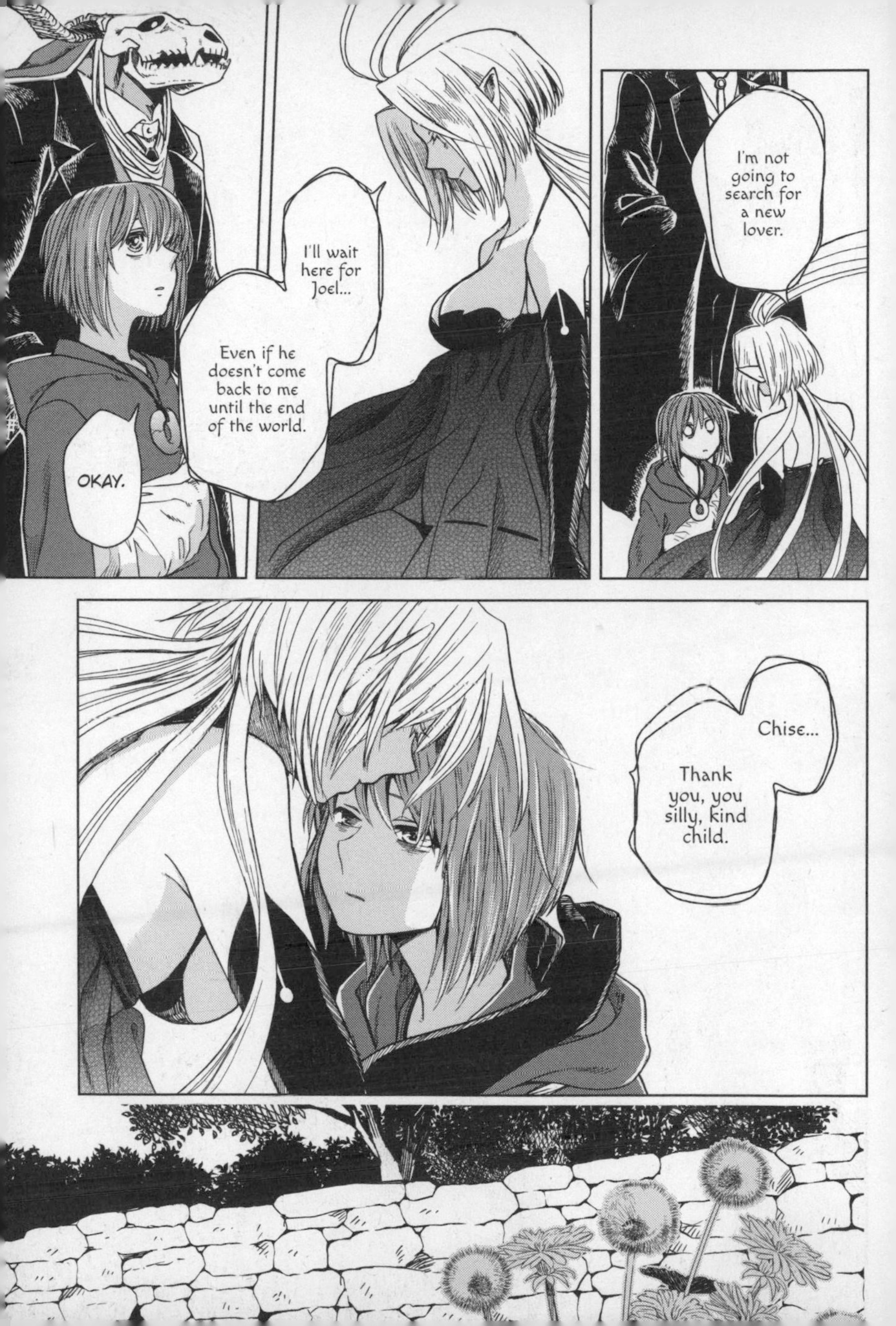
I'm not going to search for a new lover.
I'll wait here for Joel...
Even if he doesn't come back to me until the end of the world.
OKAY.
Chise...
Thank you, you silly, kind child.

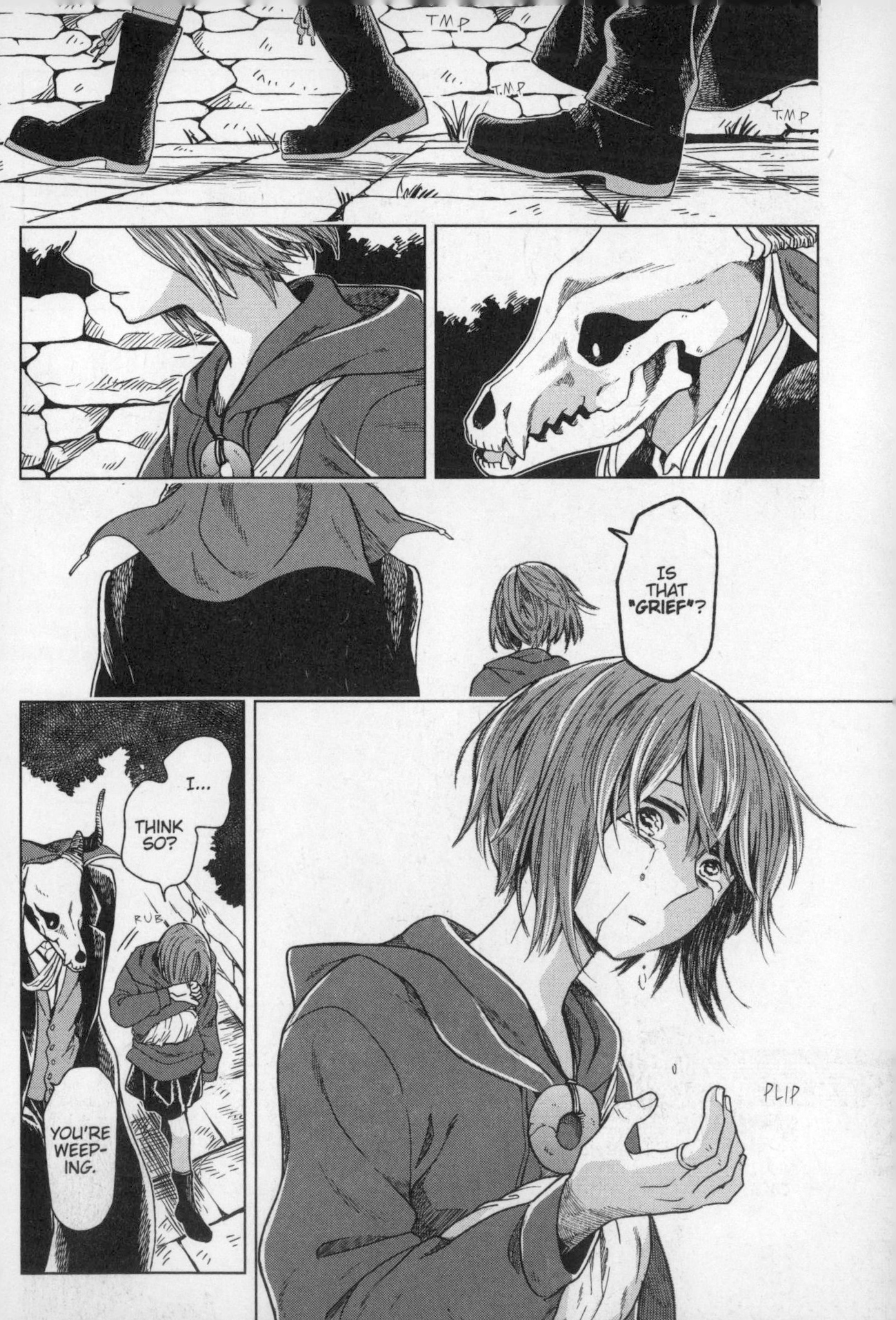
TMP
T.M.P
TMP
IS THAT "GRIEF"?
PLIP
I...
THINK SO?
RUB
YOU'RE WEEPING.

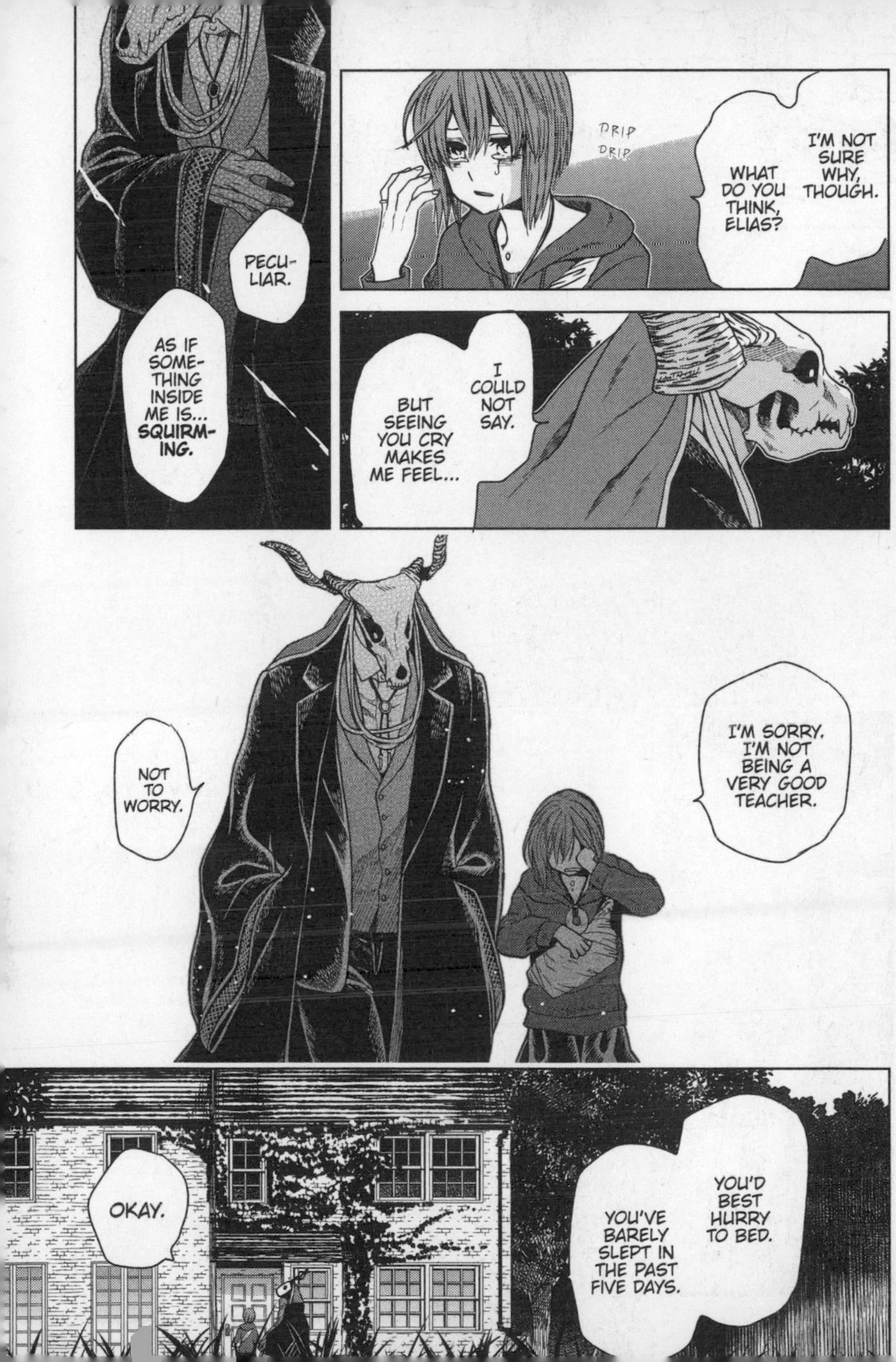
I'M NOT SURE WHY, THOUGH.
WHAT DO YOU THINK, ELIAS?
DRIP DRIP
I COULD NOT SAY.
BUT SEEING YOU CRY MAKES ME FEEL...
PECULIAR.
AS IF SOMETHING INSIDE ME IS... **SQUIRMING.**
I'M SORRY. I'M NOT BEING A VERY GOOD TEACHER.
NOT TO WORRY.
YOU'D BEST HURRY TO BED.
YOU'VE BARELY SLEPT IN THE PAST FIVE DAYS.
OKAY.

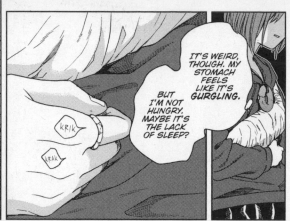

IT'S WEIRD, THOUGH. MY STOMACH FEELS LIKE IT'S GURGLING.

BUT I'M NOT HUNGRY. MAYBE IT'S THE LACK OF SLEEP?

KRIK

KRAK

SWING!

HI!

FWP

WHAT BRINGS YOU HERE?

OBERON ?!

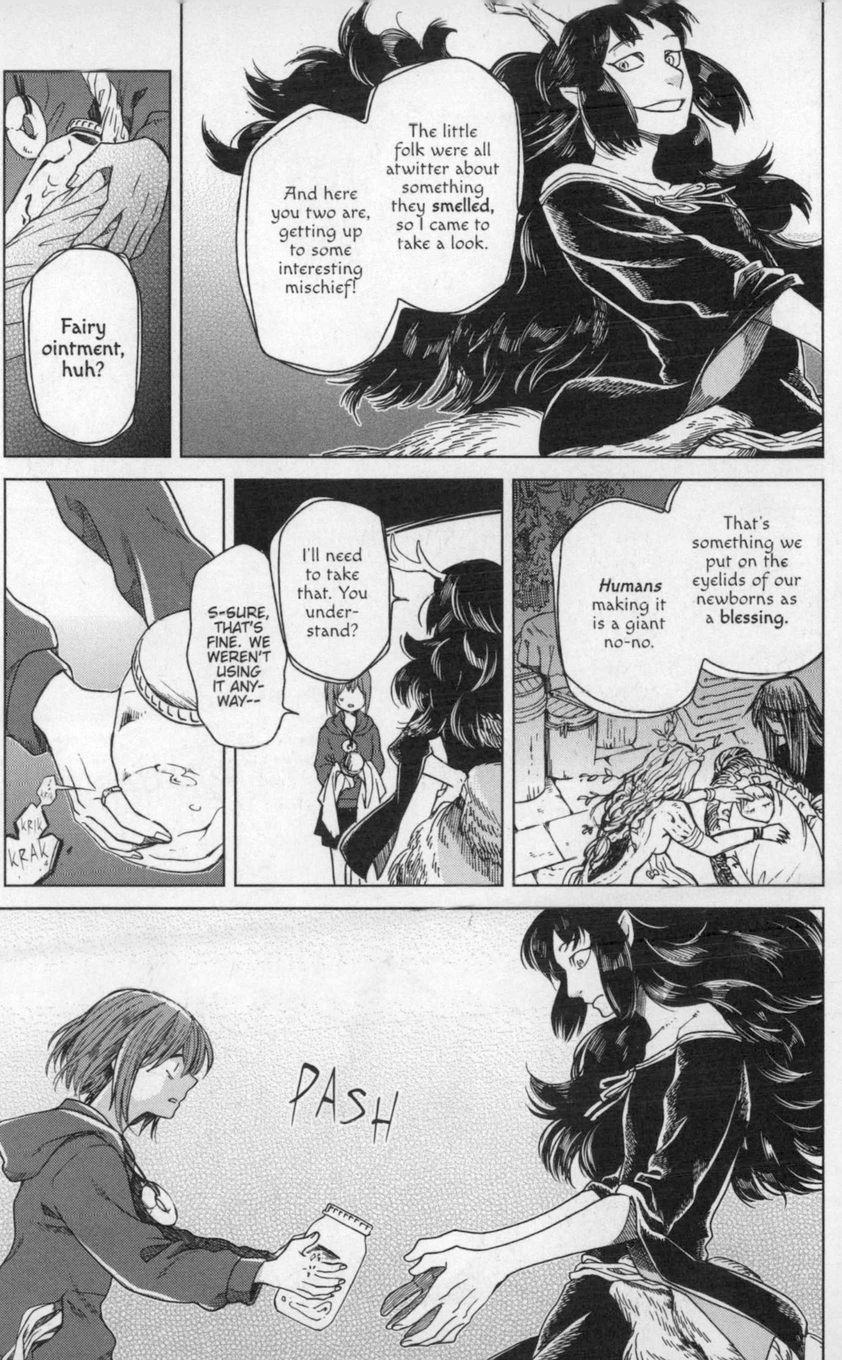
The little folk were all atwitter about something they smelled, so I came to take a look.
And here you two are, getting up to some interesting mischief!
Fairy ointment, huh?
That's something we put on the eyelids of our newborns as a blessing.
Humans making it is a giant no-no.
I'll need to take that. You understand?
S-SURE, THAT'S FINE. WE WEREN'T USING IT ANYWAY--
KRIK
KRAK
PASH

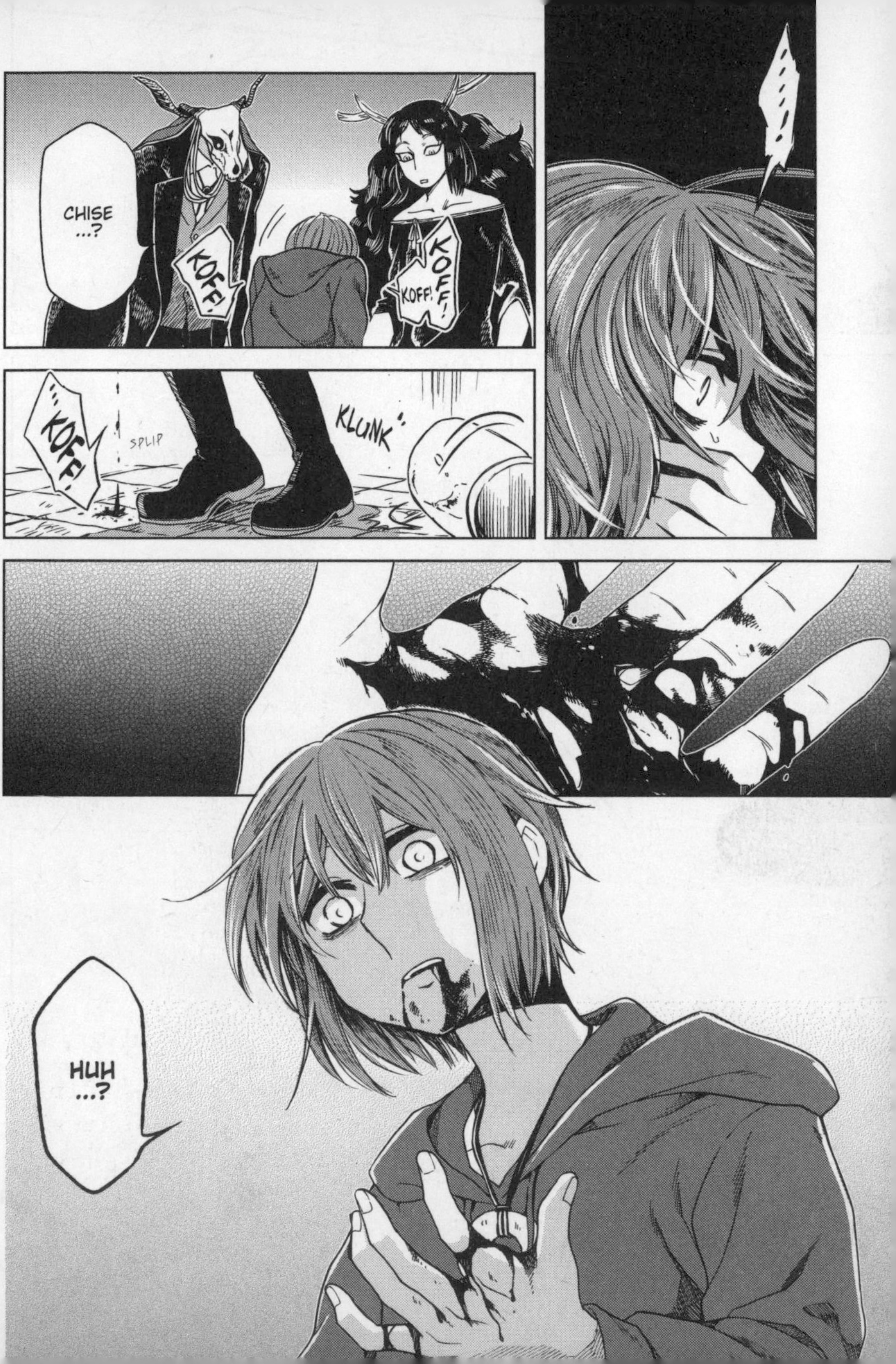
...!
KOFF! KOFF!
KOFF!
CHISE ...?
KLUNK
SPLIP
...KOFF!
HUH ...?

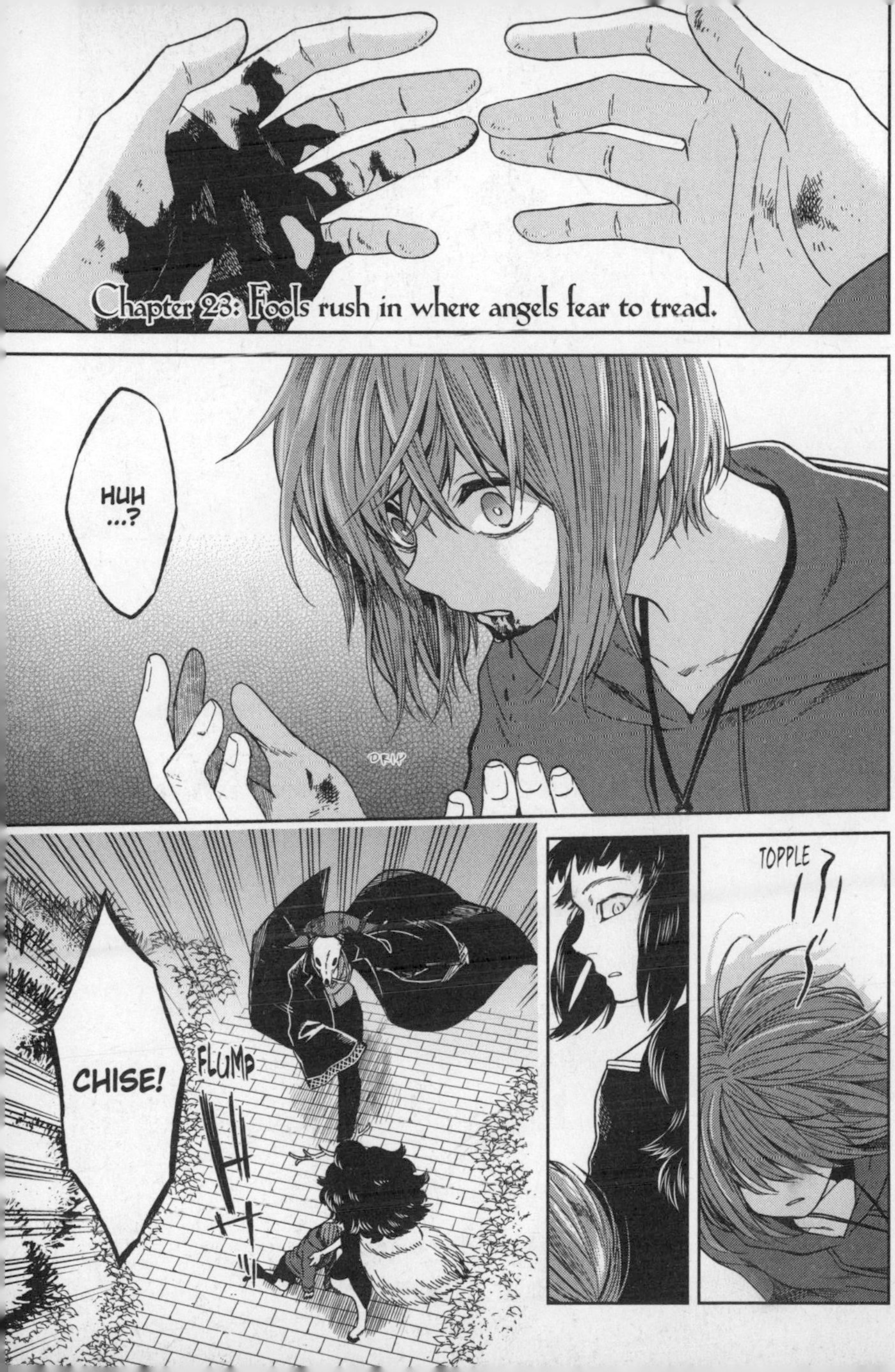
Chapter 23: Fools rush in where angels fear to tread.
HUH ...?
DRIP
TOPPLE
CHISE!
FLUMP

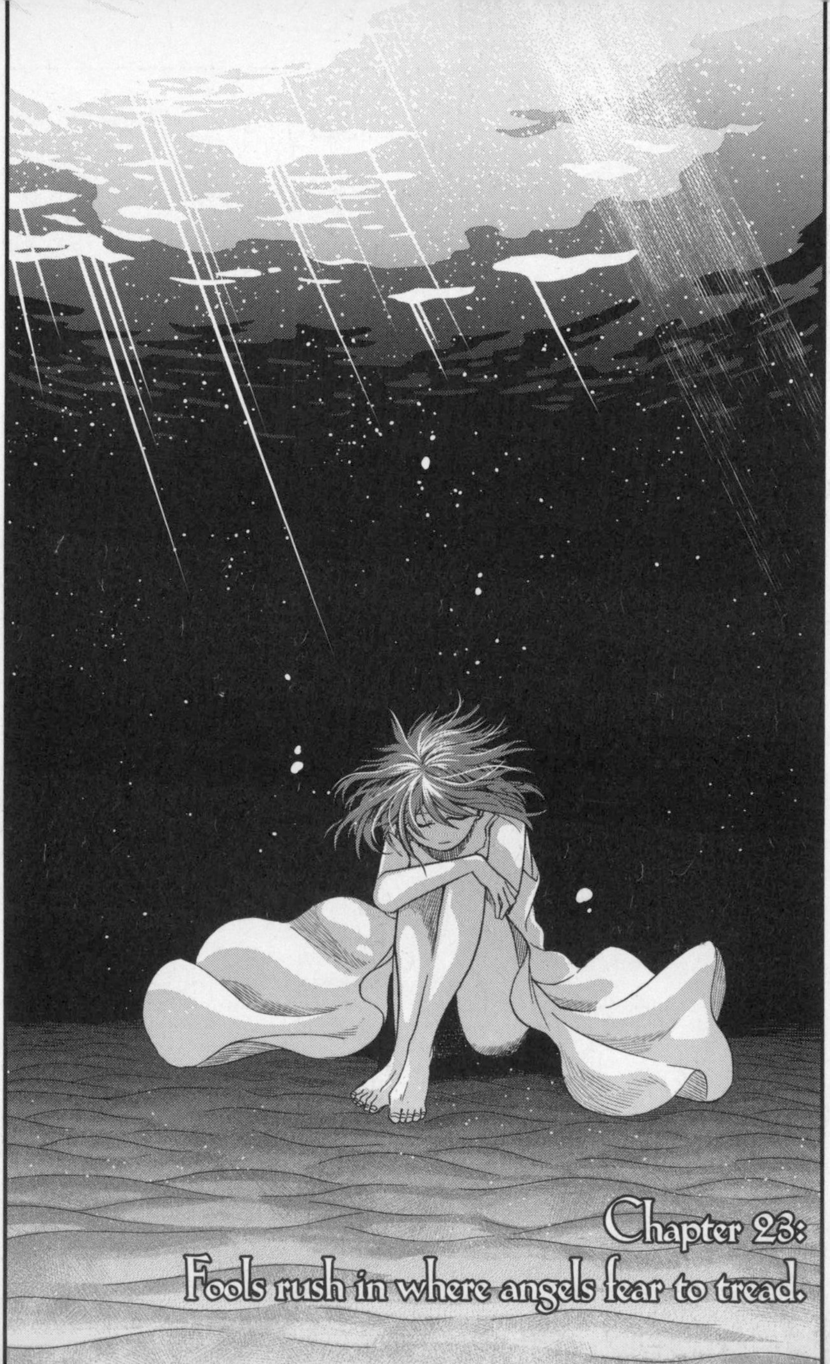
Chapter 23:
Fools rush in where angels fear to tread.

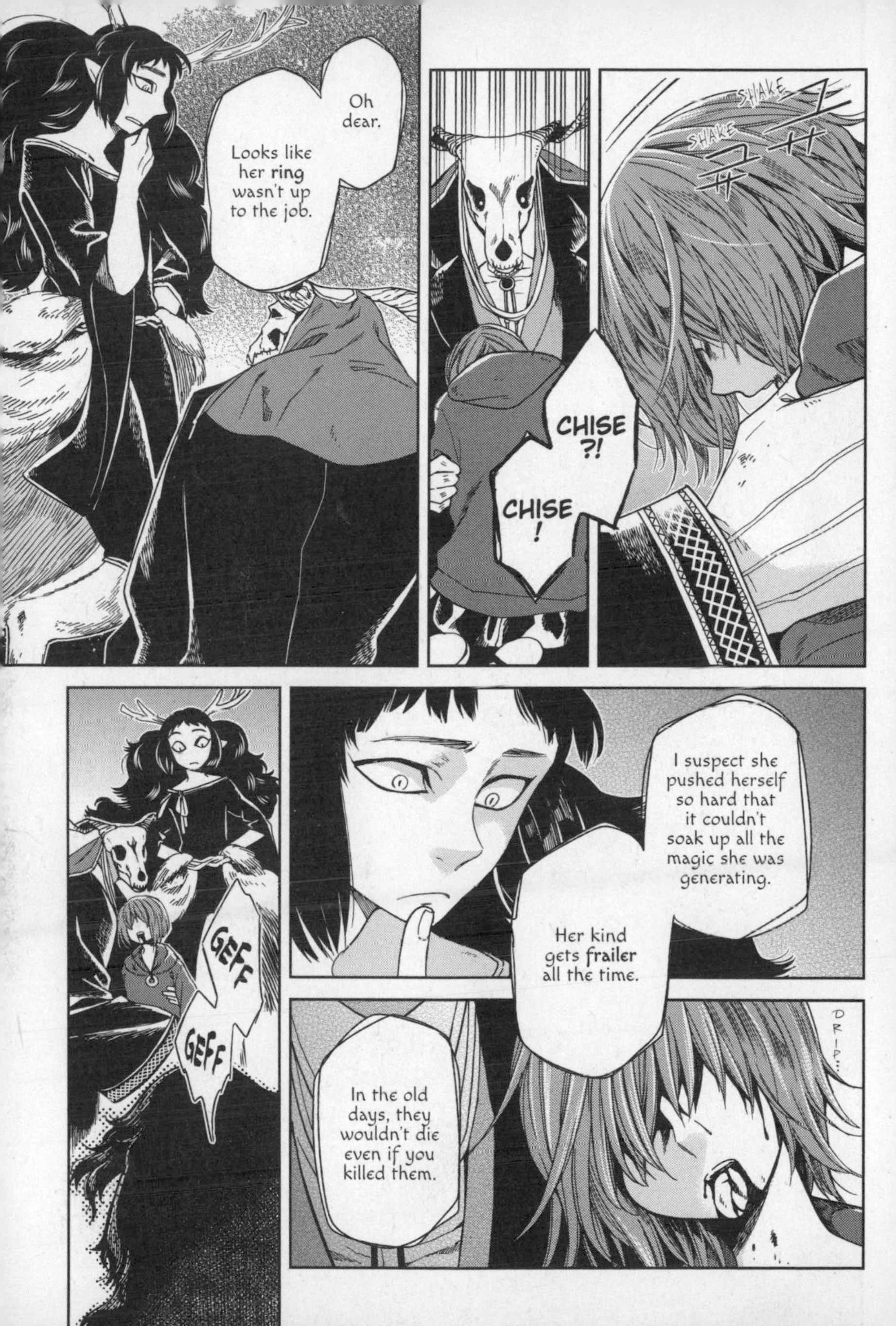
SHAKE
SHAKE
CHISE?!
CHISE!
Oh dear.
Looks like her ring wasn't up to the job.
I suspect she pushed herself so hard that it couldn't soak up all the magic she was generating.
Her kind gets frailer all the time.
DRIP...
In the old days, they wouldn't die even if you killed them.
GEFF
GEFF

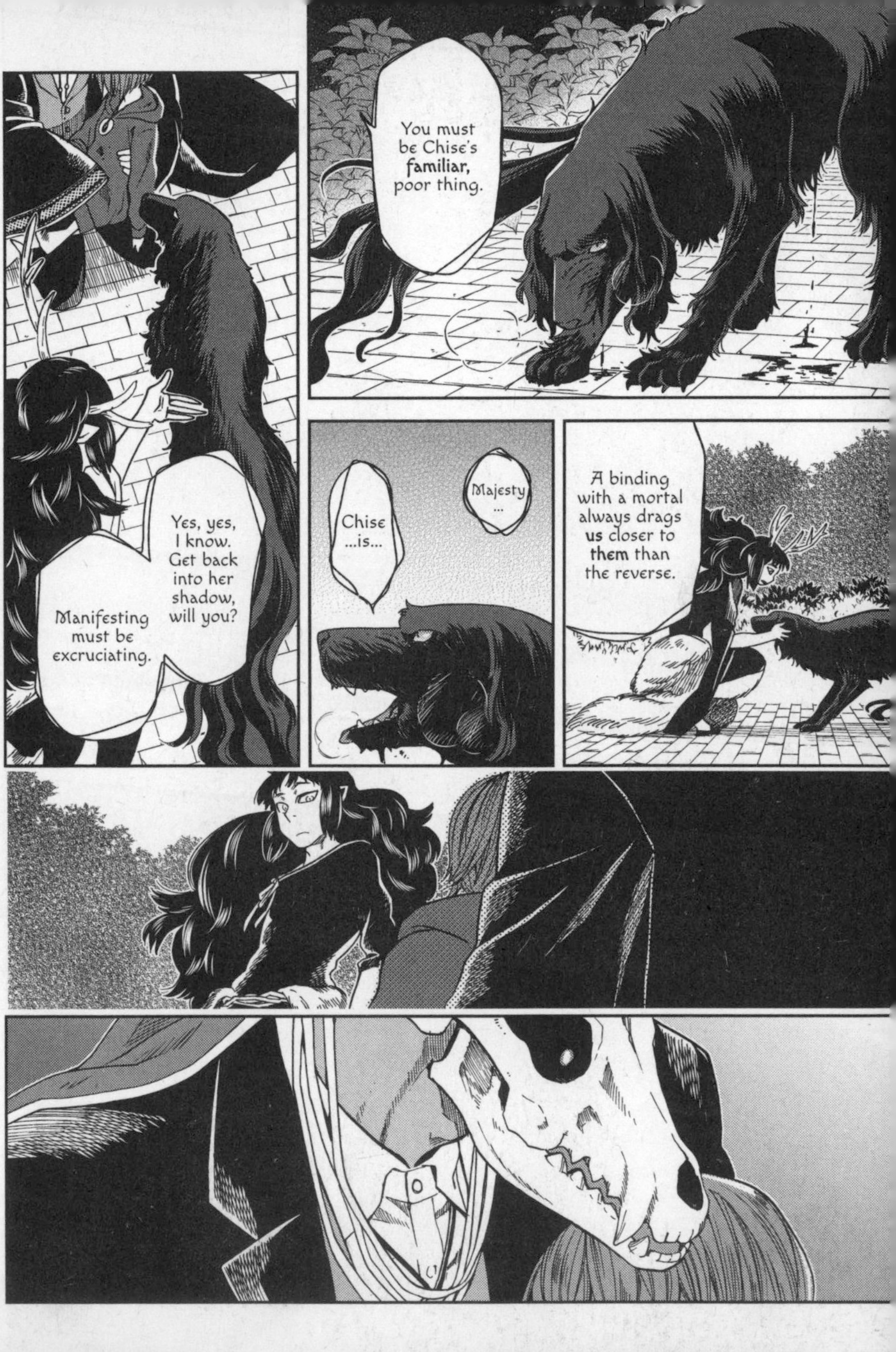
You must be Chise's familiar, poor thing.
A binding with a mortal always drags us closer to them than the reverse.
Majesty ...
Chise ...is...
Yes, yes, I know. Get back into her shadow, will you?
Manifesting must be excruciating.

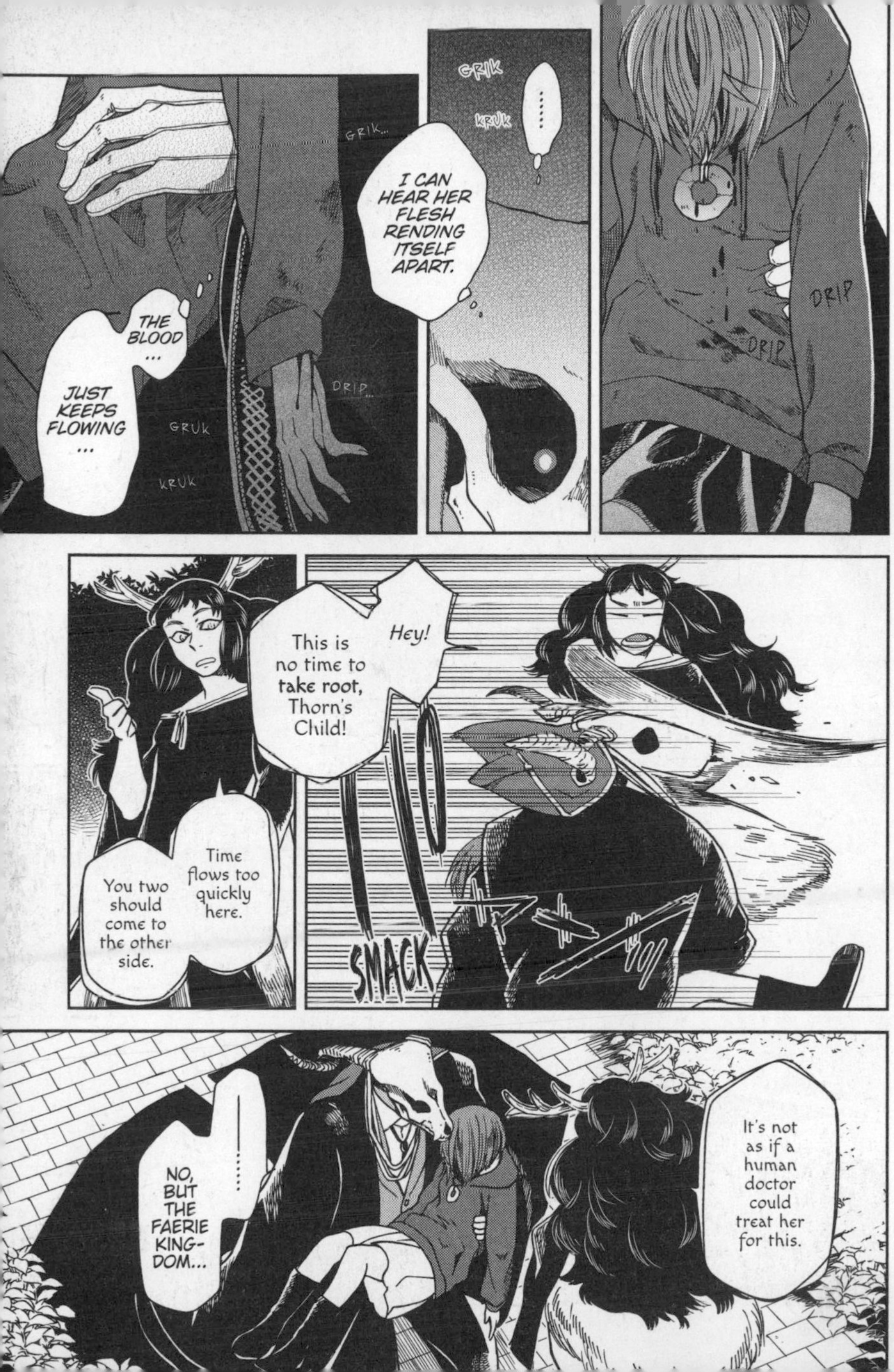
DRIP
DRIP
GRIK
KRUK
......
I CAN HEAR HER FLESH RENDING ITSELF APART.
GRIK...
THE BLOOD ...
JUST KEEPS FLOWING ...
DRIP...
GRUK
KRUK
Hey!
This is no time to take root, Thorn's Child!
SMACK
Time flows too quickly here.
You two should come to the other side.
It's not as if a human doctor could treat her for this.
......
NO, BUT THE FAERIE KING-DOM...

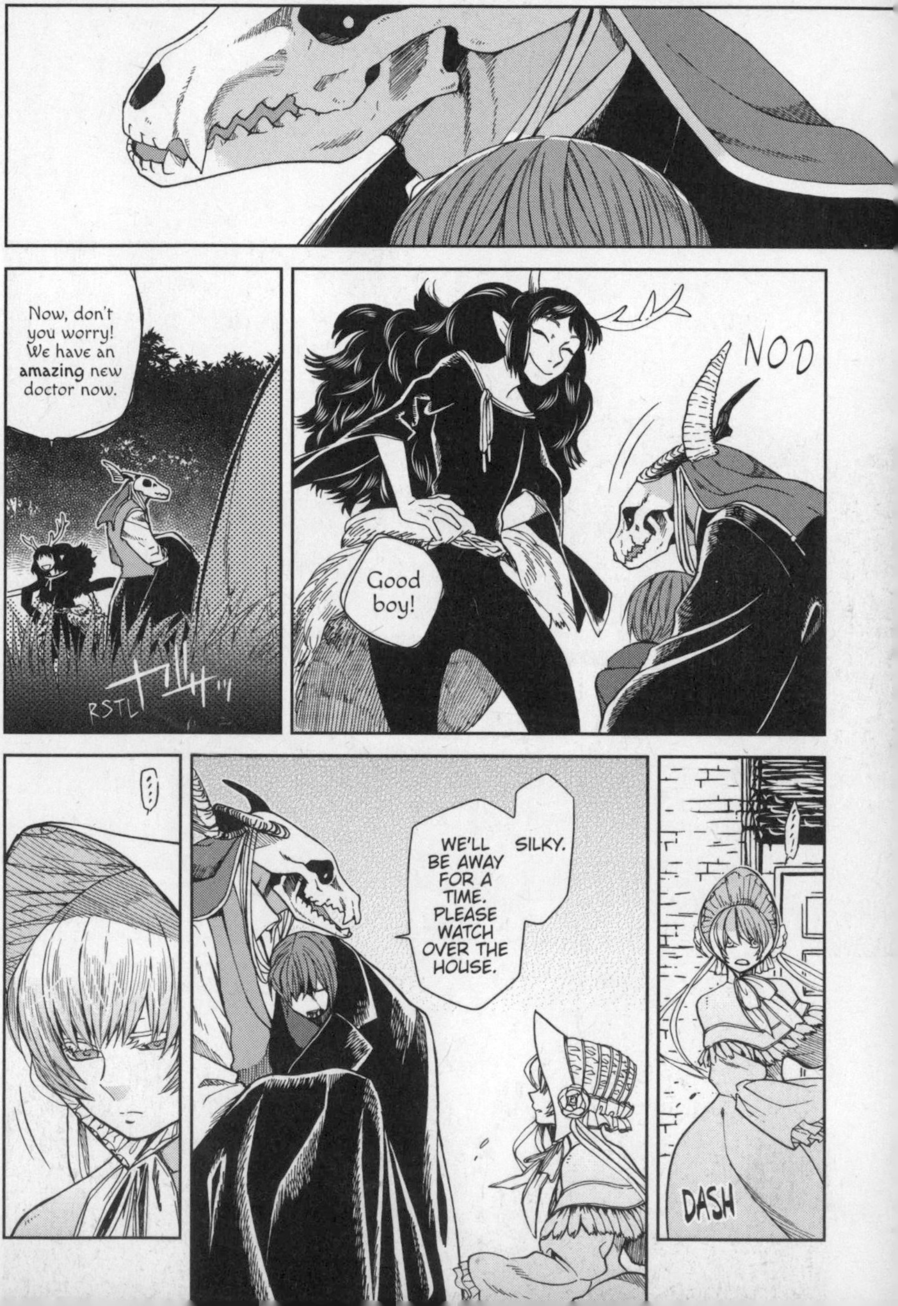

NOD
Good boy!
Now, don't you worry! We have an **amazing** new doctor now.
RSTL
DASH
SILKY. WE'LL BE AWAY FOR A TIME. PLEASE WATCH OVER THE HOUSE.

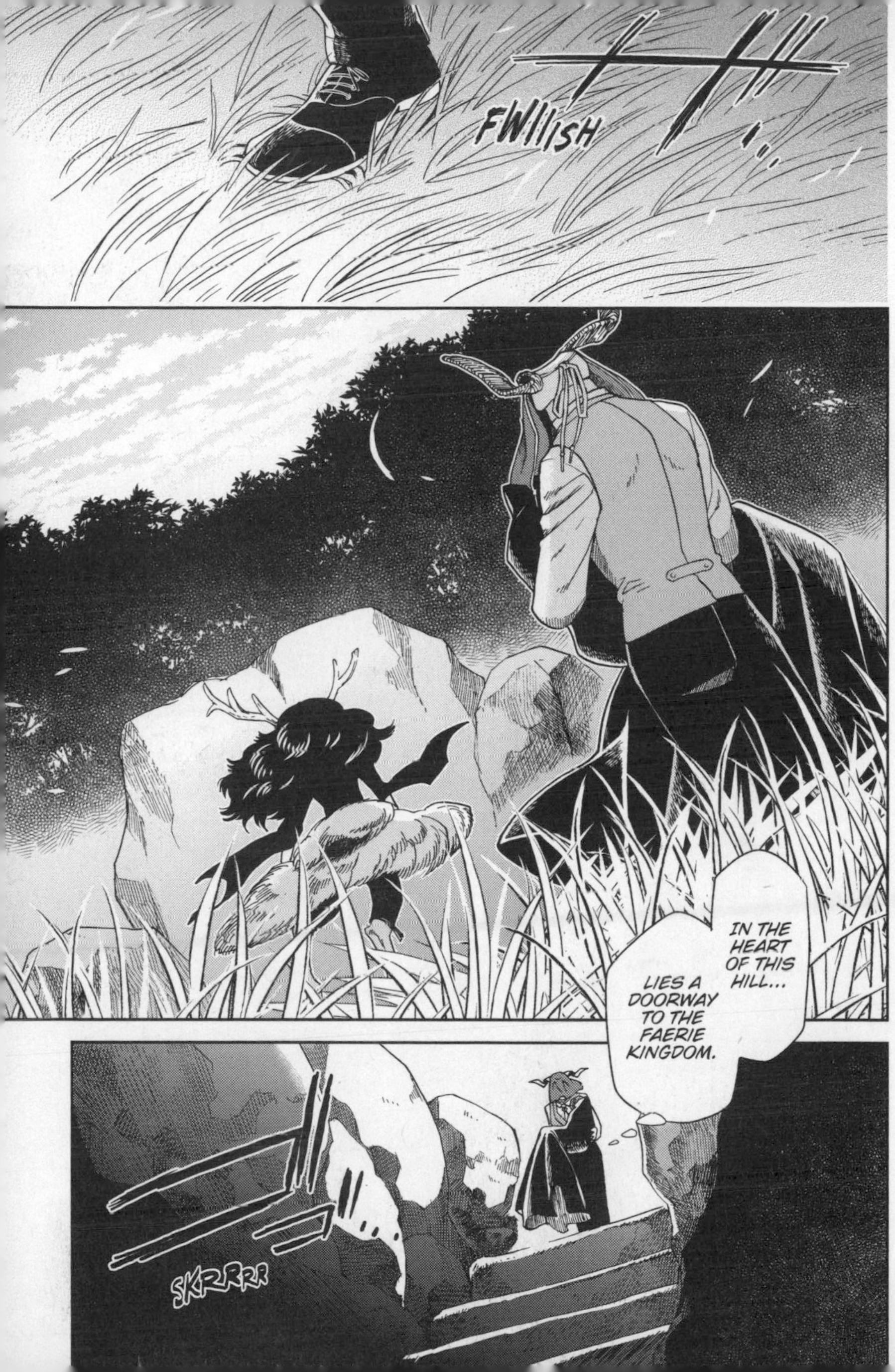
FWIIISH
IN THE HEART OF THIS HILL...
LIES A DOORWAY TO THE FAERIE KINGDOM.
SKRRRR

WHEN YOU CAME HERE BEFORE, I REACHED OUT TO STOP YOU.

NOW, I AM CARRYING YOU **ACROSS** THE THRESHOLD.

WHAT A STRANGE TURN OF FATE.

TOK

SWOoooooo

Half-thing.

Look! It's the failure.

Half-ling.

It stinks. oh yes.

TOK

TOK

TOK

But it brings a robin.

Yes.

Precious.

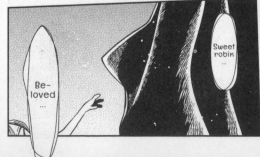

Sweet robin ...

Beloved ...

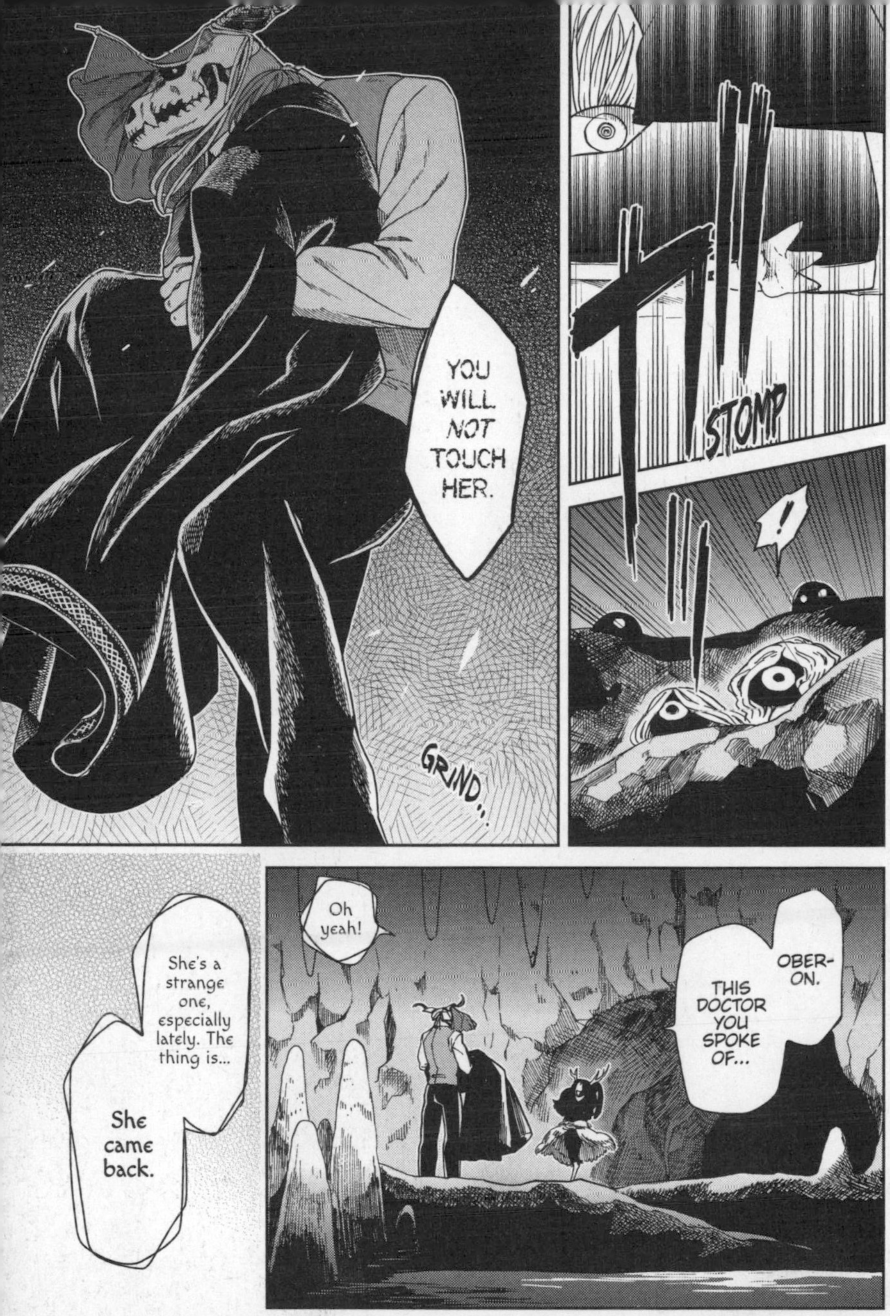
STOMP
!
YOU WILL NOT TOUCH HER.
GRIND...
OBER-ON.
THIS DOCTOR YOU SPOKE OF...
Oh yeah!
She's a strange one, especially lately. The thing is...
She came back.

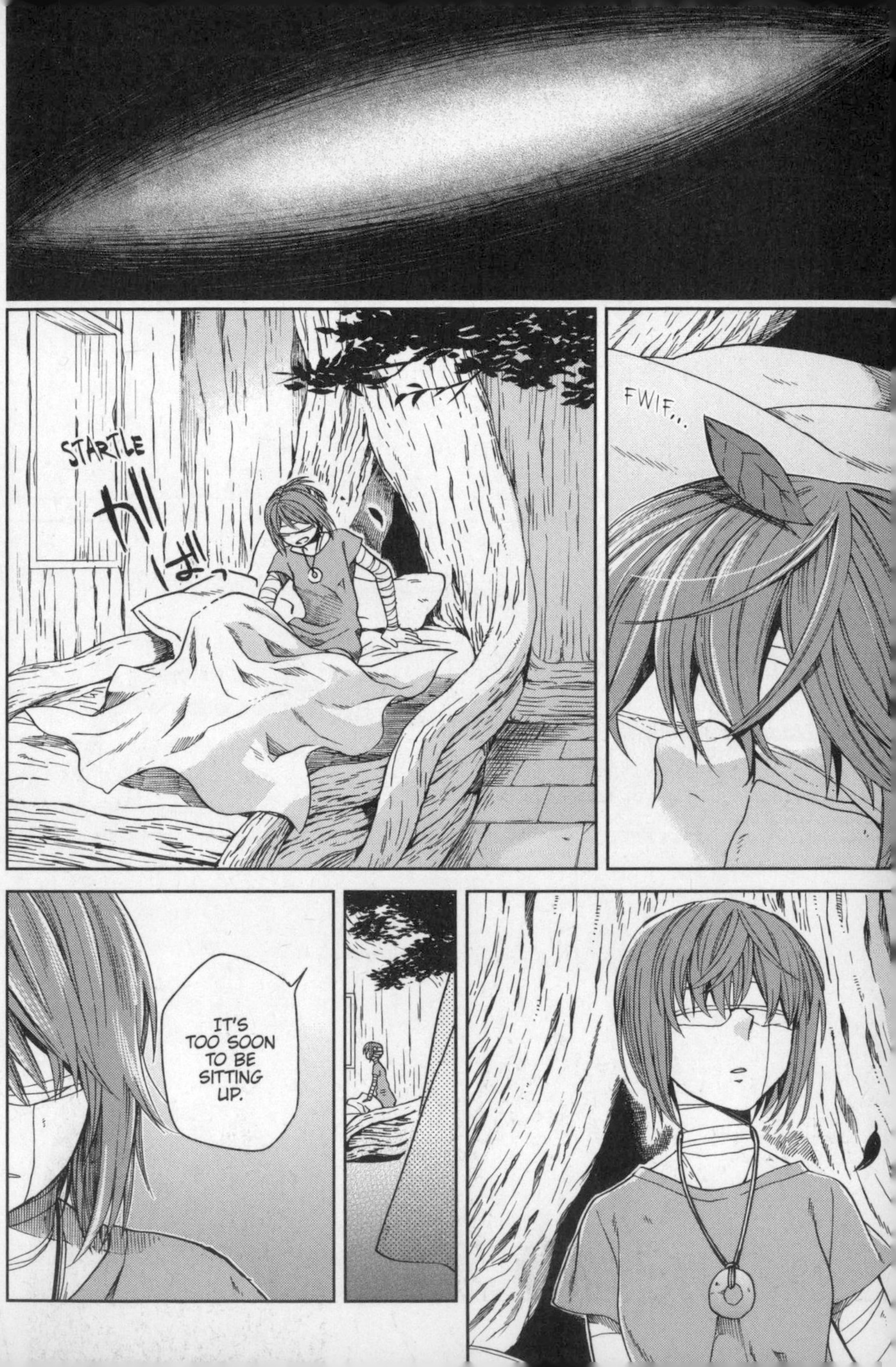
FWIF...
STARTLE
IT'S TOO SOON TO BE SITTING UP.

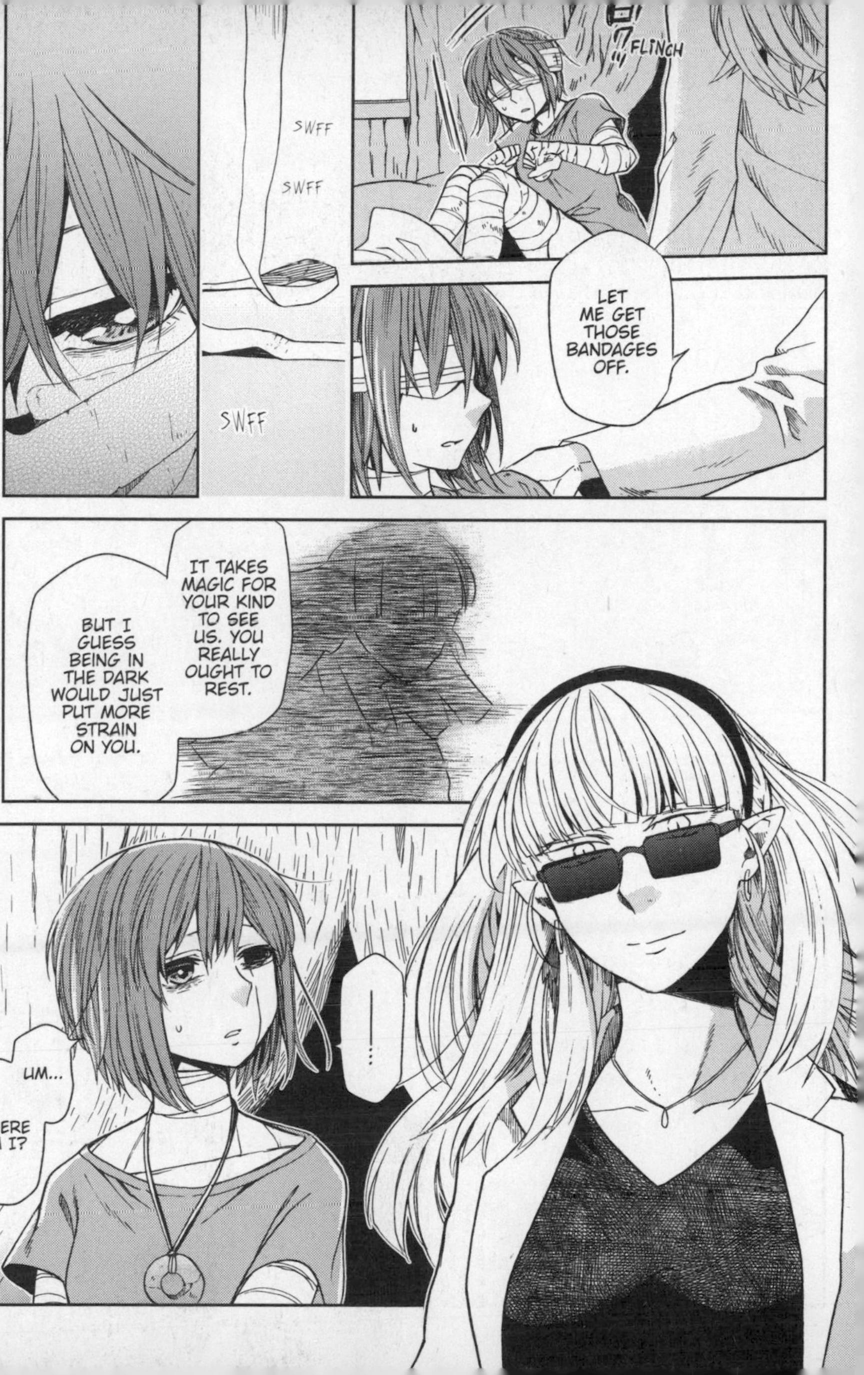
FLINCH
LET ME GET THOSE BANDAGES OFF.
SWFF
SWFF
SWFF
IT TAKES MAGIC FOR YOUR KIND TO SEE US. YOU REALLY OUGHT TO REST.
BUT I GUESS BEING IN THE DARK WOULD JUST PUT MORE STRAIN ON YOU.
...!
UM...
WHERE AM I?

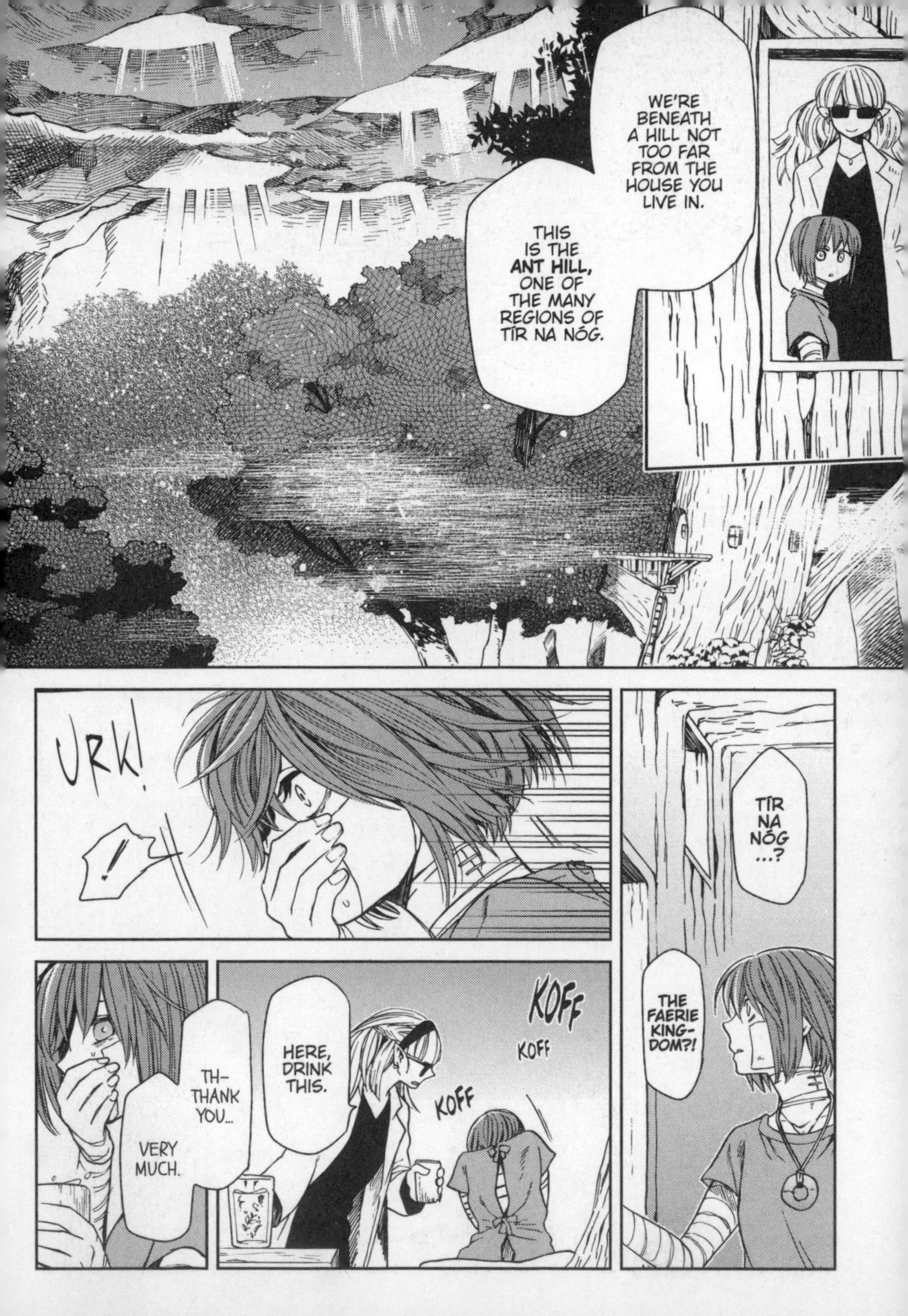
WE'RE BENEATH A HILL NOT TOO FAR FROM THE HOUSE YOU LIVE IN.
THIS IS THE **ANT HILL,** ONE OF THE MANY REGIONS OF TÍR NA NÓG.
TÍR NA NÓG...?
THE FAERIE KING-DOM?!
URK!
!
KOFF
KOFF
KOFF
HERE, DRINK THIS.
TH-THANK YOU...
VERY MUCH.

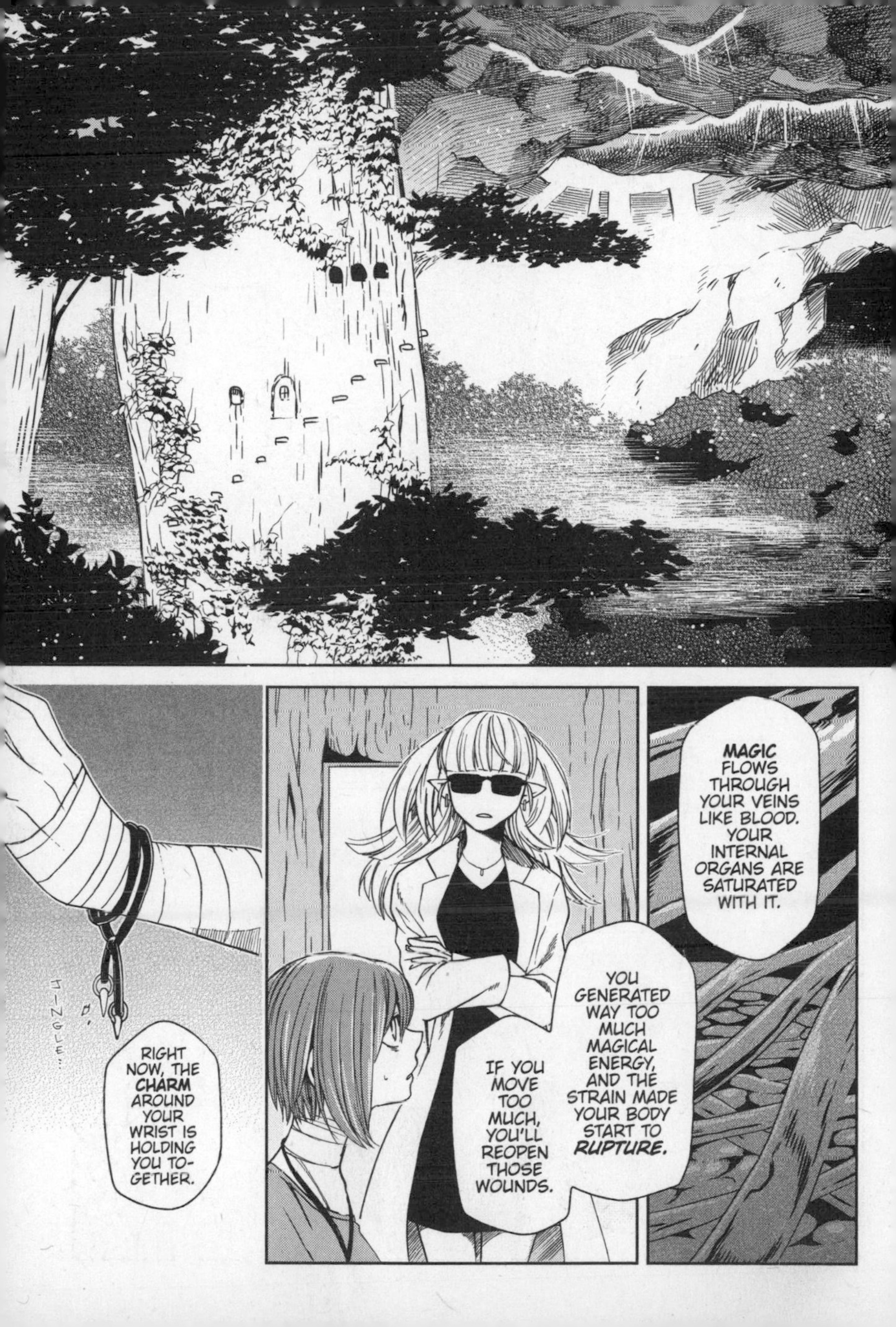
MAGIC FLOWS THROUGH YOUR VEINS LIKE BLOOD. YOUR INTERNAL ORGANS ARE SATURATED WITH IT.
YOU GENERATED WAY TOO MUCH MAGICAL ENERGY, AND THE STRAIN MADE YOUR BODY START TO RUPTURE.
IF YOU MOVE TOO MUCH, YOU'LL REOPEN THOSE WOUNDS.
JINGLE...
RIGHT NOW, THE CHARM AROUND YOUR WRIST IS HOLDING YOU TO-GETHER.

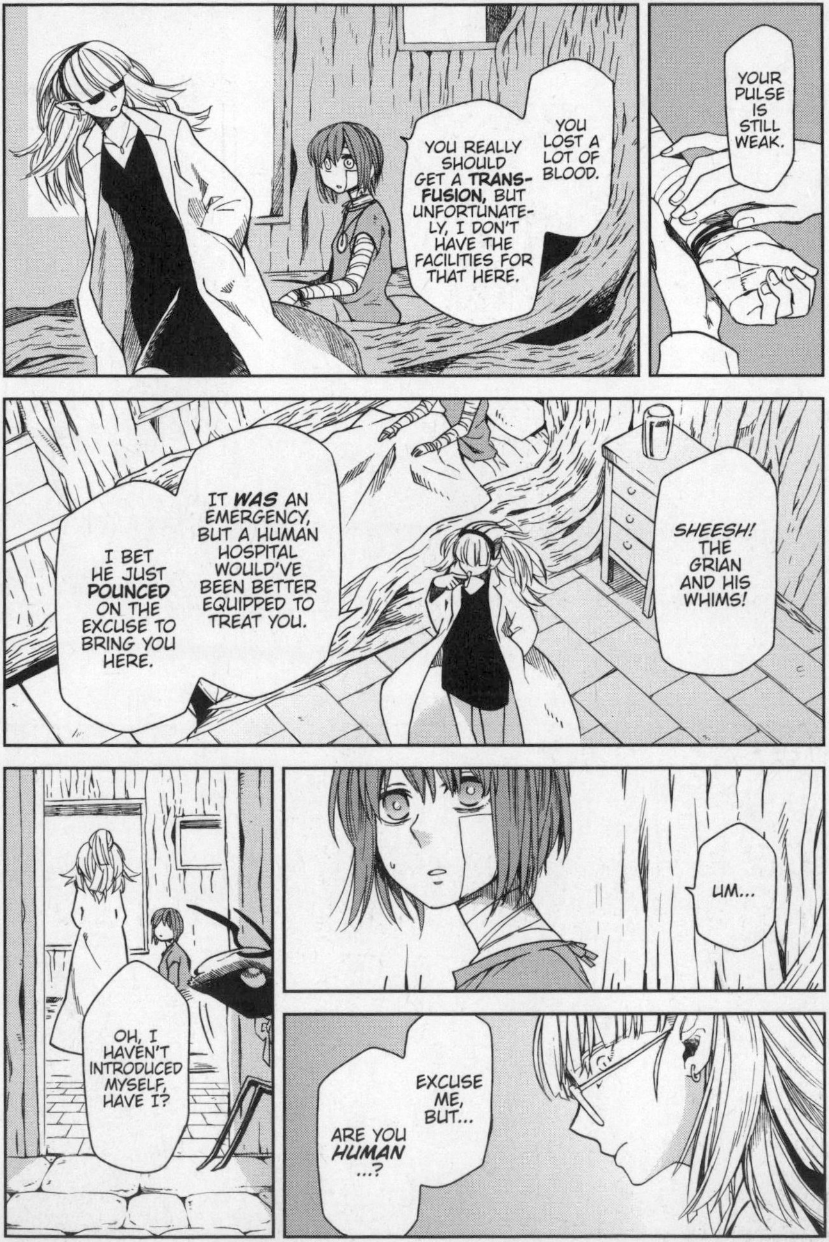
YOUR PULSE IS STILL WEAK.
YOU LOST A LOT OF BLOOD.
YOU REALLY SHOULD GET A TRANSFUSION, BUT UNFORTUNATELY, I DON'T HAVE THE FACILITIES FOR THAT HERE.
SHEESH! THE GRIAN AND HIS WHIMS!
IT WAS AN EMERGENCY, BUT A HUMAN HOSPITAL WOULD'VE BEEN BETTER EQUIPPED TO TREAT YOU.
I BET HE JUST POUNCED ON THE EXCUSE TO BRING YOU HERE.
UM...
EXCUSE ME, BUT...
ARE YOU HUMAN ...?
OH, I HAVEN'T INTRODUCED MYSELF, HAVE I?

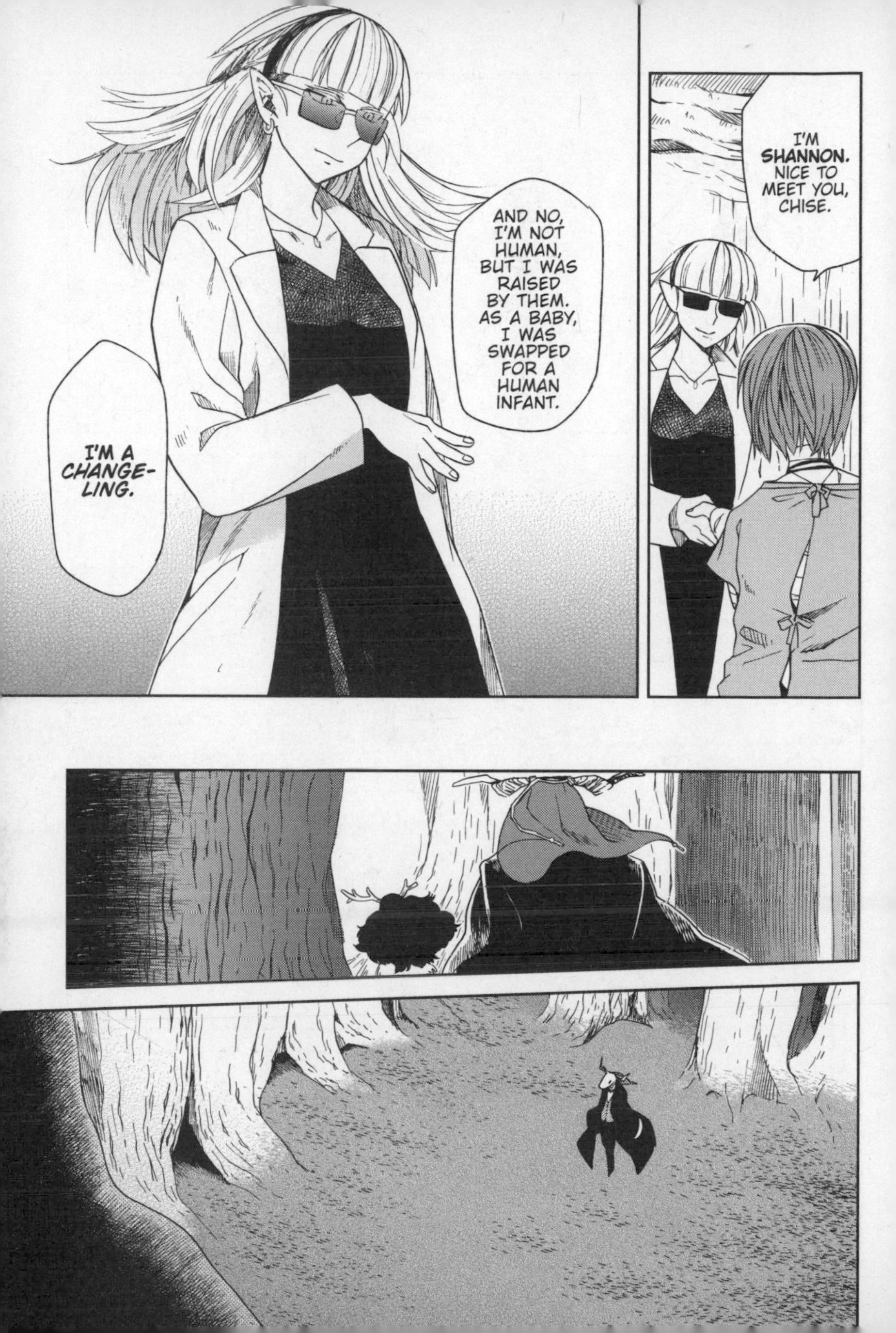
I'M SHANNON. NICE TO MEET YOU, CHISE.
AND NO, I'M NOT HUMAN, BUT I WAS RAISED BY THEM. AS A BABY, I WAS SWAPPED FOR A HUMAN INFANT.
I'M A CHANGE-LING.

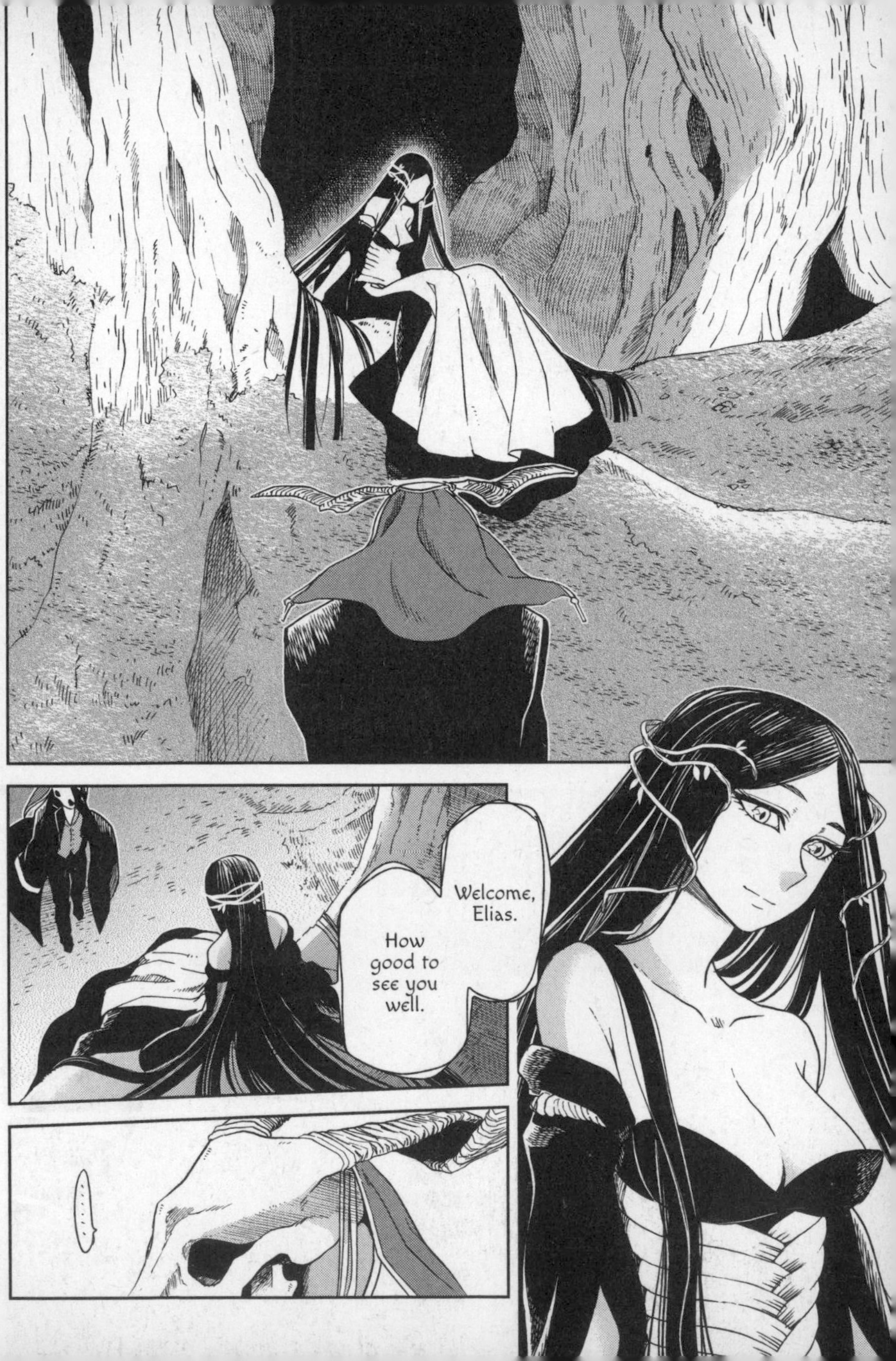
Welcome, Elias.
How good to see you well.
......

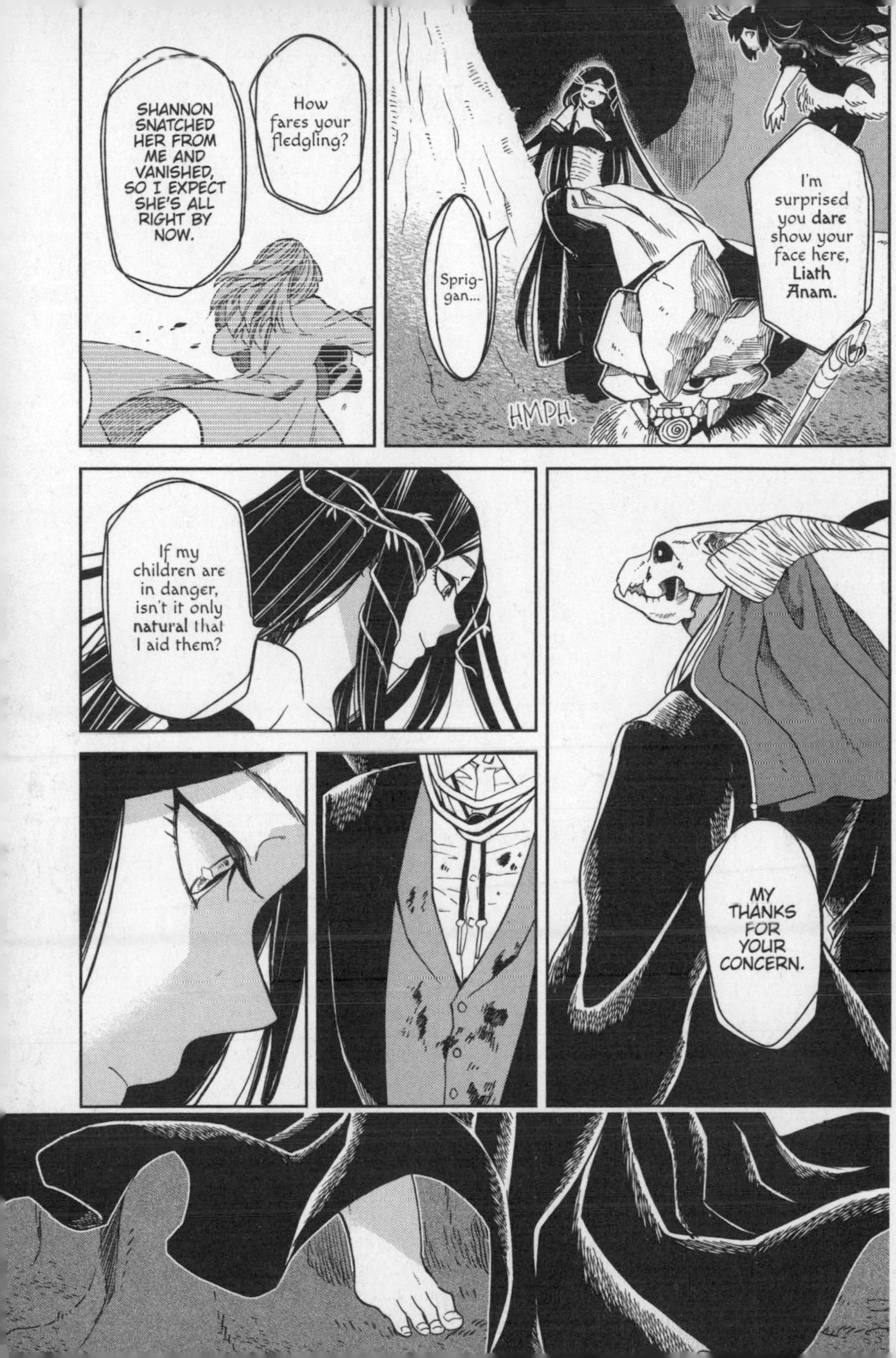
I'm surprised you dare show your face here, Liath Anam.
Sprig-gan...
HMPH.
How fares your fledgling?
SHANNON SNATCHED HER FROM ME AND VANISHED, SO I EXPECT SHE'S ALL RIGHT BY NOW.
MY THANKS FOR YOUR CONCERN.
If my children are in danger, isn't it only natural that I aid them?

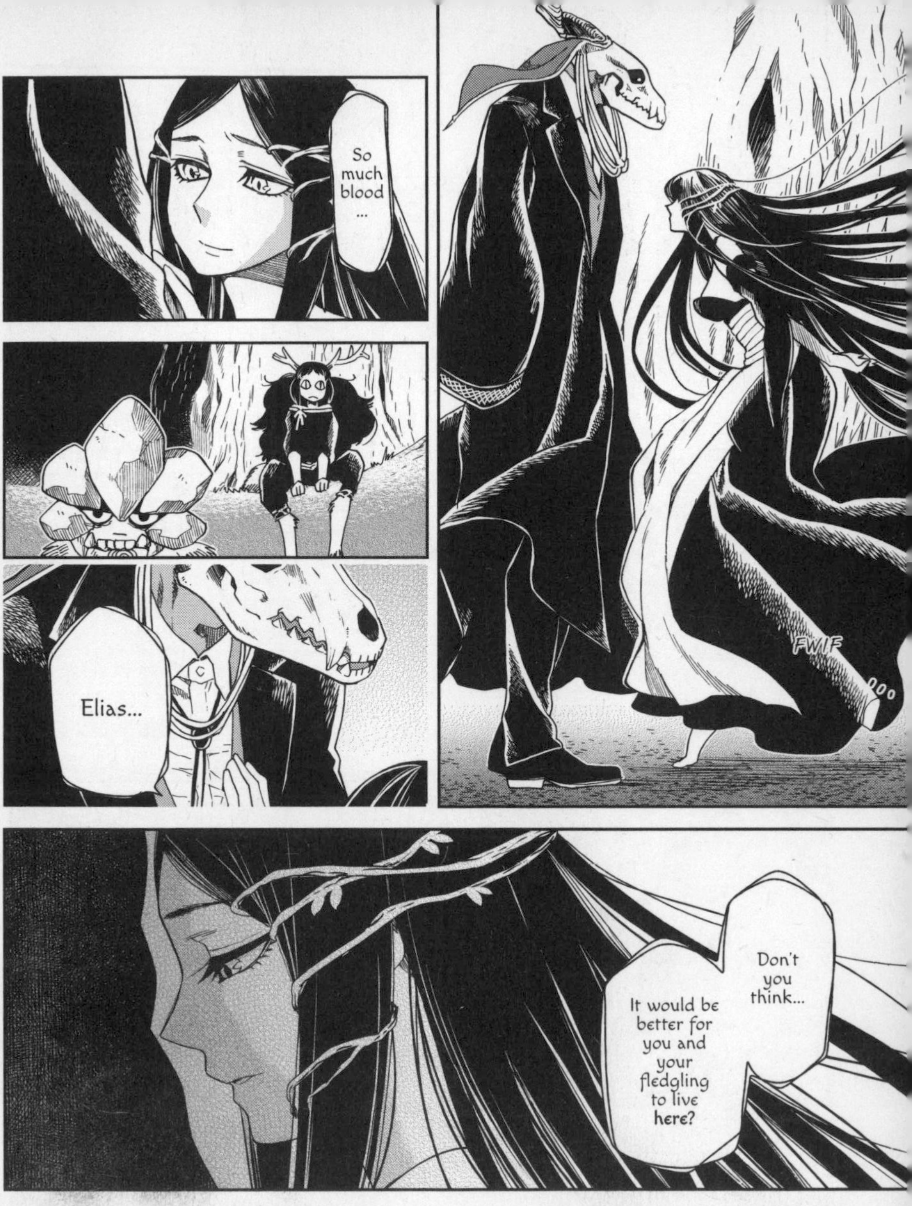
FWIF
So much blood ...
Elias...
Don't you think...
It would be better for you and your fledgling to live here?

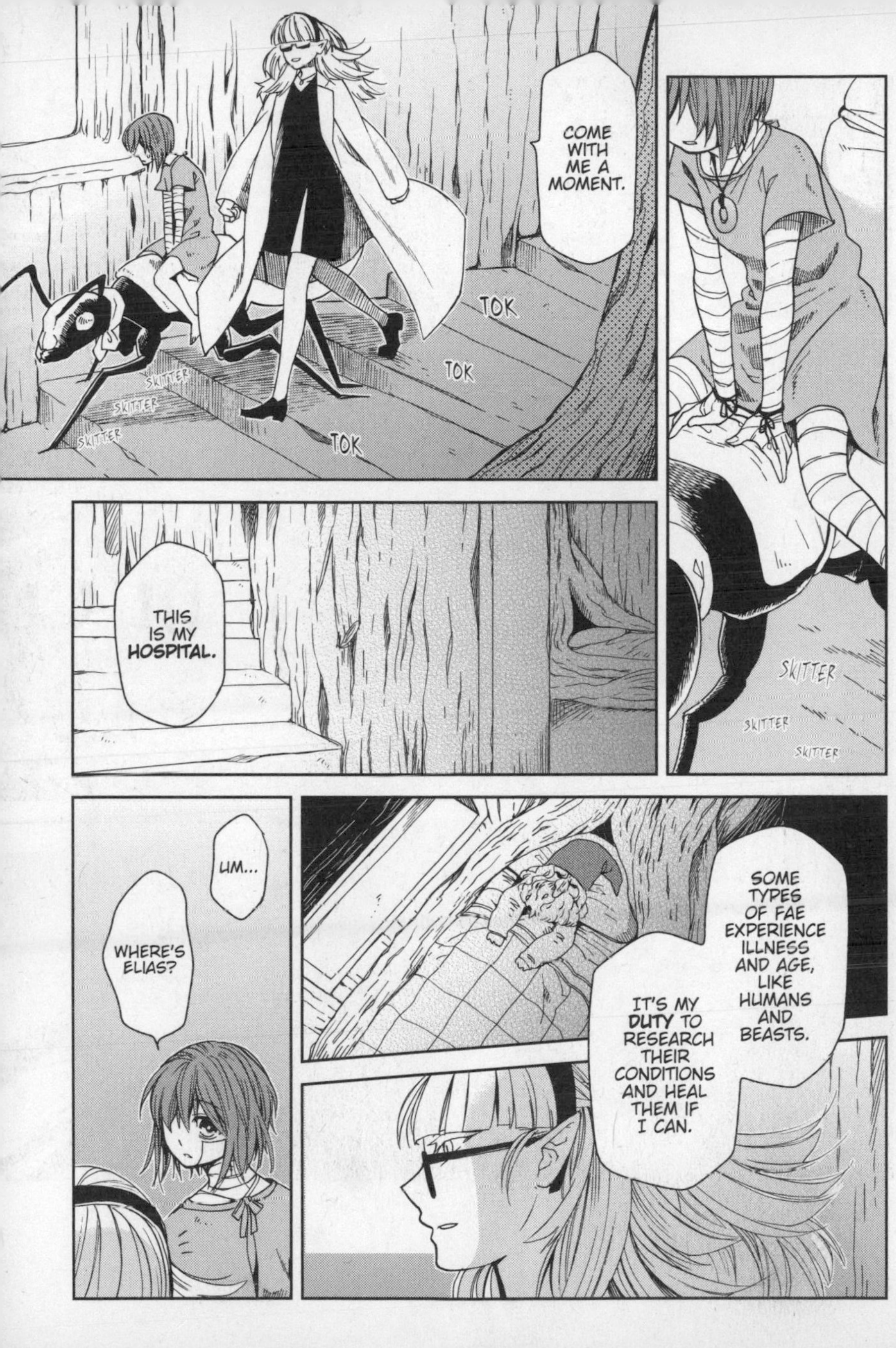
...
SKITTER
SKITTER
SKITTER
COME WITH ME A MOMENT.
TOK
TOK
TOK
SKITTER
SKITTER
SKITTER
THIS IS MY **HOSPITAL.**
...
SOME TYPES OF FAE EXPERIENCE ILLNESS AND AGE, LIKE HUMANS AND BEASTS.
IT'S MY **DUTY** TO RESEARCH THEIR CONDITIONS AND HEAL THEM IF I CAN.
UM...
WHERE'S ELIAS?

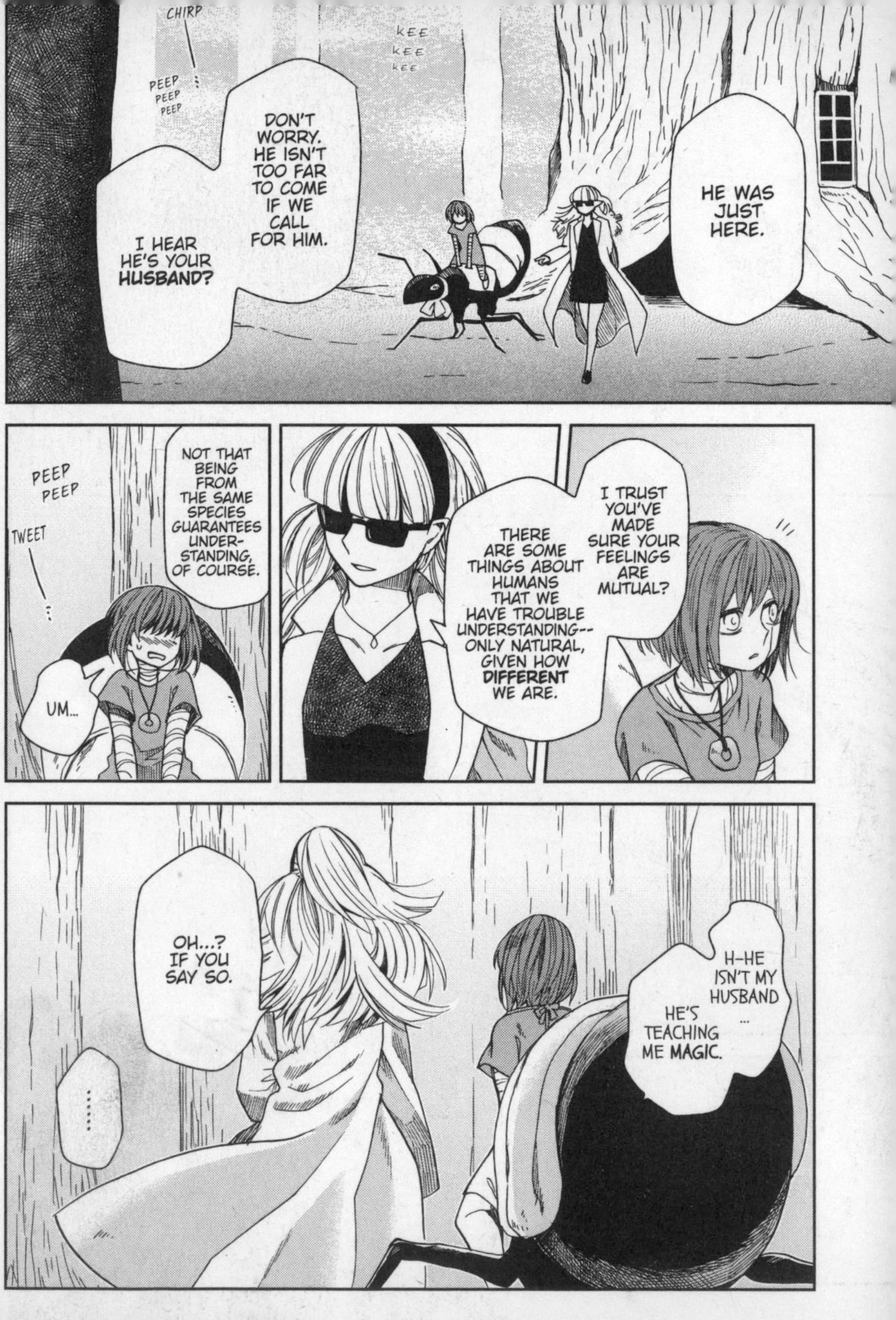
HE WAS JUST HERE.
KEE KEE KEE
DON'T WORRY. HE ISN'T TOO FAR TO COME IF WE CALL FOR HIM.
I HEAR HE'S YOUR HUSBAND?
CHIRP
PEEP PEEP PEEP
I TRUST YOU'VE MADE SURE YOUR FEELINGS ARE MUTUAL?
THERE ARE SOME THINGS ABOUT HUMANS THAT WE HAVE TROUBLE UNDERSTANDING-- ONLY NATURAL, GIVEN HOW DIFFERENT WE ARE.
NOT THAT BEING FROM THE SAME SPECIES GUARANTEES UNDER-STANDING, OF COURSE.
PEEP PEEP
TWEET
UM...
H-HE ISN'T MY HUSBAND ...
HE'S TEACHING ME MAGIC.
OH...? IF YOU SAY SO.
......

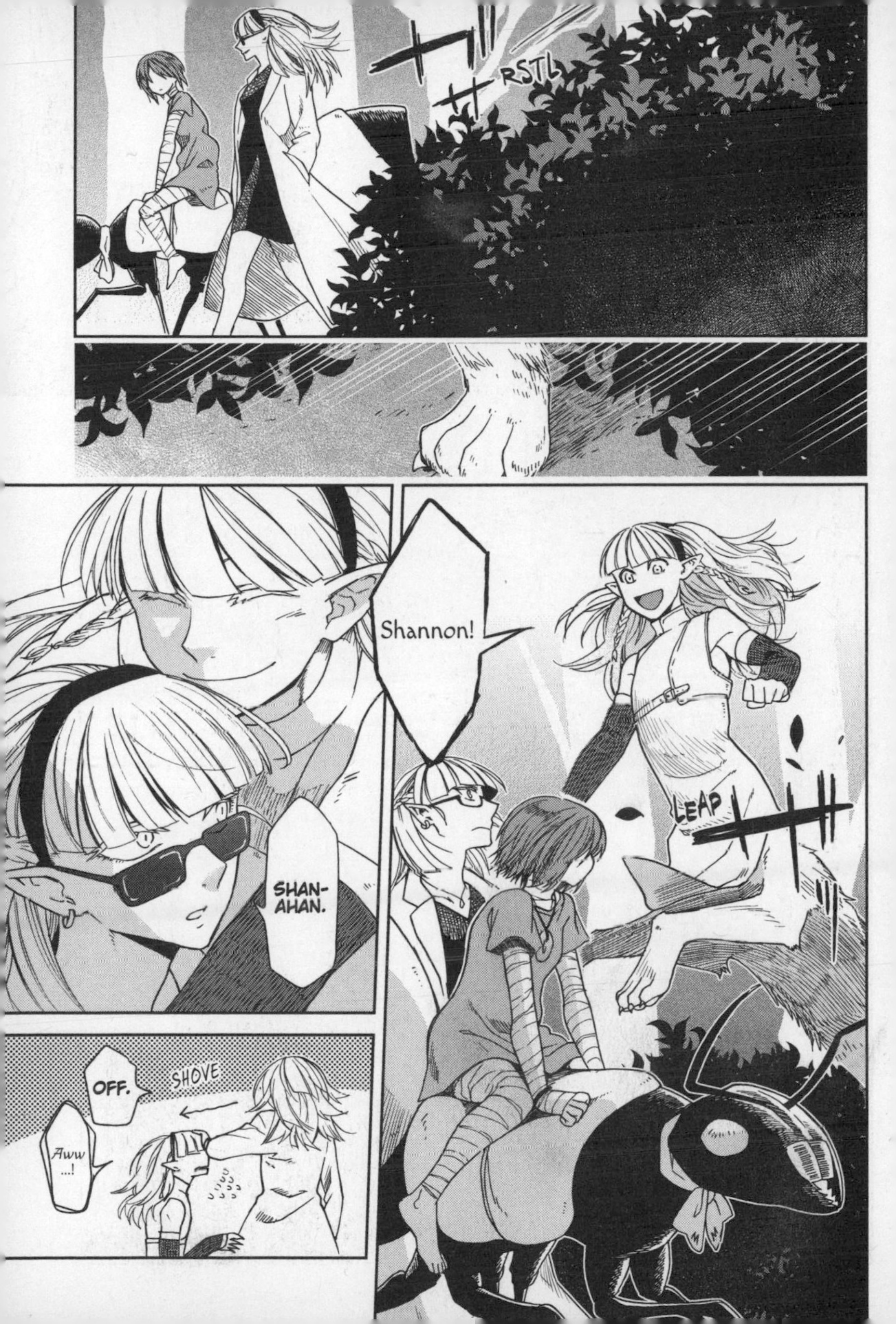
RSTL
Shannon!
LEAP
SHAN-AHAN.
OFF.
SHOVE
Aww ...!

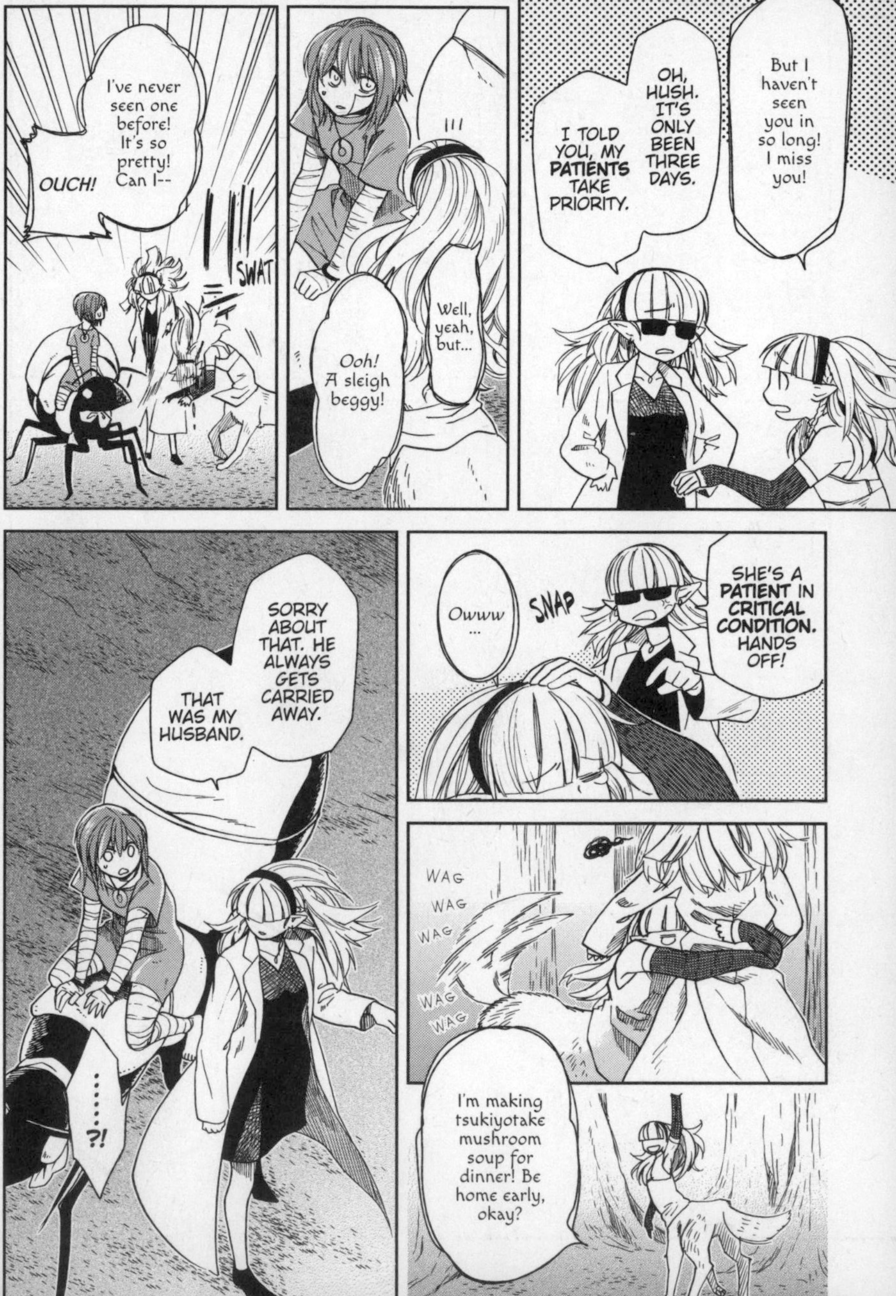
But I haven't seen you in so long! I miss you!
OH, HUSH. IT'S ONLY BEEN THREE DAYS.
I TOLD YOU, MY PATIENTS TAKE PRIORITY.
Well, yeah, but...
Ooh! A sleigh beggy!
I've never seen one before! It's so pretty! Can I--
SWAT
OUCH!
SHE'S A PATIENT IN CRITICAL CONDITION. HANDS OFF!
SNAP
Owww...
WAG
WAG
WAG
WAG
WAG
I'm making tsukiyotake mushroom soup for dinner! Be home early, okay?
SORRY ABOUT THAT. HE ALWAYS GETS CARRIED AWAY.
THAT WAS MY HUSBAND.
......?!

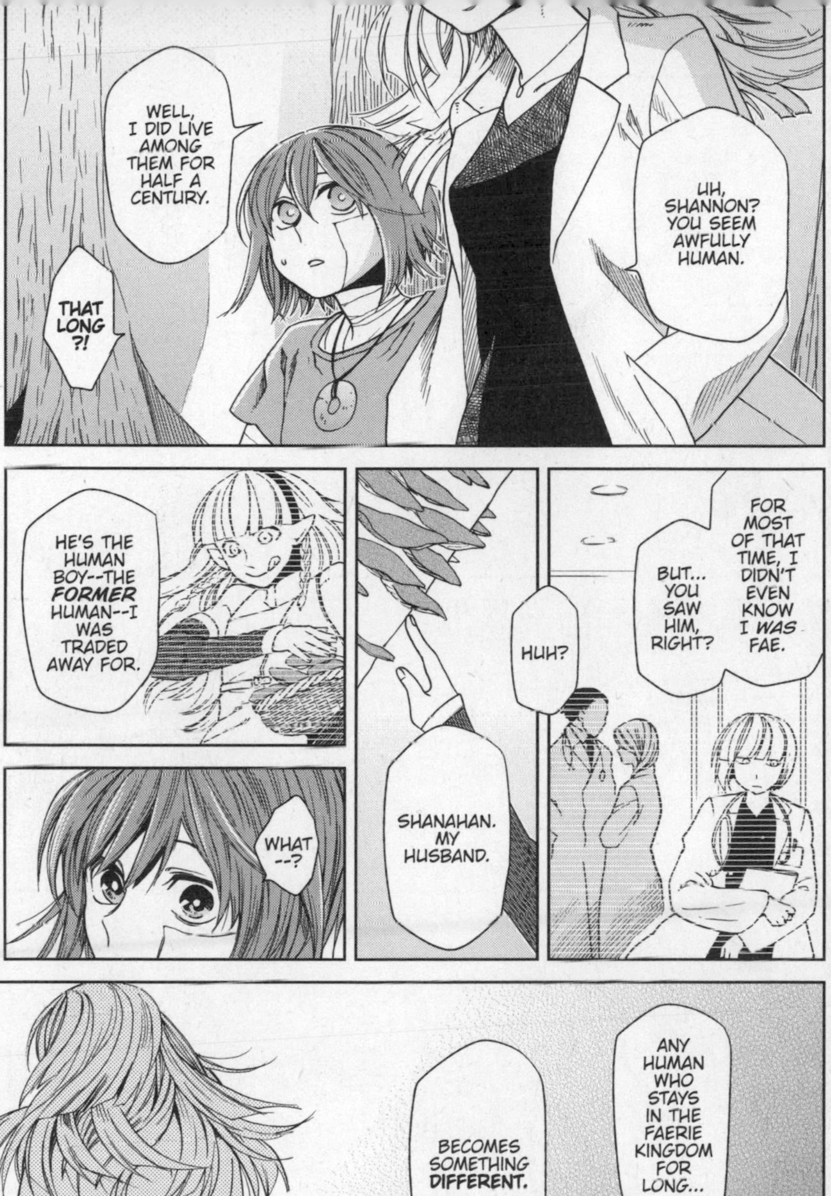
UH, SHANNON? YOU SEEM AWFULLY HUMAN.
WELL, I DID LIVE AMONG THEM FOR HALF A CENTURY.
THAT LONG ?!
FOR MOST OF THAT TIME, I DIDN'T EVEN KNOW I *WAS* FAE.
BUT... YOU SAW HIM, RIGHT?
HUH?
SHANAHAN. MY HUSBAND.
HE'S THE HUMAN BOY--THE ***FORMER*** HUMAN--I WAS TRADED AWAY FOR.
WHAT --?
ANY HUMAN WHO STAYS IN THE FAERIE KINGDOM FOR LONG...
BECOMES SOMETHING **DIFFERENT.**

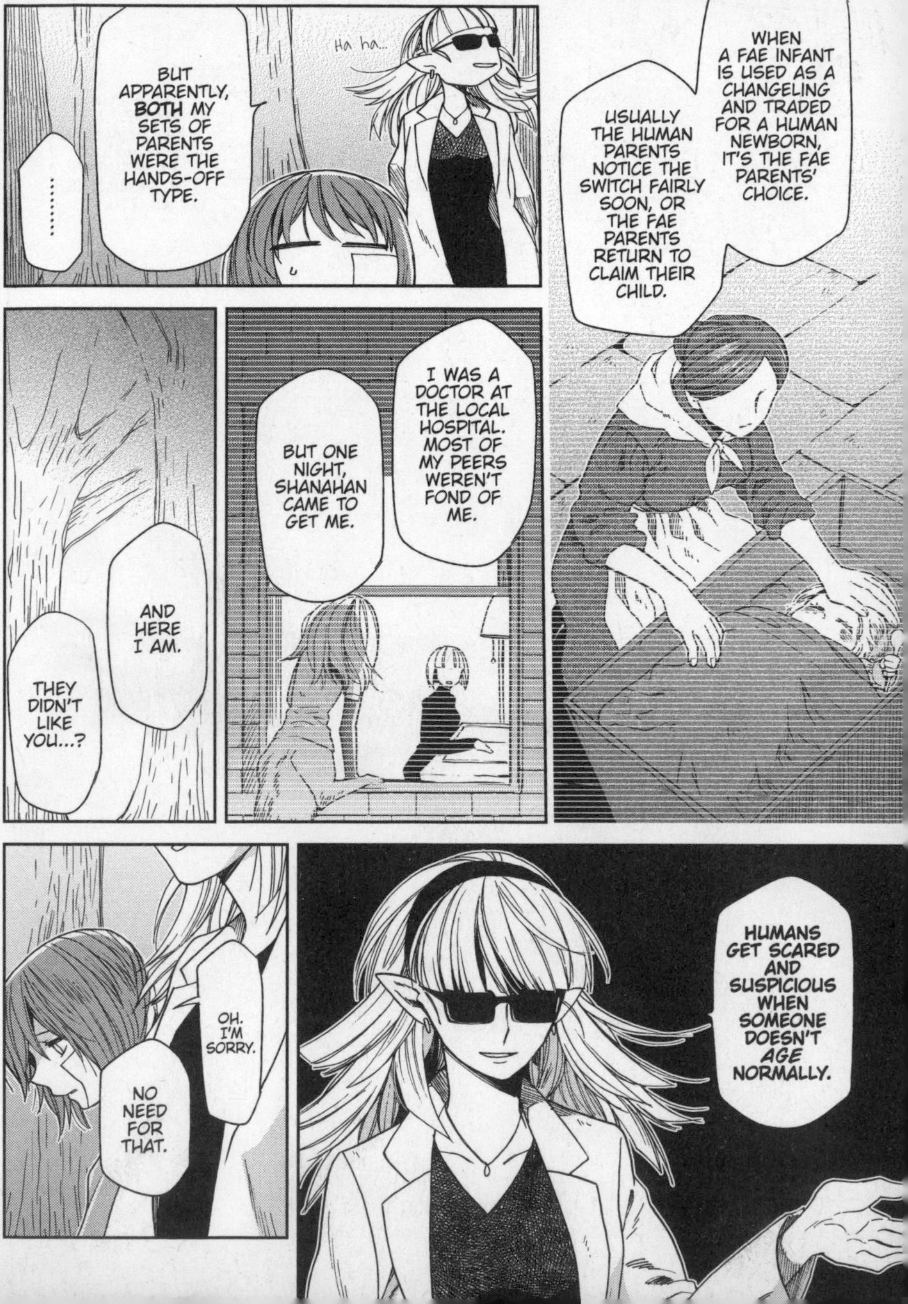
WHEN A FAE INFANT IS USED AS A CHANGELING AND TRADED FOR A HUMAN NEWBORN, IT'S THE FAE PARENTS' CHOICE.
USUALLY THE HUMAN PARENTS NOTICE THE SWITCH FAIRLY SOON, OR THE FAE PARENTS RETURN TO CLAIM THEIR CHILD.
Ha ha...
BUT APPARENTLY, **BOTH** MY SETS OF PARENTS WERE THE HANDS-OFF TYPE.
......
I WAS A DOCTOR AT THE LOCAL HOSPITAL. MOST OF MY PEERS WEREN'T FOND OF ME.
BUT ONE NIGHT, SHANAHAN CAME TO GET ME.
AND HERE I AM.
THEY DIDN'T LIKE YOU...?
HUMANS GET SCARED AND SUSPICIOUS WHEN SOMEONE DOESN'T *AGE* NORMALLY.
OH. I'M SORRY.
NO NEED FOR THAT.

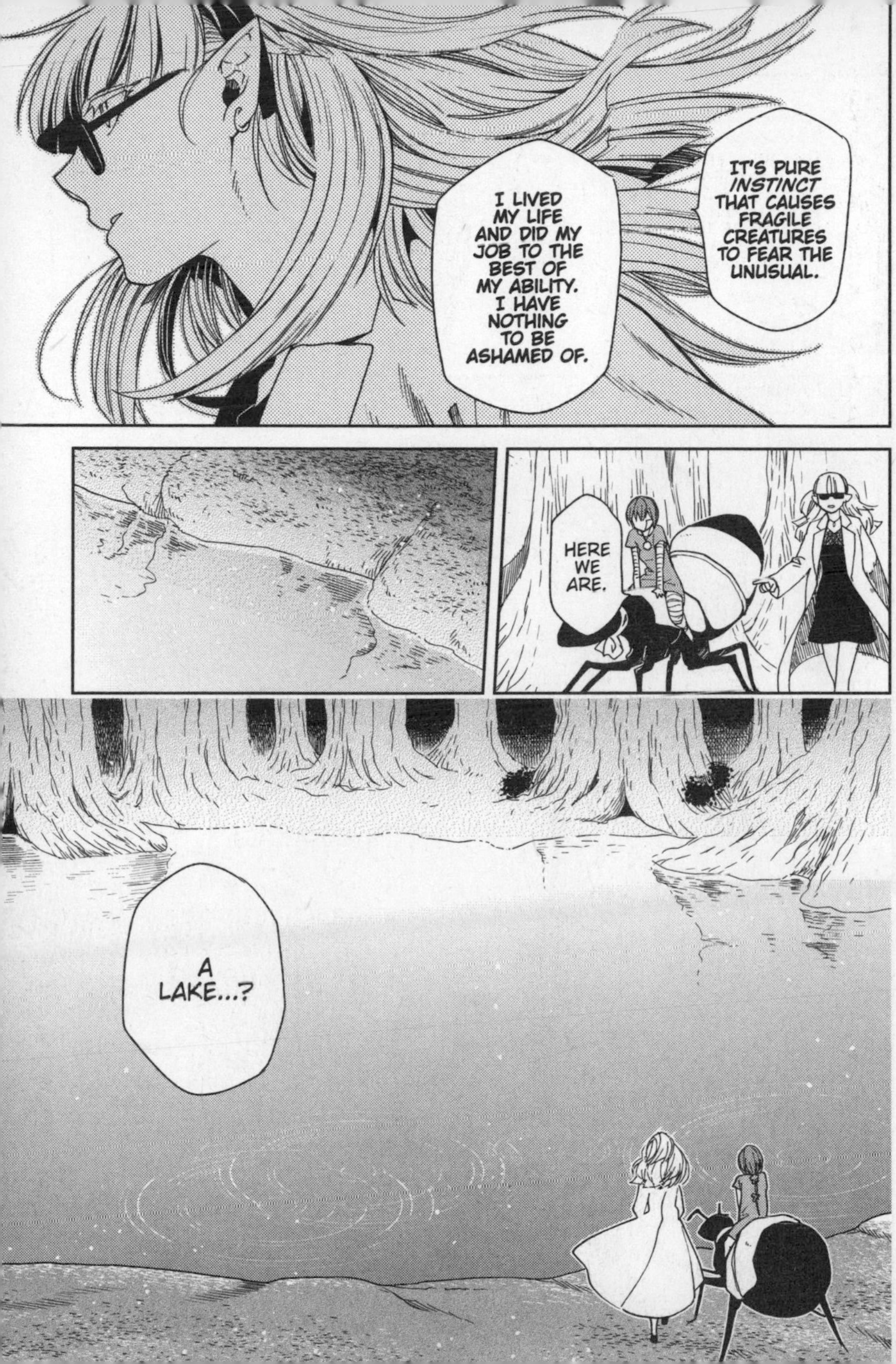
IT'S PURE *INSTINCT* THAT CAUSES FRAGILE CREATURES TO FEAR THE UNUSUAL.
I LIVED MY LIFE AND DID MY JOB TO THE BEST OF MY ABILITY. I HAVE NOTHING TO BE ASHAMED OF.
HERE WE ARE.
A LAKE...?

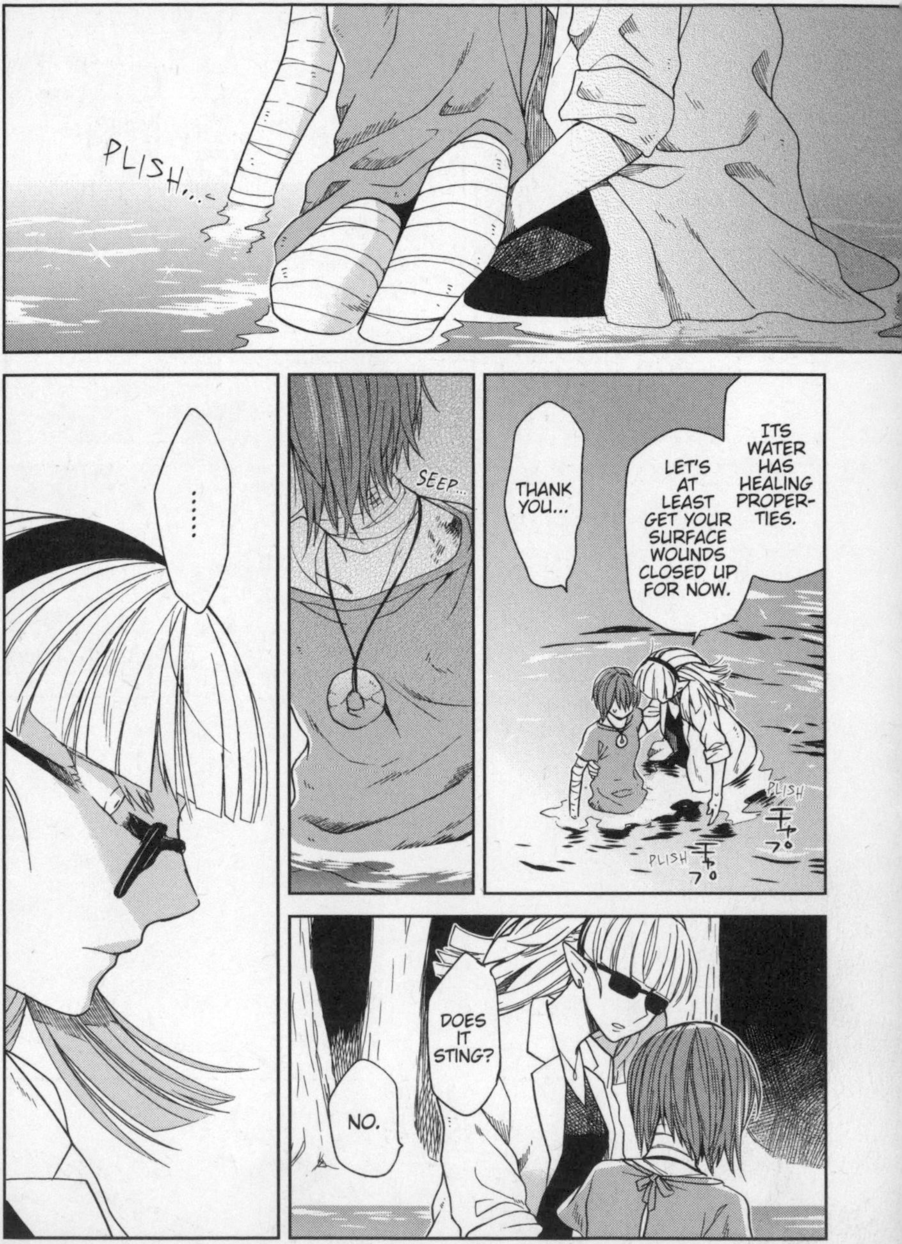
PLISH...
ITS WATER HAS HEALING PROPER-TIES.
LET'S AT LEAST GET YOUR SURFACE WOUNDS CLOSED UP FOR NOW.
THANK YOU...
PLISH
チャプ
PLISH
チャプ
SEEP...
DOES IT STING?
NO.
......

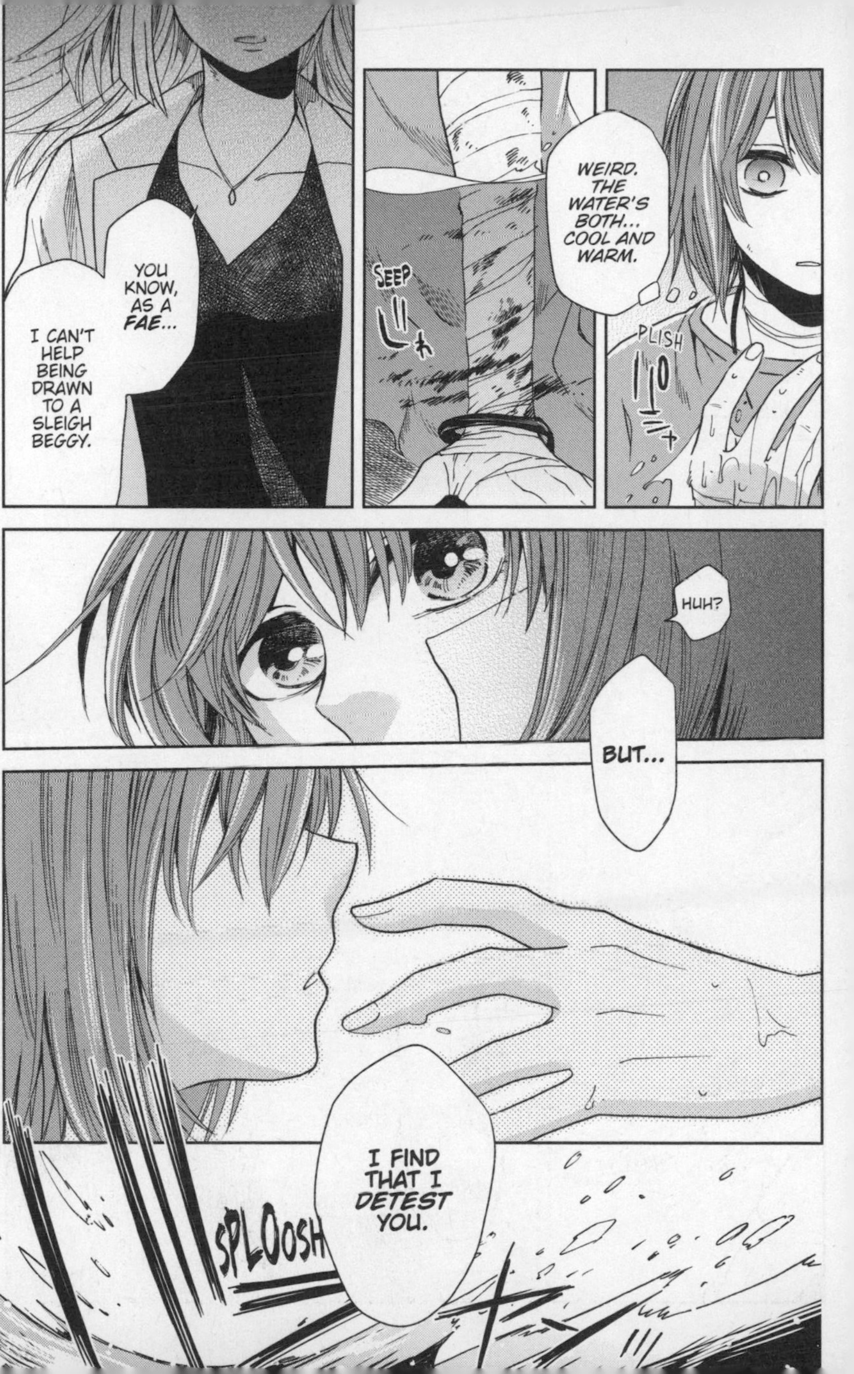
WEIRD. THE WATER'S BOTH... COOL AND WARM.
PLISH
SEEP
YOU KNOW, AS A *FAE*...
I CAN'T HELP BEING DRAWN TO A SLEIGH BEGGY.
HUH?
BUT...
I FIND THAT I *DETEST* YOU.
SPLOOSH

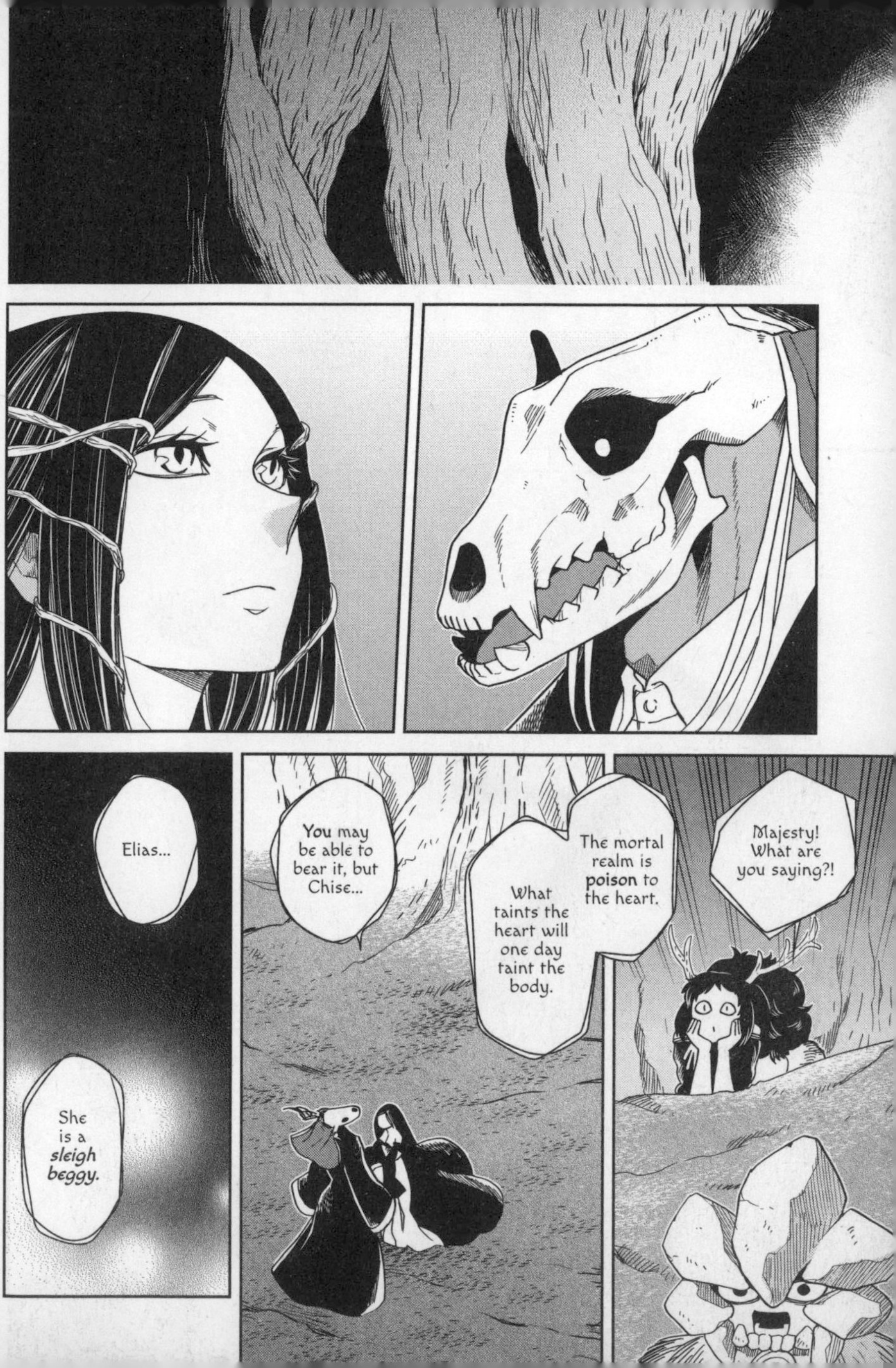
Majesty! What are you saying?!
The mortal realm is poison to the heart.
What taints the heart will one day taint the body.
You may be able to bear it, but Chise...
Elias...
She is a sleigh beggy.

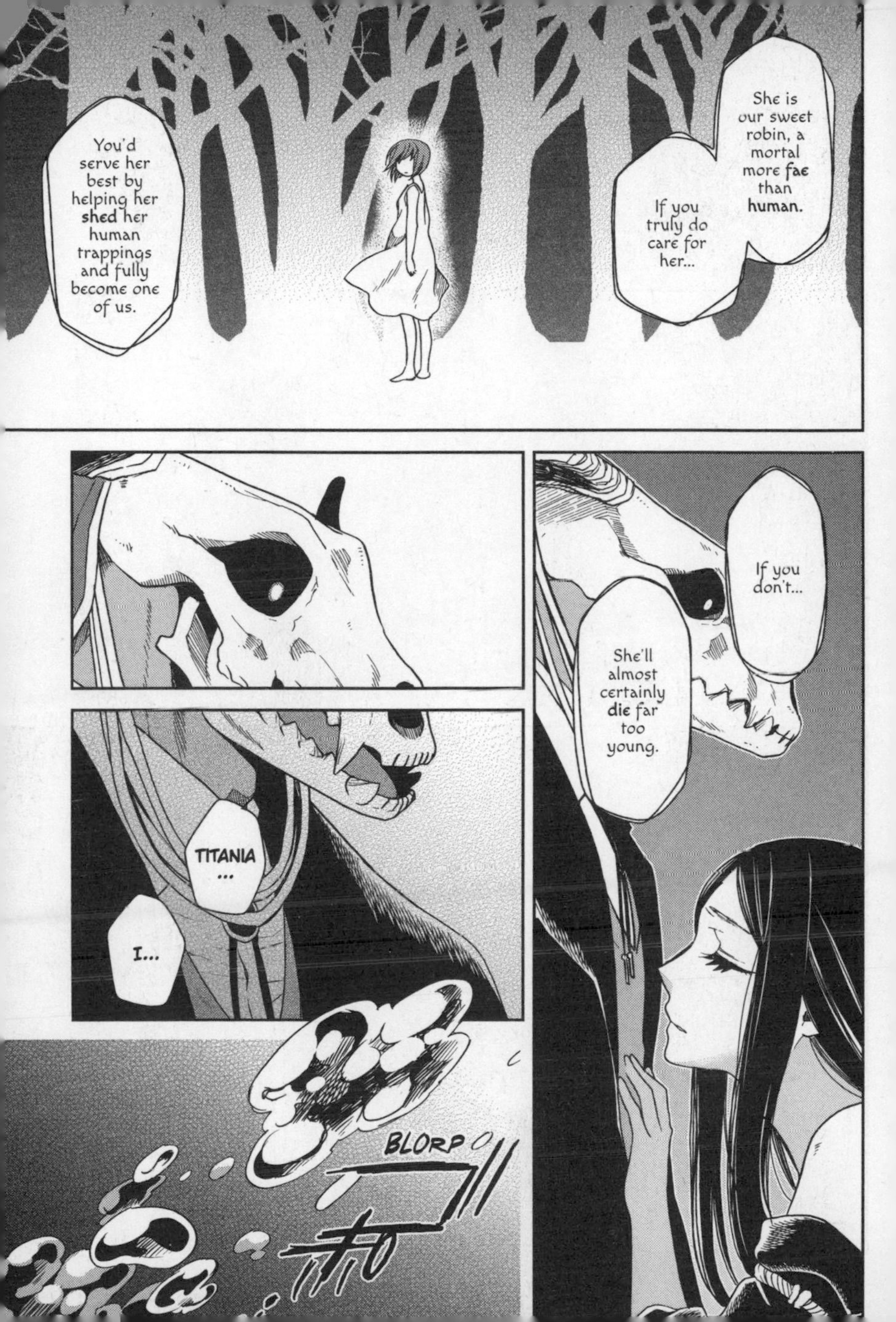
She is our sweet robin, a mortal more fae than human.
If you truly do care for her...
You'd serve her best by helping her shed her human trappings and fully become one of us.
If you don't...
She'll almost certainly die far too young.
TITANIA...
I...
BLORP

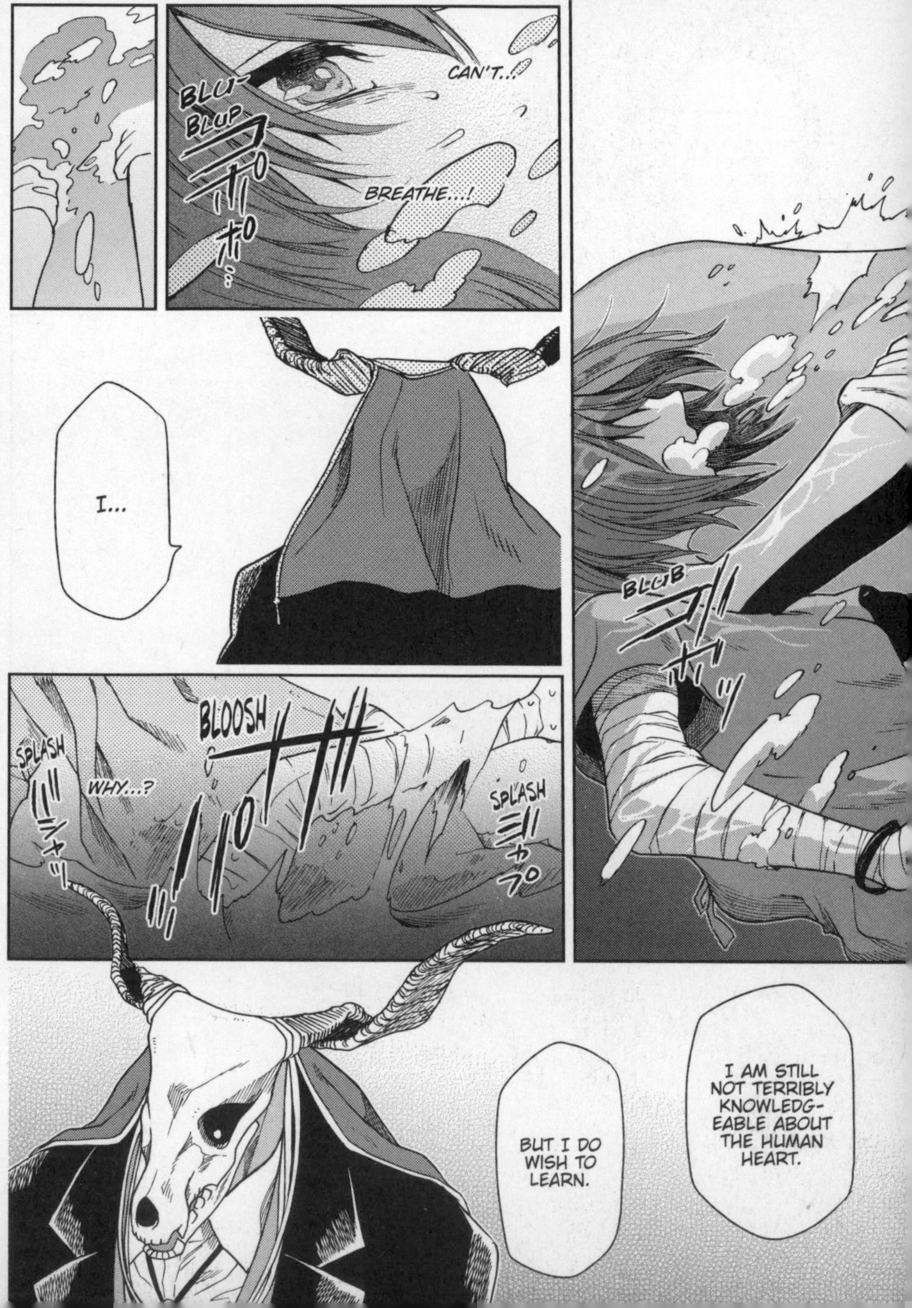
BLUB
CAN'T...
BLU-BLUP
BREATHE...!
I...
BLOOSH
SPLASH
WHY...?
SPLASH
I AM STILL NOT TERRIBLY KNOWLEDG-EABLE ABOUT THE HUMAN HEART.
BUT I DO WISH TO LEARN.

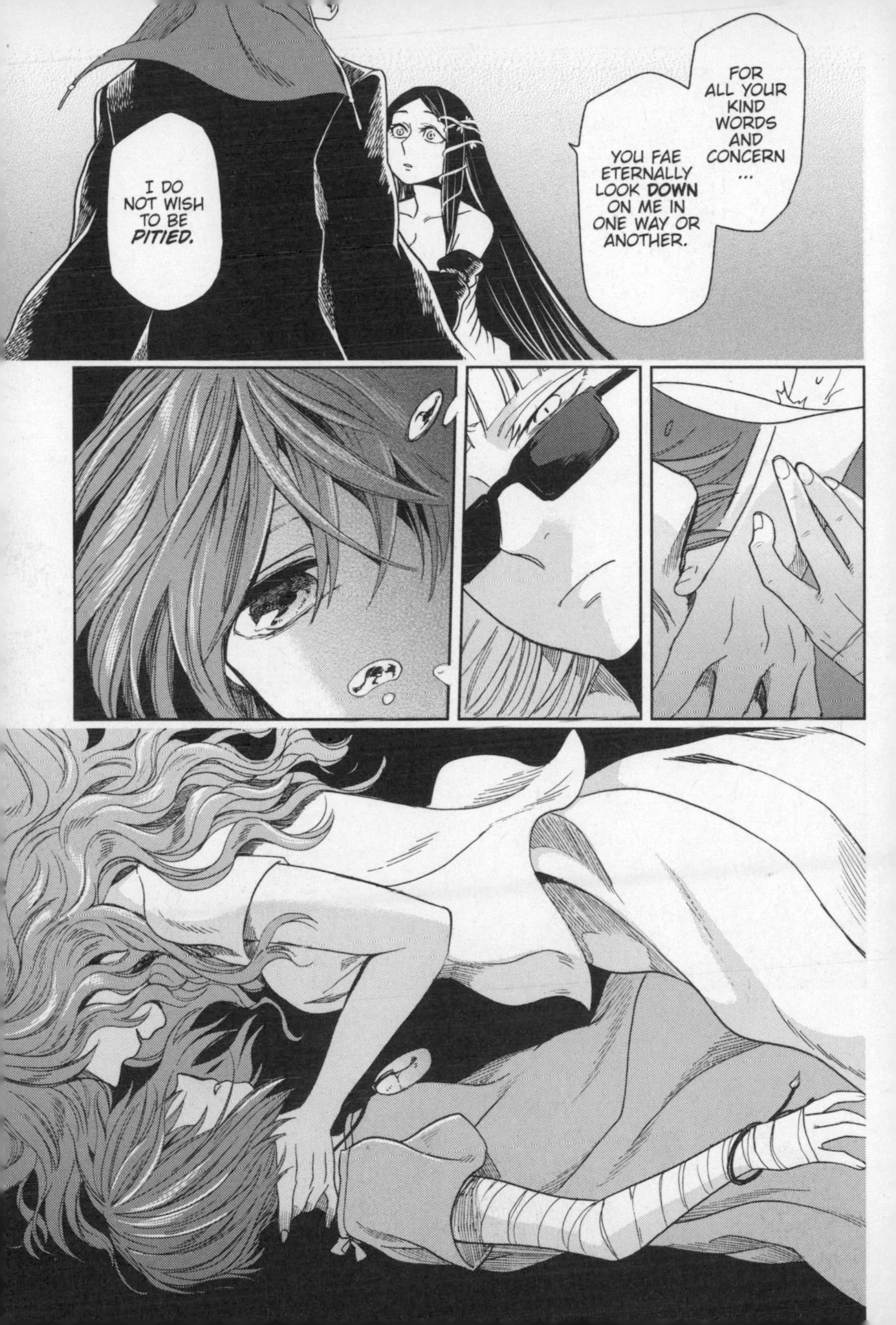
FOR ALL YOUR KIND WORDS AND CONCERN ...
YOU FAE ETERNALLY LOOK DOWN ON ME IN ONE WAY OR ANOTHER.
I DO NOT WISH TO BE PITIED.

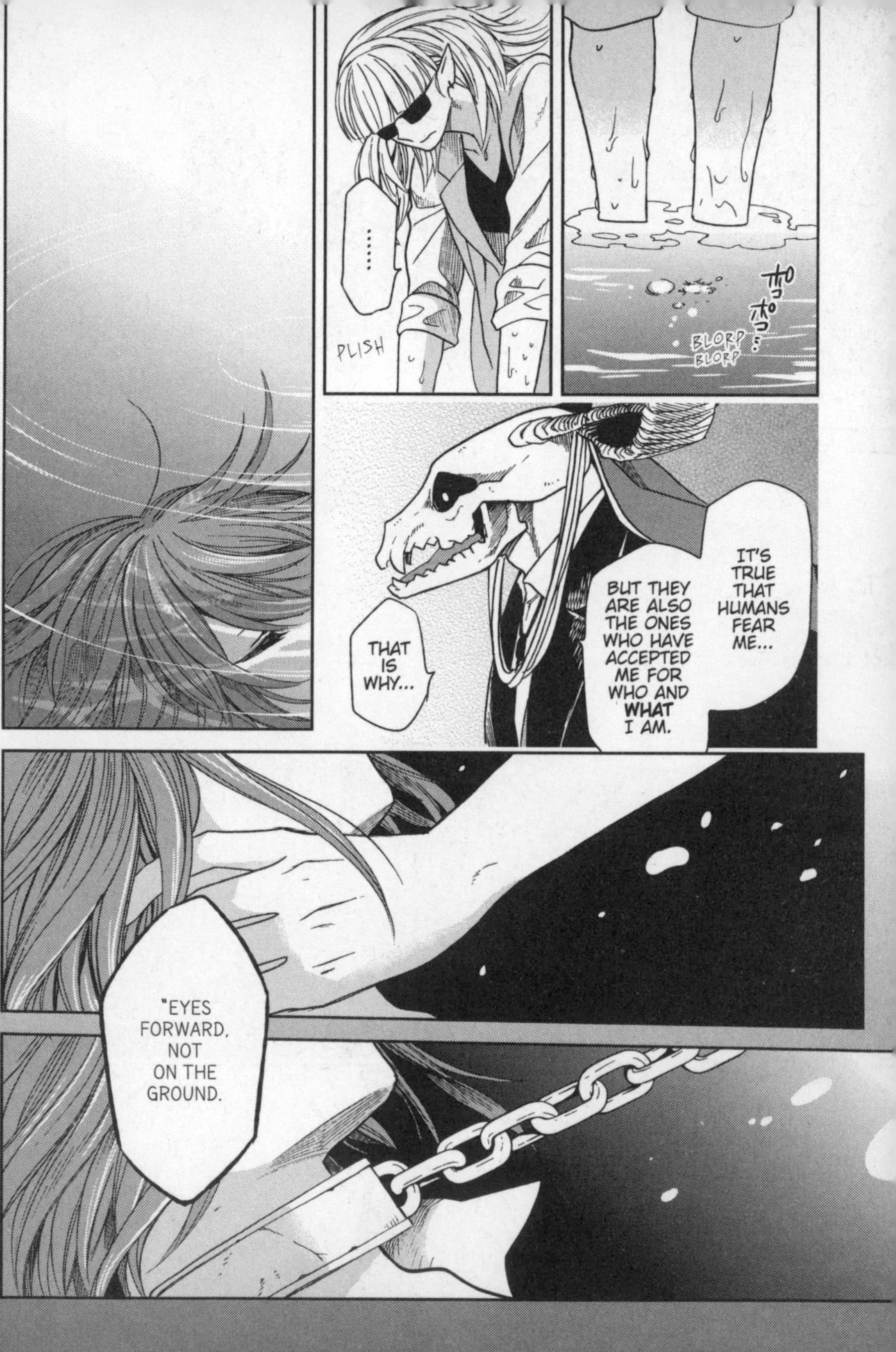
ポコポコ…
BLORP BLORP
......
PLISH
IT'S TRUE THAT HUMANS FEAR ME...
BUT THEY ARE ALSO THE ONES WHO HAVE ACCEPTED ME FOR WHO AND **WHAT** I AM.
THAT IS WHY...
"EYES FORWARD, NOT ON THE GROUND.

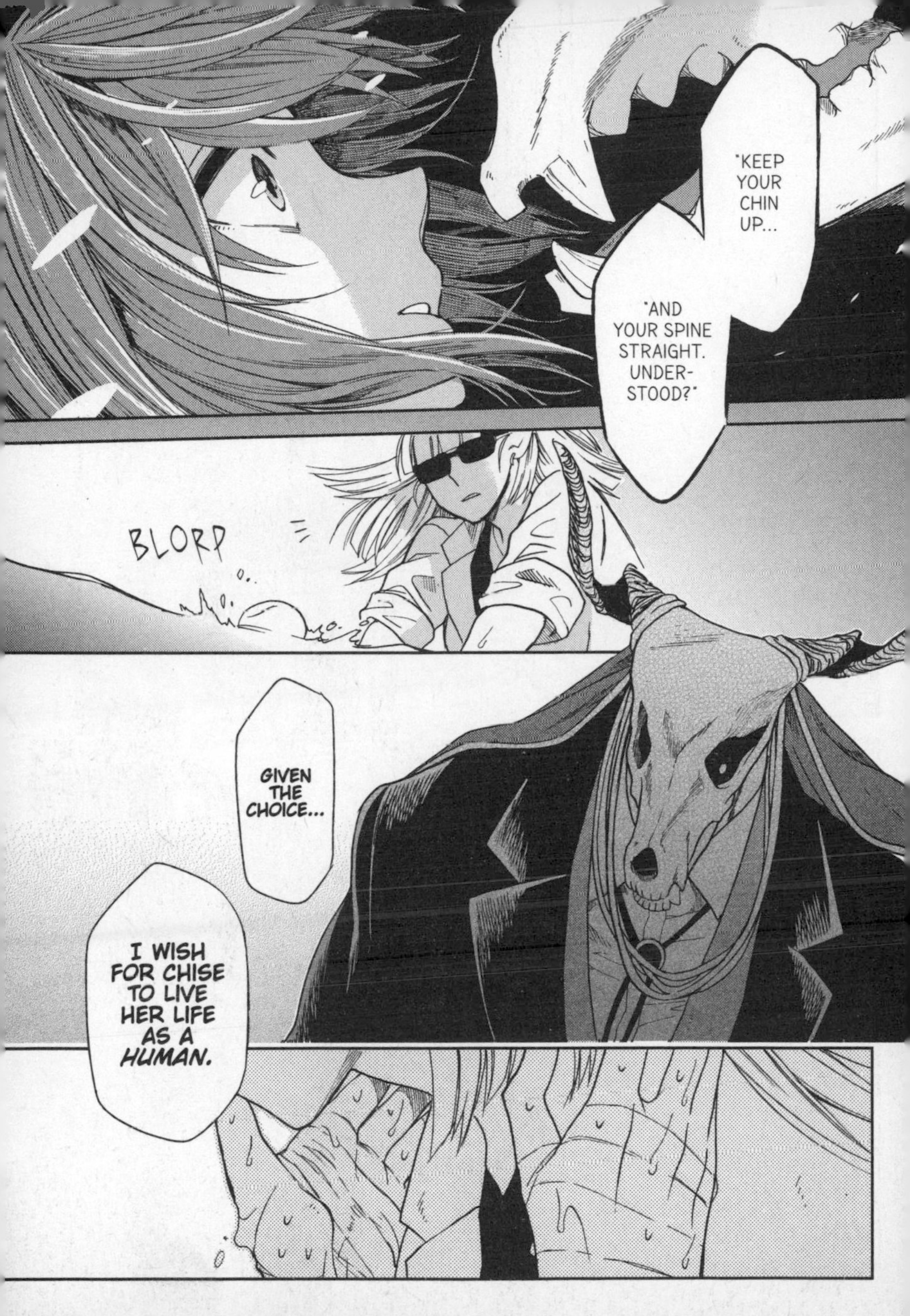
"KEEP YOUR CHIN UP...
"AND YOUR SPINE STRAIGHT. UNDER-STOOD?"
BLORP
GIVEN THE CHOICE...
I WISH FOR CHISE TO LIVE HER LIFE AS A HUMAN.

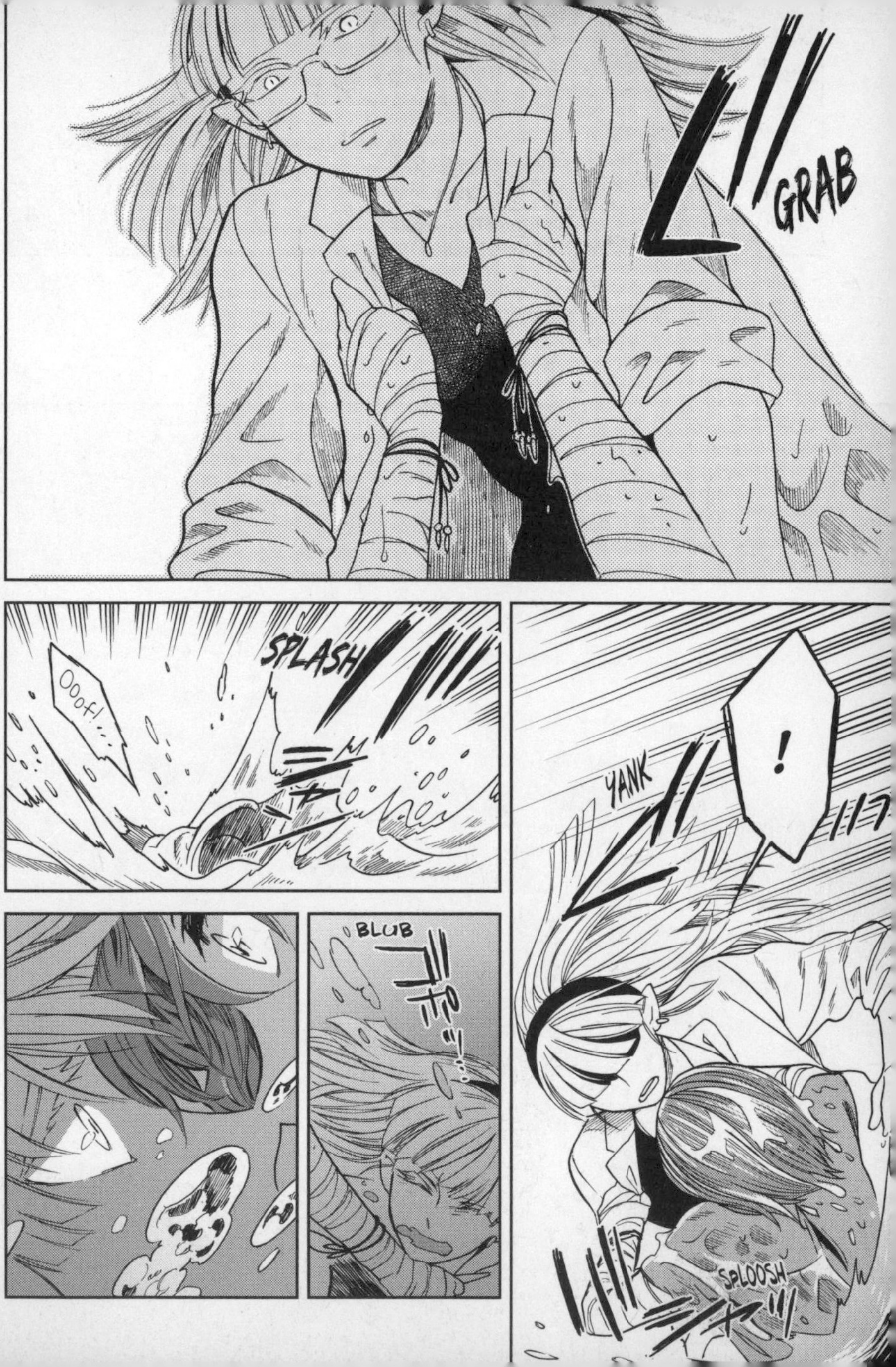
GRAB
!
YANK
SPLOOSH
SPLASH
Ooof!...
BLUB

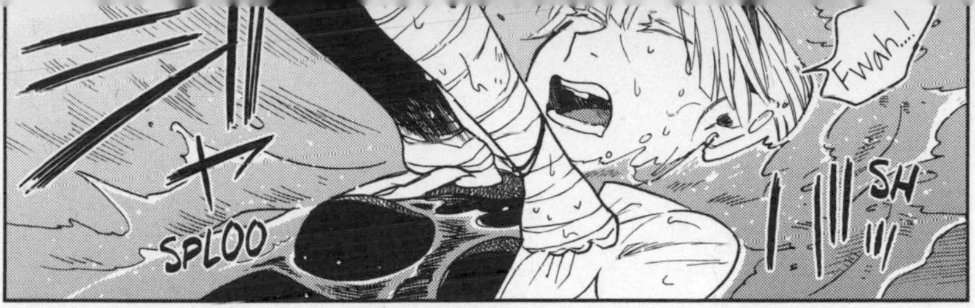
Fwah...!
SH
SPLOO
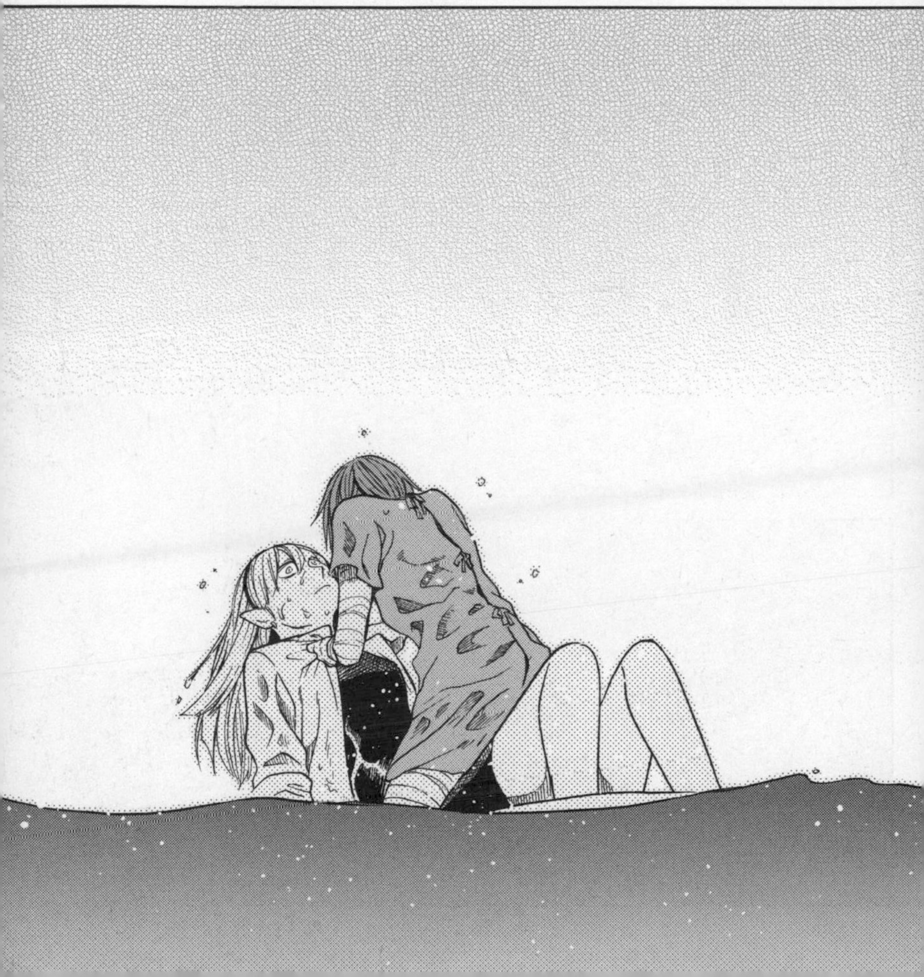

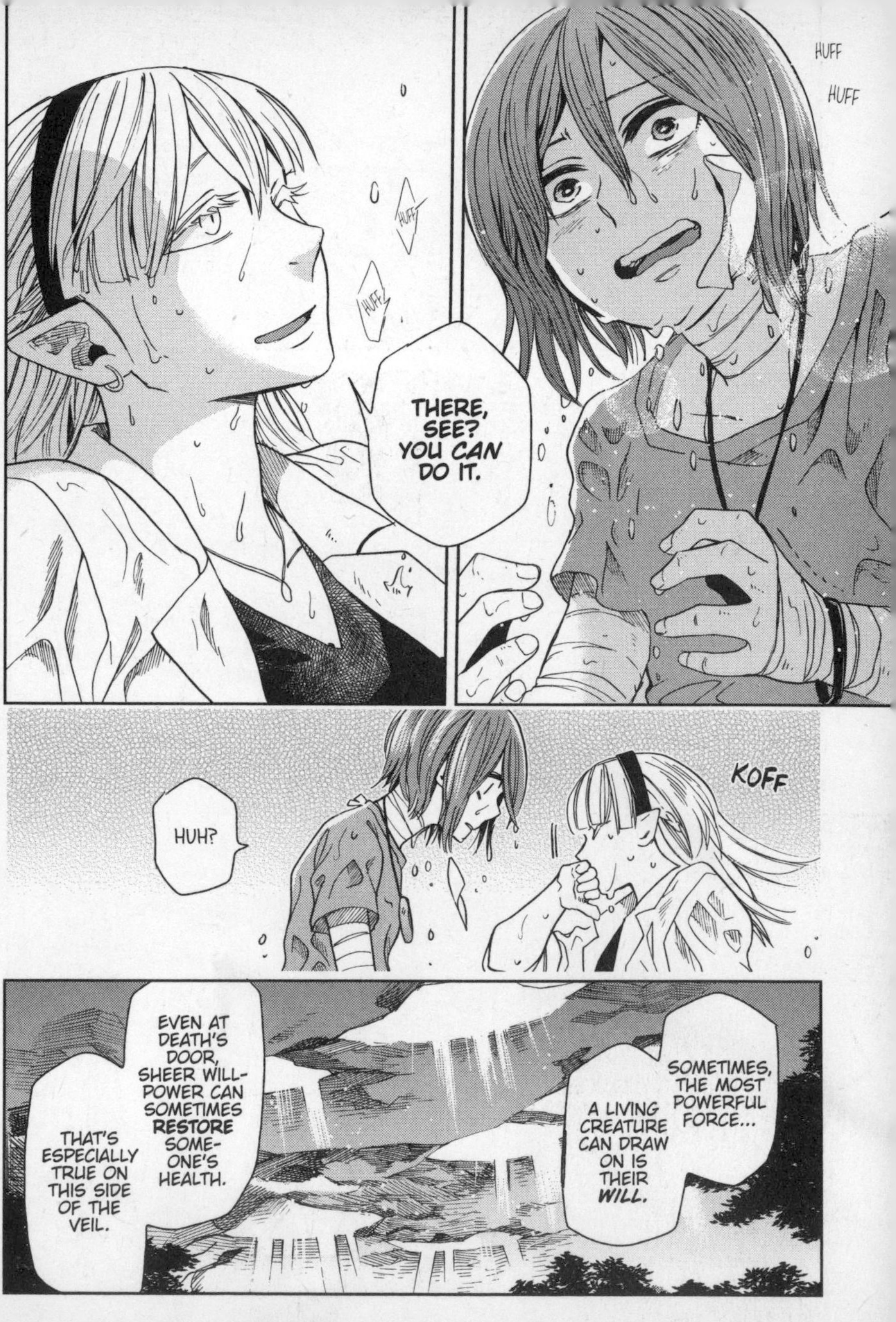
HUFF
HUFF
HUFF
HUFF
THERE, SEE? YOU CAN DO IT.
KOFF
HUH?
SOMETIMES, THE MOST POWERFUL FORCE...
A LIVING CREATURE CAN DRAW ON IS THEIR WILL.
EVEN AT DEATH'S DOOR, SHEER WILL-POWER CAN SOMETIMES RESTORE SOME-ONE'S HEALTH.
THAT'S ESPECIALLY TRUE ON THIS SIDE OF THE VEIL.

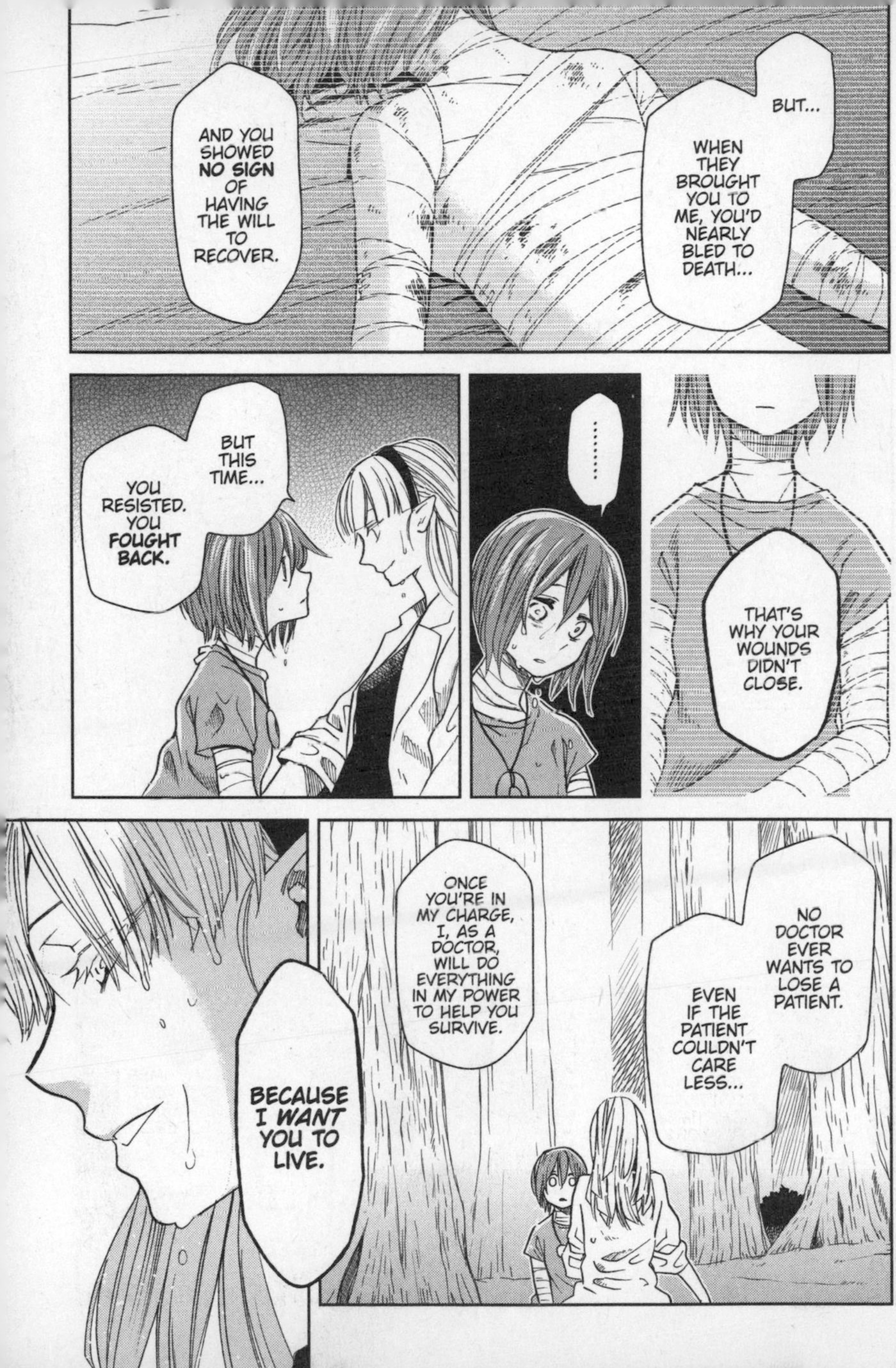
BUT...
WHEN THEY BROUGHT YOU TO ME, YOU'D NEARLY BLED TO DEATH...
AND YOU SHOWED **NO SIGN** OF HAVING THE WILL TO RECOVER.
THAT'S WHY YOUR WOUNDS DIDN'T CLOSE.
......
BUT THIS TIME...
YOU RESISTED. YOU **FOUGHT BACK.**
NO DOCTOR EVER WANTS TO LOSE A PATIENT.
EVEN IF THE PATIENT COULDN'T CARE LESS...
ONCE YOU'RE IN MY CHARGE, I, AS A DOCTOR, WILL DO EVERYTHING IN MY POWER TO HELP YOU SURVIVE.
BECAUSE I *WANT* YOU TO LIVE.

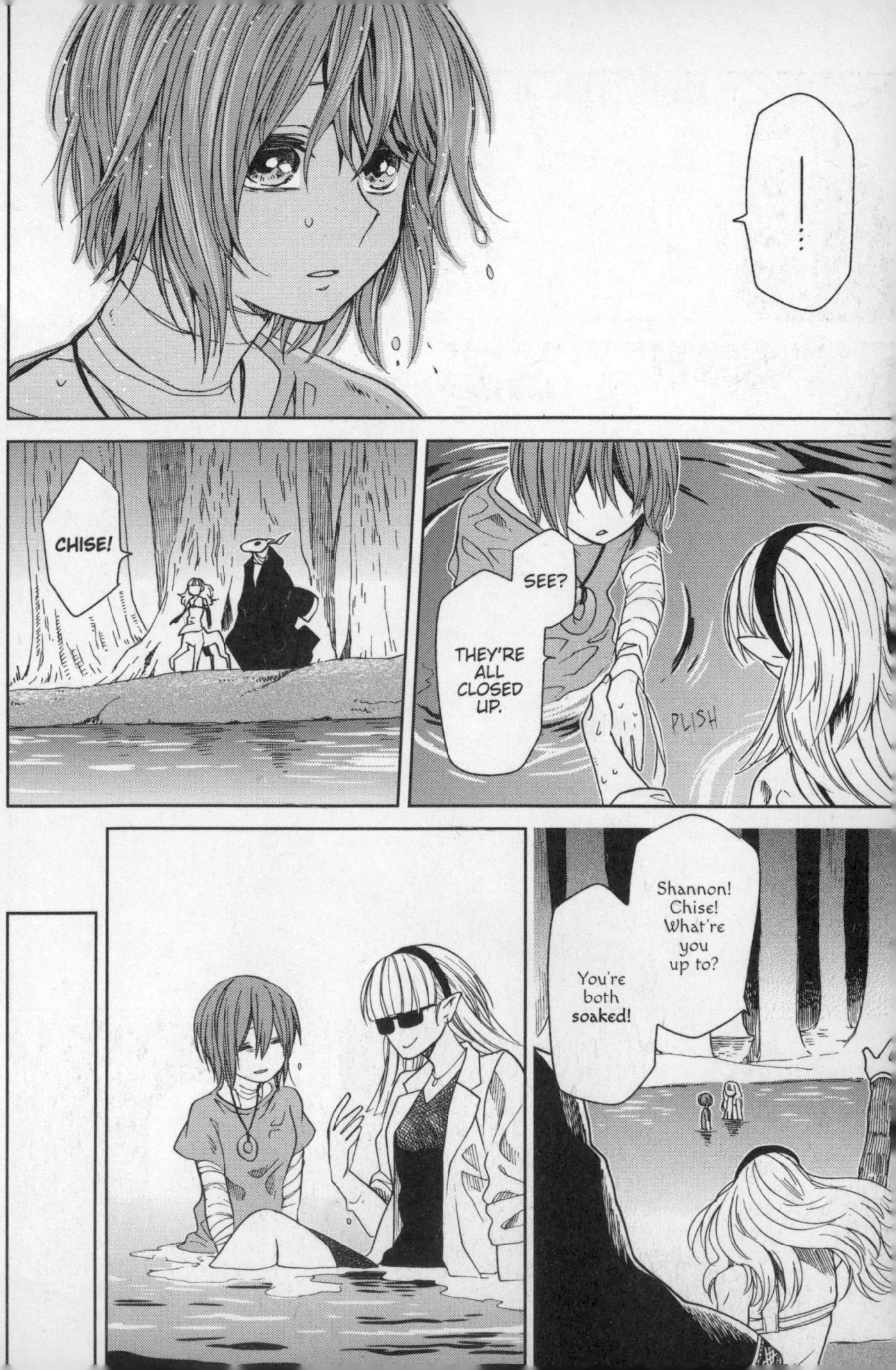
—…!
SEE?
THEY'RE ALL CLOSED UP.
PLISH
CHISE!
Shannon! Chise! What're you up to?
You're both soaked!

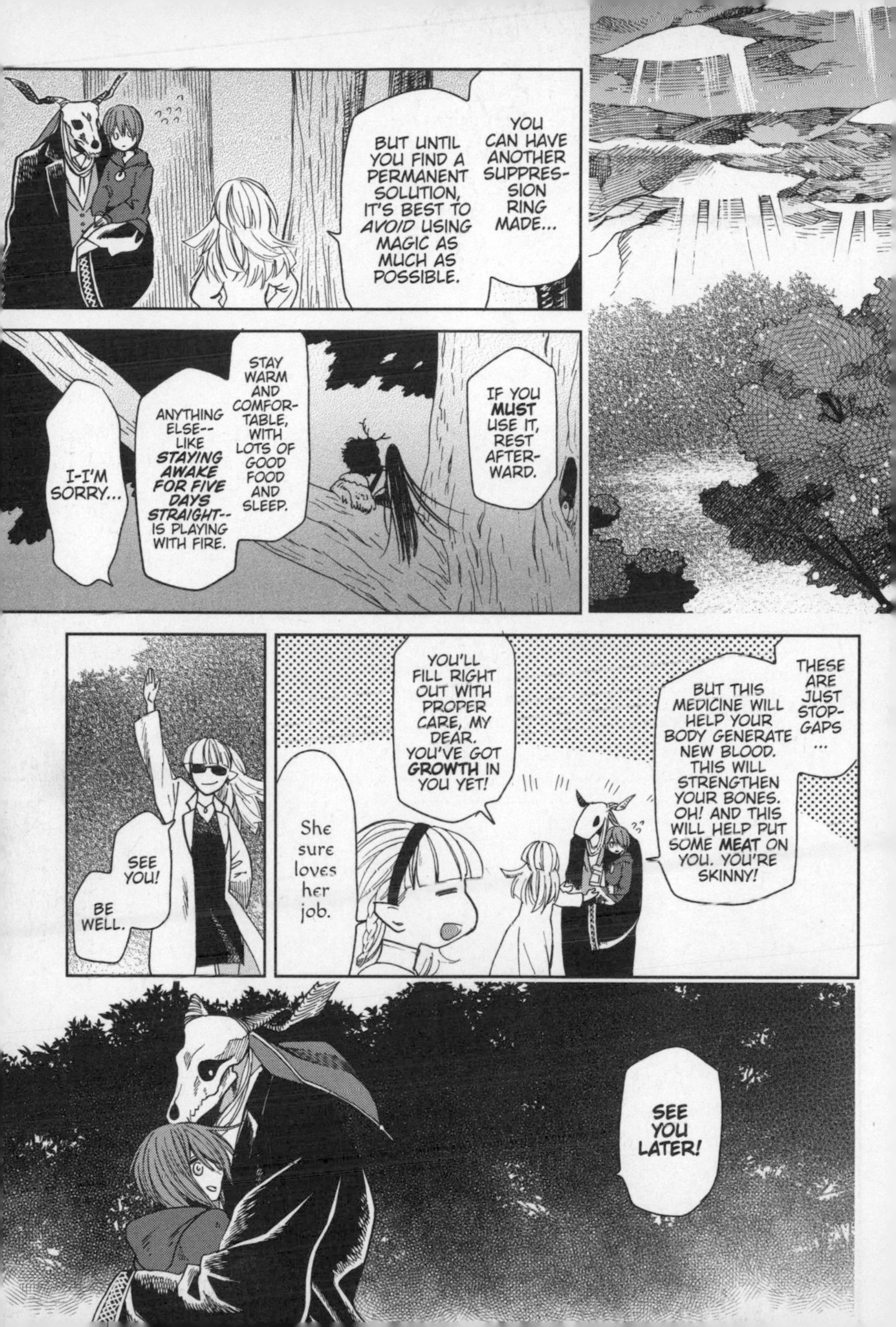

YOU CAN HAVE ANOTHER SUPPRESSION RING MADE...
BUT UNTIL YOU FIND A PERMANENT SOLUTION, IT'S BEST TO *AVOID* USING MAGIC AS MUCH AS POSSIBLE.
IF YOU **MUST** USE IT, REST AFTERWARD.
STAY WARM AND COMFORTABLE, WITH LOTS OF GOOD FOOD AND SLEEP.
ANYTHING ELSE--LIKE **STAYING AWAKE FOR FIVE DAYS STRAIGHT**--IS PLAYING WITH FIRE.
I-I'M SORRY...
THESE ARE JUST STOPGAPS...
BUT THIS MEDICINE WILL HELP YOUR BODY GENERATE NEW BLOOD. THIS WILL STRENGTHEN YOUR BONES. OH! AND THIS WILL HELP PUT SOME **MEAT** ON YOU. YOU'RE SKINNY!
YOU'LL FILL RIGHT OUT WITH PROPER CARE, MY DEAR. YOU'VE GOT **GROWTH** IN YOU YET!
She sure loves her job.
SEE YOU!
BE WELL.
SEE YOU LATER!

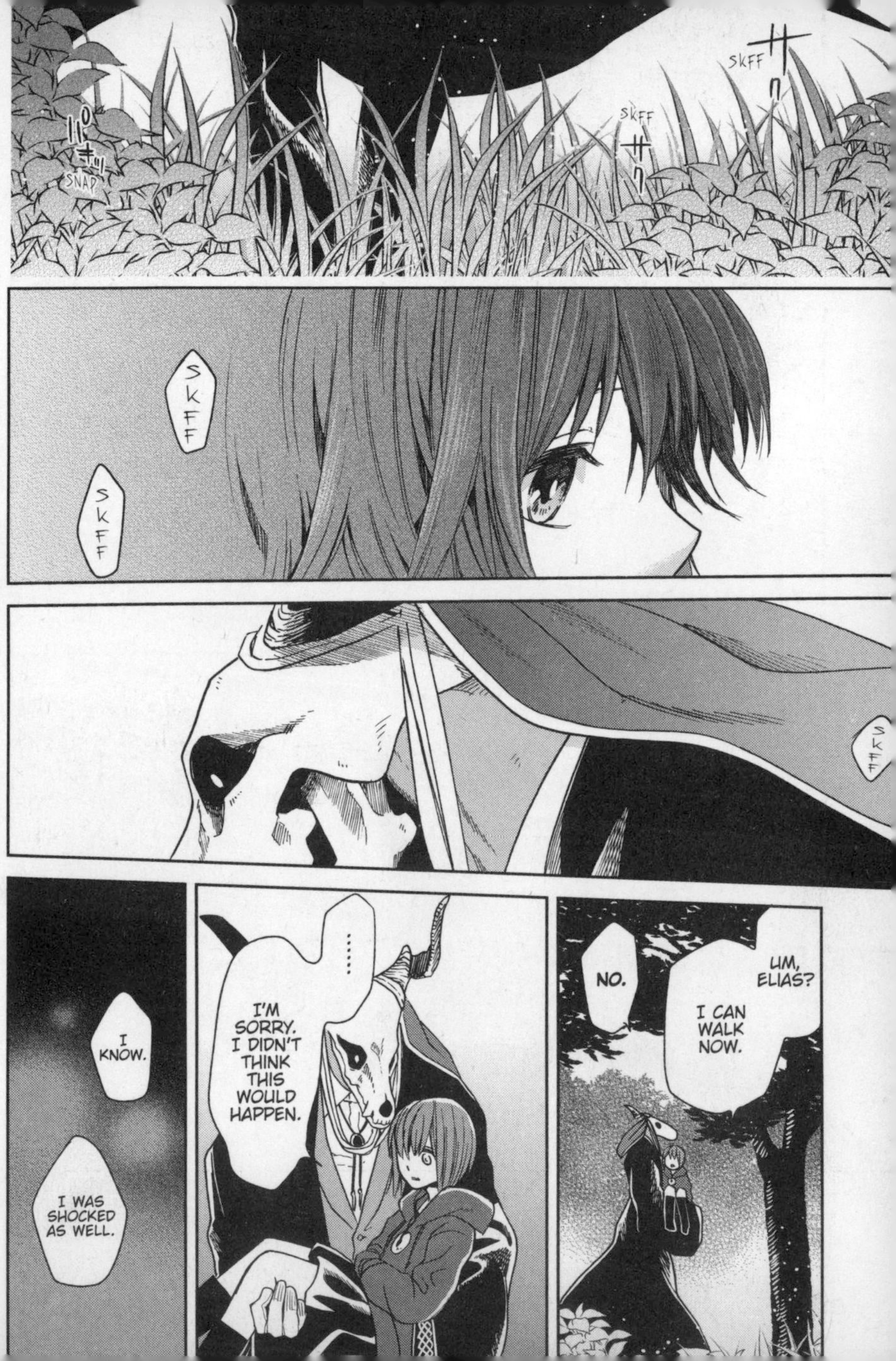
サク
SKFF
サク
SKFF
パキッ
SNAP
SKFF
SKFF
SKFF
UM, ELIAS?
I CAN WALK NOW.
NO.
.....
I'M SORRY. I DIDN'T THINK THIS WOULD HAPPEN.
I KNOW.
I WAS SHOCKED AS WELL.

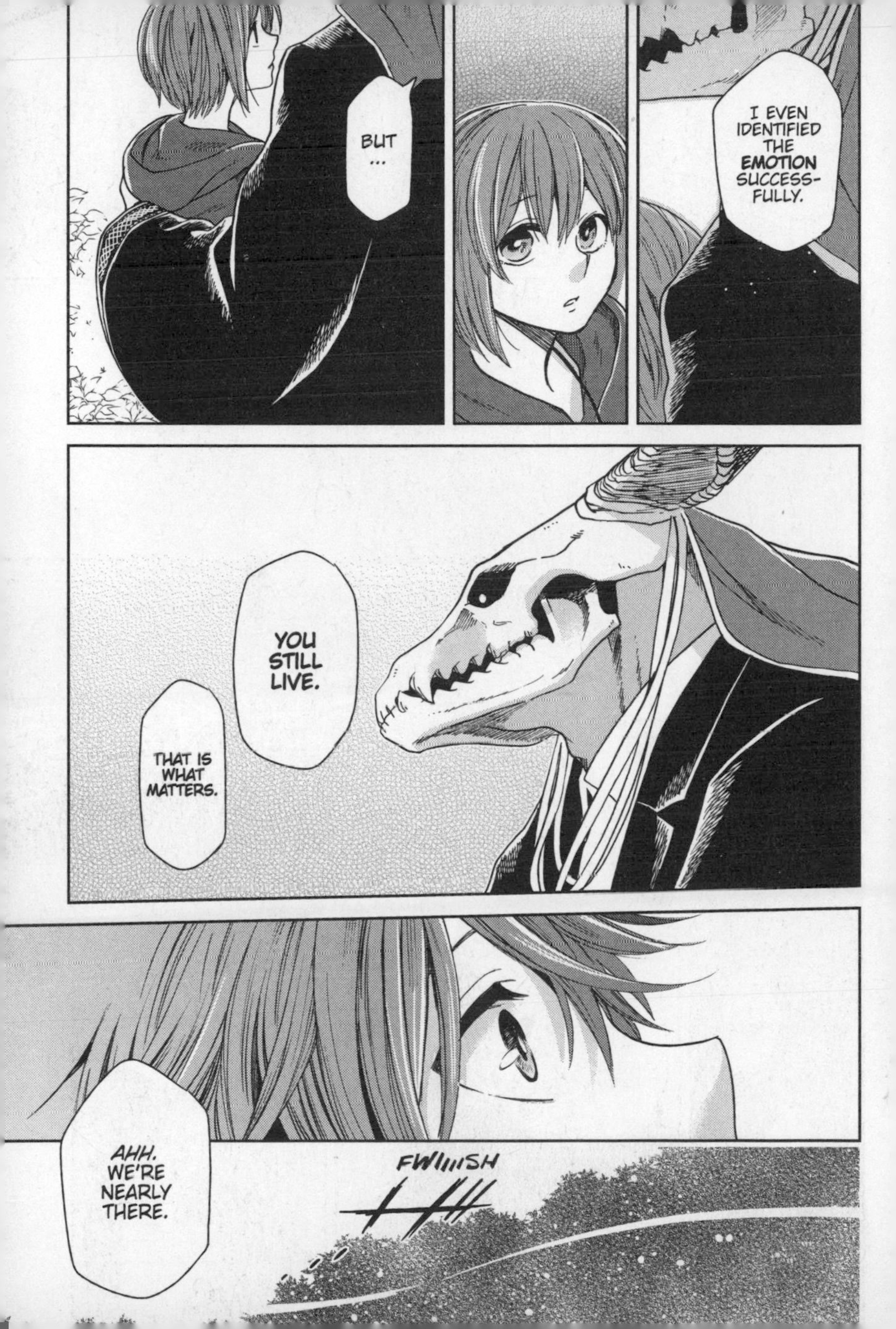
I EVEN IDENTIFIED THE EMOTION SUCCESS-FULLY.
BUT ...
YOU STILL LIVE.
THAT IS WHAT MATTERS.
AHH. WE'RE NEARLY THERE.
FWIIIISH

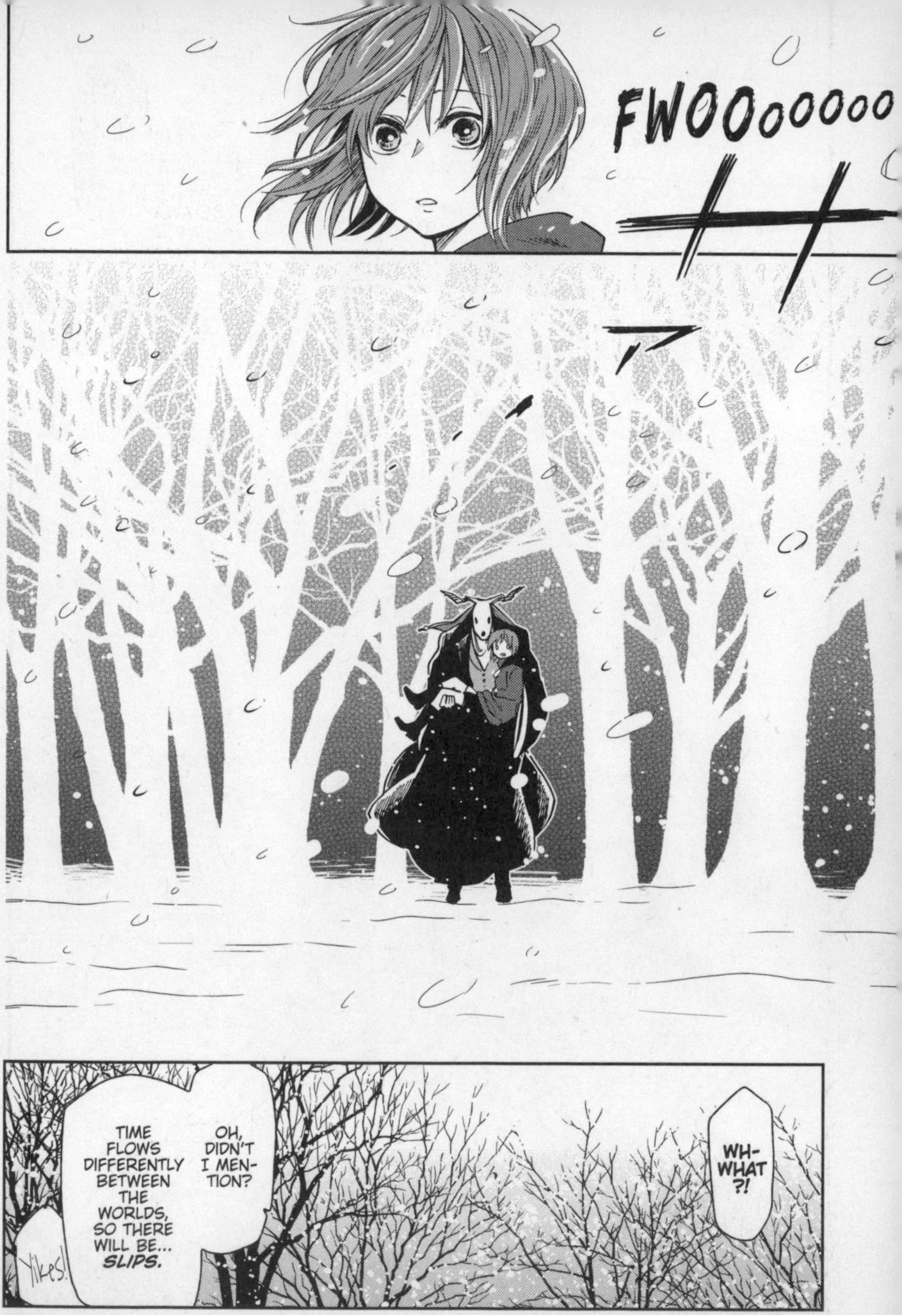
FWOOoooooo
WH-WHAT?!
OH, DIDN'T I MENTION?
TIME FLOWS DIFFERENTLY BETWEEN THE WORLDS, SO THERE WILL BE... **SLIPS.**
Yikes!

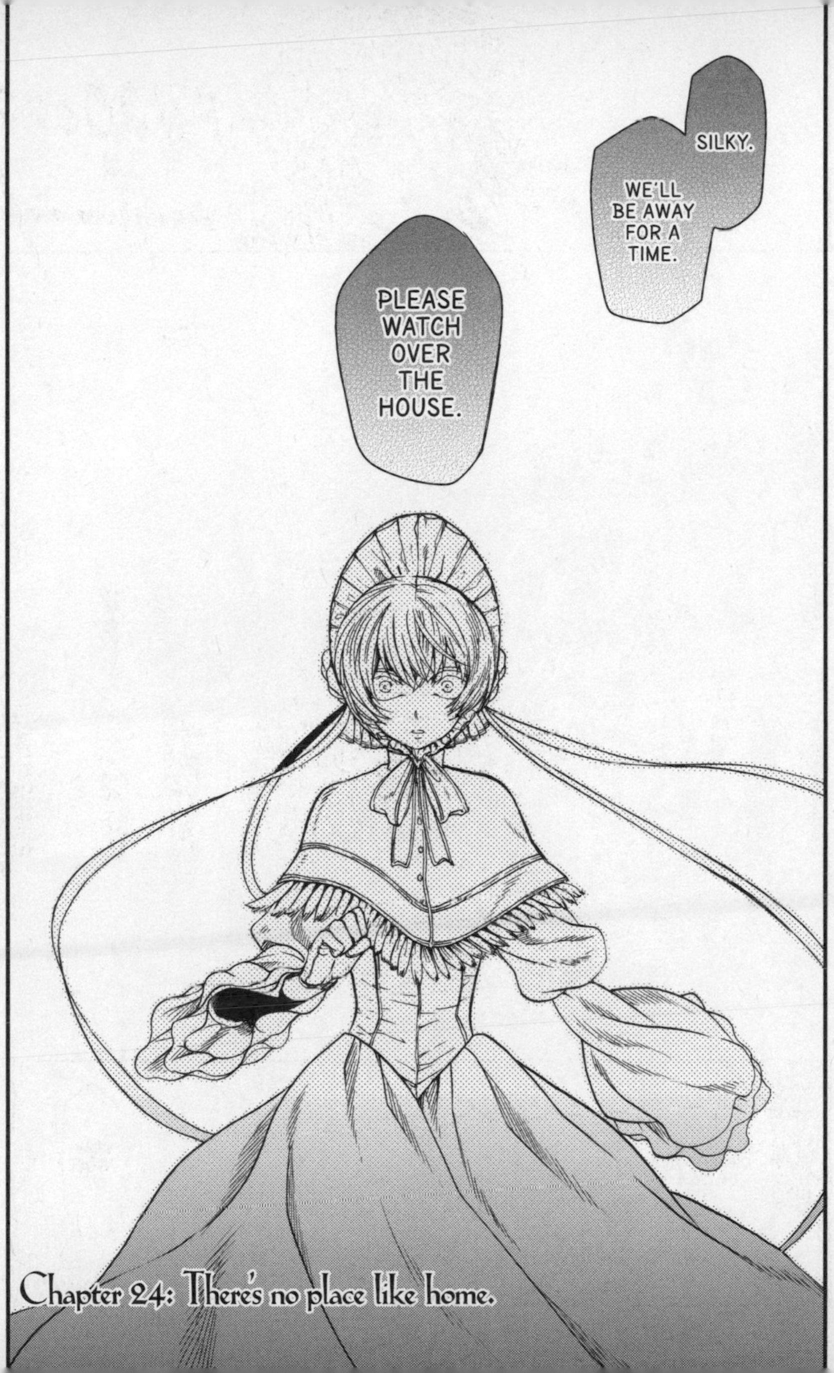
SILKY.
WE'LL BE AWAY FOR A TIME.
PLEASE WATCH OVER THE HOUSE.

Chapter 24: There's no place like home.

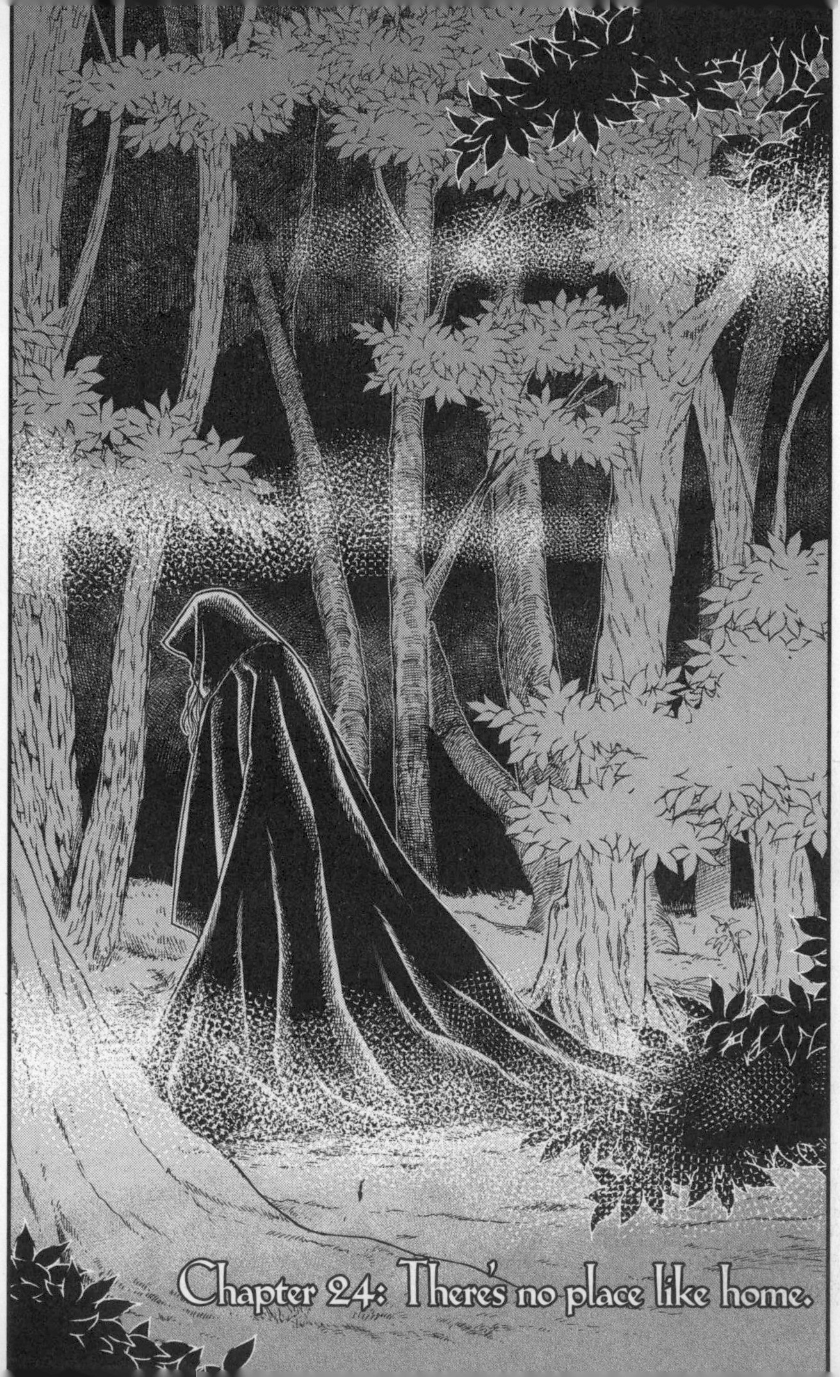
Chapter 24: There's no place like home.

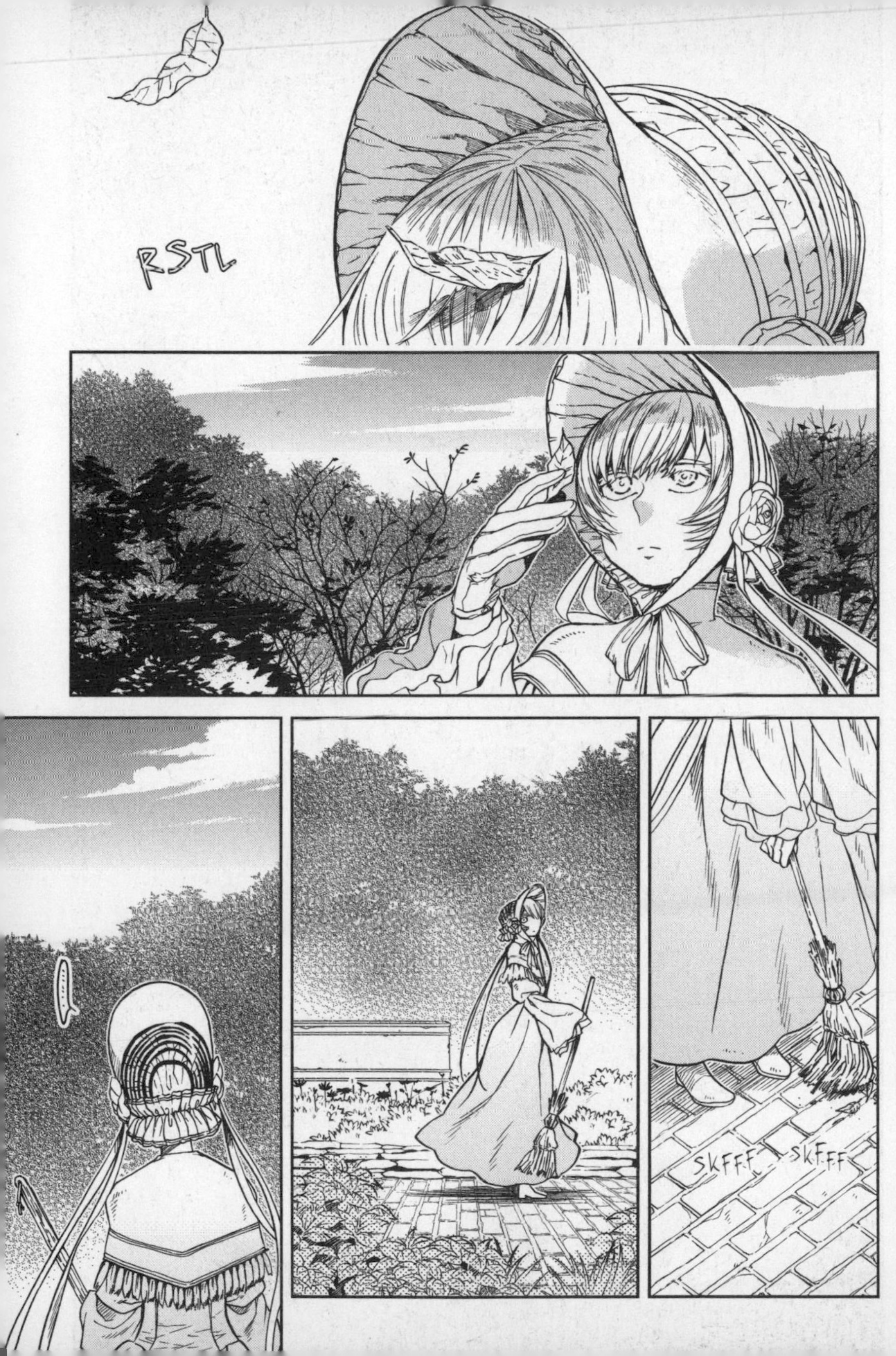
RSTL
SKFFF SKFFF
......

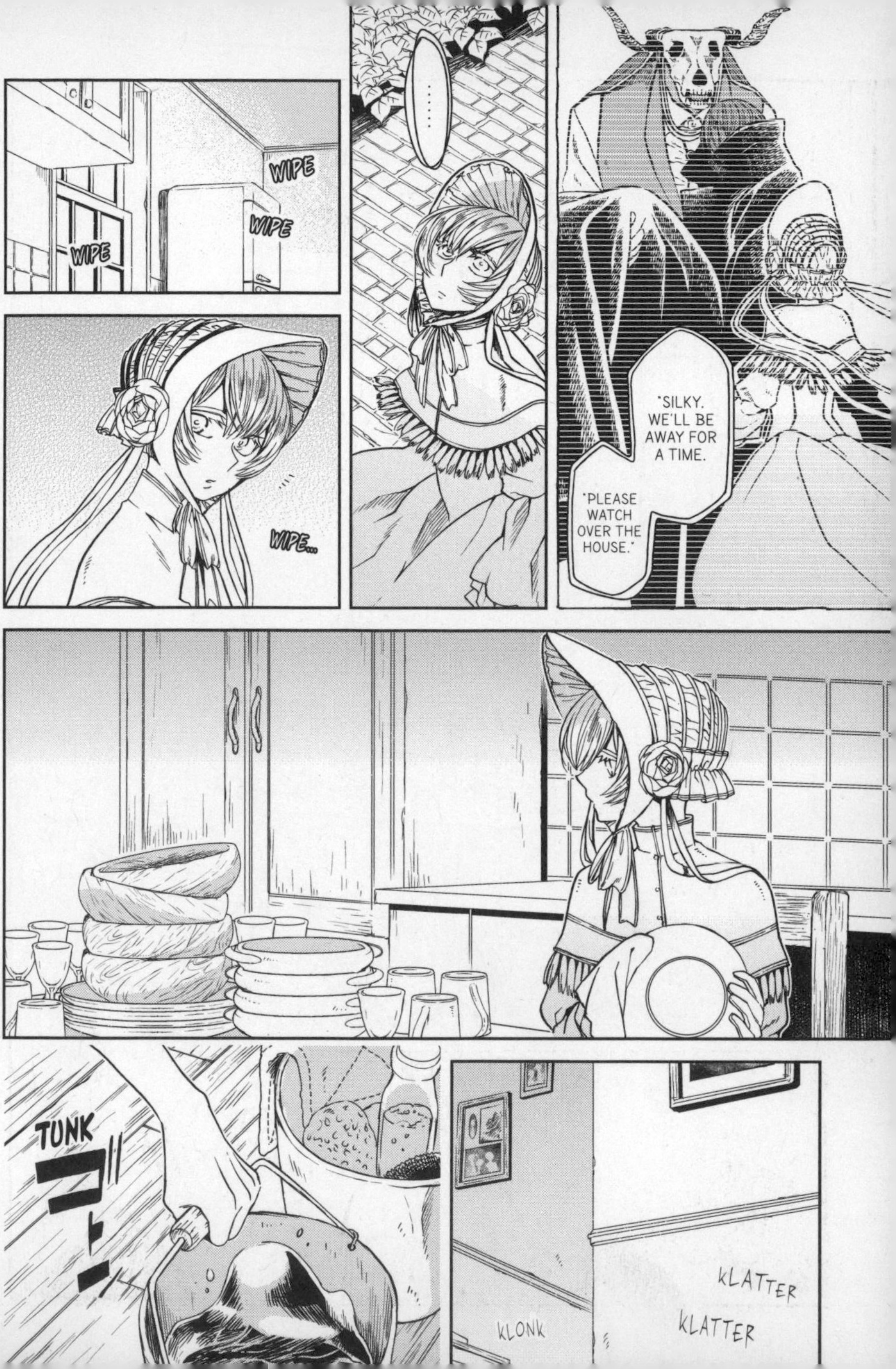
"SILKY. WE'LL BE AWAY FOR A TIME.
"PLEASE WATCH OVER THE HOUSE."
......
WIPE
WIPE
WIPE
WIPE...
KLATTER
KLATTER
KLONK
TUNK

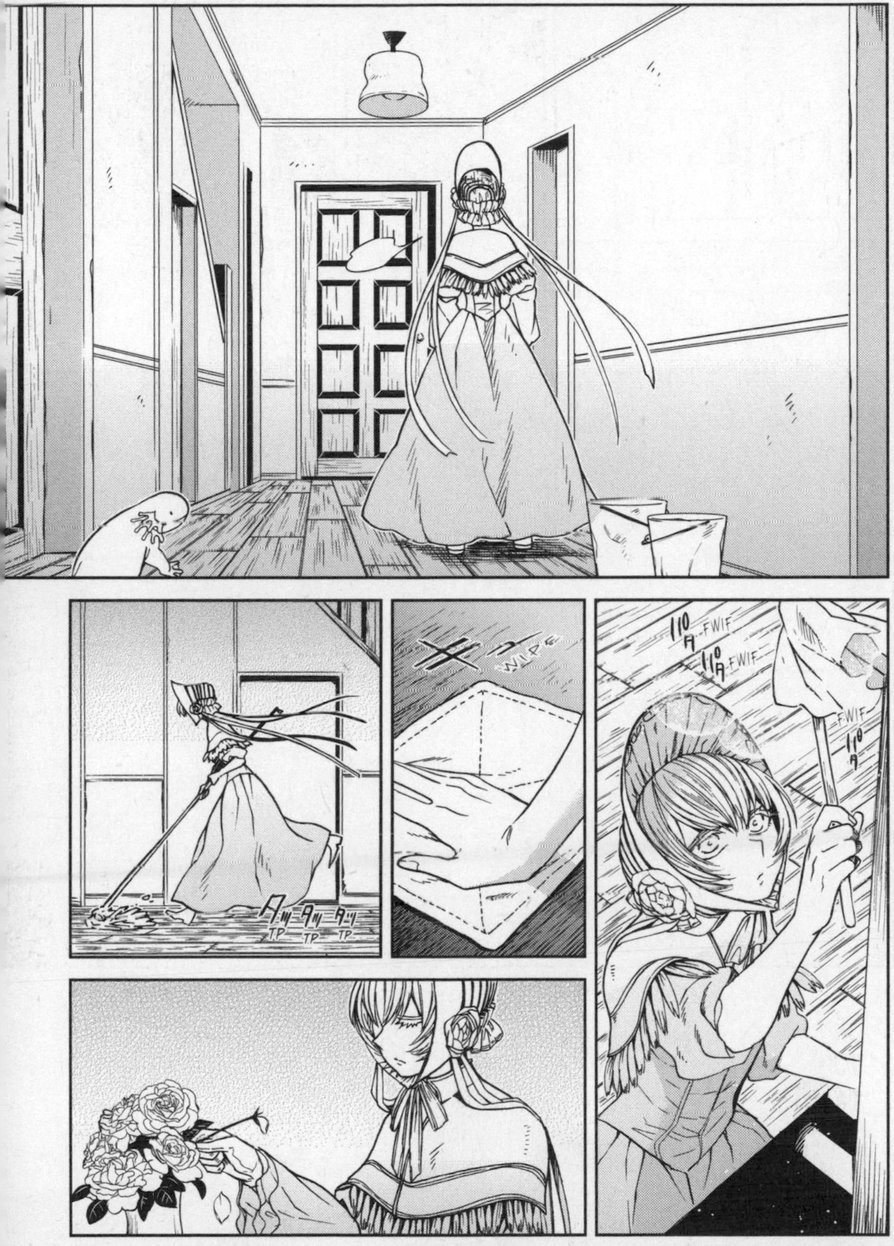
FWIF
FWIF
FWIF
WIPE
TP
TP
TP

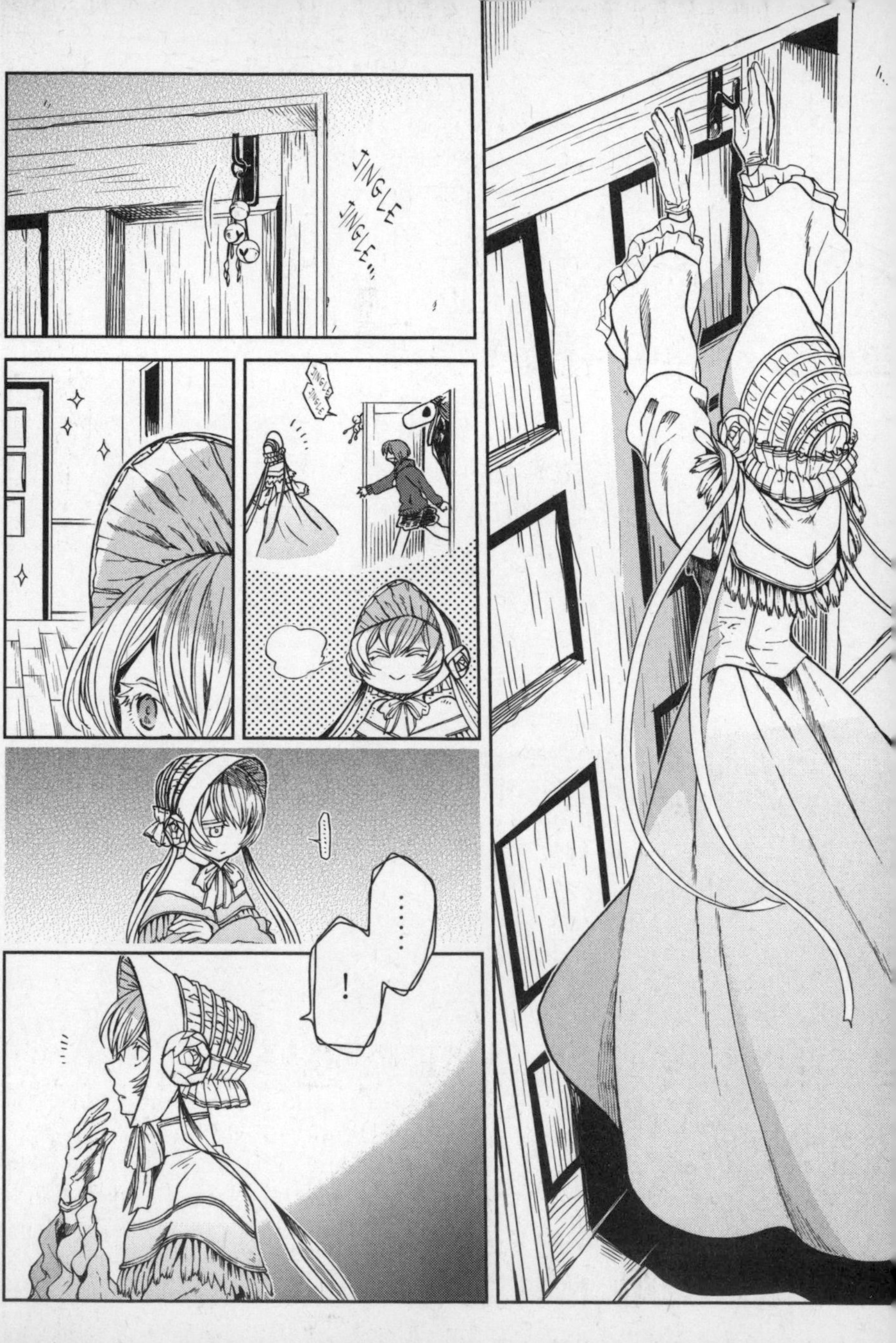
JINGLE JINGLE...
JINGLE JINGLE
......!
......!

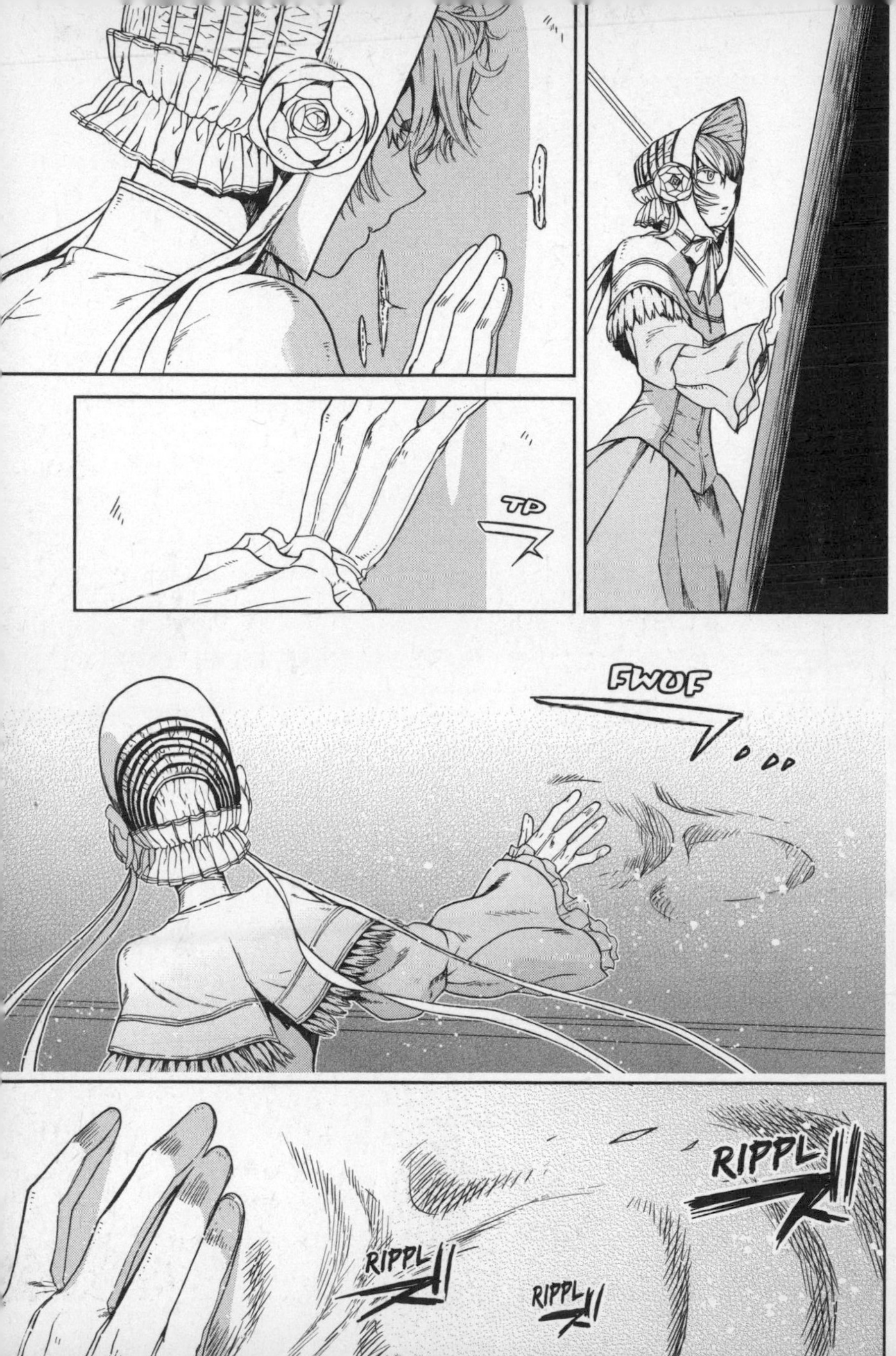
TP
FWOF
RIPPL
RIPPL
RIPPL

RIPPL

RIPPL

RIPPL

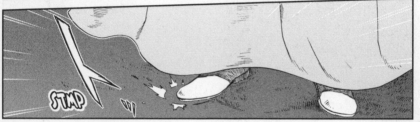

STMP

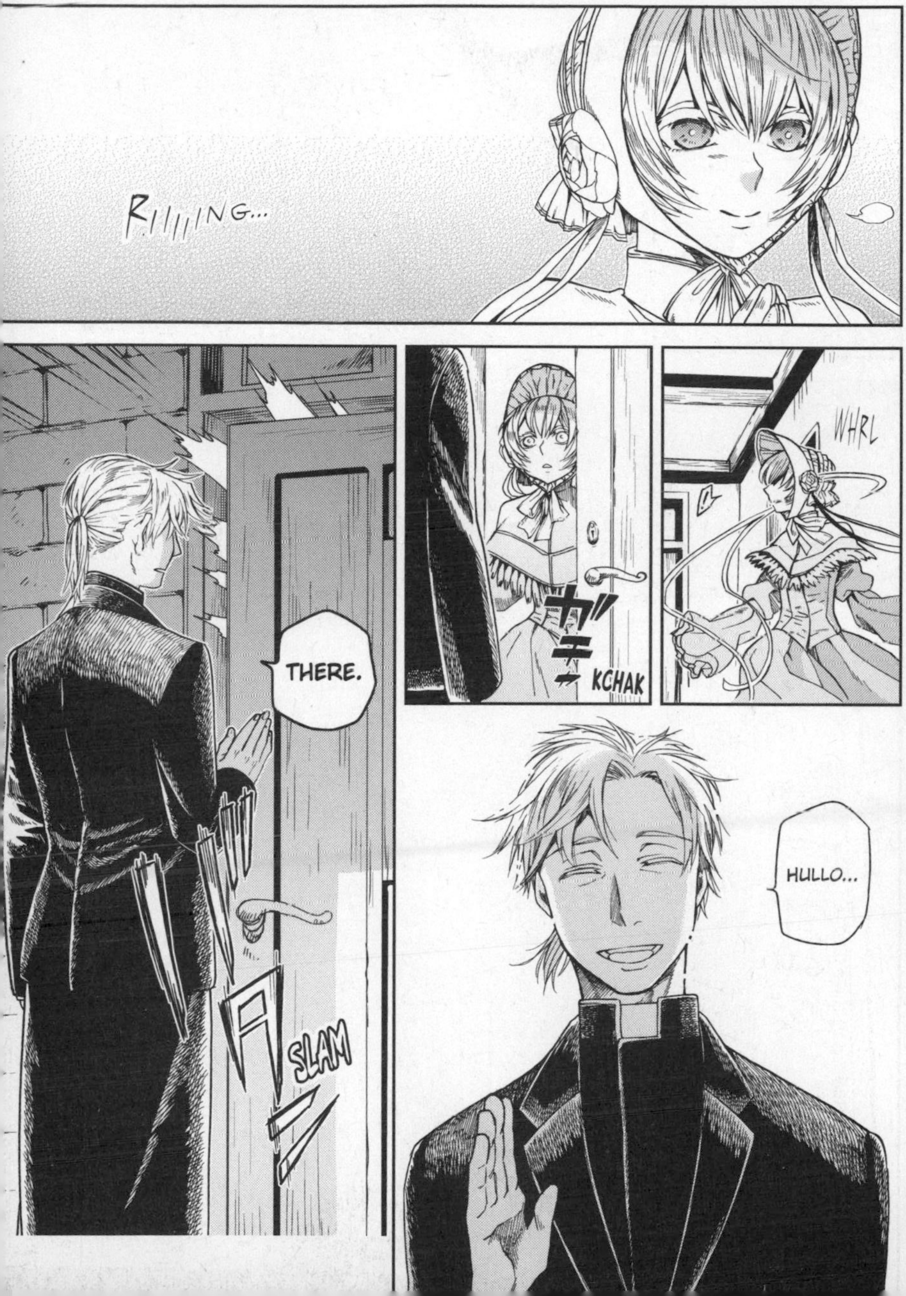
RIIIING...
WHRL
KCHAK
HULLO...
THERE.
SLAM

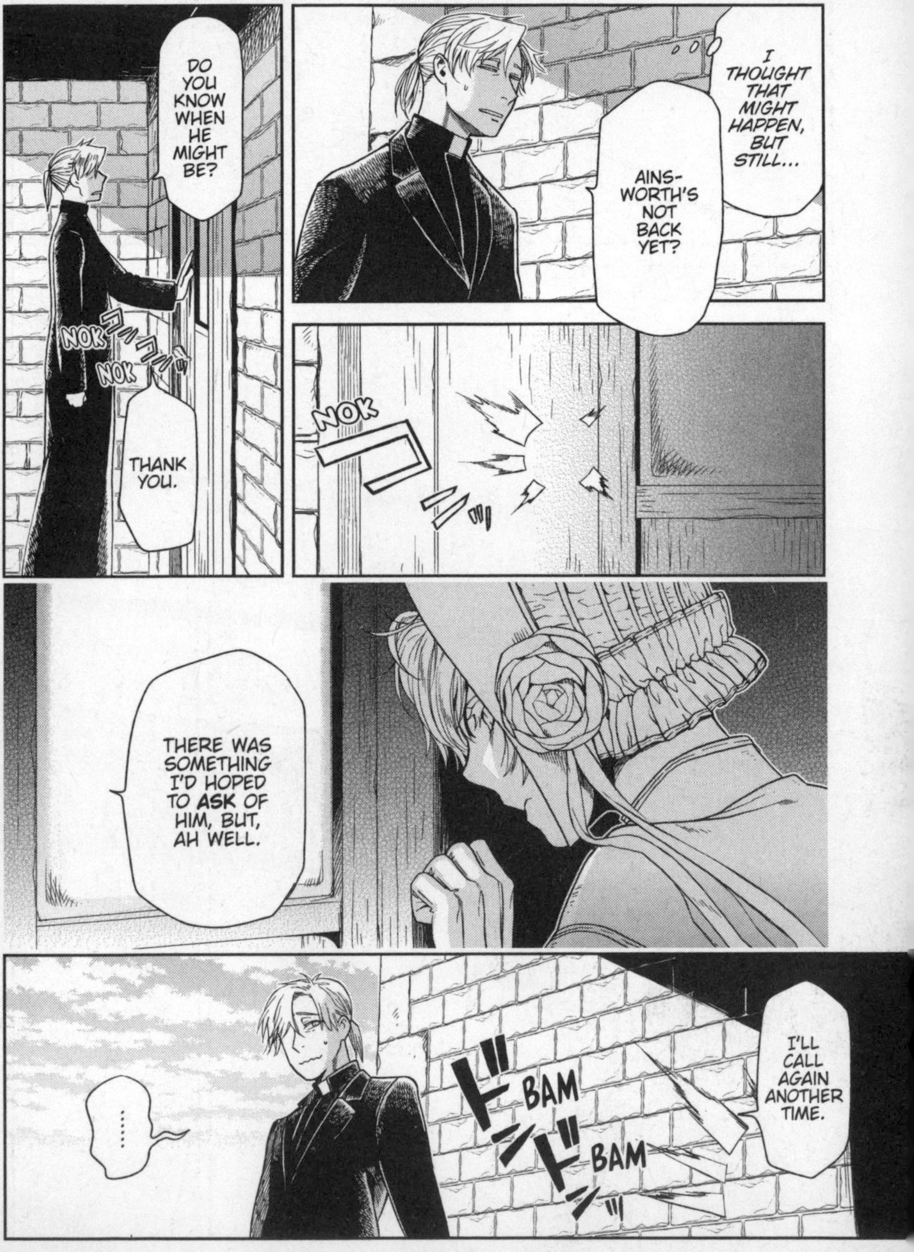
I THOUGHT THAT MIGHT HAPPEN, BUT STILL...
AINS-WORTH'S NOT BACK YET?
NOK
DO YOU KNOW WHEN HE MIGHT BE?
NOK
NOK
THANK YOU.
THERE WAS SOMETHING I'D HOPED TO **ASK** OF HIM, BUT, AH WELL.
I'LL CALL AGAIN ANOTHER TIME.
BAM
BAM
......

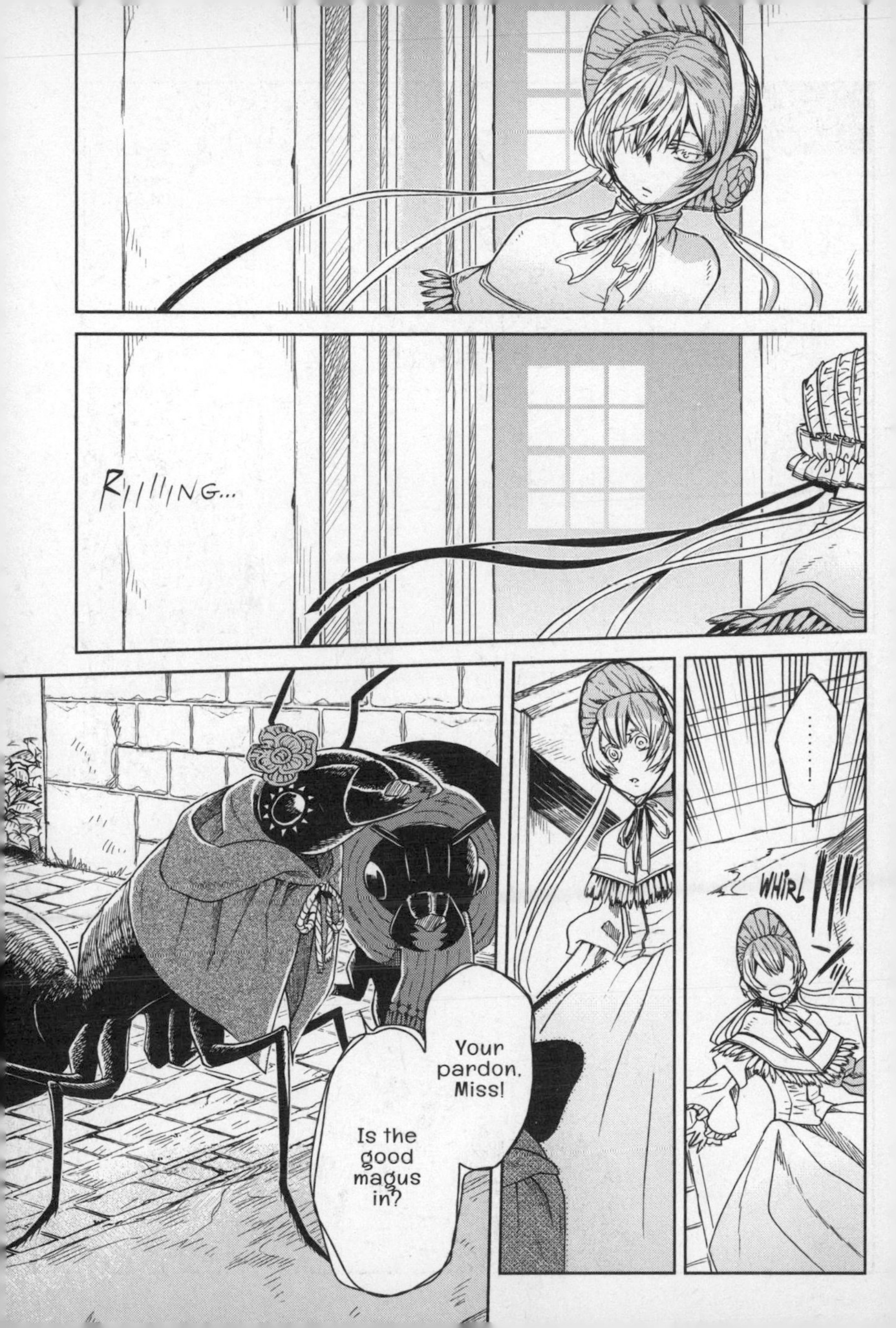
RIIIIING...
.......!
WHIRL
Your pardon, Miss!
Is the good magus in?

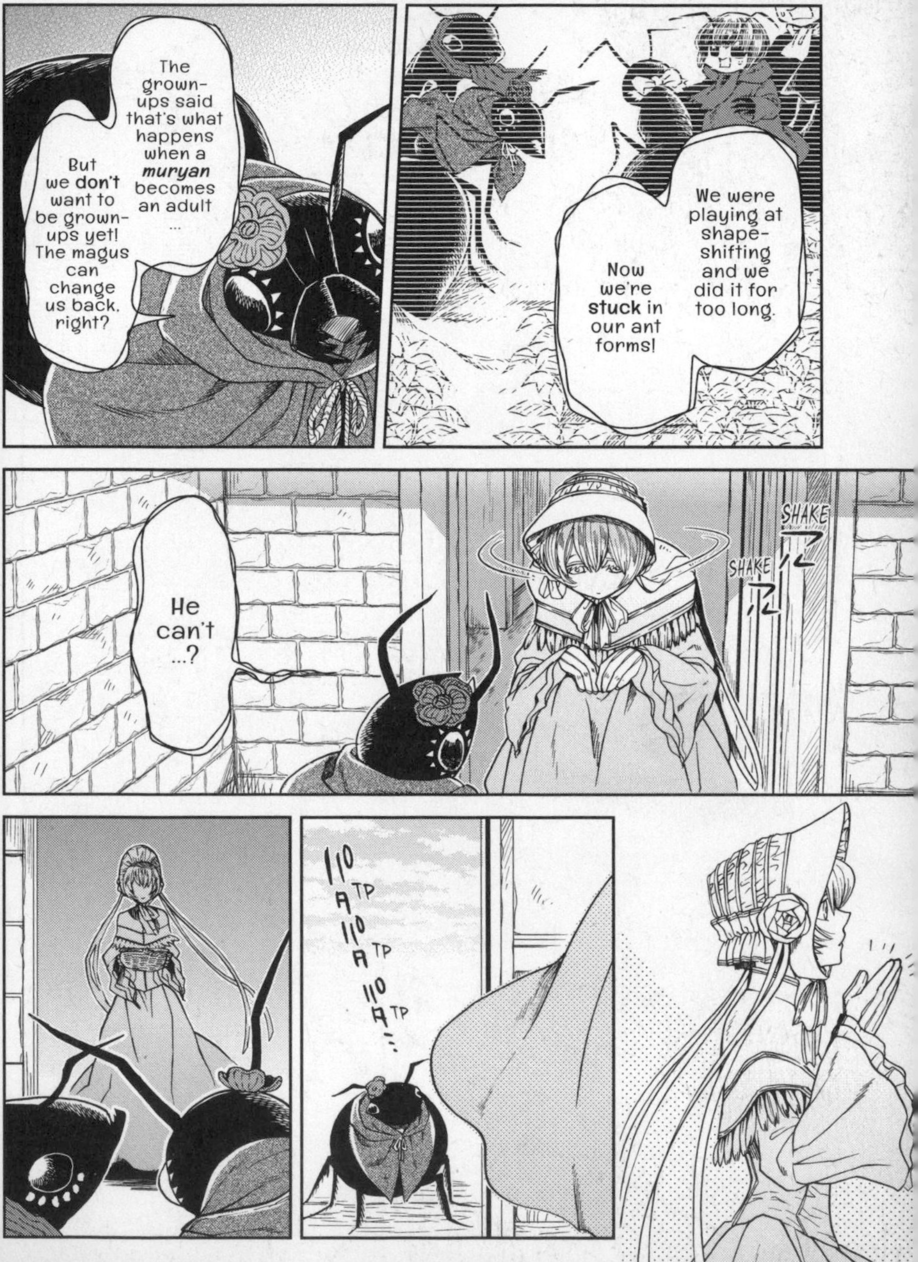
We were playing at shape-shifting and we did it for too long.
Now we're **stuck** in our ant forms!
The grown-ups said that's what happens when a *muryan* becomes an adult ...
But we **don't** want to be grown-ups yet! The magus can change us back, right?
SHAKE
SHAKE
He can't ...?
!
TP
TP
TP

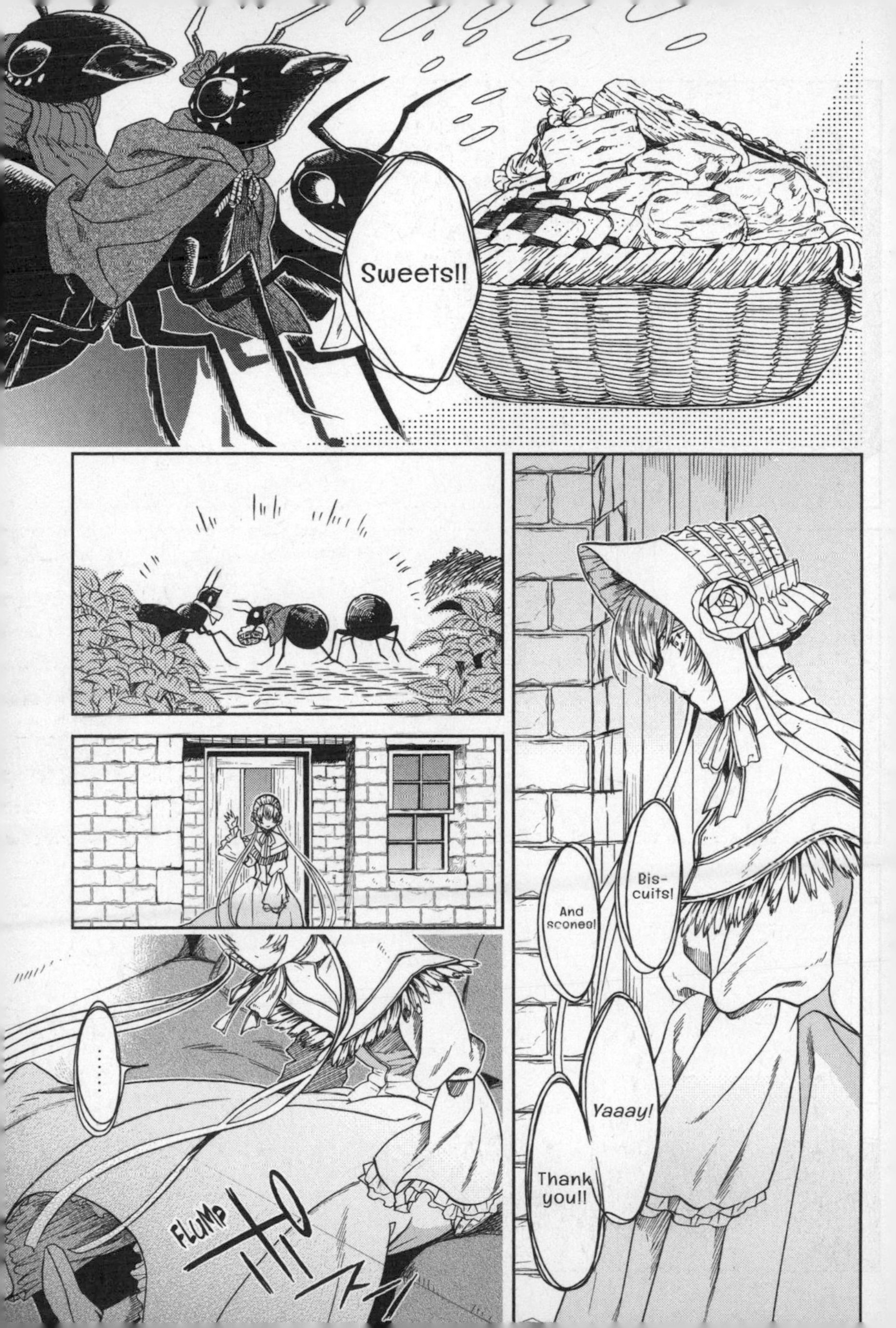
Sweets!!
Bis-cuits!
And scones!
Yaaay!
Thank you!!
......
FLUMP

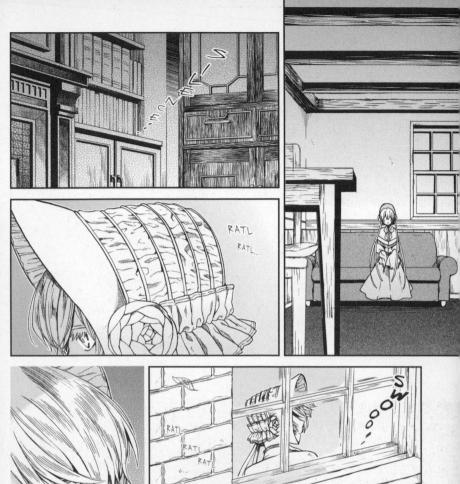

RATL
RATL...

RATL
RATL
RATL
...

SW
OOO...

SW O OO OOO...

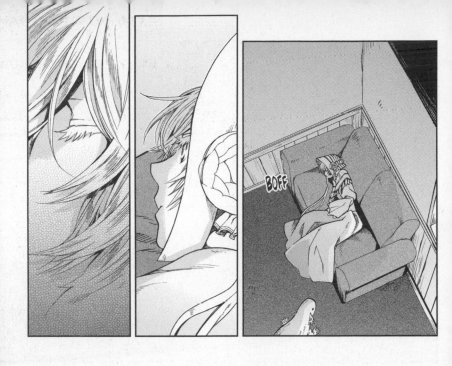

BOFF

BAU
AWOO...

HOOO
HOOOO

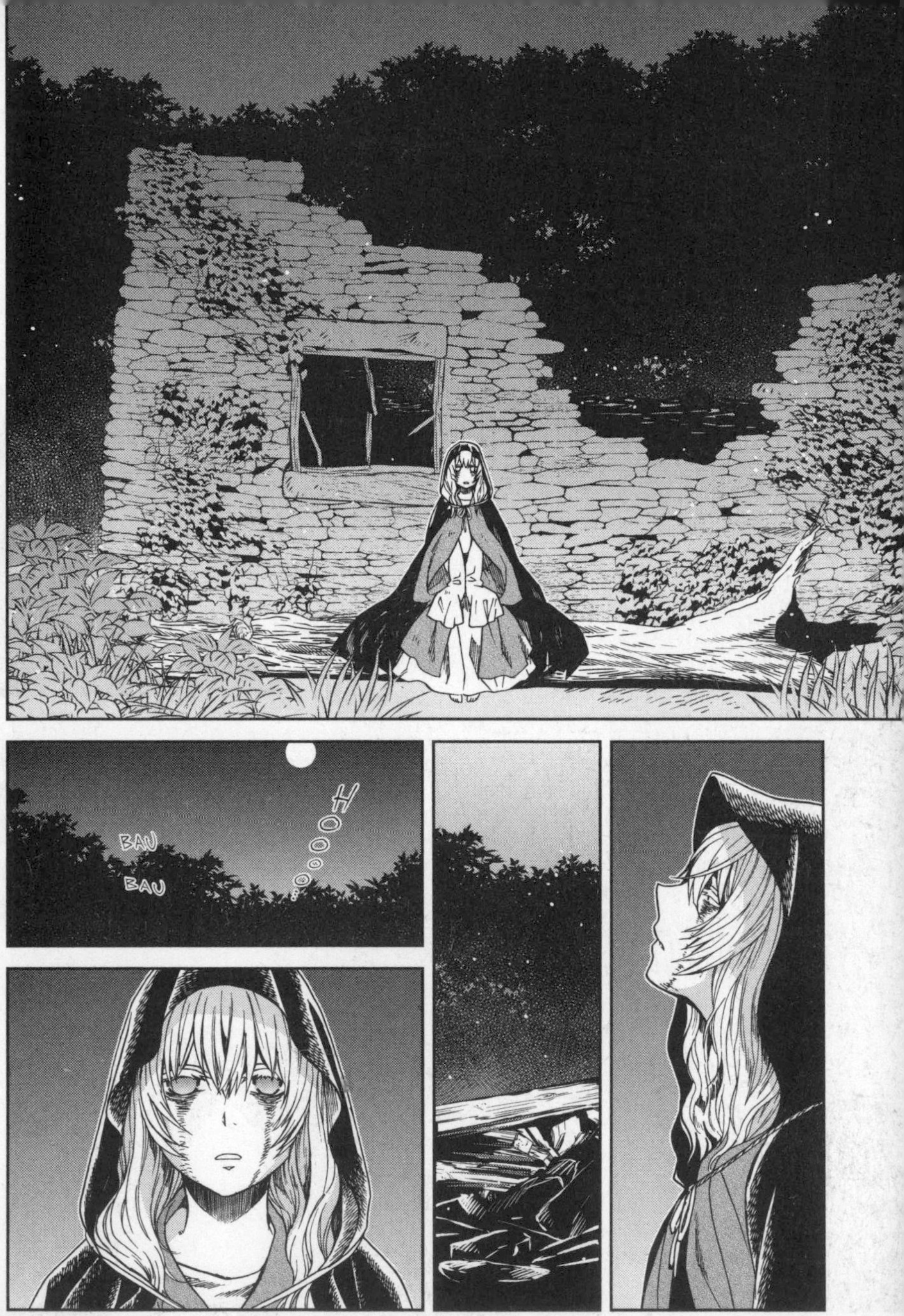
HOOOO...
BAU
BAU

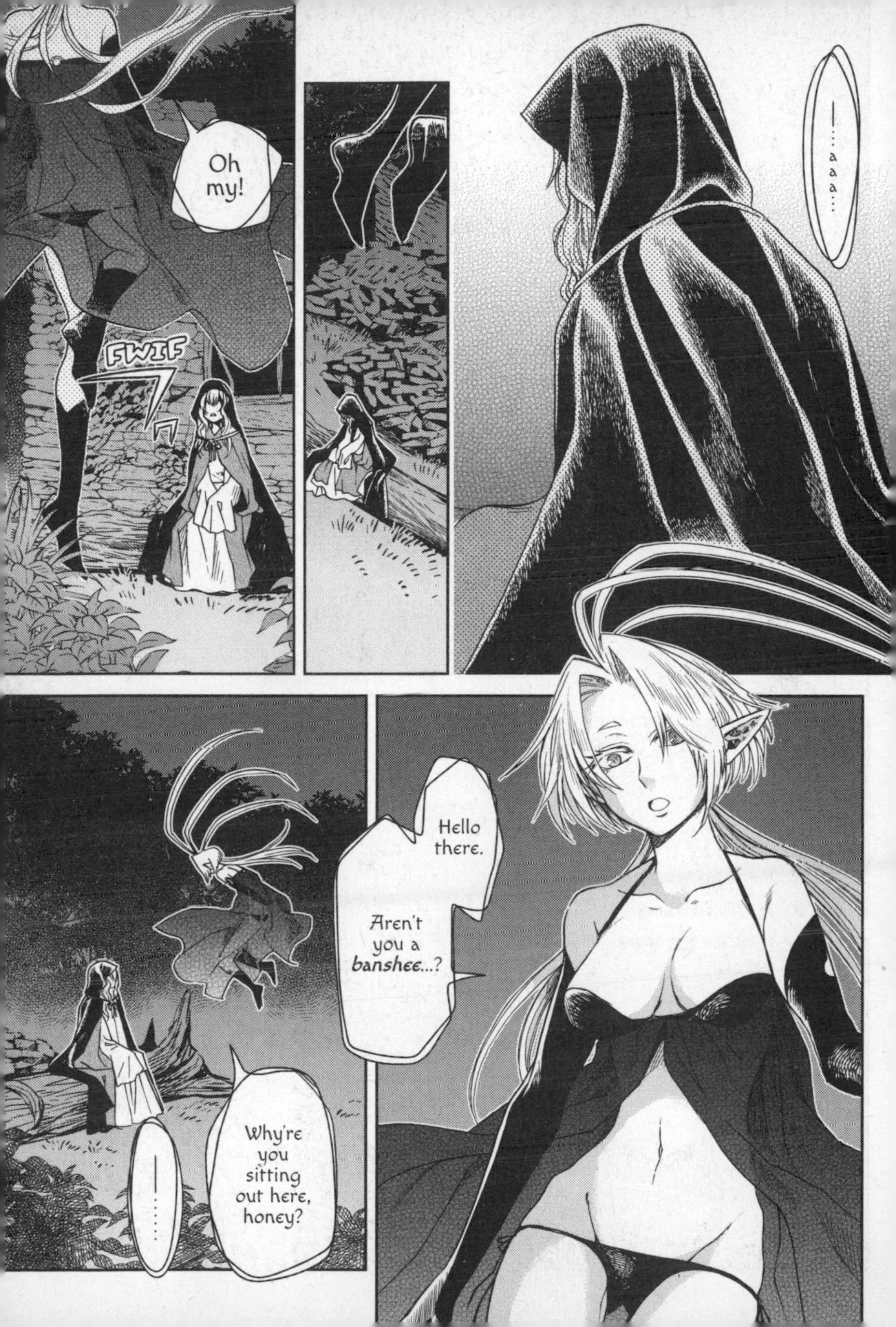
...aaa...
Oh my!
FWIF
Hello there.
Aren't you a *banshee*...?
Why're you sitting out here, honey?
......

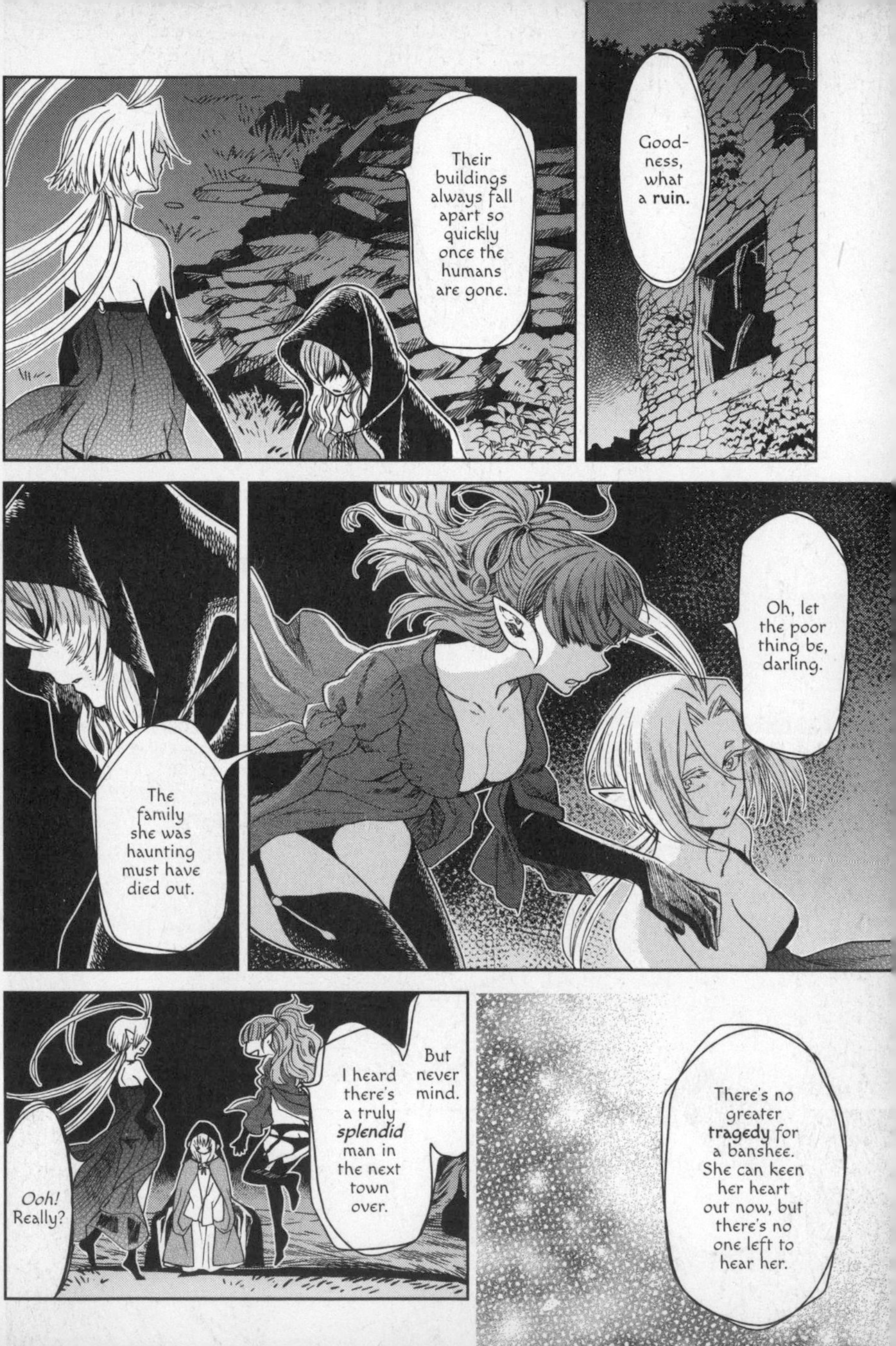
Goodness, what a **ruin.**
Their buildings always fall apart so quickly once the humans are gone.
Oh, let the poor thing be, darling.
The family she was haunting must have died out.
There's no greater **tragedy** for a banshee. She can keen her heart out now, but there's no one left to hear her.
But never mind.
I heard there's a truly ***splendid*** man in the next town over.
Ooh! Really?

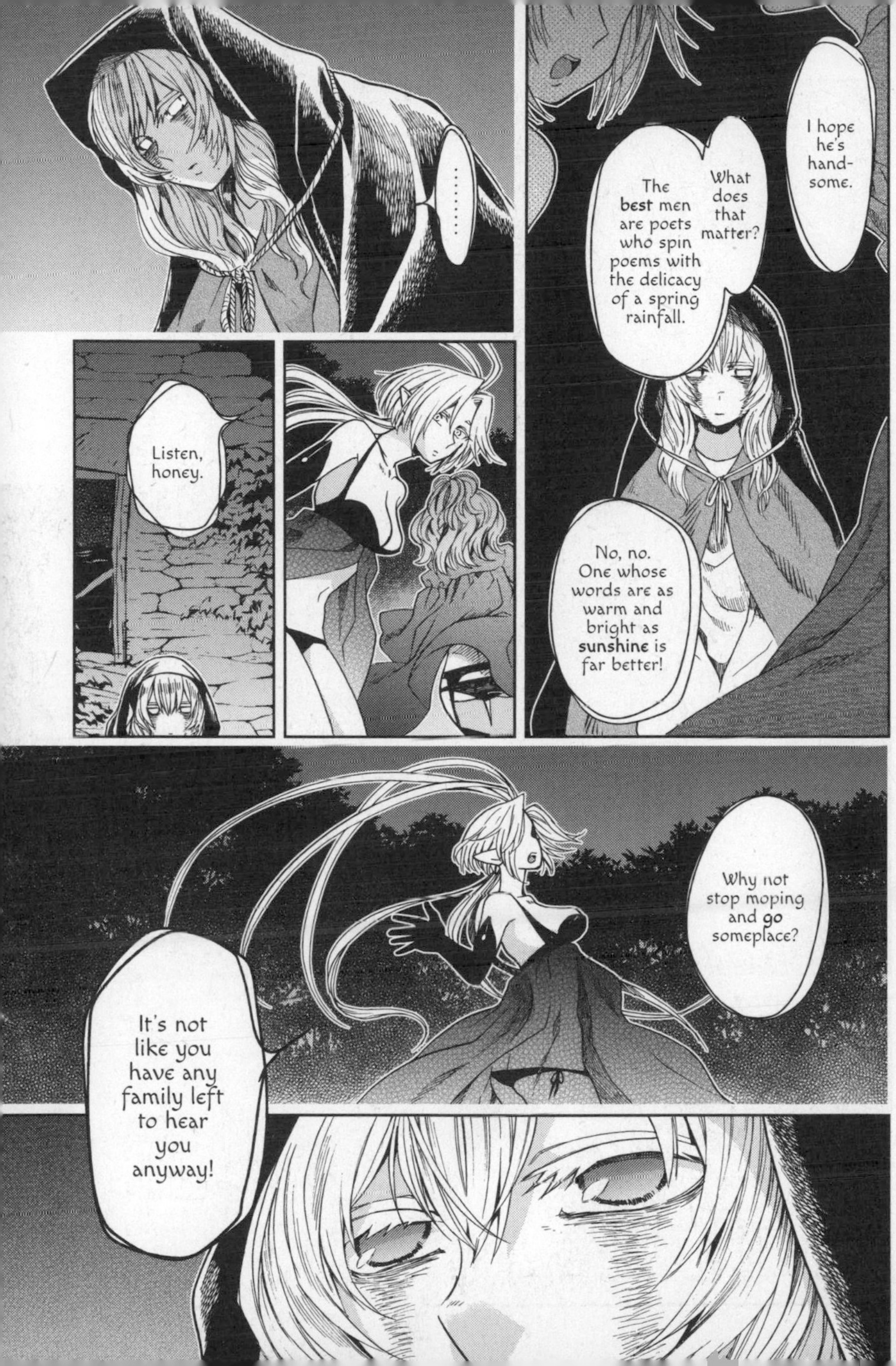
I hope he's hand-some.
What does that matter?
The best men are poets who spin poems with the delicacy of a spring rainfall.
No, no. One whose words are as warm and bright as sunshine is far better!
……
Listen, honey.
Why not stop moping and go someplace?
It's not like you have any family left to hear you anyway!

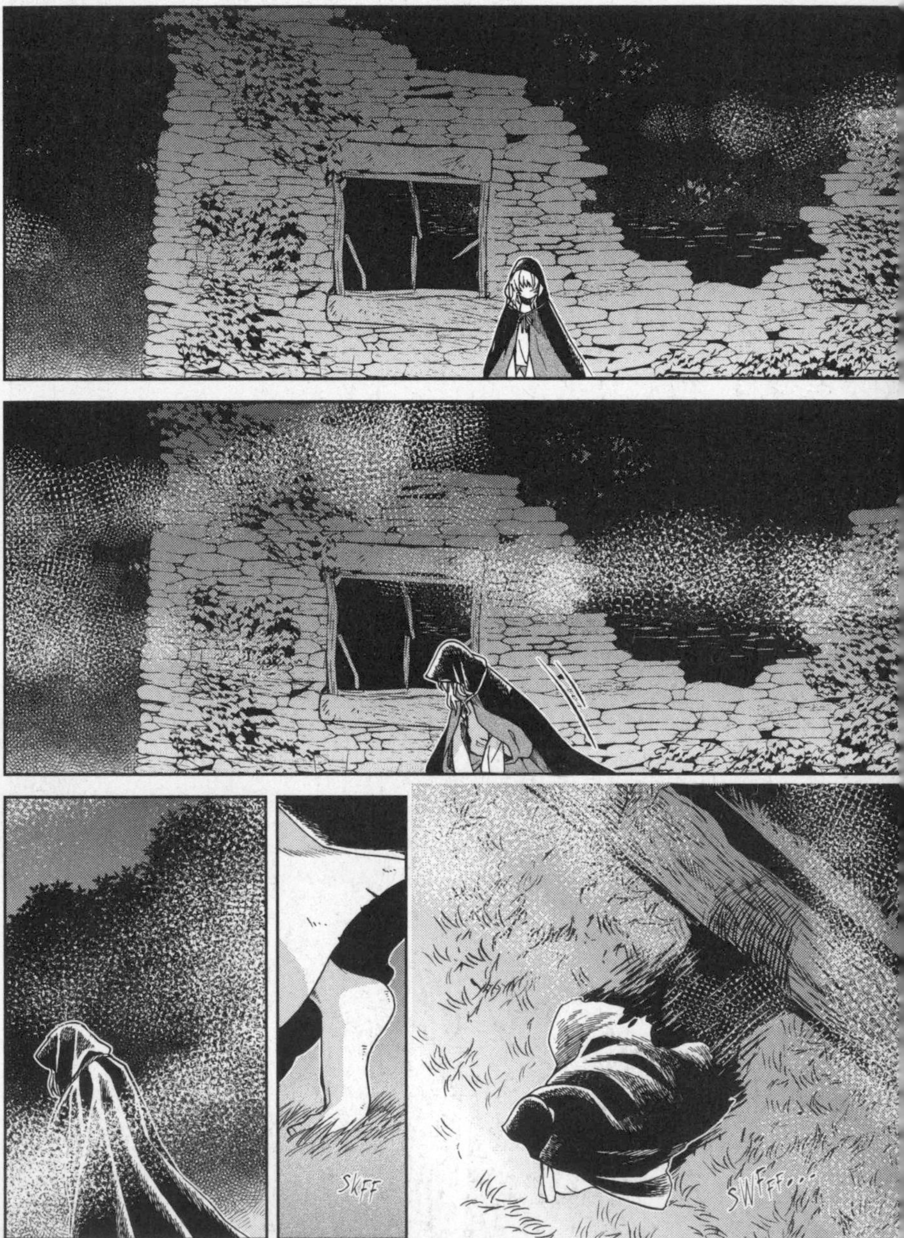
SWFFF...
...
SKFF

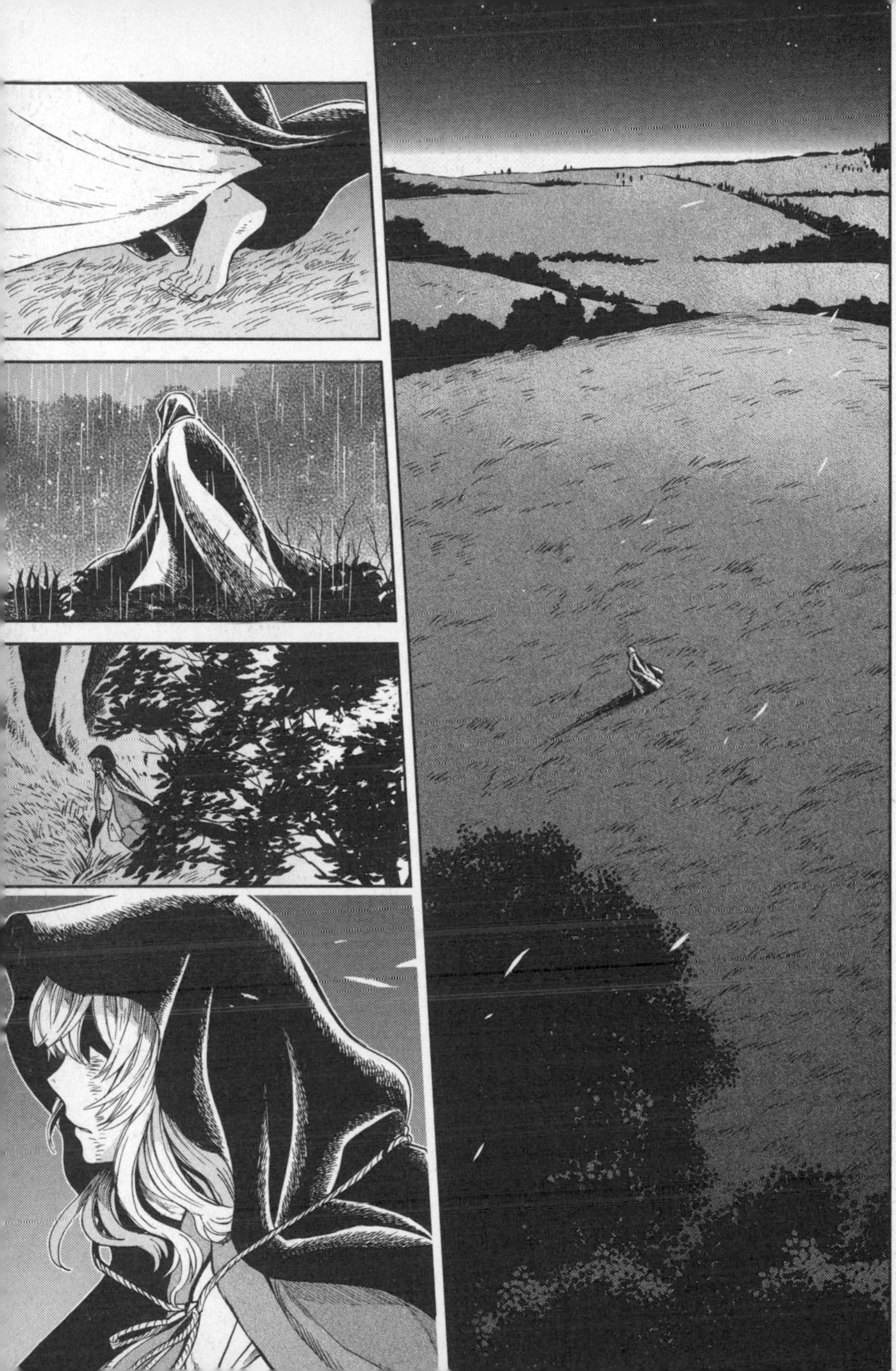

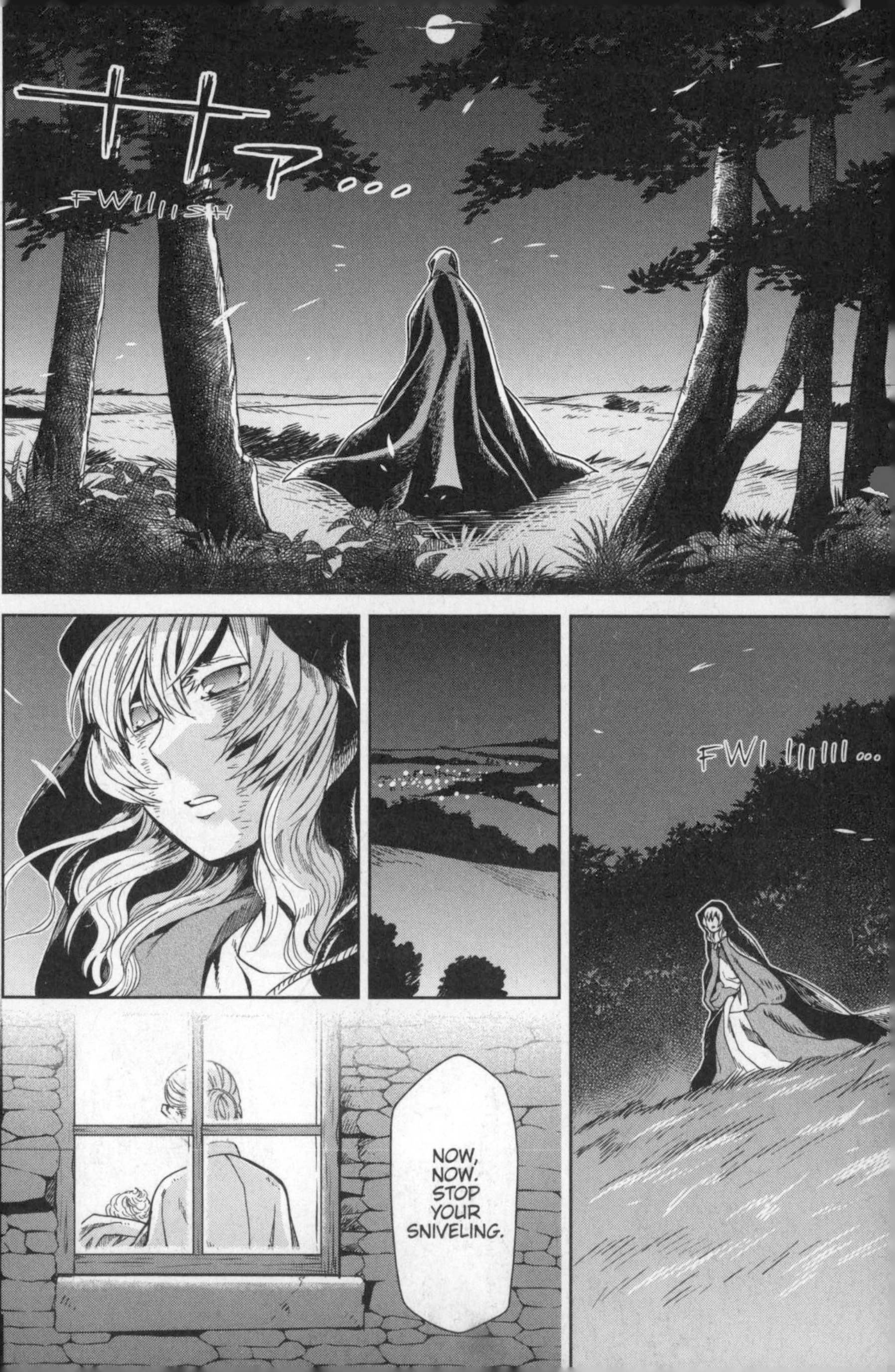
FWIIIISH
FWI IIIIII...
NOW, NOW. STOP YOUR SNIVELING.

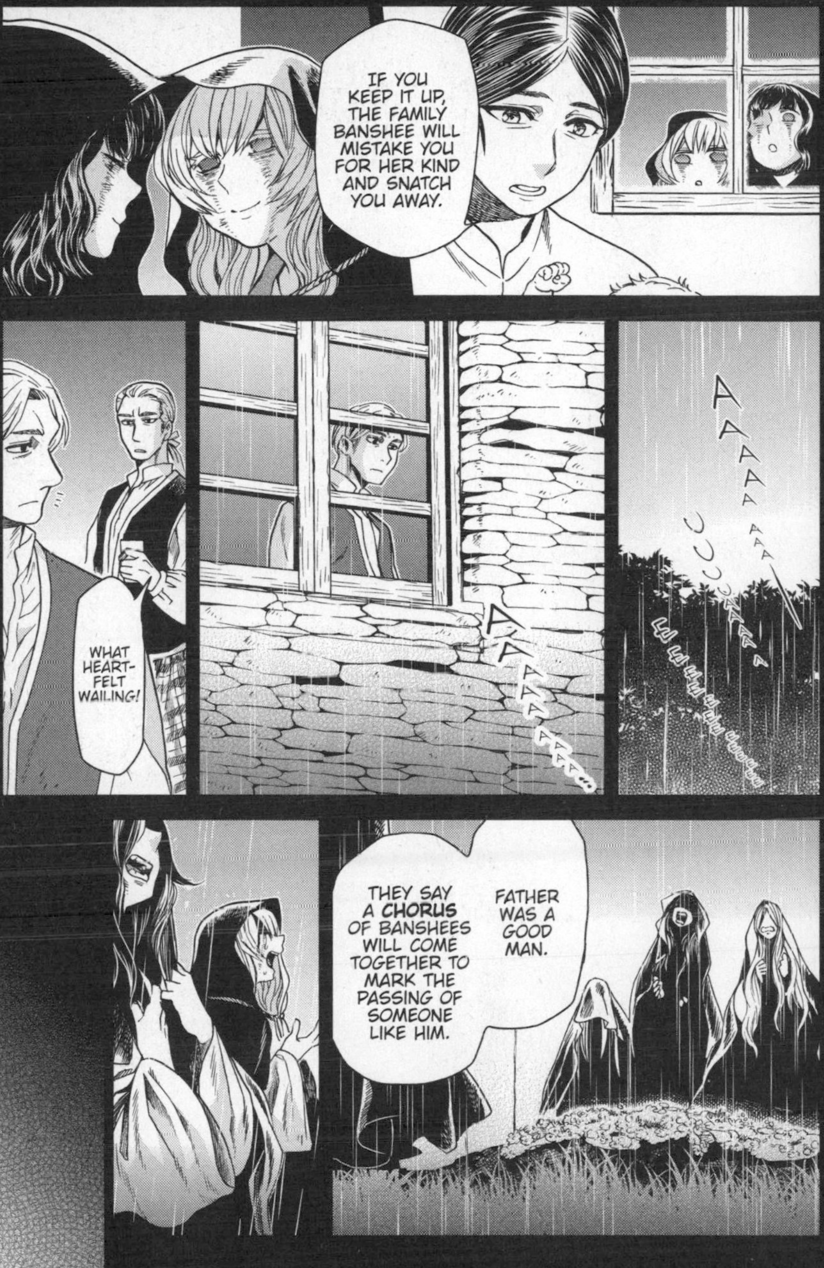
IF YOU KEEP IT UP, THE FAMILY BANSHEE WILL MISTAKE YOU FOR HER KIND AND SNATCH YOU AWAY.
AAAAAAA
UUUUUAAAAA
EEEEEEEEE...
AAAAAA...
WHAT HEART-FELT WAILING!
FATHER WAS A GOOD MAN.
THEY SAY A **CHORUS** OF BANSHEES WILL COME TOGETHER TO MARK THE PASSING OF SOMEONE LIKE HIM.

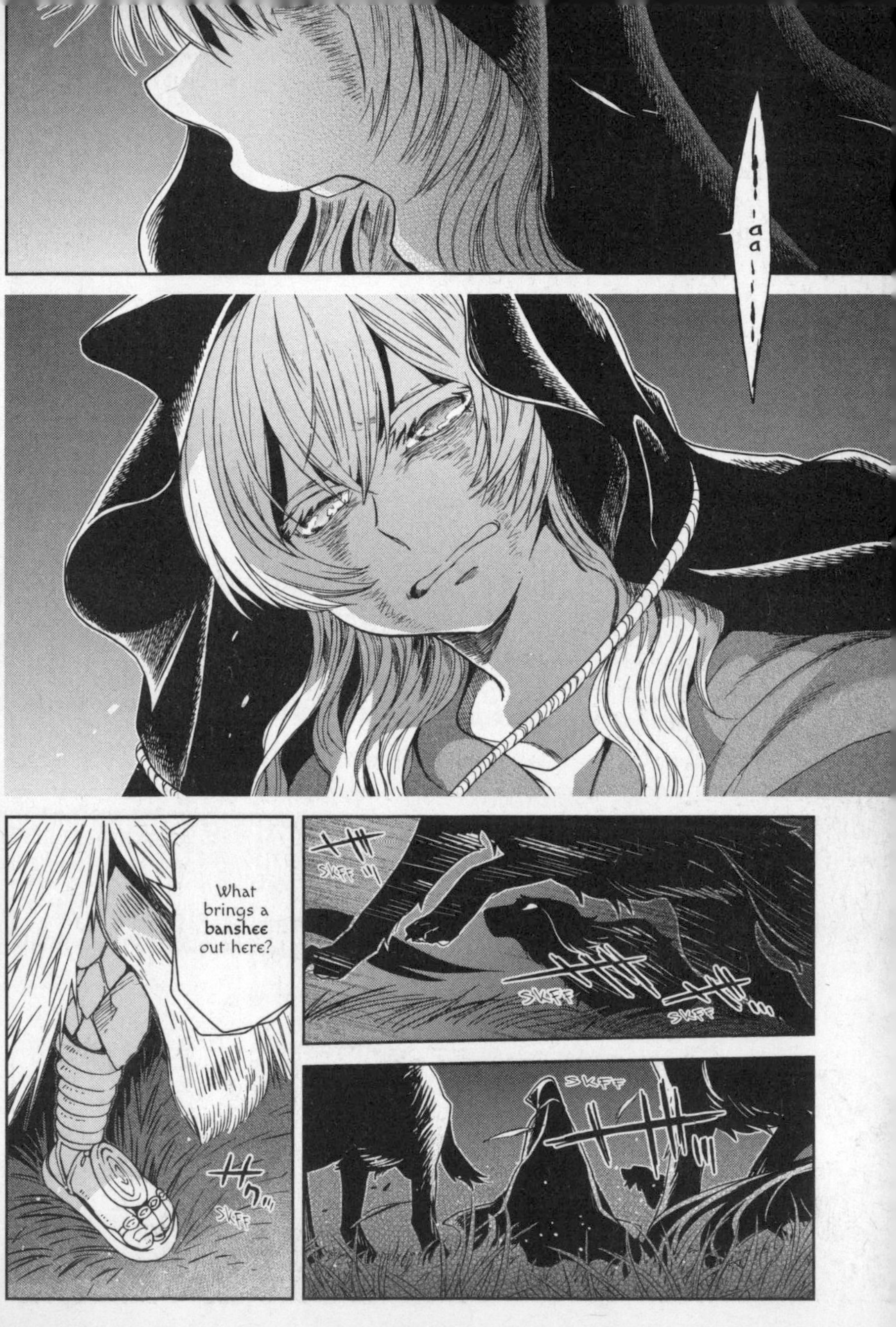
aa
SKFF
SKFF
SKFF
SKFF
What brings a banshee out here?
SKFF

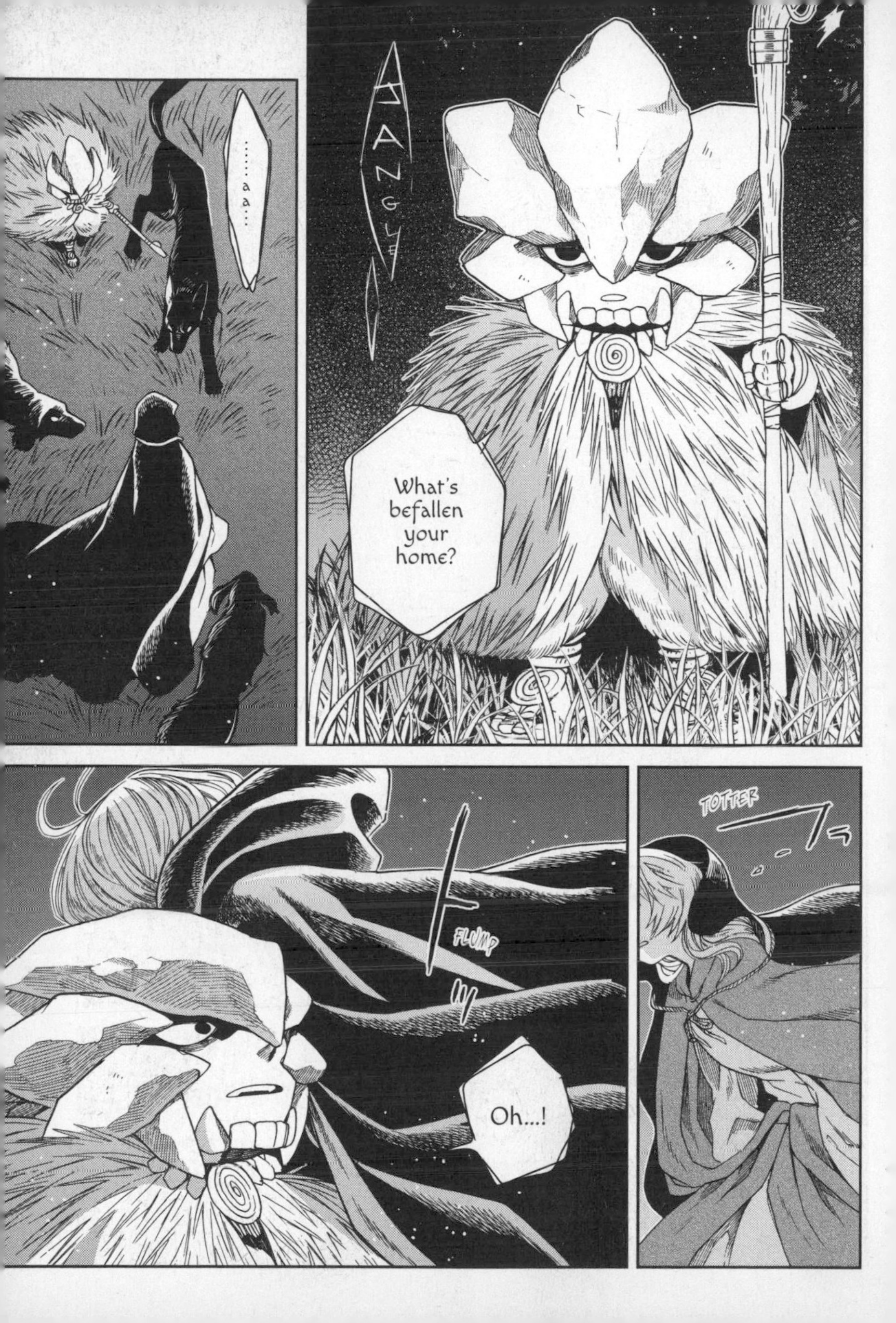
SANGLE
What's befallen your home?
......a a...
TOTTER
FLUMP
Oh...!

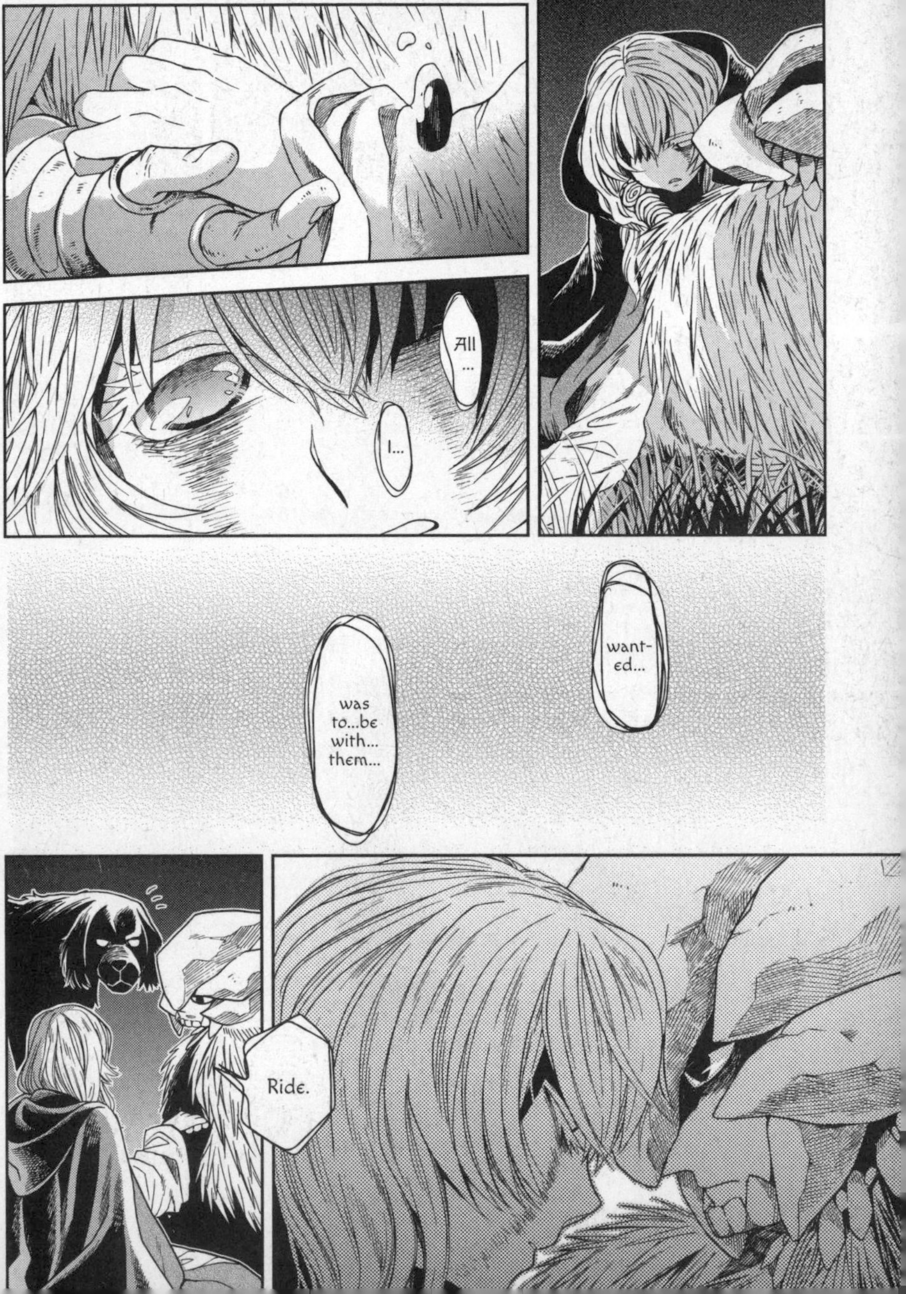
All ...
I...
want-ed...
was to...be with... them...
Ride.

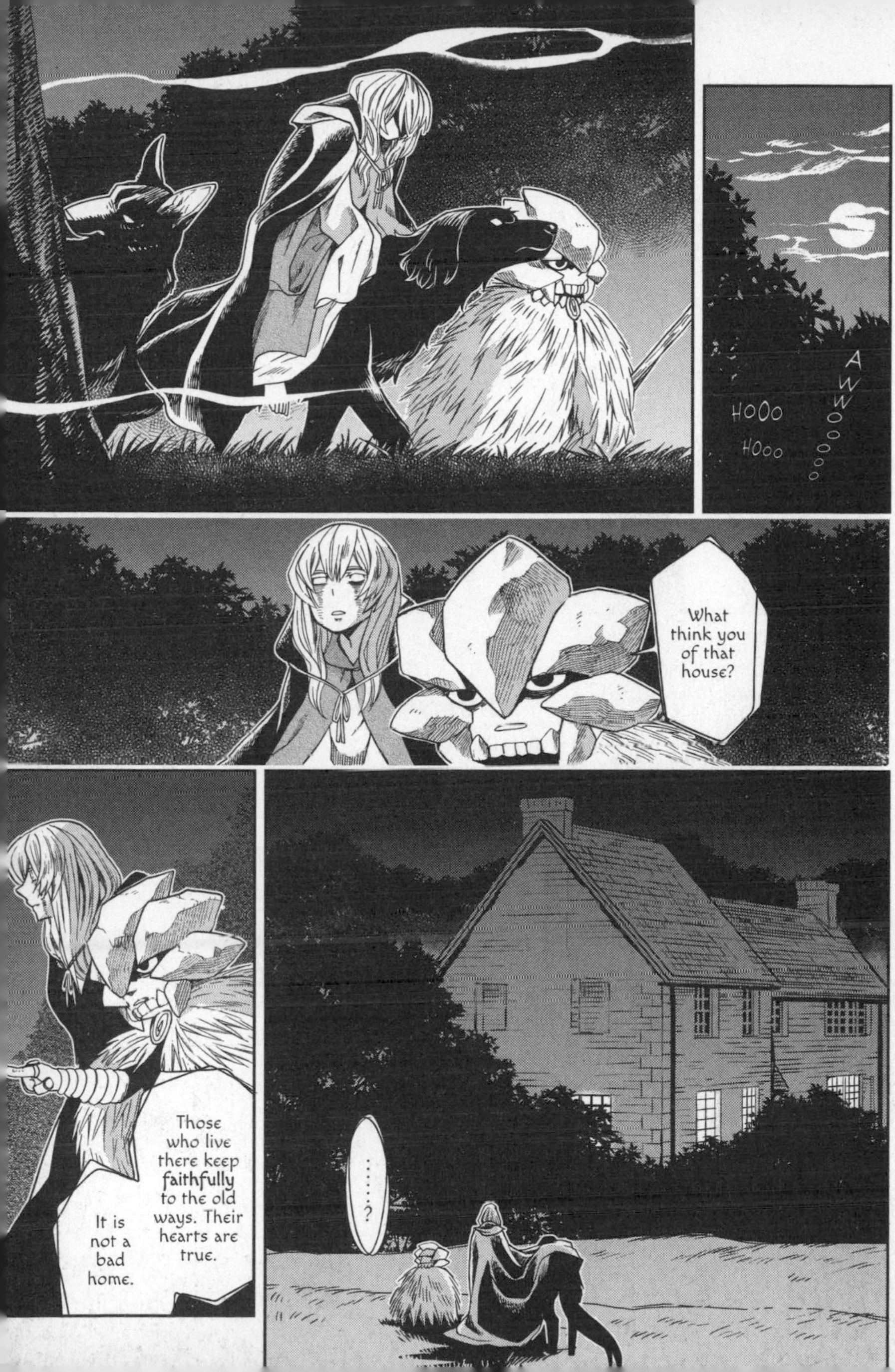
HOOO
HOOO
AWWOOOOO
What think you of that house?
......?
Those who live there keep **faithfully** to the old ways. Their hearts are true.
It is not a bad home.

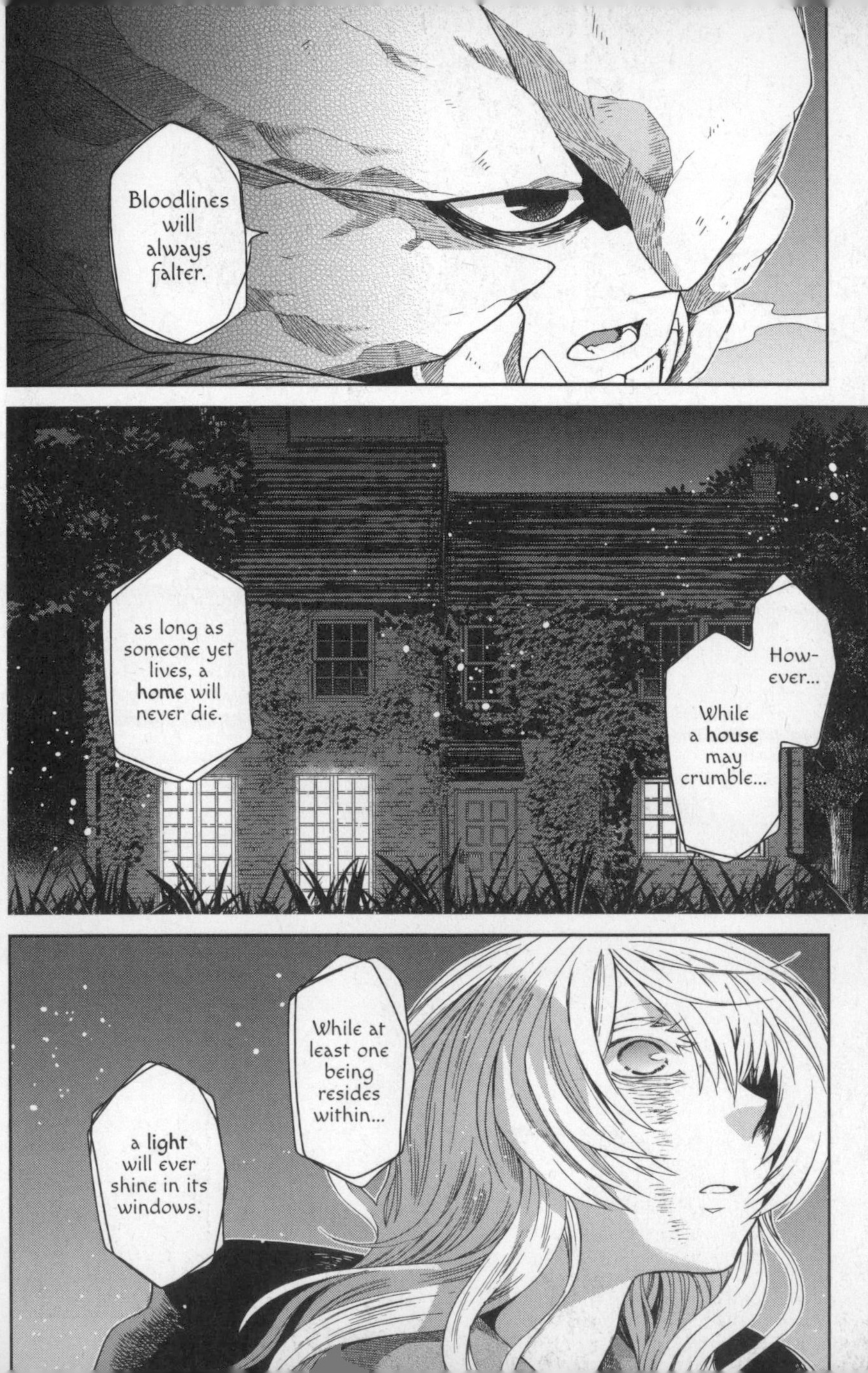
Bloodlines will always falter.
However...
While a house may crumble...
as long as someone yet lives, a home will never die.
While at least one being resides within...
a light will ever shine in its windows.

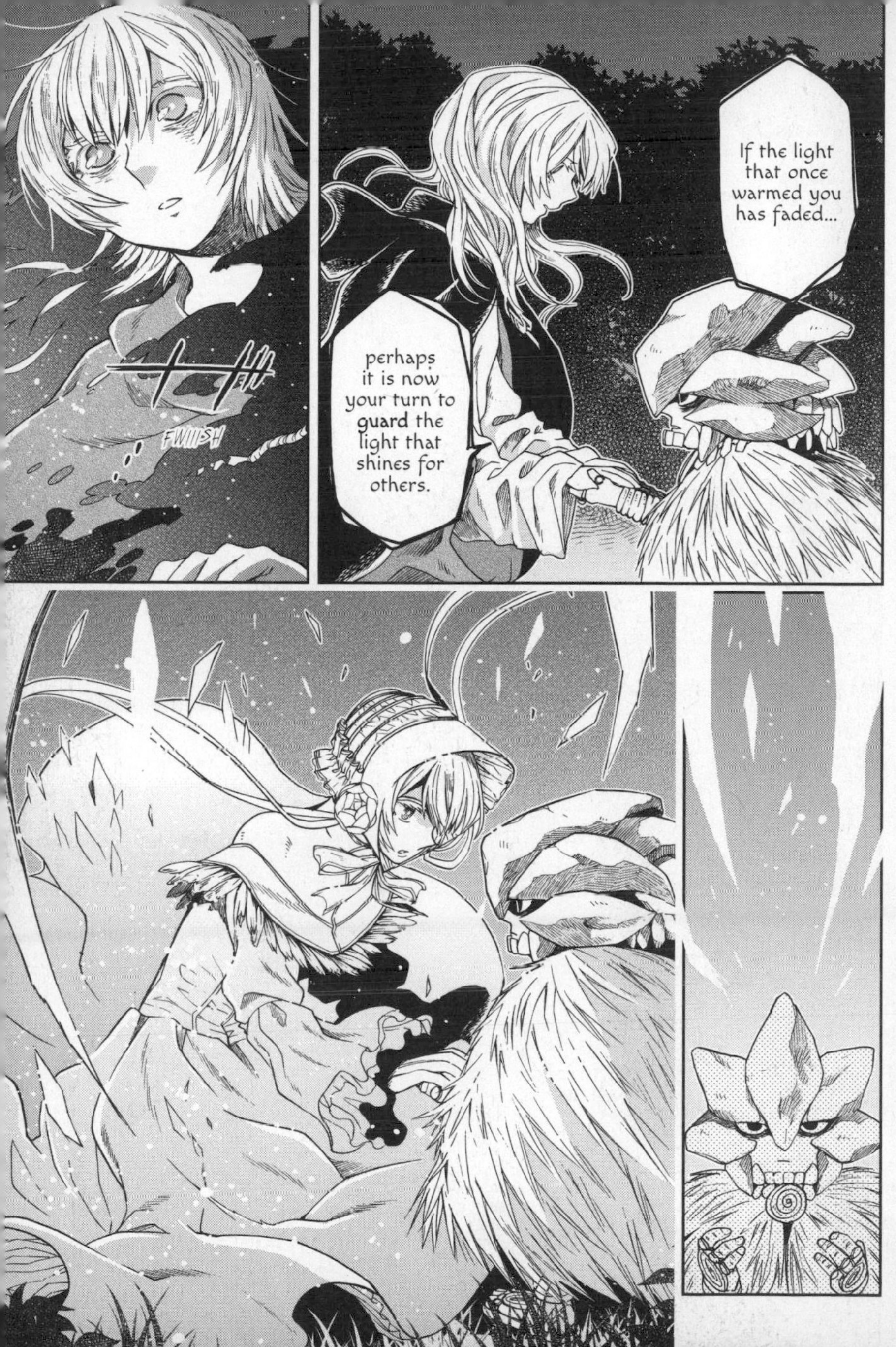
If the light that once warmed you has faded...
perhaps it is now your turn to **guard** the light that shines for others.
FWIIISH

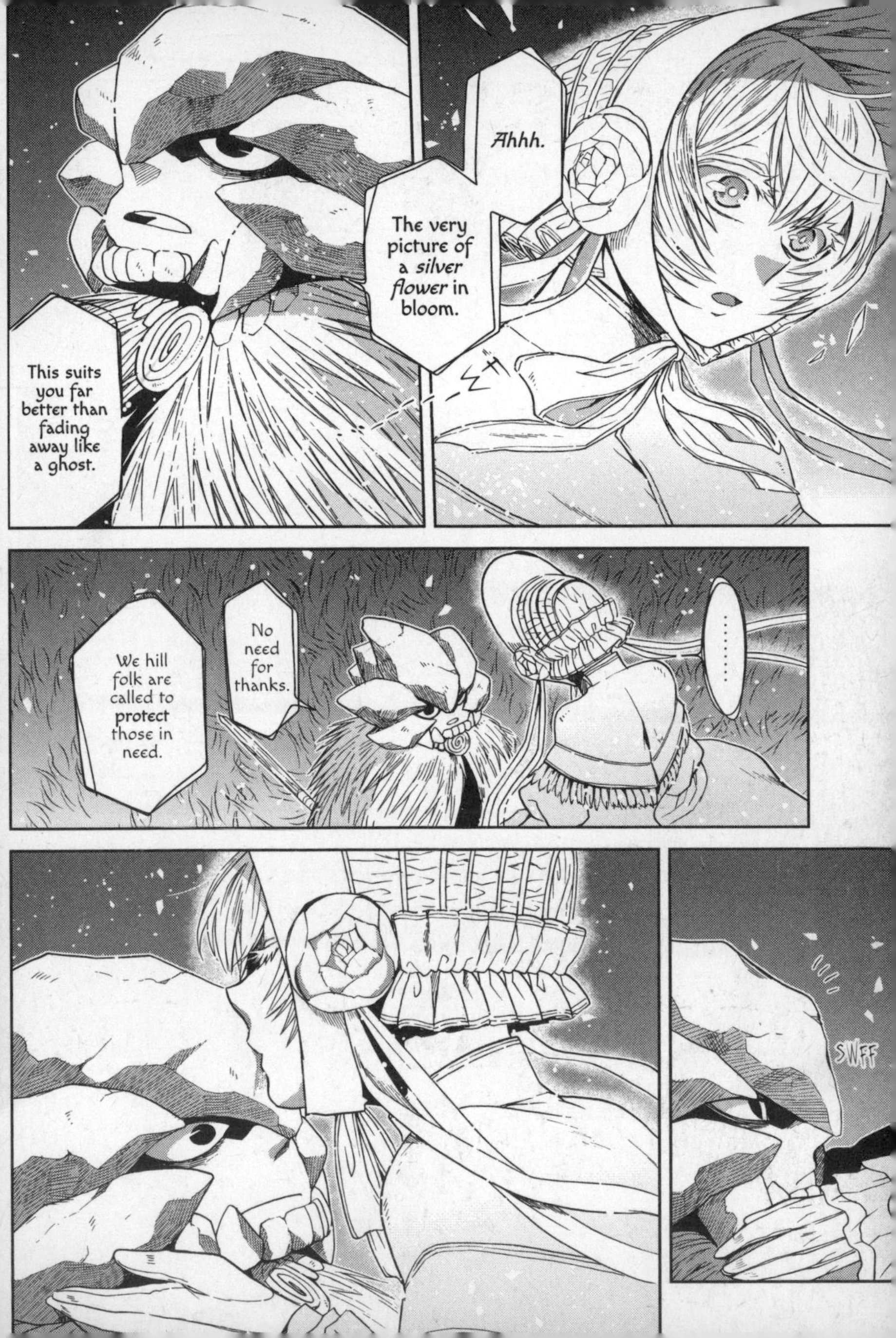
Ahhh.
The very picture of a *silver flower* in bloom.
This suits you far better than fading away like a ghost.
......
No need for thanks.
We hill folk are called to **protect** those in need.
SWFF

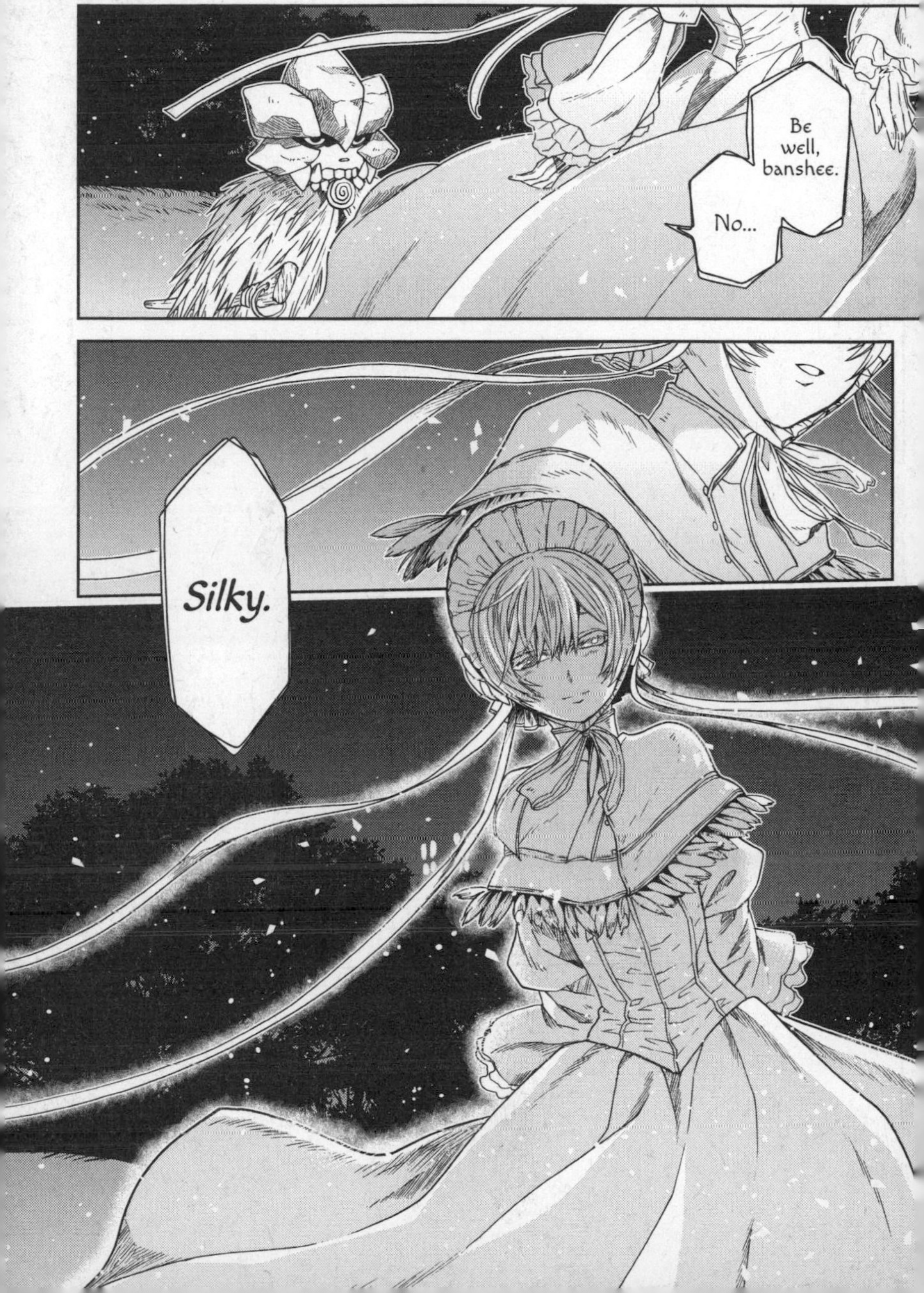
Be well, banshee.
No...
Silky.

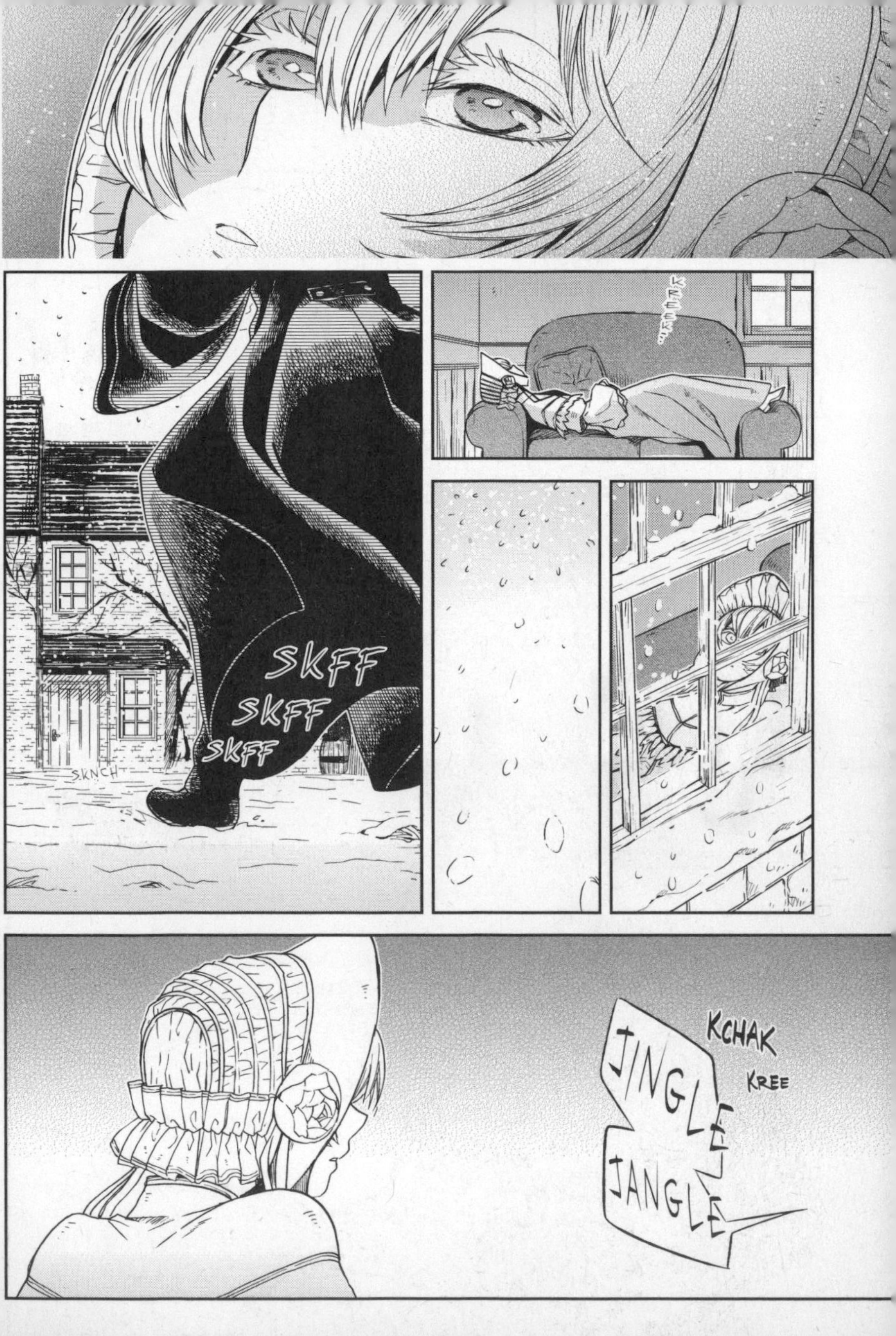
KREEK...
SKFF
SKFF
SKFF
SKNCH
KCHAK
KREE
JINGLE JANGLE

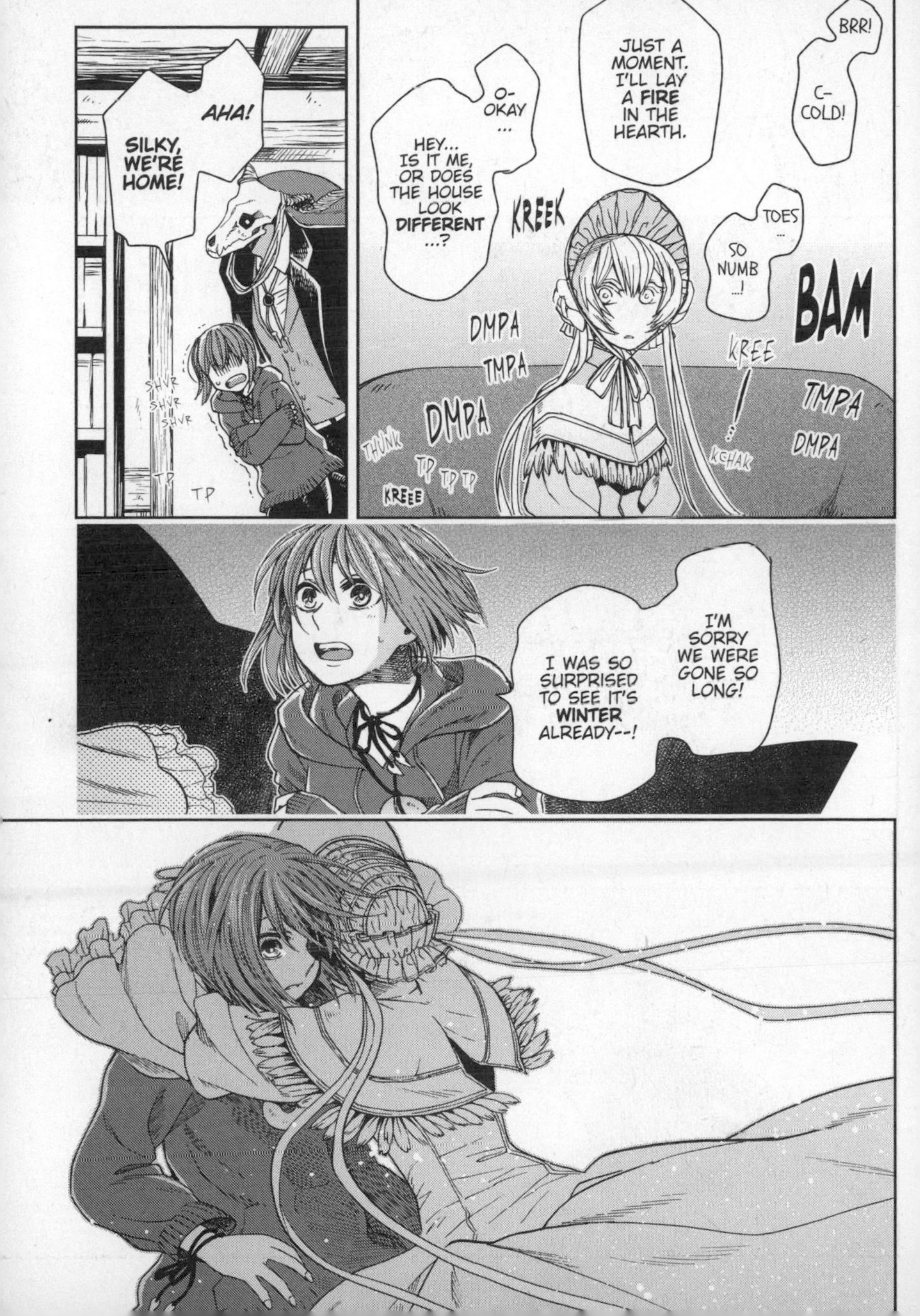
BRR!
C-COLD!
JUST A MOMENT. I'LL LAY A **FIRE** IN THE HEARTH.
TOES ...
SO NUMB ...!
BAM
O-OKAY ...
HEY... IS IT ME, OR DOES THE HOUSE LOOK **DIFFERENT** ...?
KREEK
KREE
DMPA
TMPA
DMPA
KCHAK
TMPA
DMPA
THUNK
TP TP TP
KREEE
AHA!
SILKY, WE'RE HOME!
SHVR SHVR SHVR
TP
TP
I'M SORRY WE WERE GONE SO LONG!
I WAS SO SURPRISED TO SEE IT'S **WINTER** ALREADY--!

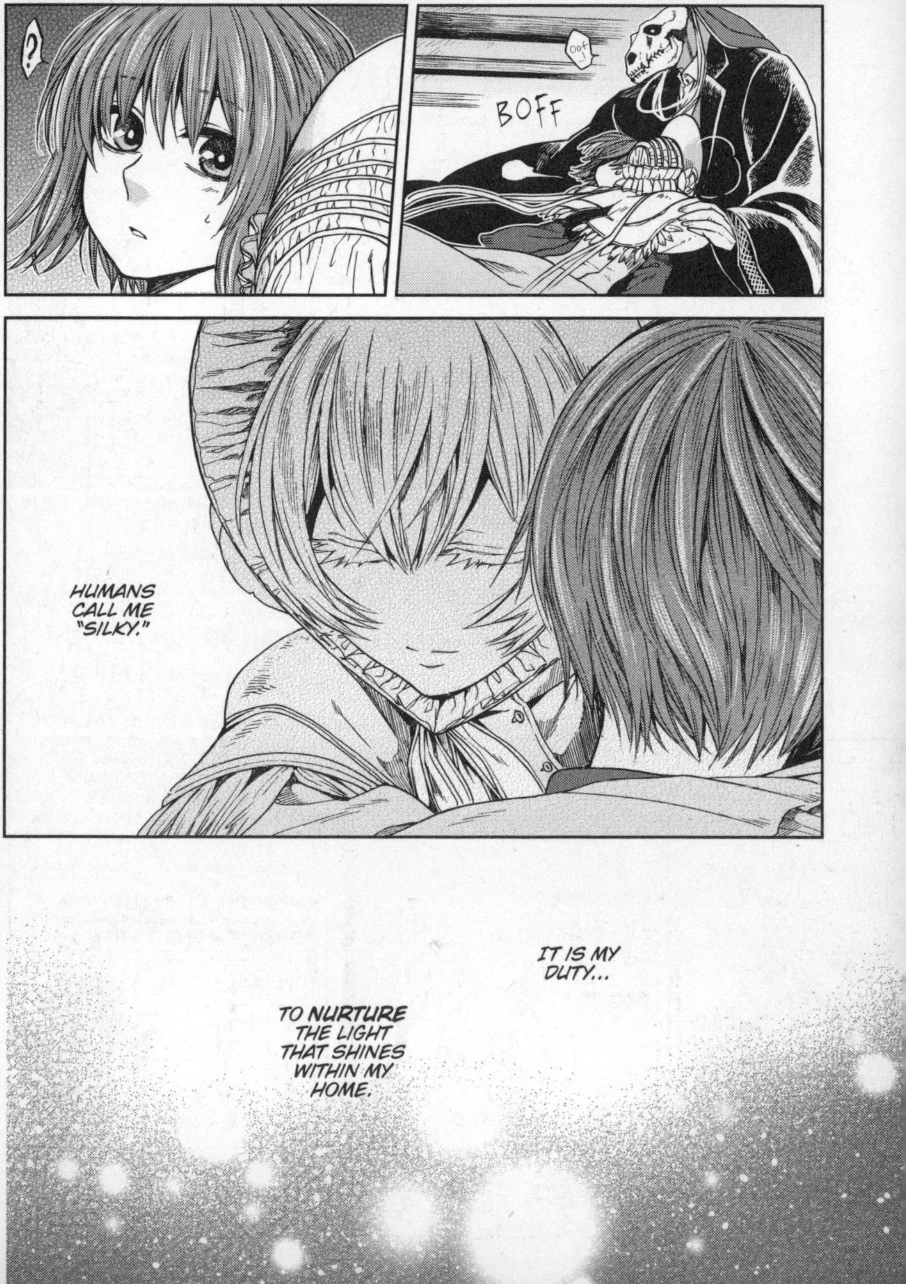
Oof..!
BOFF
?
HUMANS CALL ME "SILKY."
IT IS MY DUTY...
TO NURTURE THE LIGHT THAT SHINES WITHIN MY HOME.

Chapter 25: Even the longest night has an end.

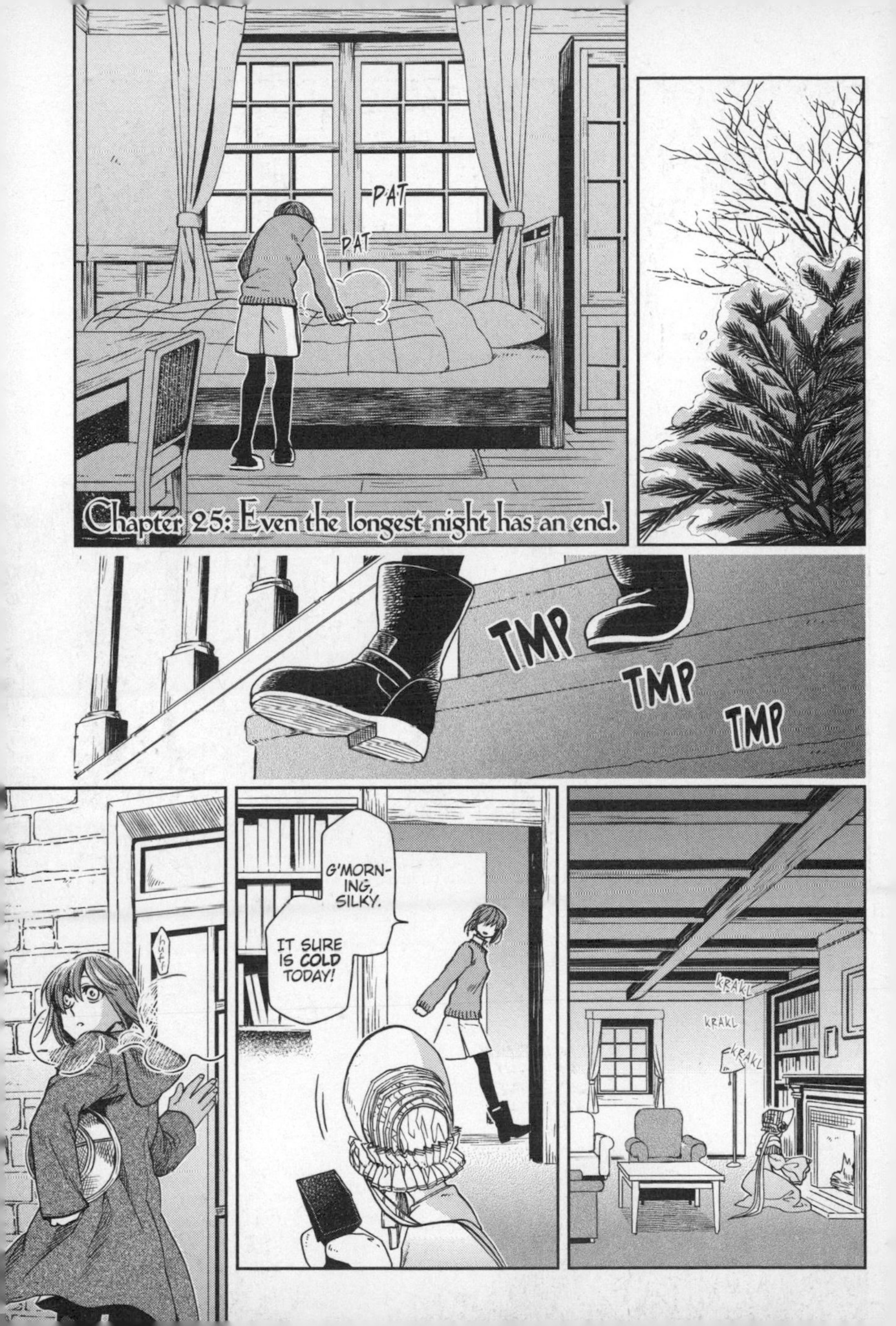
PAT
PAT
TMP
TMP
TMP
KRAKL
KRAKL
KRAKL
G'MORNING, SILKY.
IT SURE IS COLD TODAY!

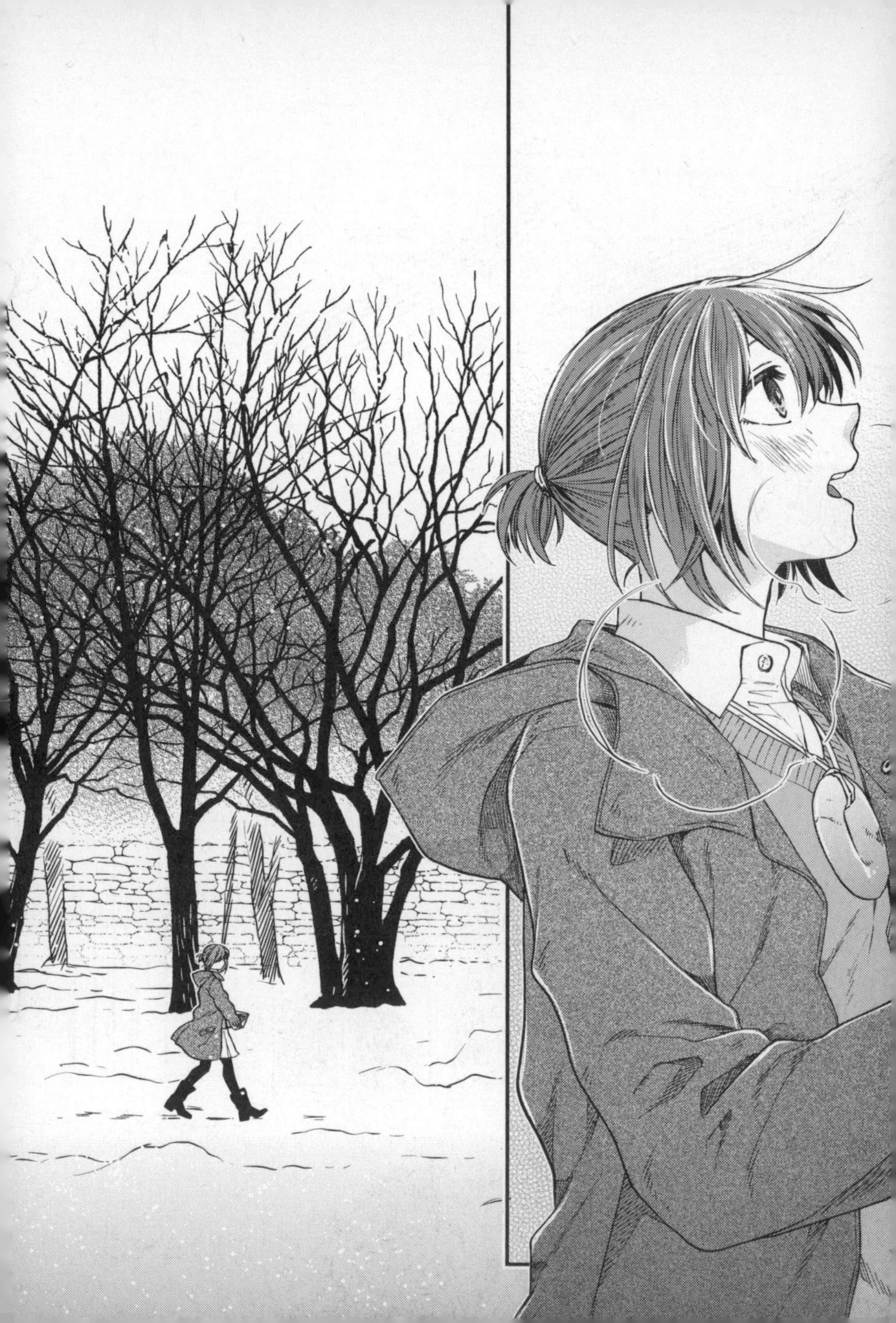

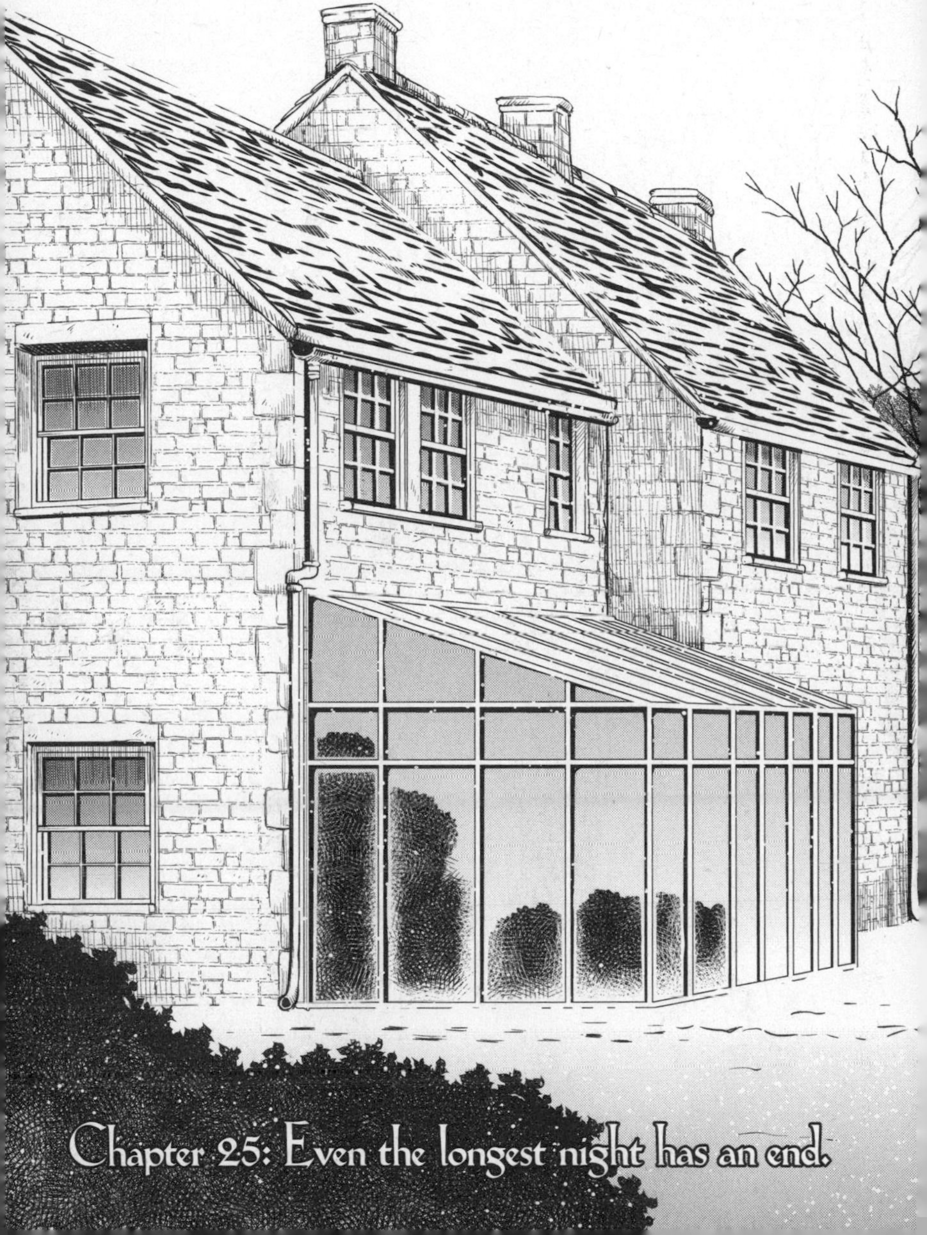

Chapter 25: Even the longest night has an end.

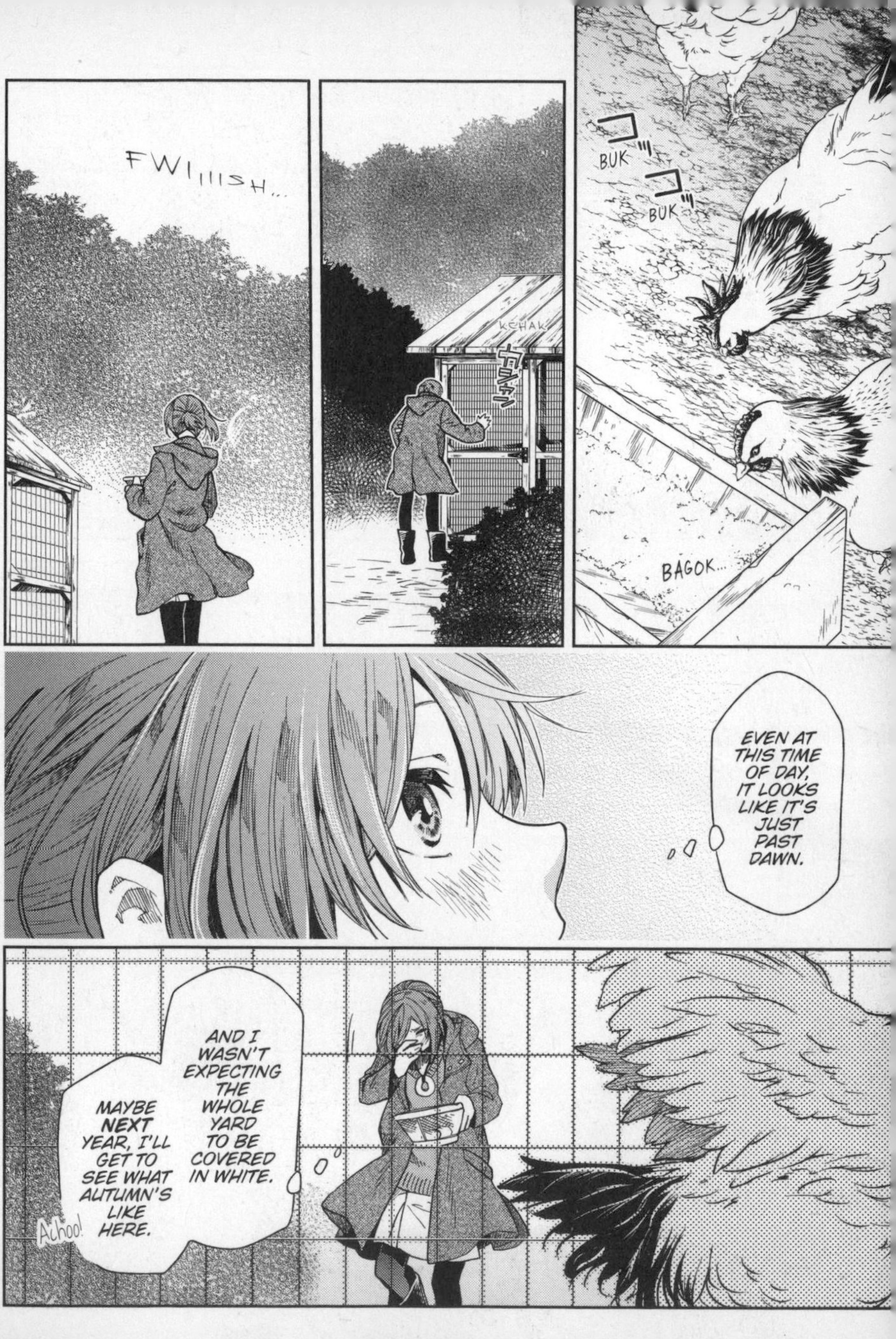
BUK
BUK
BAGOK...
KCHAK
FWIIIISH...
EVEN AT THIS TIME OF DAY, IT LOOKS LIKE IT'S JUST PAST DAWN.
AND I WASN'T EXPECTING THE WHOLE YARD TO BE COVERED IN WHITE.
MAYBE NEXT YEAR, I'LL GET TO SEE WHAT AUTUMN'S LIKE HERE.
Achoo!

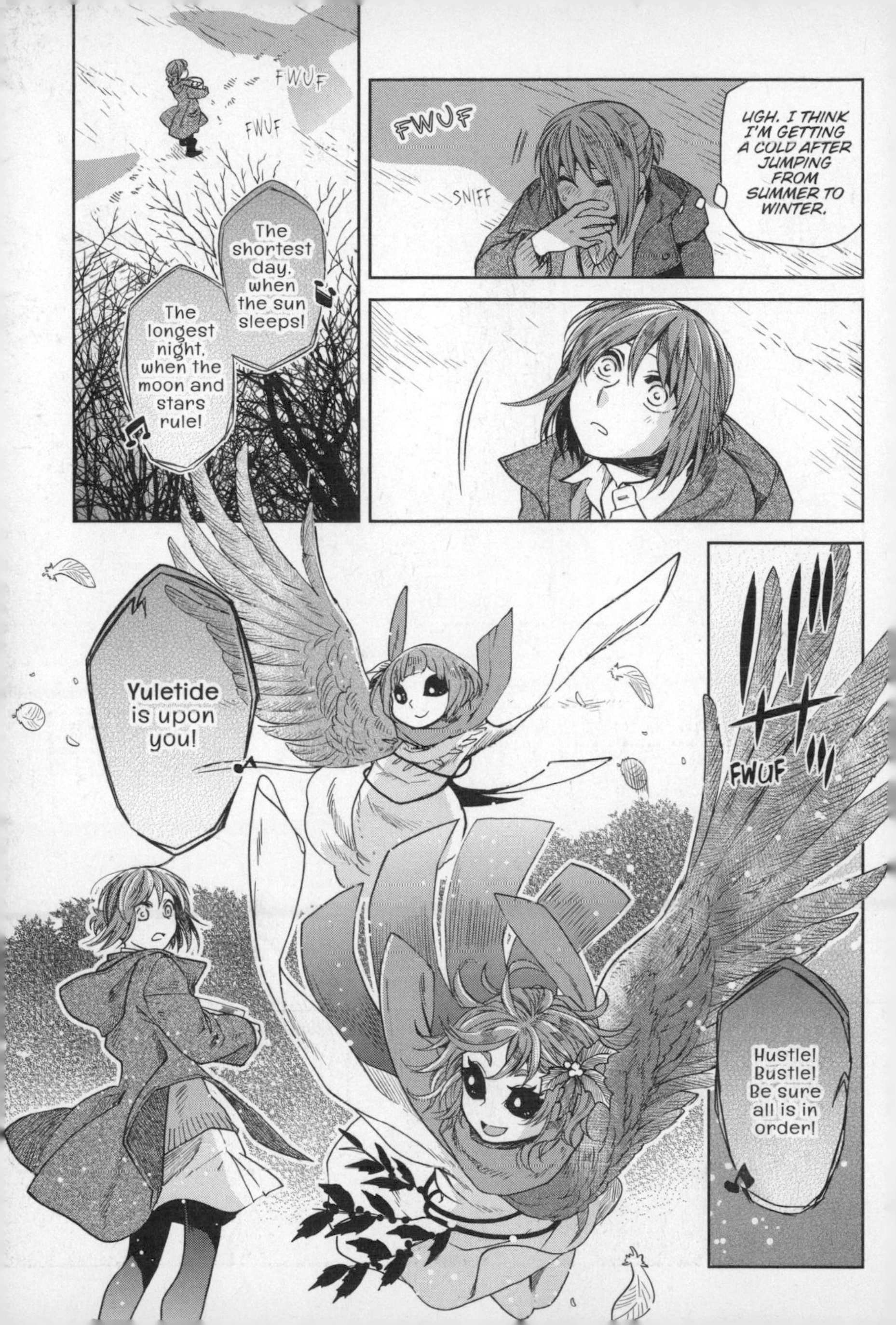

UGH. I THINK I'M GETTING A COLD AFTER JUMPING FROM SUMMER TO WINTER.
FWUF
SNIFF
FWUF
FWUF
The shortest day, when the sun sleeps!
The longest night, when the moon and stars rule!
!!
FWUF
Hustle! Bustle! Be sure all is in order!
Yuletide is upon you!

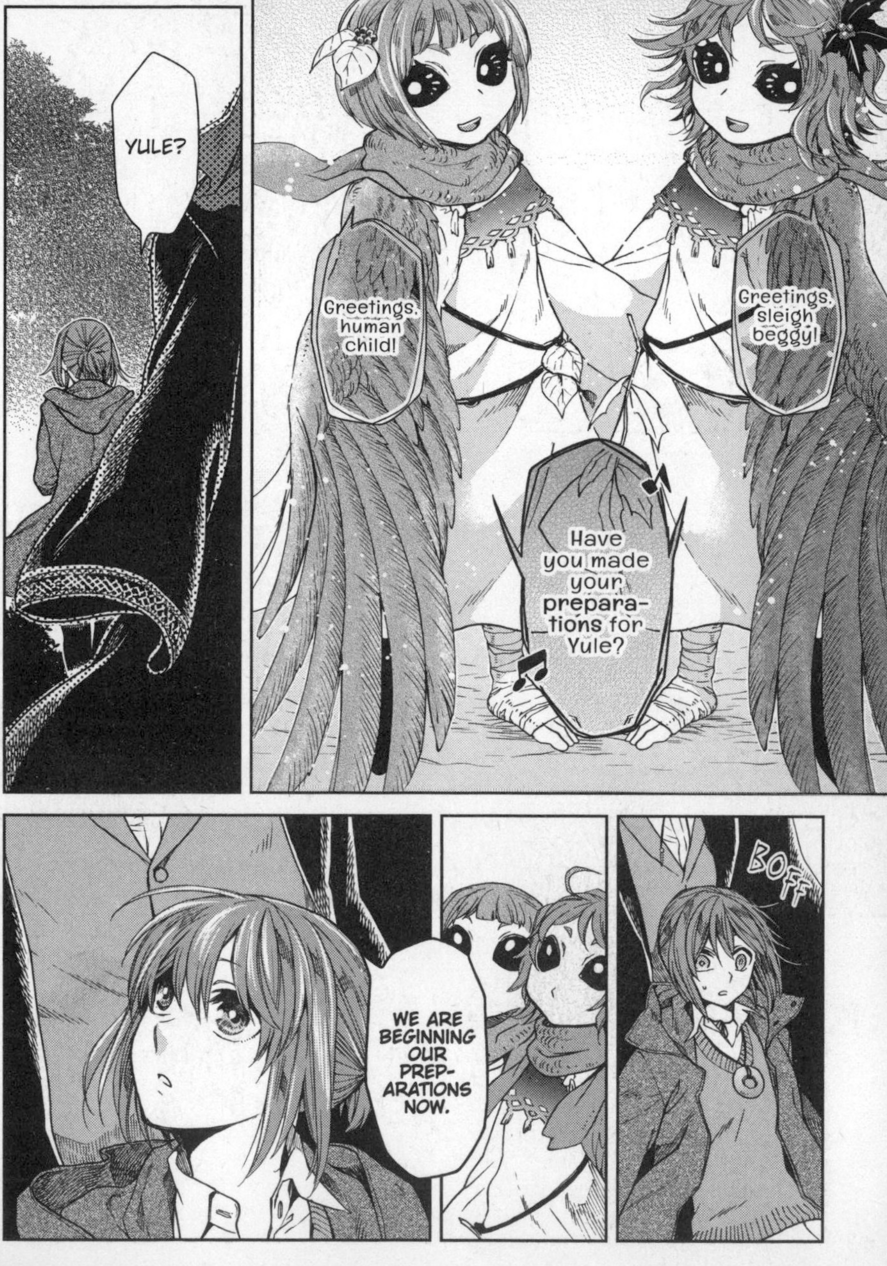
Greetings, sleigh beggy!
Greetings, human child!
Have you made your preparations for Yule?
YULE?
BOFF
WE ARE BEGINNING OUR PREPARATIONS NOW.

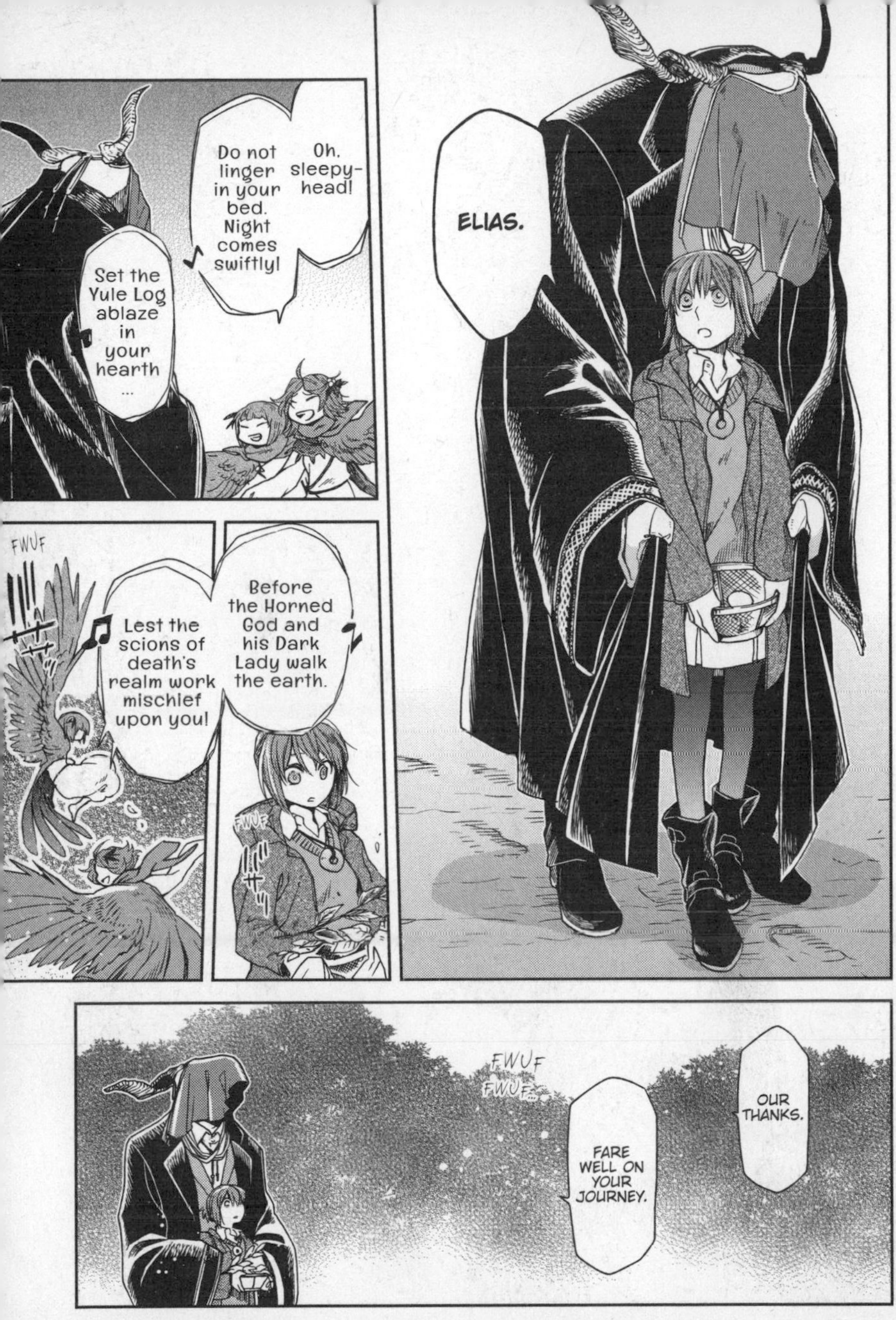
ELIAS.
Oh. sleepy-head!
Do not linger in your bed. Night comes swiftly!
Set the Yule Log ablaze in your hearth ...
Before the Horned God and his Dark Lady walk the earth.
FWUF
Lest the scions of death's realm work mischief upon you!
FWUF
FWUF
FWUF...
OUR THANKS.
FARE WELL ON YOUR JOURNEY.

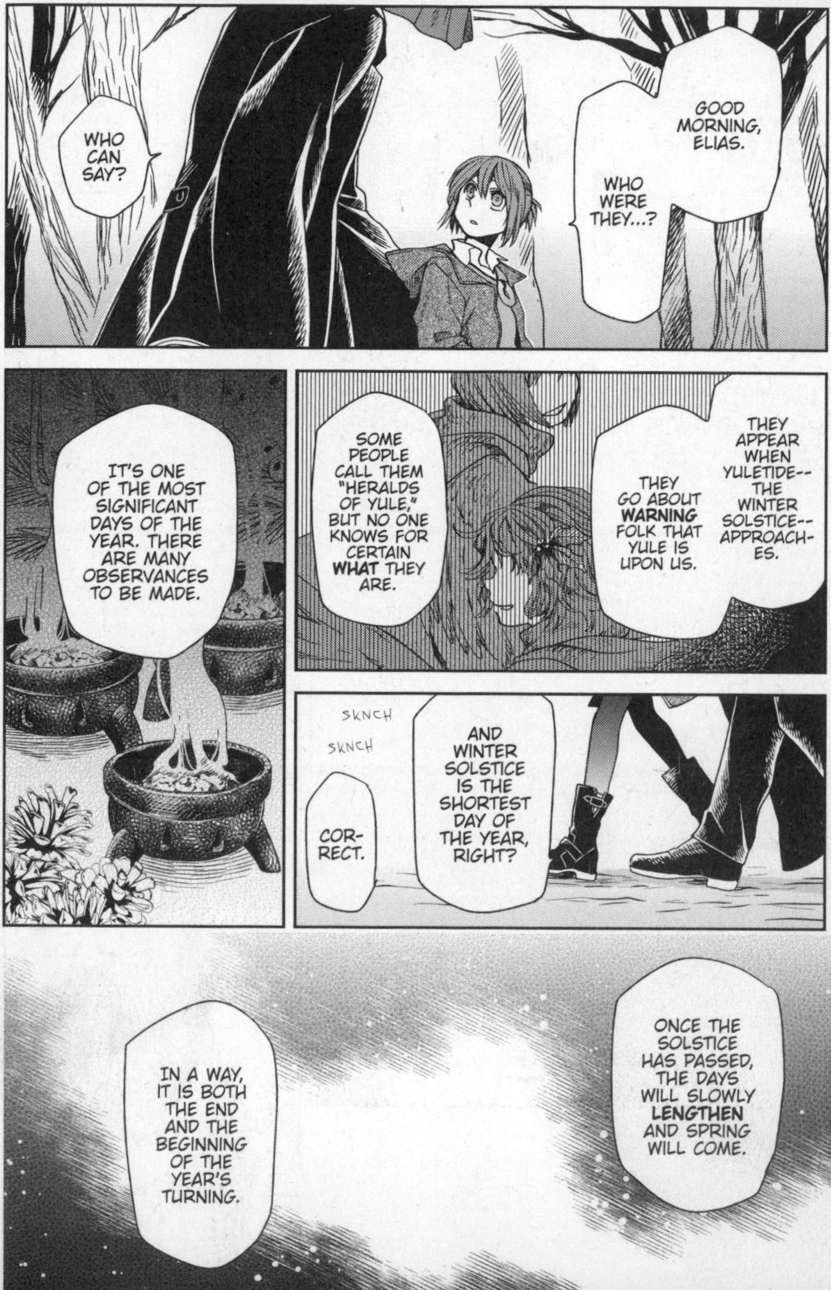
GOOD MORNING, ELIAS.
WHO WERE THEY...?
WHO CAN SAY?
THEY APPEAR WHEN YULETIDE--THE WINTER SOLSTICE--APPROACHES.
THEY GO ABOUT **WARNING** FOLK THAT YULE IS UPON US.
SOME PEOPLE CALL THEM "HERALDS OF YULE," BUT NO ONE KNOWS FOR CERTAIN **WHAT** THEY ARE.
AND WINTER SOLSTICE IS THE SHORTEST DAY OF THE YEAR, RIGHT?
SKNCH
SKNCH
CORRECT.
IT'S ONE OF THE MOST SIGNIFICANT DAYS OF THE YEAR. THERE ARE MANY OBSERVANCES TO BE MADE.
ONCE THE SOLSTICE HAS PASSED, THE DAYS WILL SLOWLY **LENGTHEN** AND SPRING WILL COME.
IN A WAY, IT IS BOTH THE END AND THE BEGINNING OF THE YEAR'S TURNING.

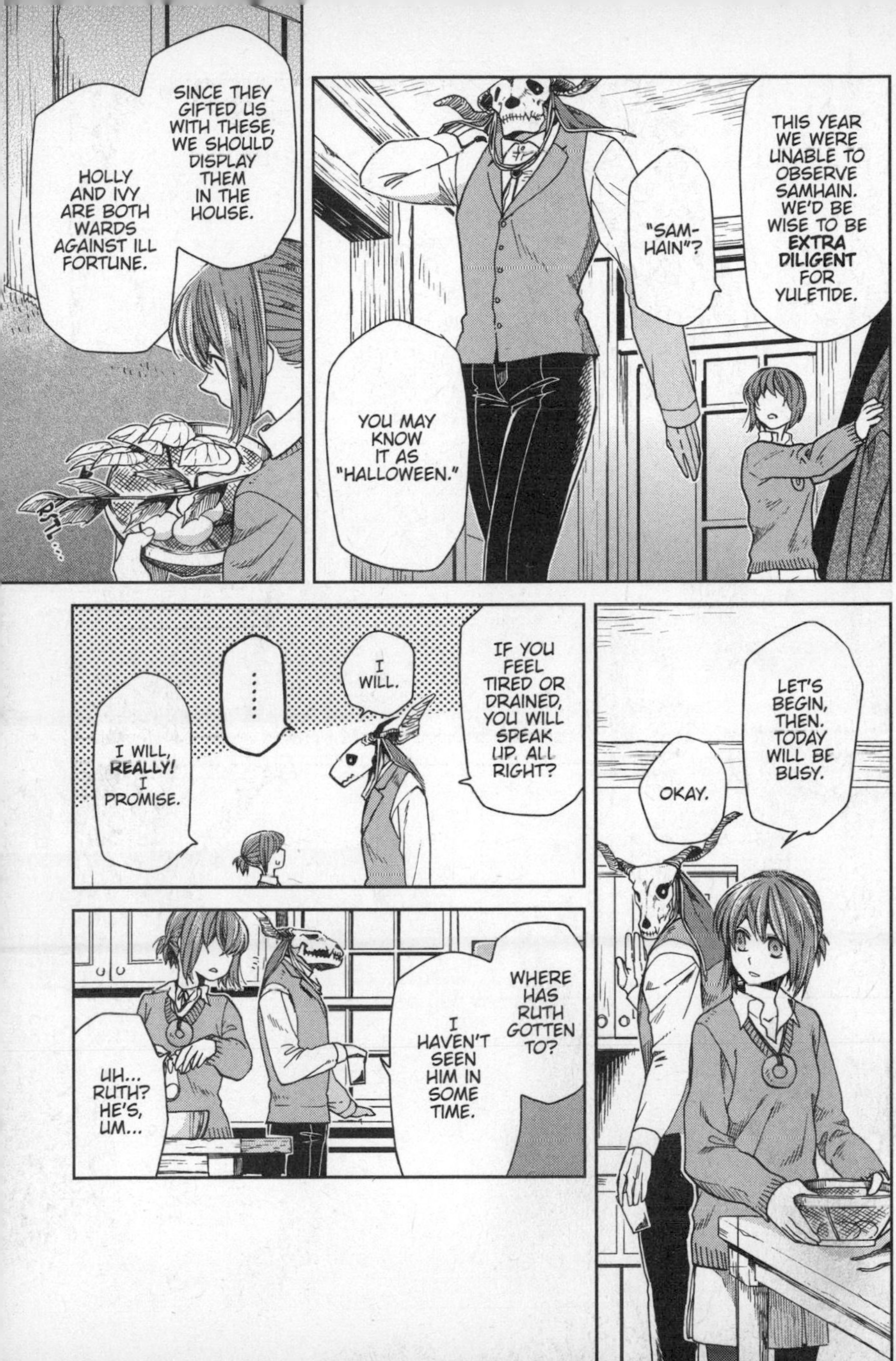
THIS YEAR WE WERE UNABLE TO OBSERVE SAMHAIN. WE'D BE WISE TO BE **EXTRA DILIGENT** FOR YULETIDE.
"SAM-HAIN"?
YOU MAY KNOW IT AS "HALLOWEEN."
SINCE THEY GIFTED US WITH THESE, WE SHOULD DISPLAY THEM IN THE HOUSE.
HOLLY AND IVY ARE BOTH WARDS AGAINST ILL FORTUNE.
RSTL...
LET'S BEGIN, THEN. TODAY WILL BE BUSY.
OKAY.
IF YOU FEEL TIRED OR DRAINED, YOU WILL SPEAK UP. ALL RIGHT?
I WILL.
......
I WILL, **REALLY!** I PROMISE.
WHERE HAS RUTH GOTTEN TO?
I HAVEN'T SEEN HIM IN SOME TIME.
UH... RUTH? HE'S, UM...

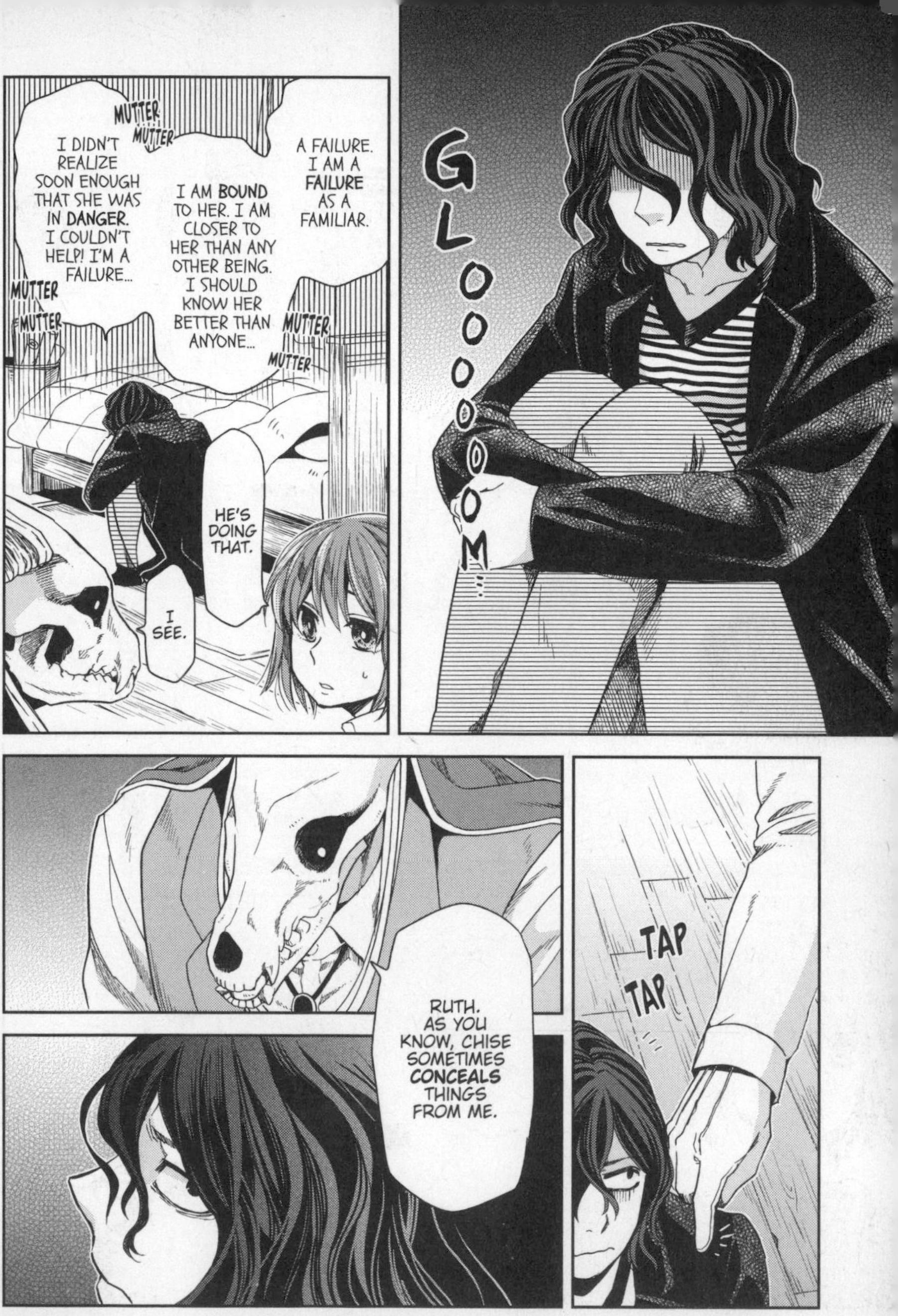
GLOOOOOOOOM...
MUTTER MUTTER
I DIDN'T REALIZE SOON ENOUGH THAT SHE WAS IN DANGER. I COULDN'T HELP! I'M A FAILURE...
I AM BOUND TO HER. I AM CLOSER TO HER THAN ANY OTHER BEING. I SHOULD KNOW HER BETTER THAN ANYONE...
A FAILURE. I AM A FAILURE AS A FAMILIAR.
MUTTER MUTTER
MUTTER MUTTER
HE'S DOING THAT.
I SEE.
TAP TAP
RUTH. AS YOU KNOW, CHISE SOMETIMES CONCEALS THINGS FROM ME.

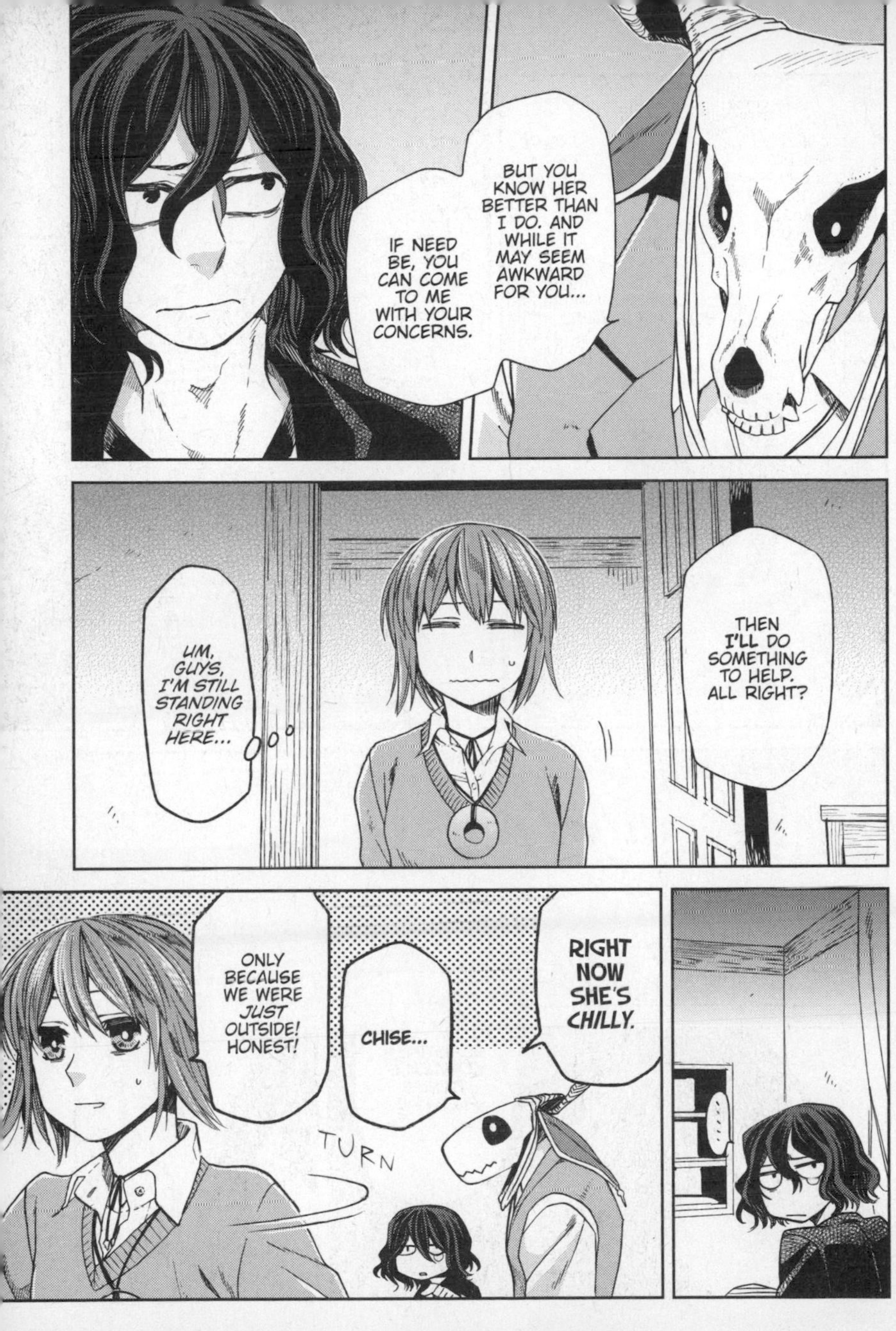
BUT YOU KNOW HER BETTER THAN I DO. AND WHILE IT MAY SEEM AWKWARD FOR YOU...
IF NEED BE, YOU CAN COME TO ME WITH YOUR CONCERNS.
THEN I'LL DO SOMETHING TO HELP. ALL RIGHT?
UM, GUYS, I'M STILL STANDING RIGHT HERE...
RIGHT NOW SHE'S *CHILLY.*
CHISE...
ONLY BECAUSE WE WERE *JUST* OUTSIDE! HONEST!
TURN

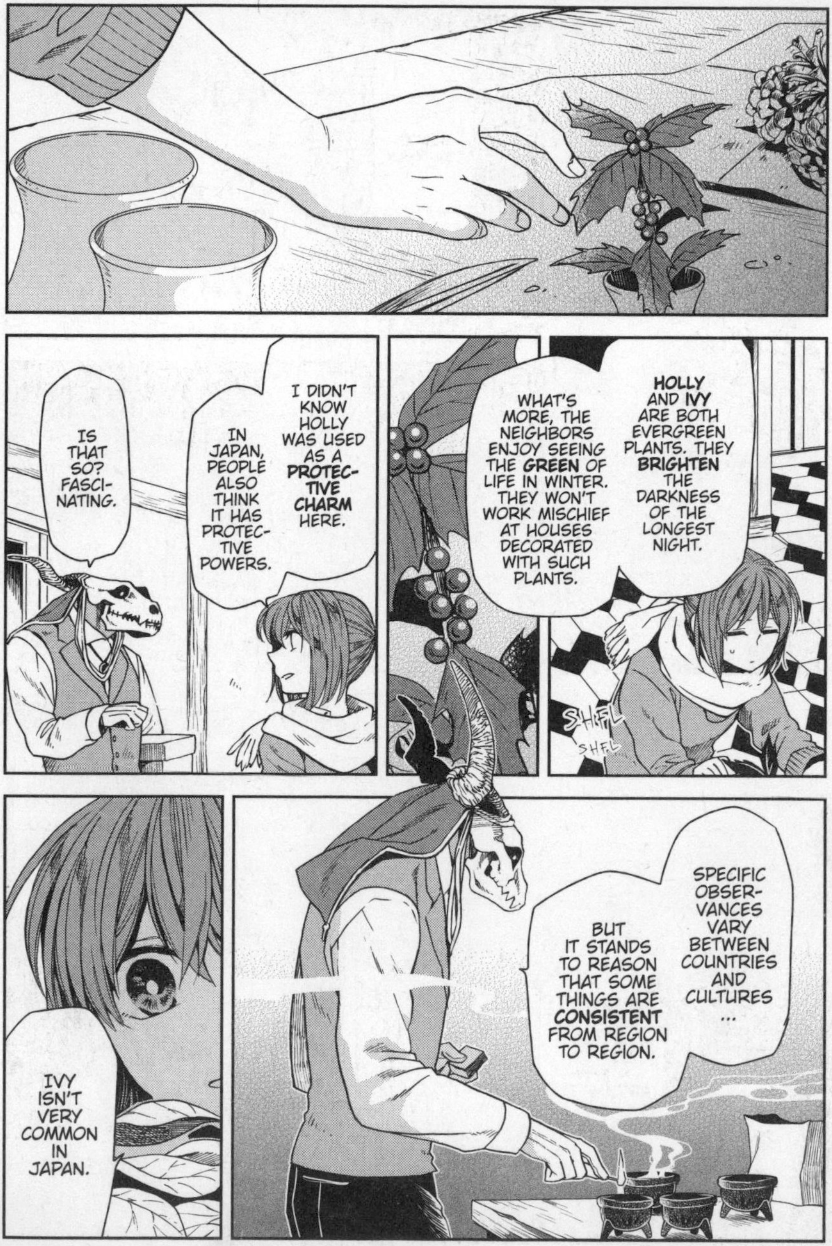
HOLLY AND IVY ARE BOTH EVERGREEN PLANTS. THEY BRIGHTEN THE DARKNESS OF THE LONGEST NIGHT.
WHAT'S MORE, THE NEIGHBORS ENJOY SEEING THE GREEN OF LIFE IN WINTER. THEY WON'T WORK MISCHIEF AT HOUSES DECORATED WITH SUCH PLANTS.
SHFL
SHFL
I DIDN'T KNOW HOLLY WAS USED AS A PROTECTIVE CHARM HERE.
IN JAPAN, PEOPLE ALSO THINK IT HAS PROTECTIVE POWERS.
IS THAT SO? FASCINATING.
SPECIFIC OBSERVANCES VARY BETWEEN COUNTRIES AND CULTURES...
BUT IT STANDS TO REASON THAT SOME THINGS ARE CONSISTENT FROM REGION TO REGION.
IVY ISN'T VERY COMMON IN JAPAN.

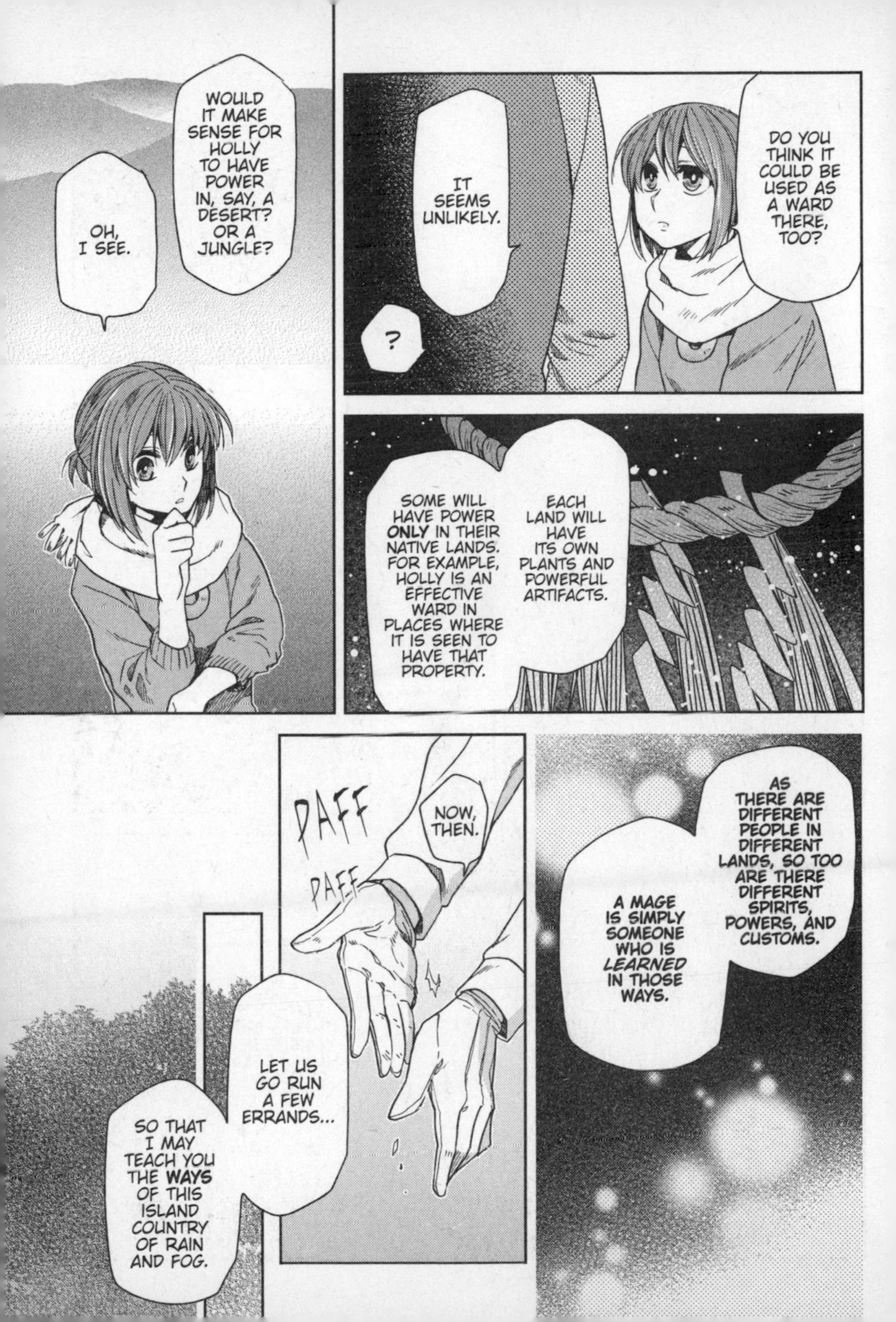
DO YOU THINK IT COULD BE USED AS A WARD THERE, TOO?
IT SEEMS UNLIKELY.
?
EACH LAND WILL HAVE ITS OWN PLANTS AND POWERFUL ARTIFACTS.
SOME WILL HAVE POWER **ONLY** IN THEIR NATIVE LANDS. FOR EXAMPLE, HOLLY IS AN EFFECTIVE WARD IN PLACES WHERE IT IS SEEN TO HAVE THAT PROPERTY.
WOULD IT MAKE SENSE FOR HOLLY TO HAVE POWER IN, SAY, A DESERT? OR A JUNGLE?
OH, I SEE.
AS THERE ARE DIFFERENT PEOPLE IN DIFFERENT LANDS, SO TOO ARE THERE DIFFERENT SPIRITS, POWERS, AND CUSTOMS.
A MAGE IS SIMPLY SOMEONE WHO IS *LEARNED* IN THOSE WAYS.
NOW, THEN.
PAFF
PAFF
LET US GO RUN A FEW ERRANDS...
SO THAT I MAY TEACH YOU THE **WAYS** OF THIS ISLAND COUNTRY OF RAIN AND FOG.

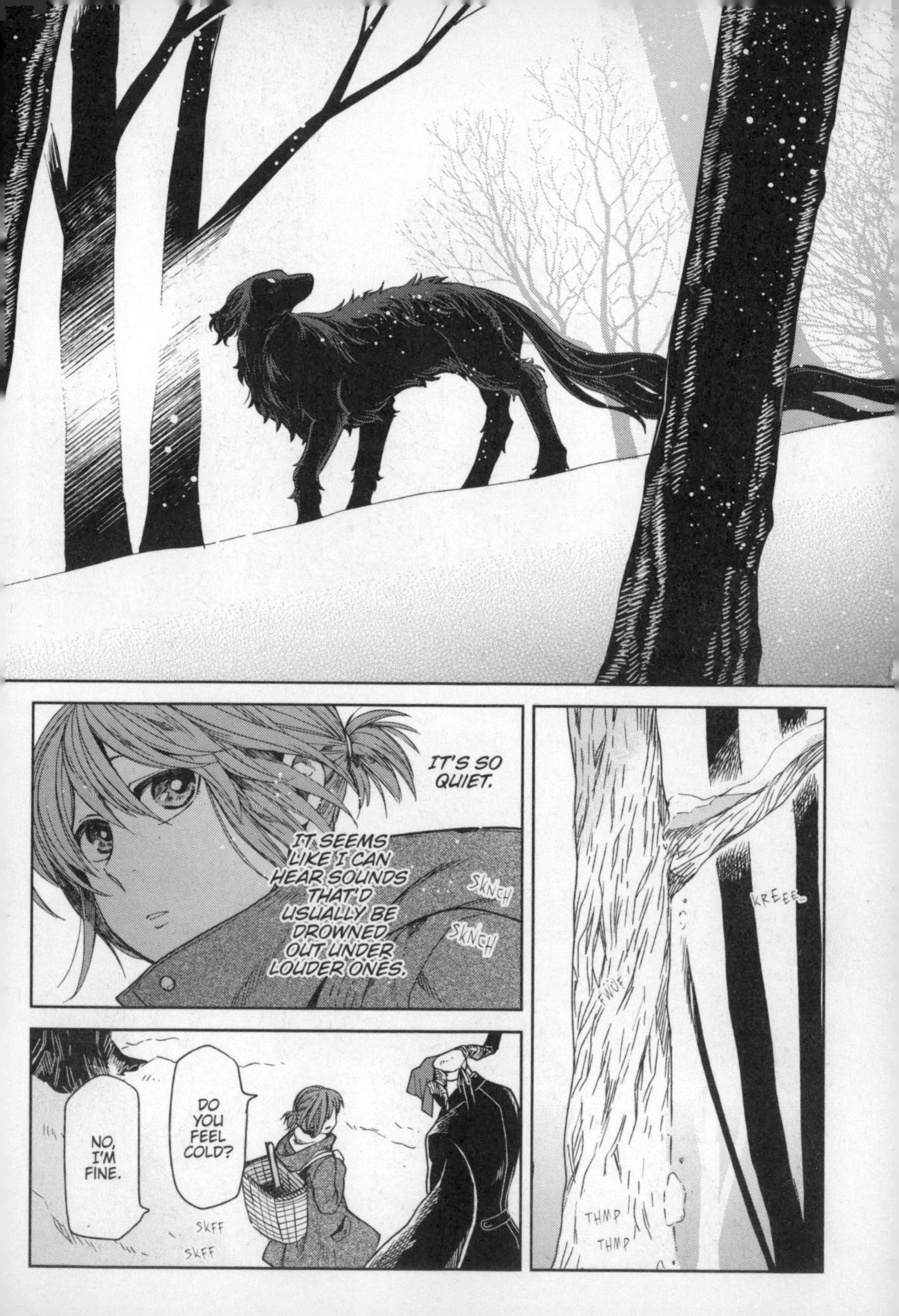
KREEE...
FWUF
THMP
THMP
IT'S SO QUIET.
IT SEEMS LIKE I CAN HEAR SOUNDS THAT'D USUALLY BE DROWNED OUT UNDER LOUDER ONES.
SKNCH
SKNCH
DO YOU FEEL COLD?
NO, I'M FINE.
SKFF
SKFF

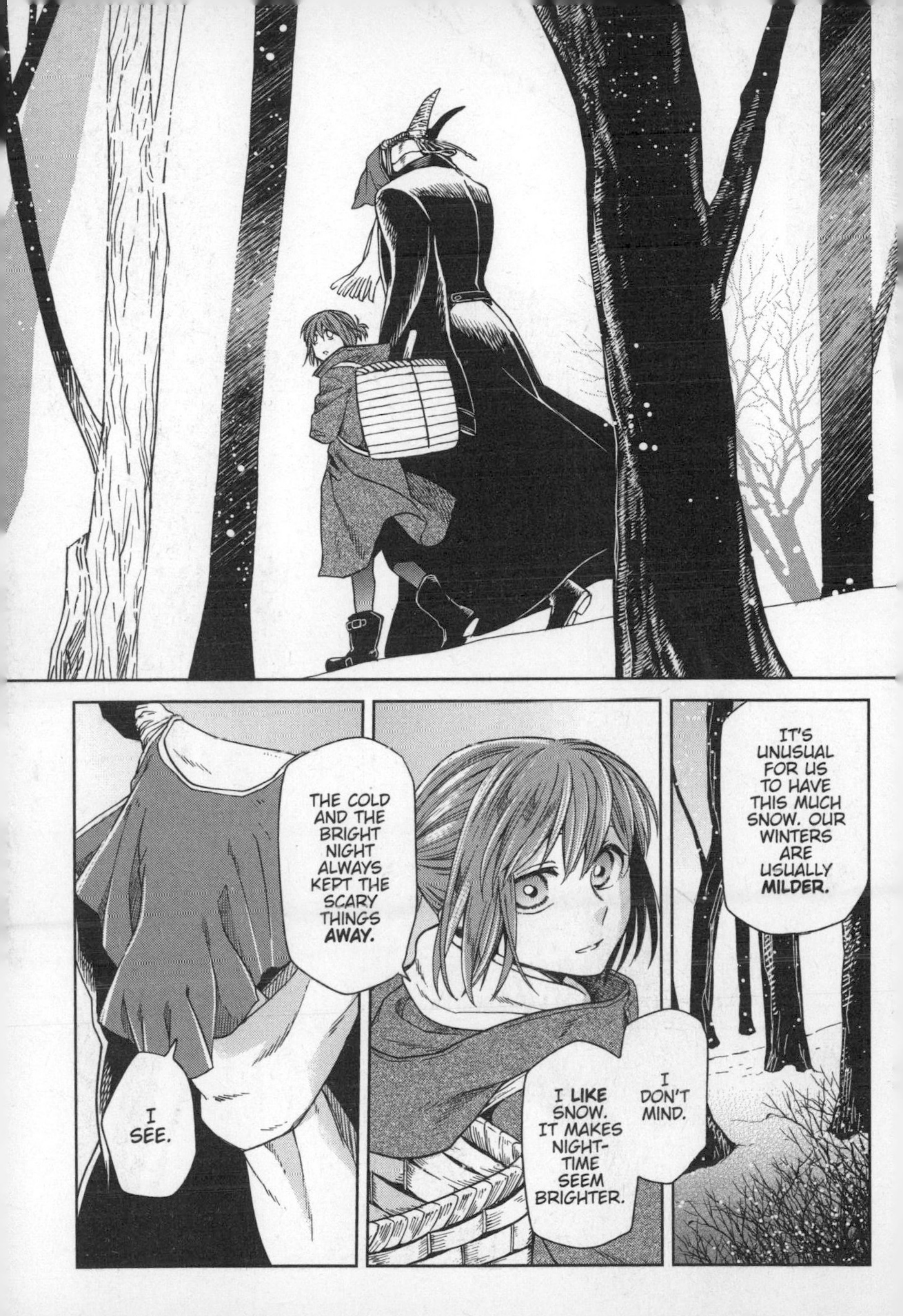
IT'S UNUSUAL FOR US TO HAVE THIS MUCH SNOW. OUR WINTERS ARE USUALLY MILDER.
I DON'T MIND.
I LIKE SNOW. IT MAKES NIGHT-TIME SEEM BRIGHTER.
THE COLD AND THE BRIGHT NIGHT ALWAYS KEPT THE SCARY THINGS AWAY.
I SEE.

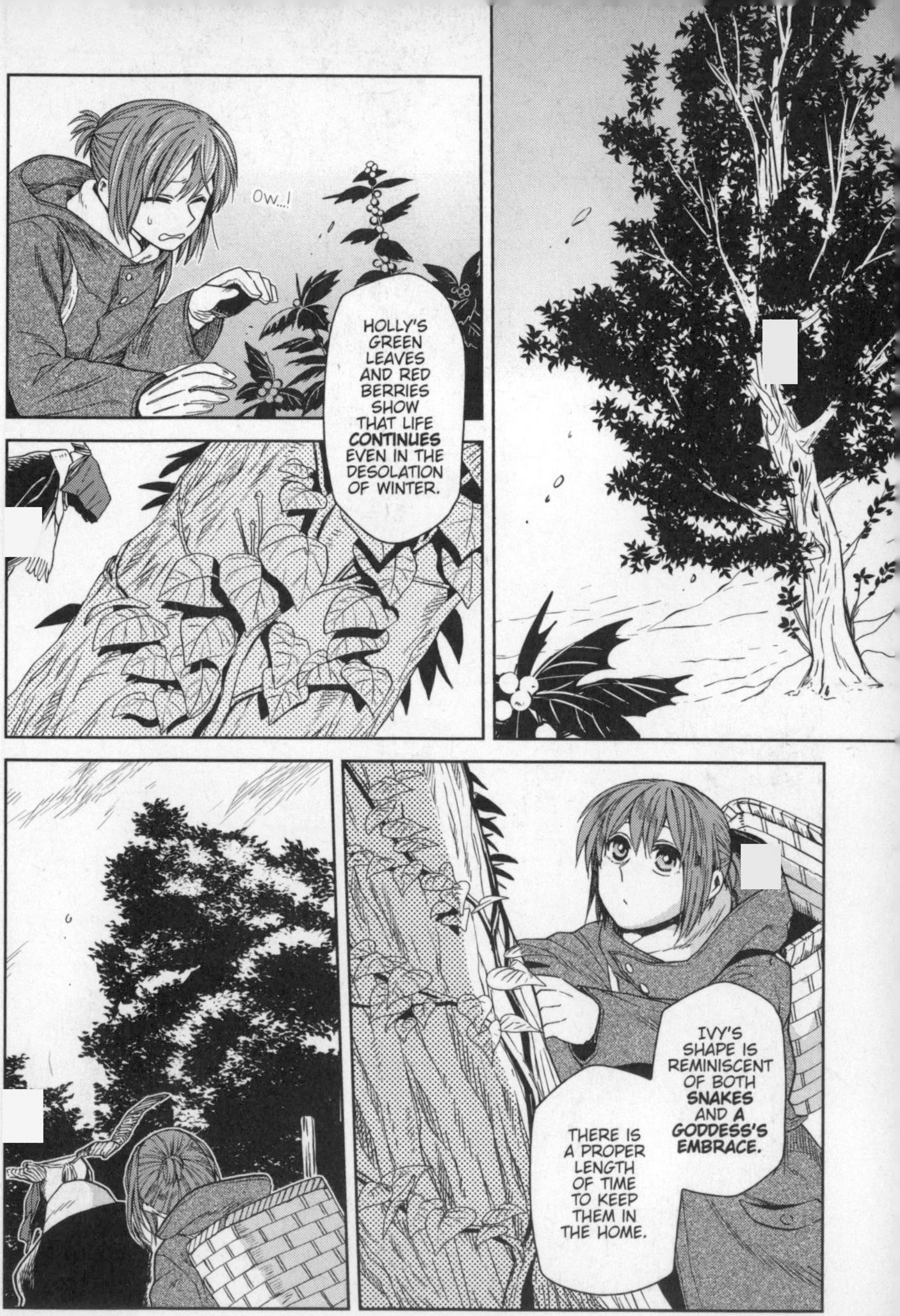
Ow...!
HOLLY'S GREEN LEAVES AND RED BERRIES SHOW THAT LIFE **CONTINUES** EVEN IN THE DESOLATION OF WINTER.
IVY'S SHAPE IS REMINISCENT OF BOTH **SNAKES** AND A **GODDESS'S EMBRACE.**
THERE IS A PROPER LENGTH OF TIME TO KEEP THEM IN THE HOME.

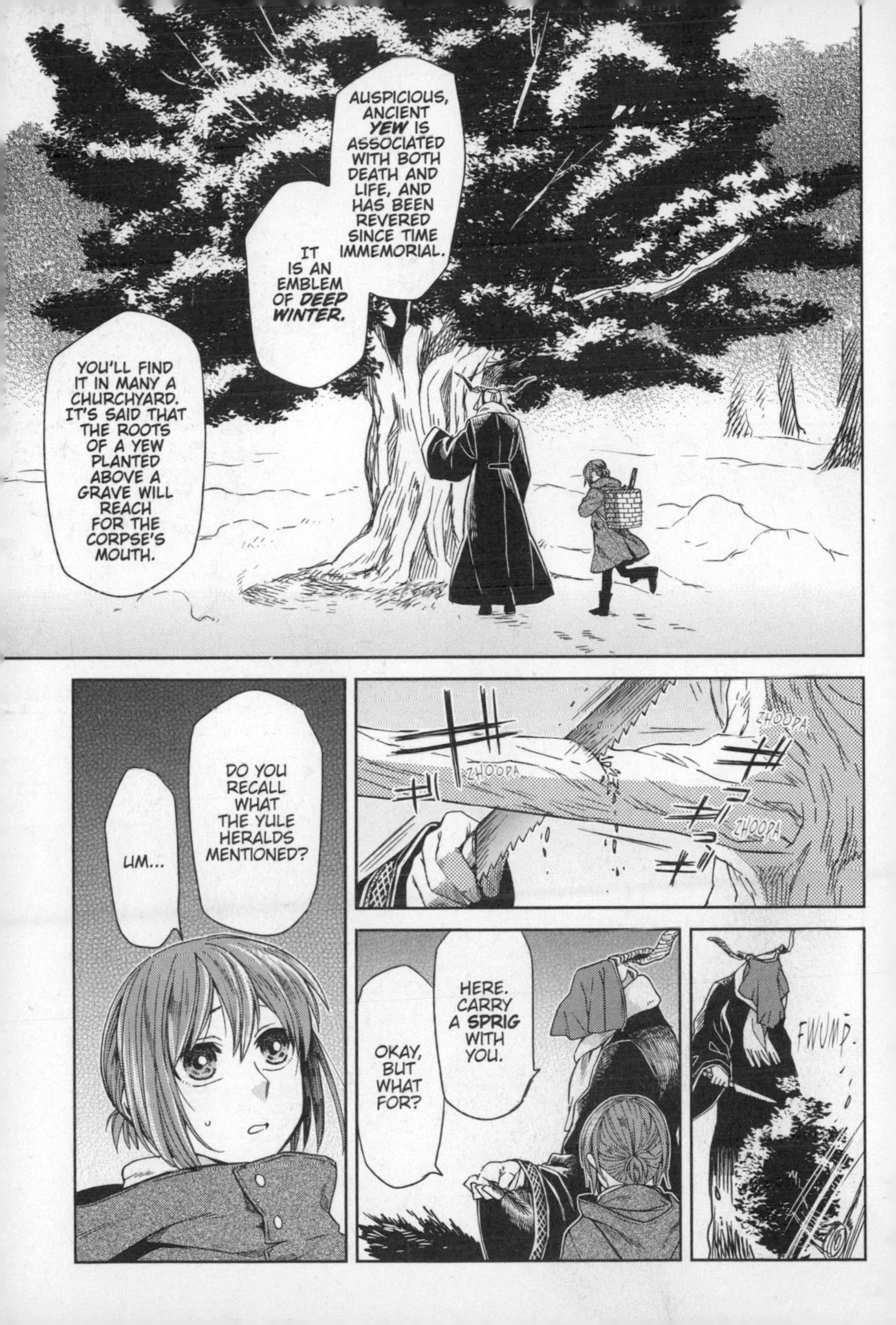
AUSPICIOUS, ANCIENT **YEW** IS ASSOCIATED WITH BOTH DEATH AND LIFE, AND HAS BEEN REVERED SINCE TIME IMMEMORIAL.
IT IS AN EMBLEM OF **DEEP WINTER.**
YOU'LL FIND IT IN MANY A CHURCHYARD. IT'S SAID THAT THE ROOTS OF A YEW PLANTED ABOVE A GRAVE WILL REACH FOR THE CORPSE'S MOUTH.
ZHOOPA
ZHOOPA
ZHOOPA
FWUMP
HERE. CARRY A **SPRIG** WITH YOU.
OKAY, BUT WHAT FOR?
DO YOU RECALL WHAT THE YULE HERALDS MENTIONED?
UM...

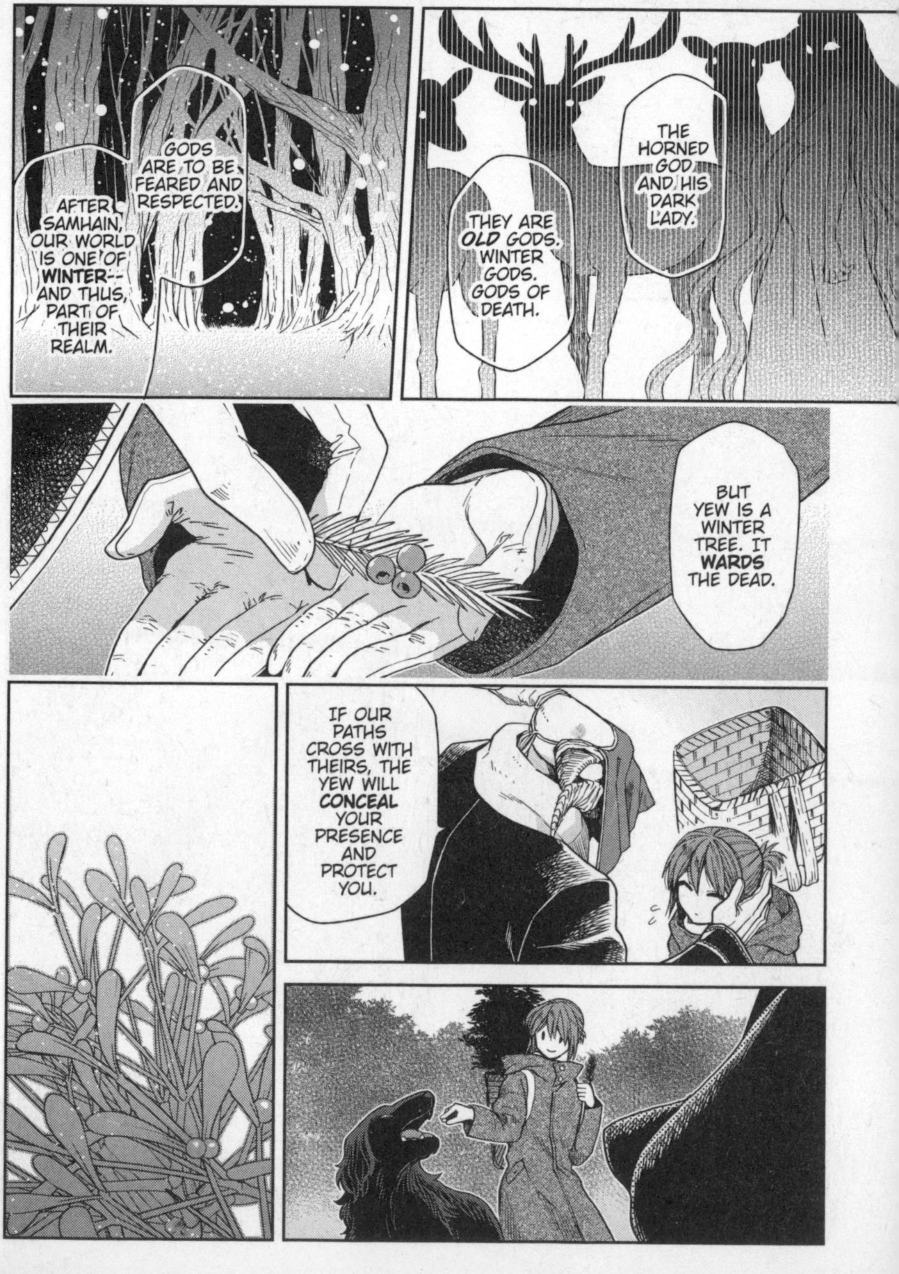
THE HORNED GOD AND HIS DARK LADY.
THEY ARE OLD GODS. WINTER GODS. GODS OF DEATH.
GODS ARE TO BE FEARED AND RESPECTED.
AFTER SAMHAIN, OUR WORLD IS ONE OF WINTER-- AND THUS, PART OF THEIR REALM.
BUT YEW IS A WINTER TREE. IT WARDS THE DEAD.
IF OUR PATHS CROSS WITH THEIRS, THE YEW WILL CONCEAL YOUR PRESENCE AND PROTECT YOU.

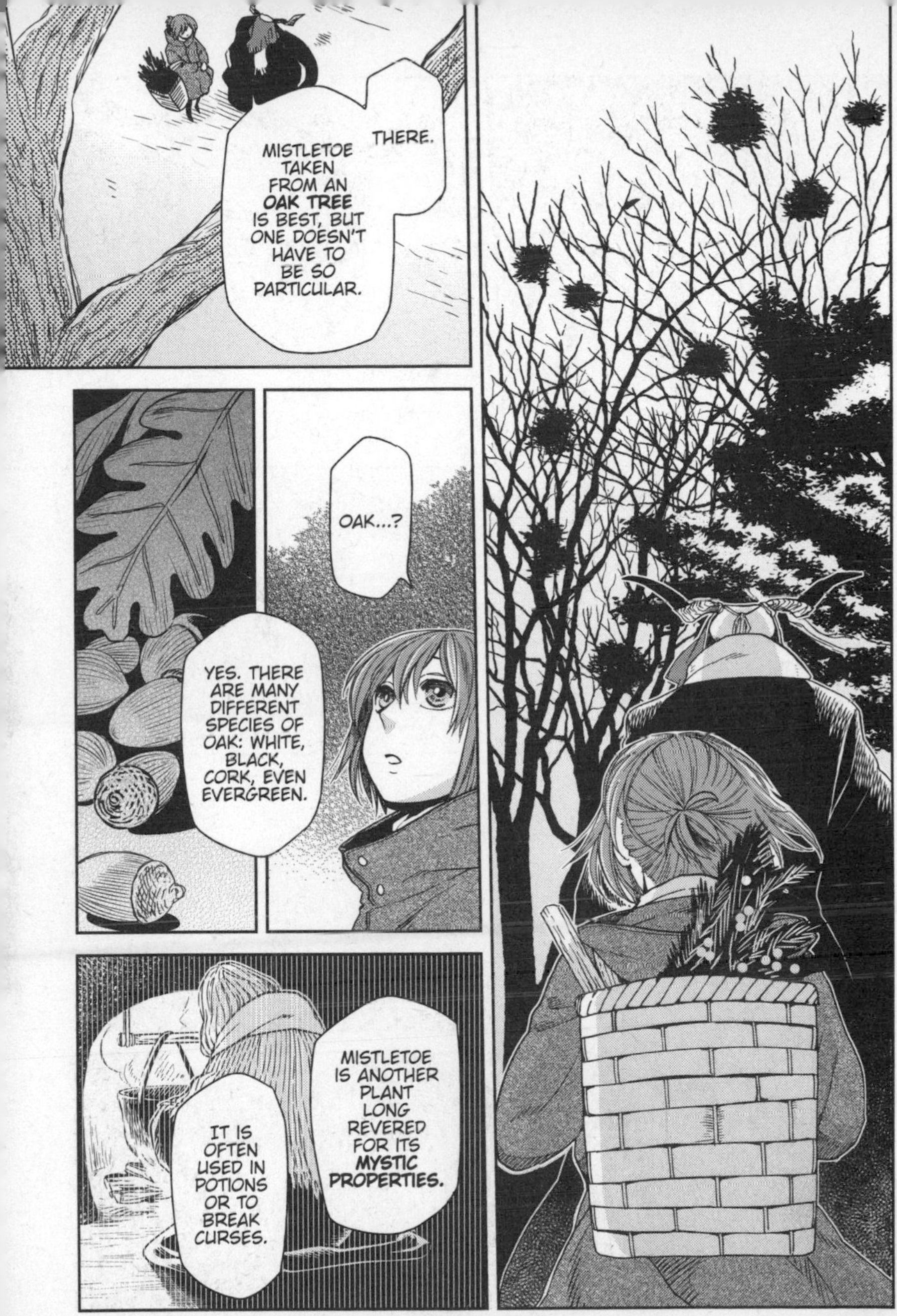
THERE.
MISTLETOE TAKEN FROM AN **OAK TREE** IS BEST, BUT ONE DOESN'T HAVE TO BE SO PARTICULAR.
OAK...?
YES. THERE ARE MANY DIFFERENT SPECIES OF OAK: WHITE, BLACK, CORK, EVEN EVERGREEN.
MISTLETOE IS ANOTHER PLANT LONG REVERED FOR ITS **MYSTIC PROPERTIES.**
IT IS OFTEN USED IN POTIONS OR TO BREAK CURSES.

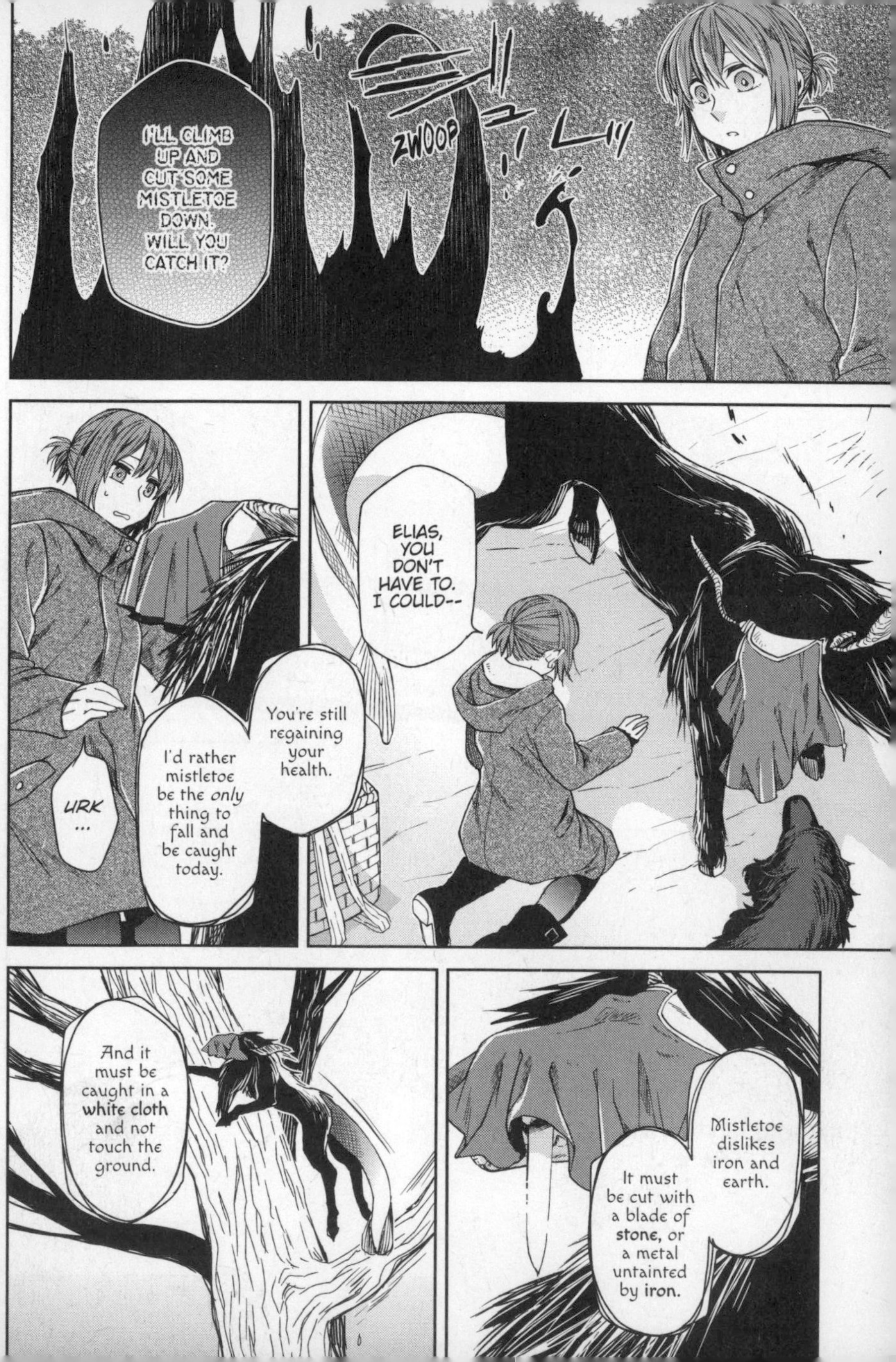
I'LL CLIMB UP AND CUT SOME MISTLETOE DOWN. WILL YOU CATCH IT?
ZWOOP
ELIAS, YOU DON'T HAVE TO. I COULD--
You're still regaining your health.
I'd rather mistletoe be the *only* thing to fall and be caught today.
URK ...
Mistletoe dislikes iron and earth.
It must be cut with a blade of **stone**, or a metal untainted by **iron**.
And it must be caught in a **white cloth** and not touch the ground.

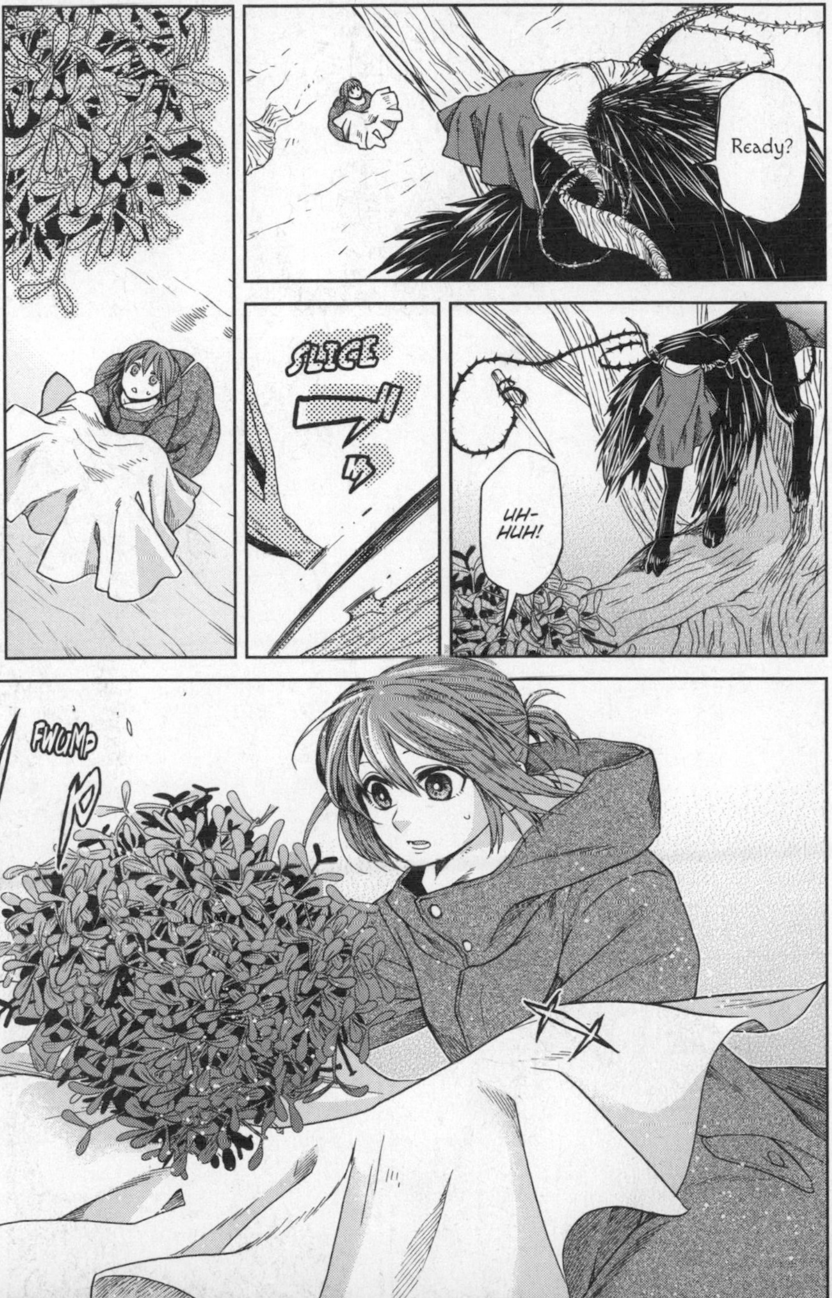
Ready?
UH-HUH!
SLICE
FWUMP

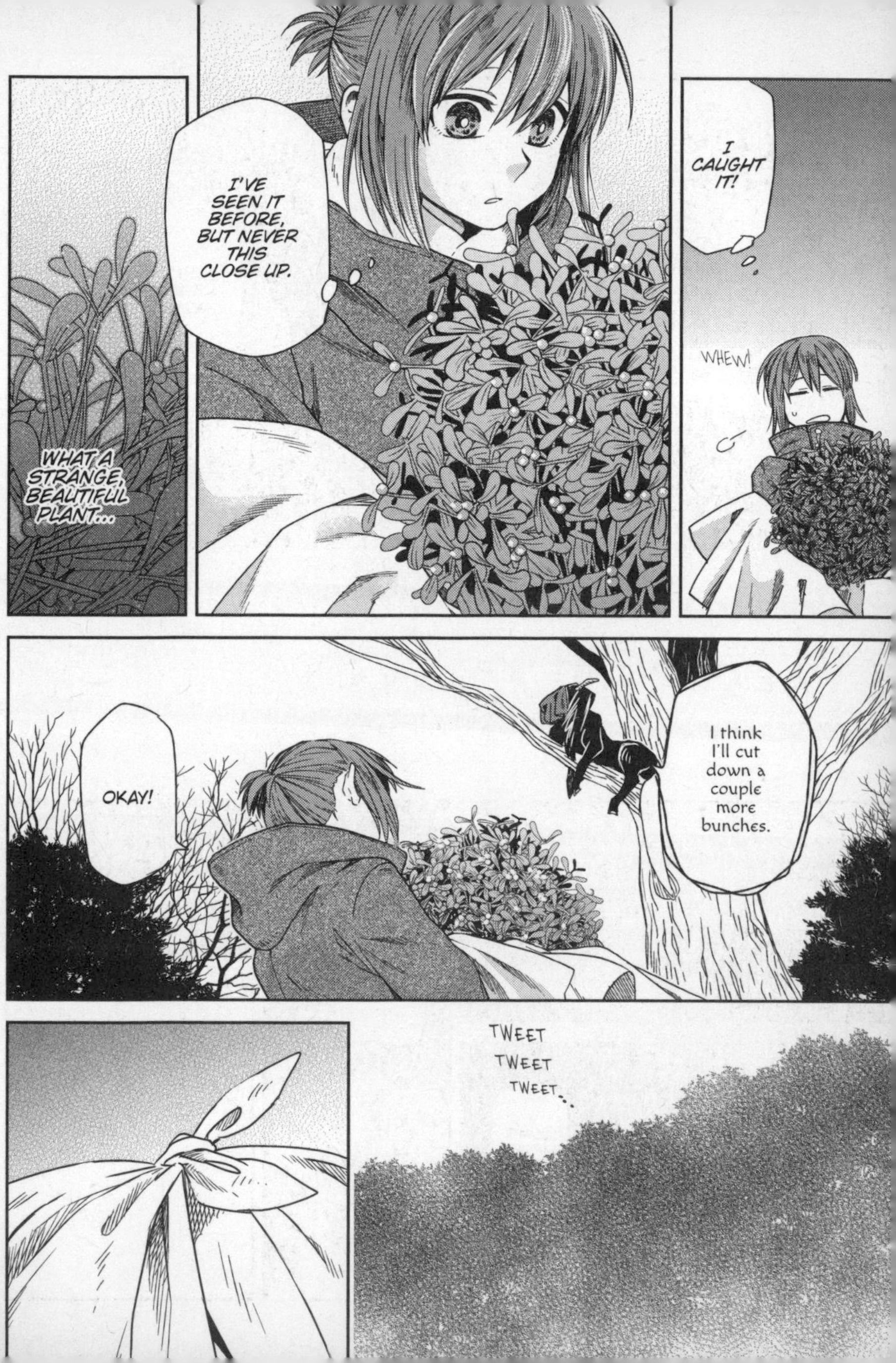
I CAUGHT IT!
WHEW!
I'VE SEEN IT BEFORE, BUT NEVER THIS CLOSE UP.
WHAT A STRANGE, BEAUTIFUL PLANT...
I think I'll cut down a couple more bunches.
OKAY!
TWEET TWEET TWEET...

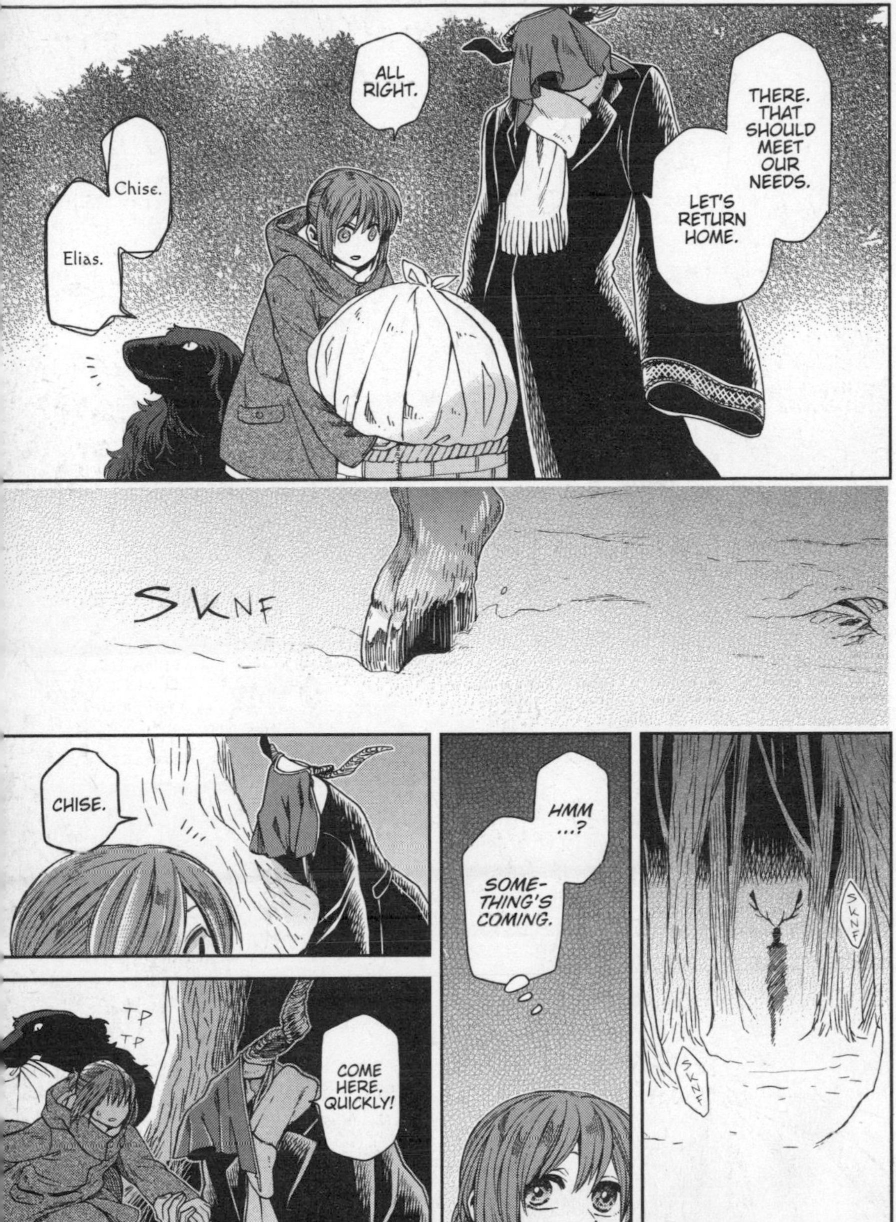
THERE. THAT SHOULD MEET OUR NEEDS.
LET'S RETURN HOME.
ALL RIGHT.
Chise.
Elias.
SKNF
SKNF
SKNF
HMM ...?
SOMETHING'S COMING.
CHISE.
COME HERE. QUICKLY!
TP TP

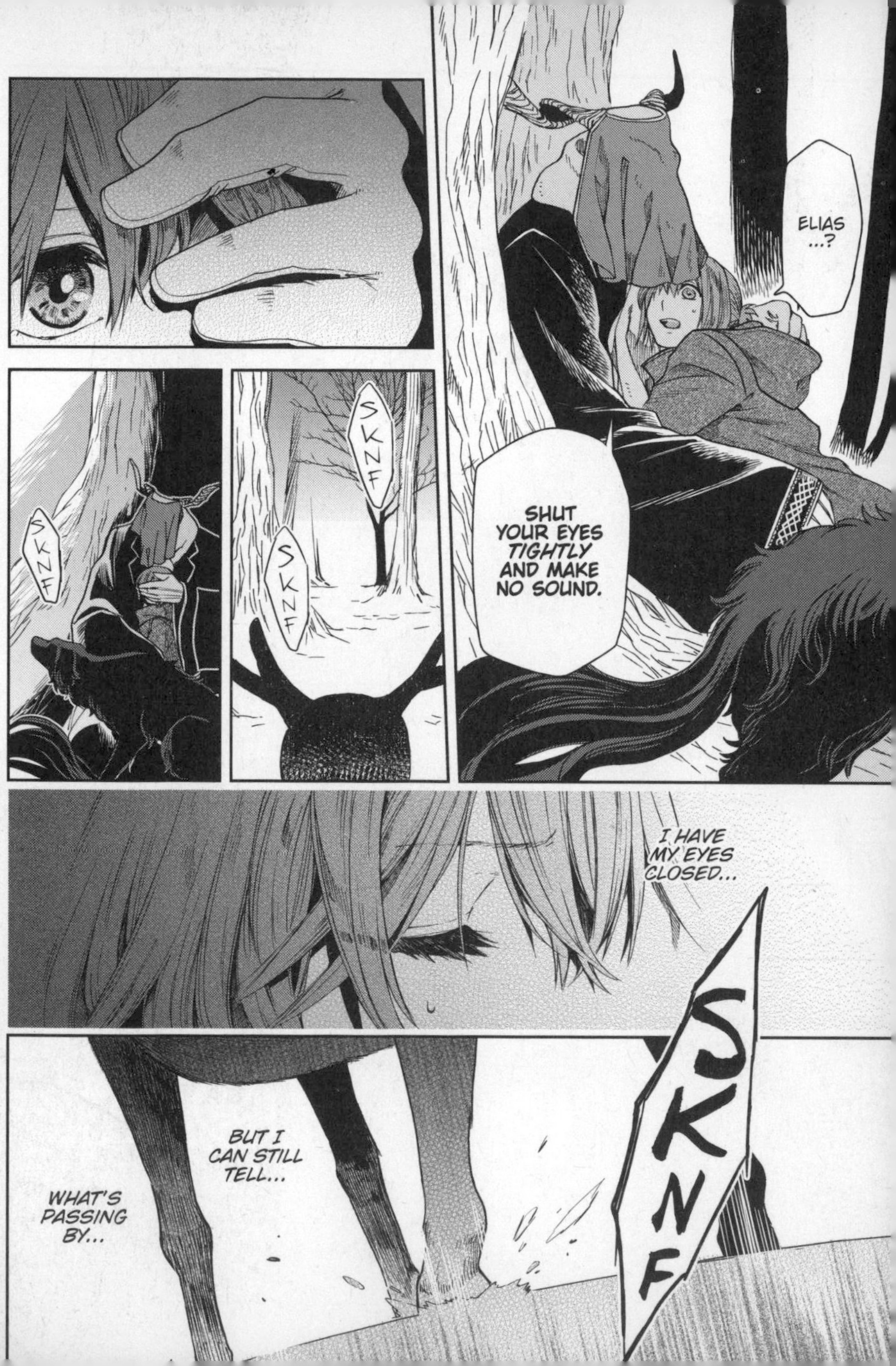
ELIAS ...?
SHUT YOUR EYES TIGHTLY AND MAKE NO SOUND.
SKNF
SKNF
SKNF
I HAVE MY EYES CLOSED...
SKNF
BUT I CAN STILL TELL...
WHAT'S PASSING BY...

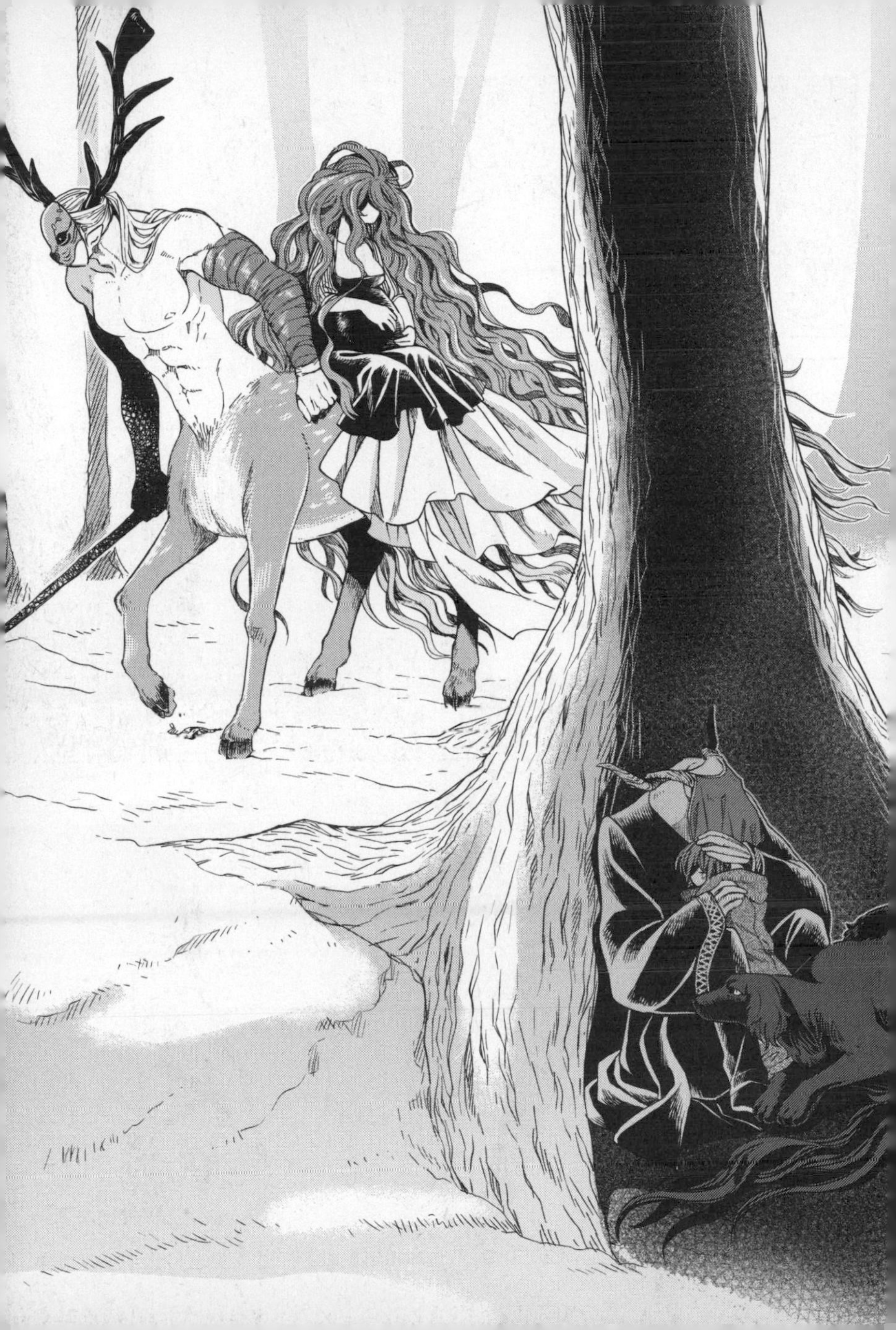

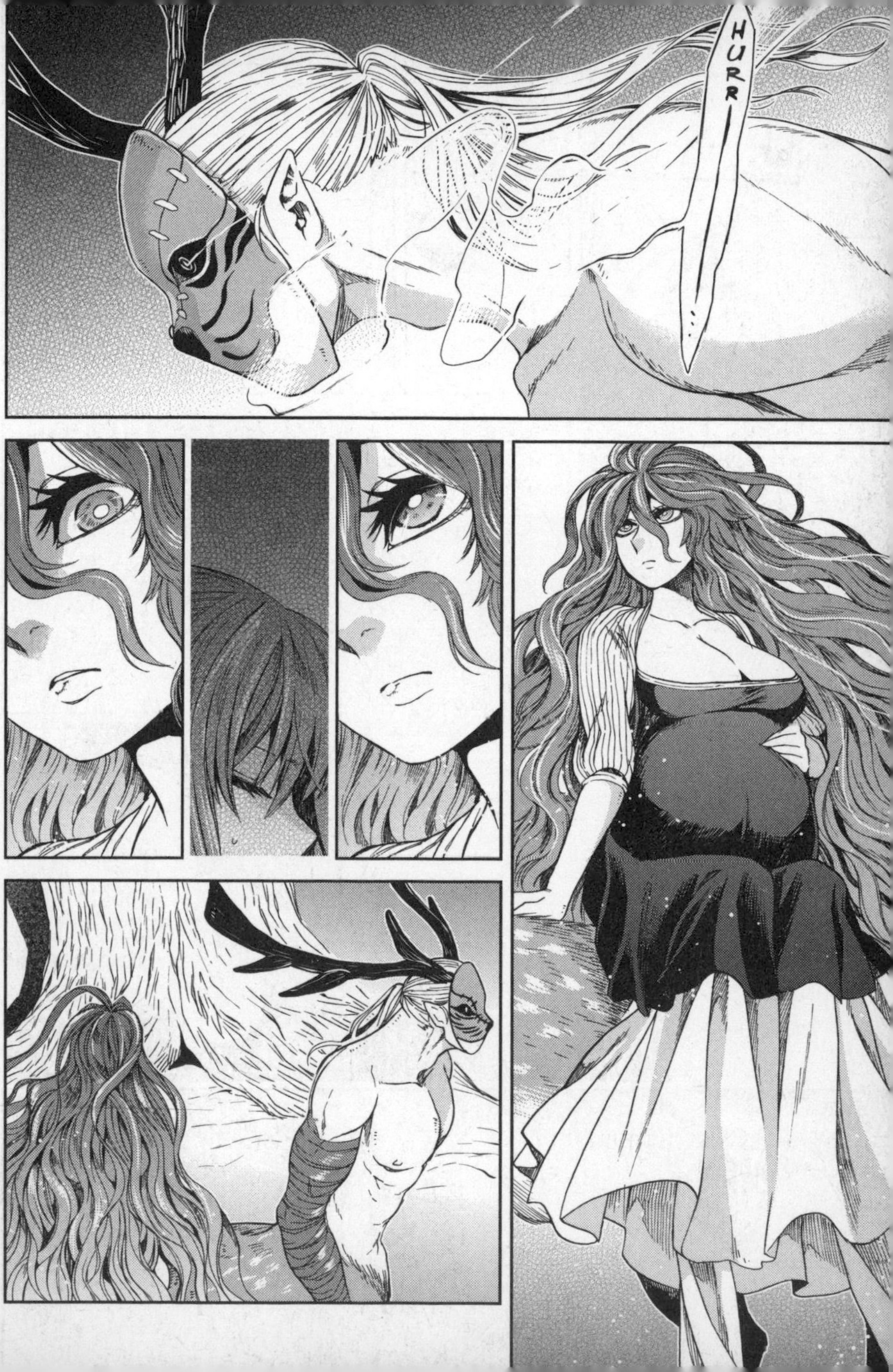
HURR

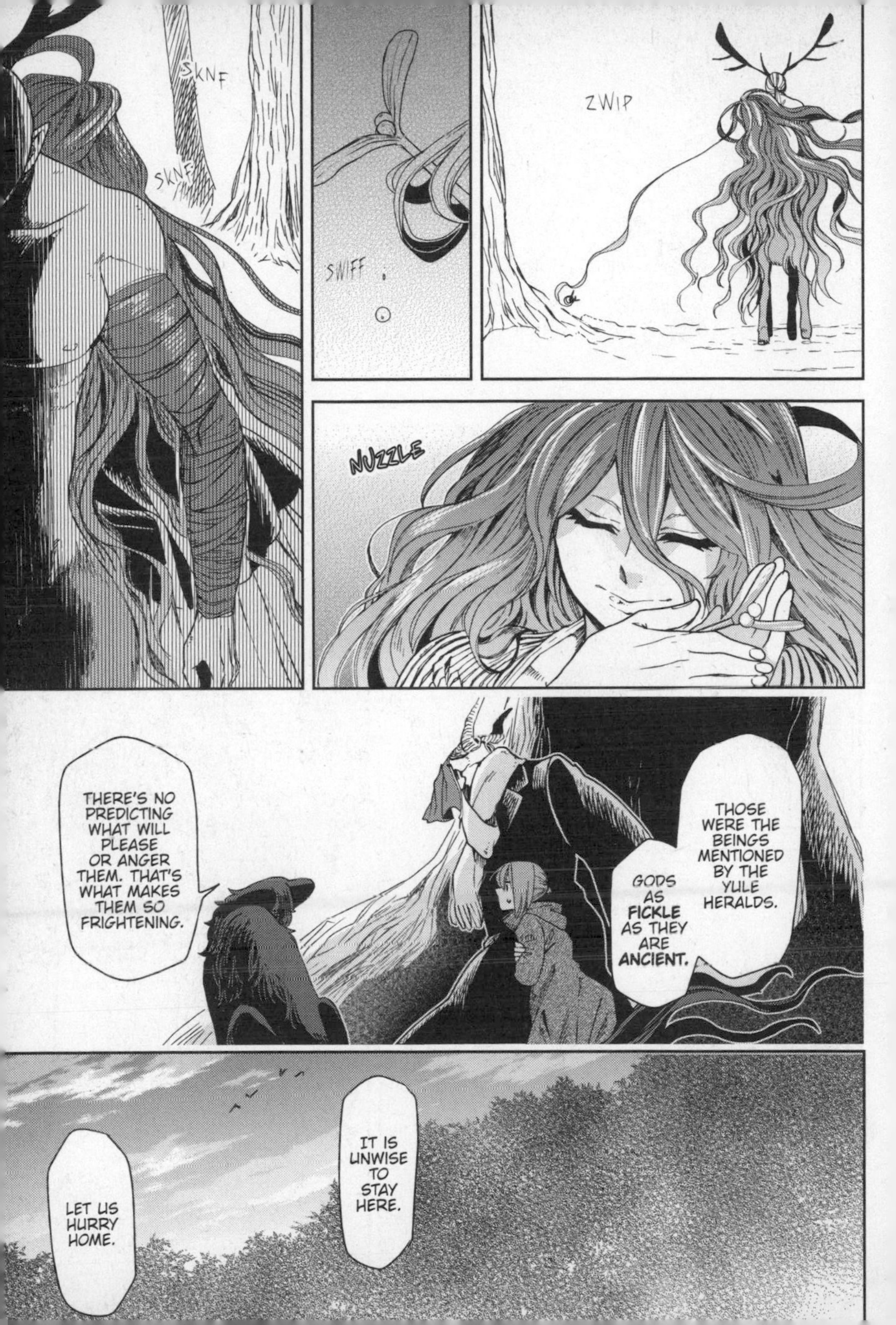
ZWIP
SWIFF
NUZZLE
SKNF
SKNF
THOSE WERE THE BEINGS MENTIONED BY THE YULE HERALDS.
GODS AS **FICKLE** AS THEY ARE **ANCIENT.**
THERE'S NO PREDICTING WHAT WILL PLEASE OR ANGER THEM. THAT'S WHAT MAKES THEM SO FRIGHTENING.
IT IS UNWISE TO STAY HERE.
LET US HURRY HOME.

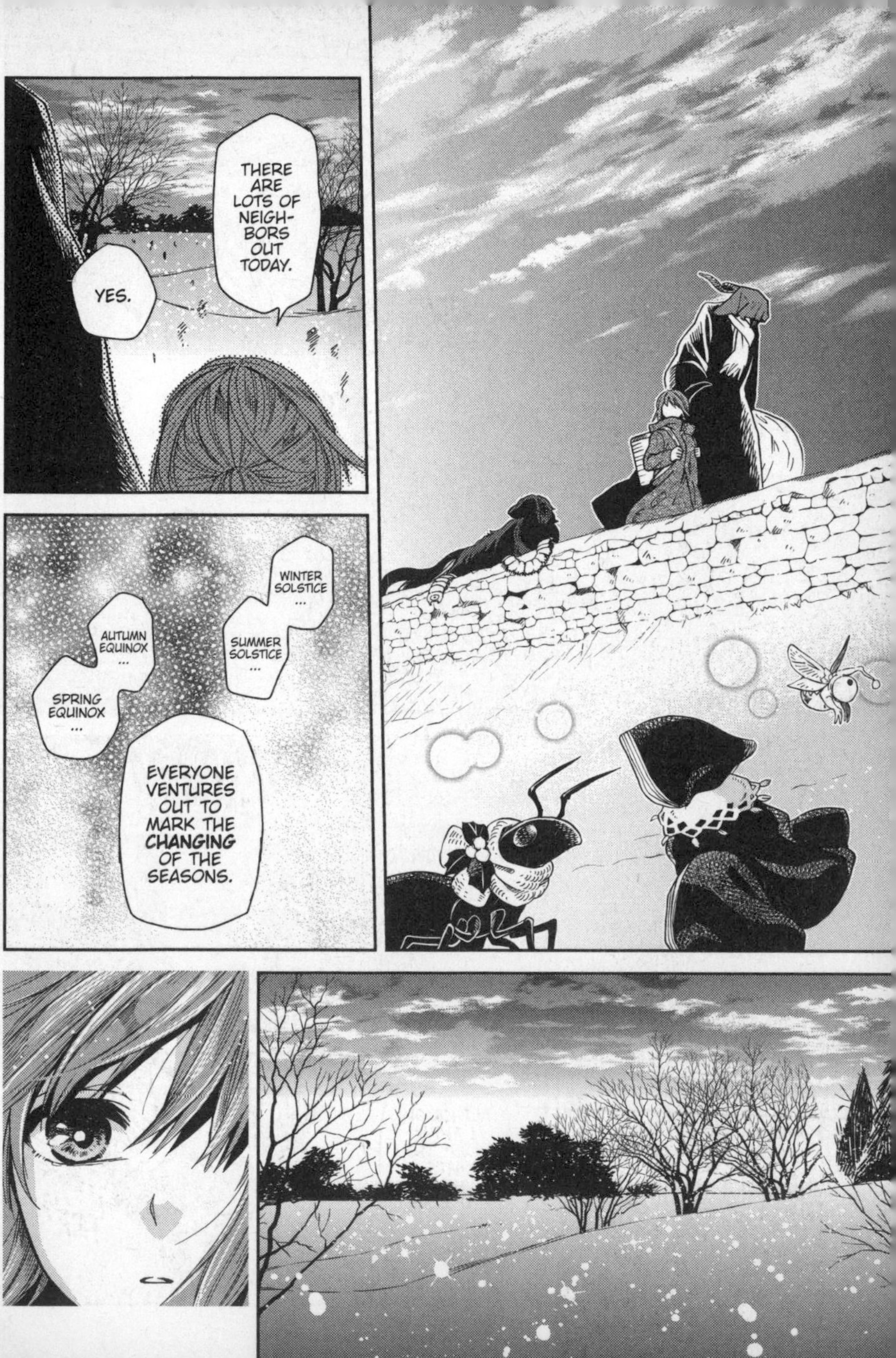
THERE ARE LOTS OF NEIGHBORS OUT TODAY.
YES.
WINTER SOLSTICE ...
SUMMER SOLSTICE ...
AUTUMN EQUINOX ...
SPRING EQUINOX ...
EVERYONE VENTURES OUT TO MARK THE **CHANGING** OF THE SEASONS.

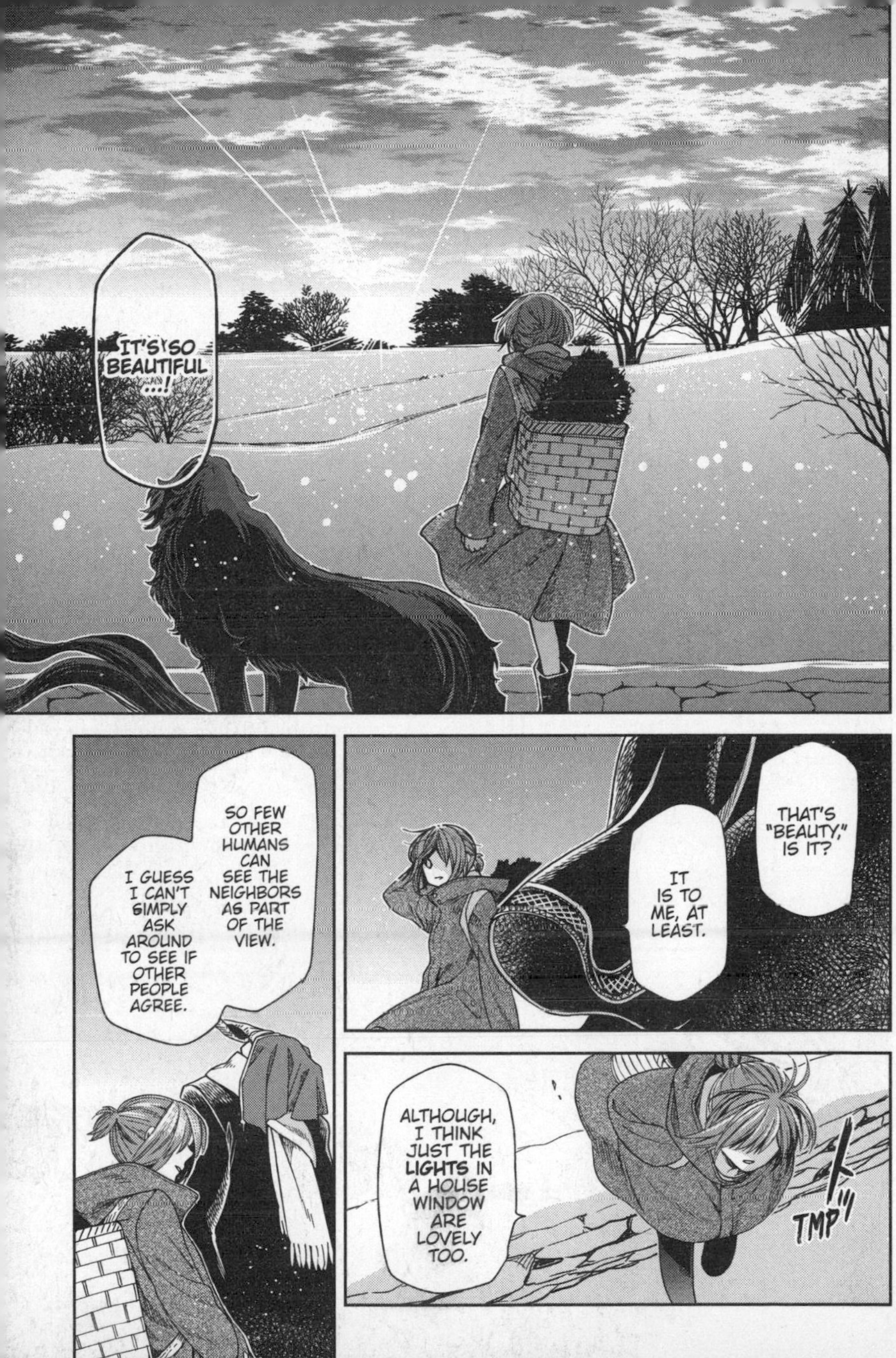
IT'S SO BEAUTIFUL ...!
THAT'S "BEAUTY," IS IT?
IT IS TO ME, AT LEAST.
ALTHOUGH, I THINK JUST THE LIGHTS IN A HOUSE WINDOW ARE LOVELY TOO.
TMP
SO FEW OTHER HUMANS CAN SEE THE NEIGHBORS AS PART OF THE VIEW.
I GUESS I CAN'T SIMPLY ASK AROUND TO SEE IF OTHER PEOPLE AGREE.

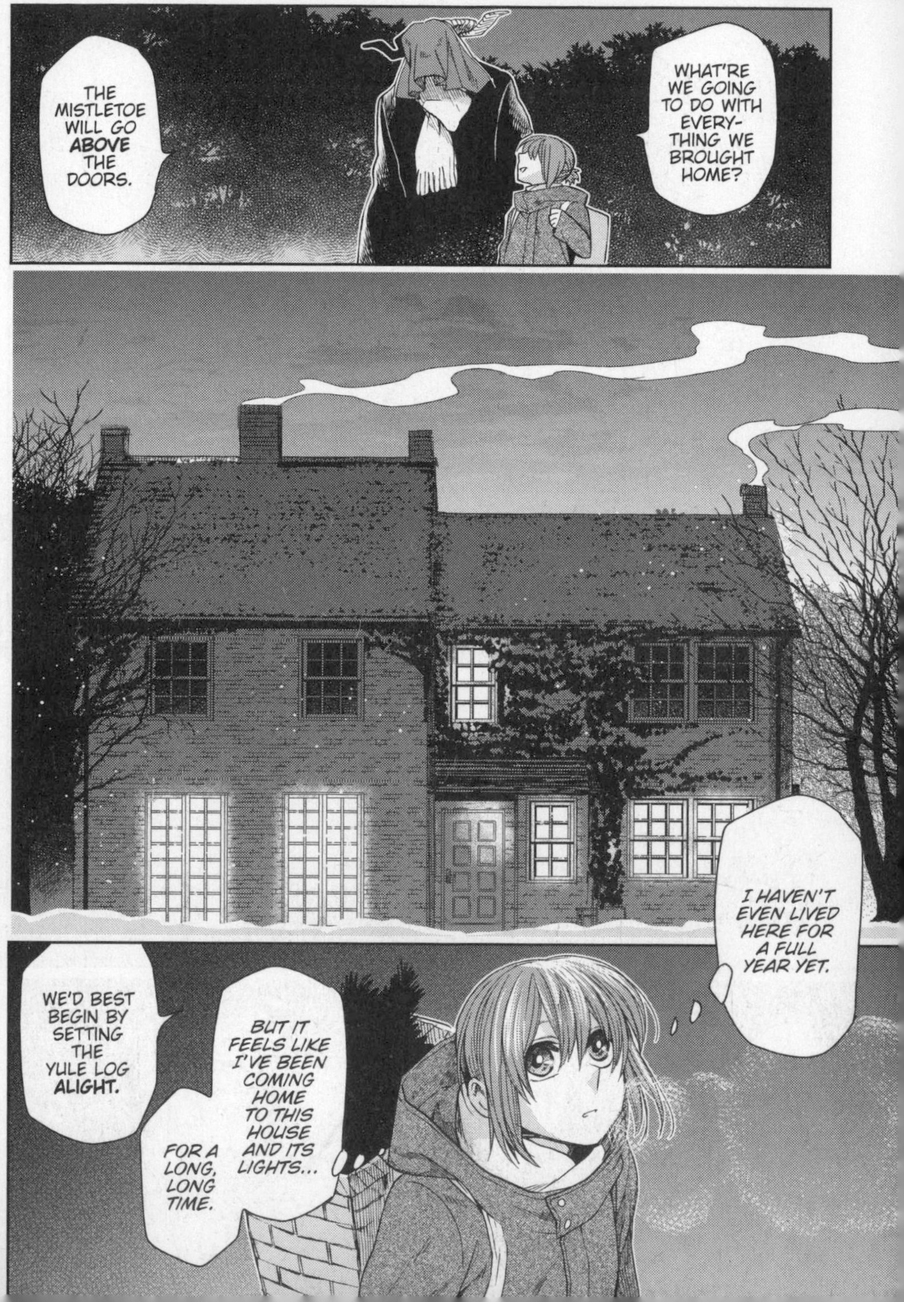
WHAT'RE WE GOING TO DO WITH EVERY-THING WE BROUGHT HOME?
THE MISTLETOE WILL GO **ABOVE** THE DOORS.
I HAVEN'T EVEN LIVED HERE FOR A FULL YEAR YET.
BUT IT FEELS LIKE I'VE BEEN COMING HOME TO THIS HOUSE AND ITS LIGHTS...
FOR A LONG, LONG TIME.
WE'D BEST BEGIN BY SETTING THE YULE LOG **ALIGHT**.

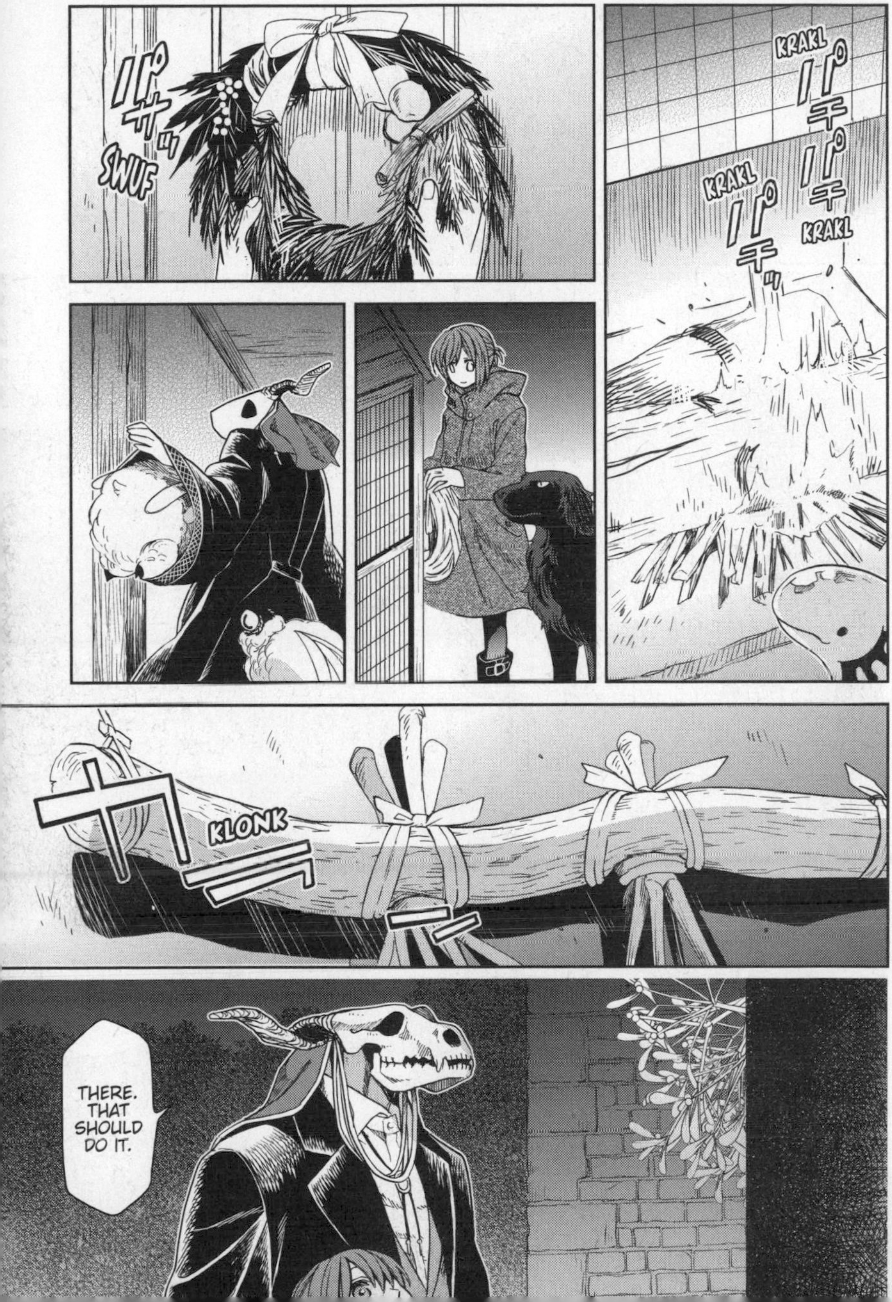
KRAKL
パチ
パチ
KRAKL
KRAKL
パチッ
パサッ
SWUF
ドン
KLONK
THERE. THAT SHOULD DO IT.

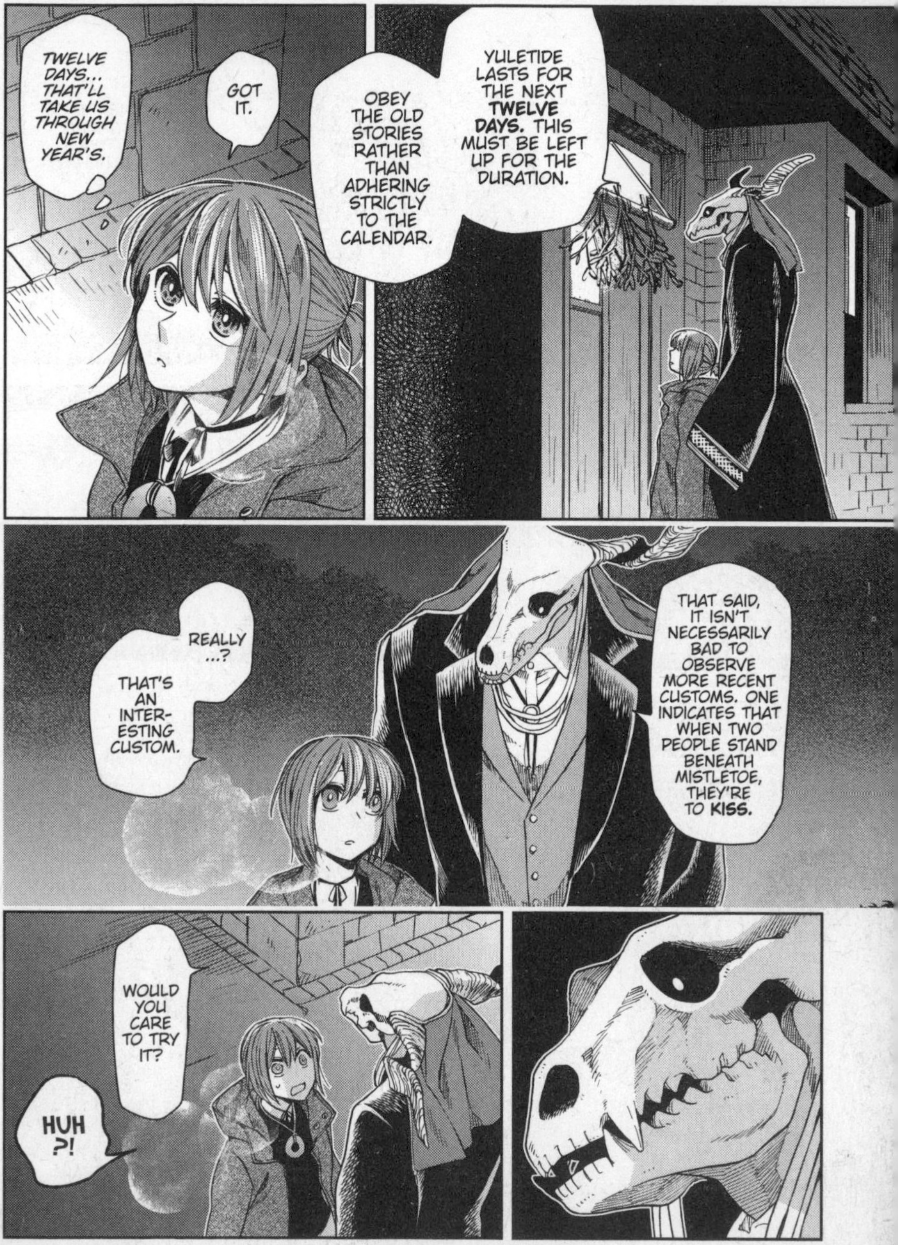
YULETIDE LASTS FOR THE NEXT TWELVE DAYS. THIS MUST BE LEFT UP FOR THE DURATION.
OBEY THE OLD STORIES RATHER THAN ADHERING STRICTLY TO THE CALENDAR.
GOT IT.
TWELVE DAYS... THAT'LL TAKE US THROUGH NEW YEAR'S.
THAT SAID, IT ISN'T NECESSARILY BAD TO OBSERVE MORE RECENT CUSTOMS. ONE INDICATES THAT WHEN TWO PEOPLE STAND BENEATH MISTLETOE, THEY'RE TO KISS.
REALLY ...?
THAT'S AN INTER-ESTING CUSTOM.
WOULD YOU CARE TO TRY IT?
HUH ?!

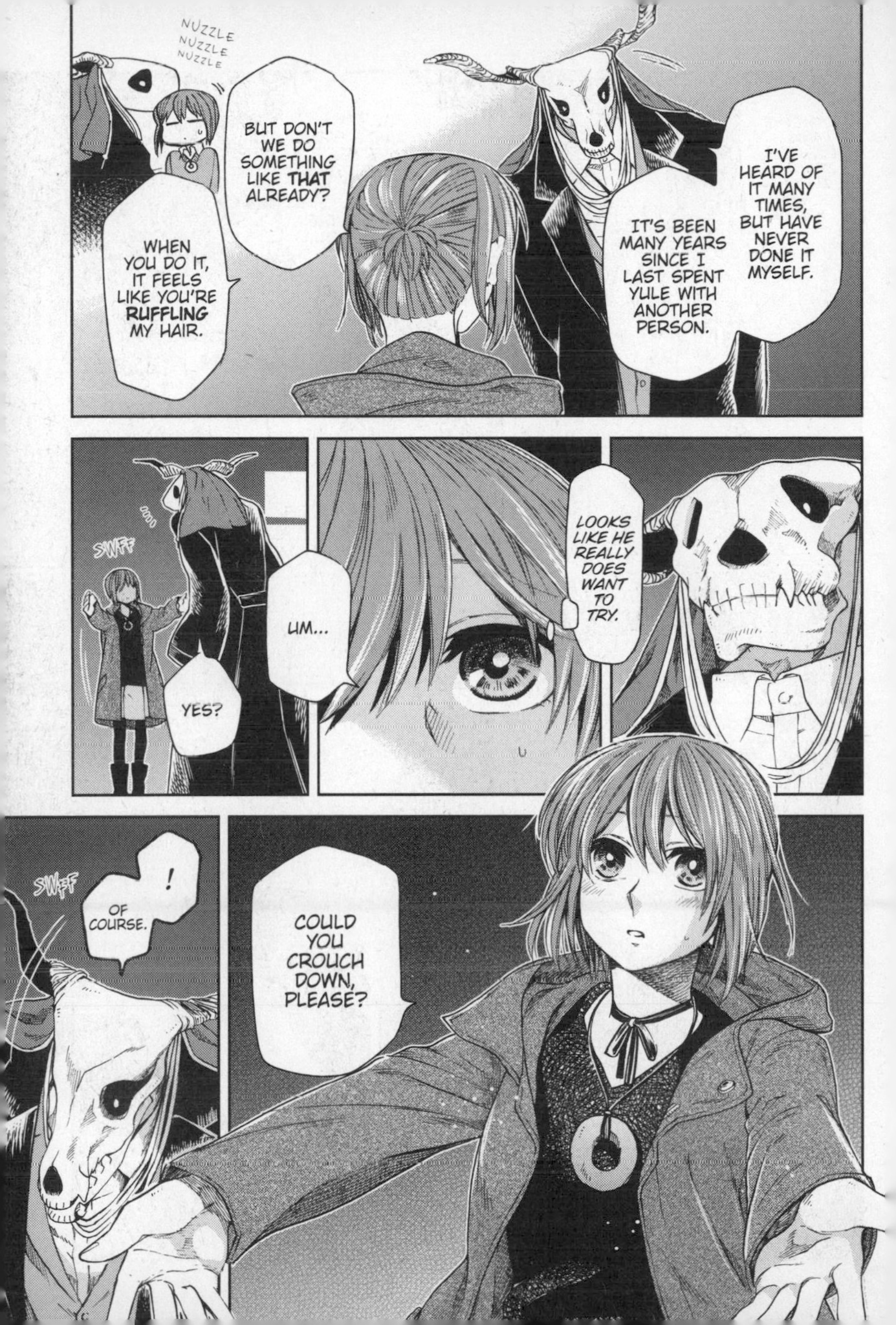
I'VE HEARD OF IT MANY TIMES, BUT HAVE NEVER DONE IT MYSELF.
IT'S BEEN MANY YEARS SINCE I LAST SPENT YULE WITH ANOTHER PERSON.
BUT DON'T WE DO SOMETHING LIKE **THAT** ALREADY?
NUZZLE NUZZLE NUZZLE
WHEN YOU DO IT, IT FEELS LIKE YOU'RE **RUFFLING** MY HAIR.
LOOKS LIKE HE REALLY DOES WANT TO TRY.
UM...
SWAFF
YES?
COULD YOU CROUCH DOWN, PLEASE?
!
OF COURSE.
SWAFF

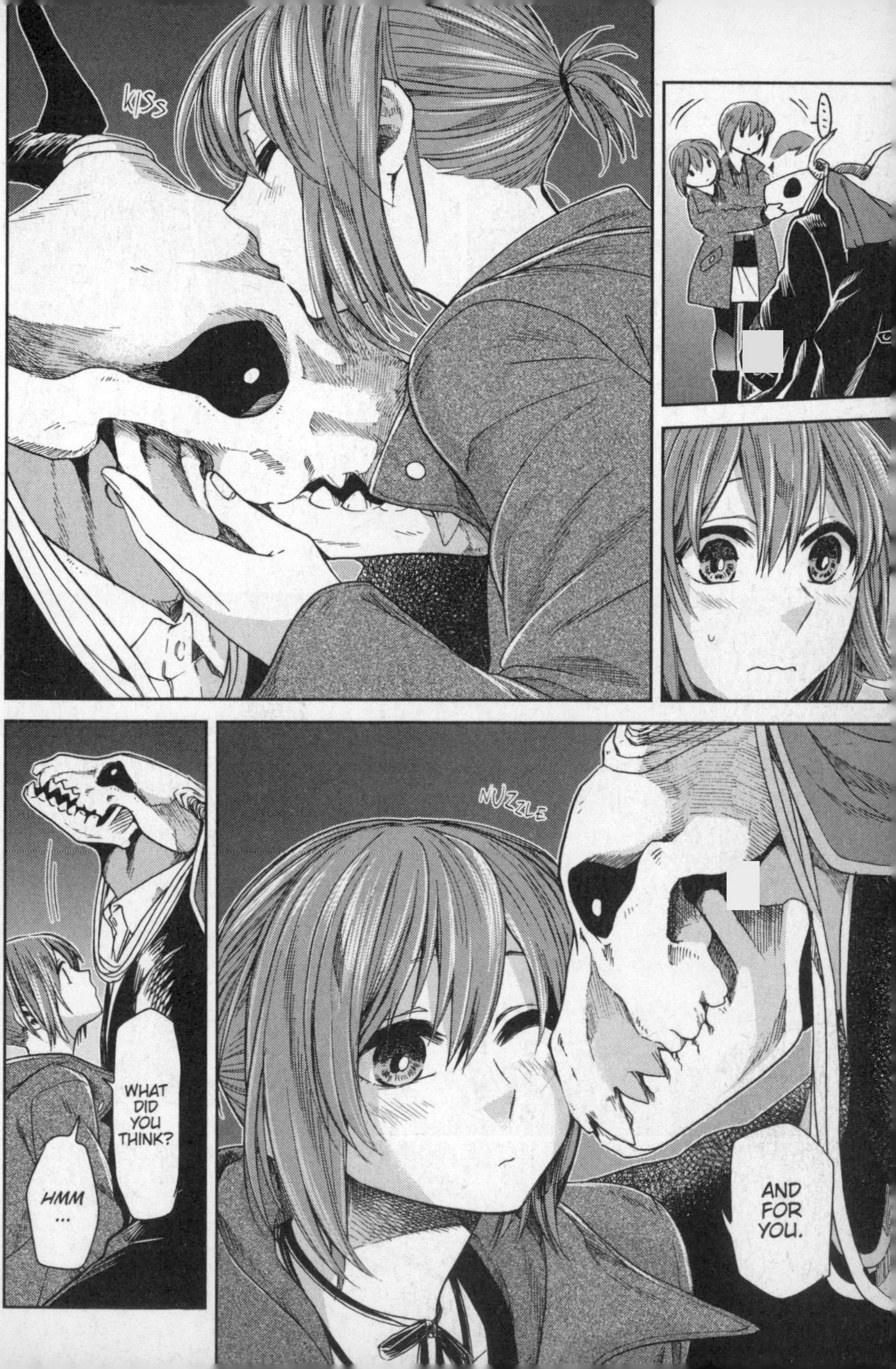
...
KISS
NUZZLE
AND FOR YOU.
WHAT DID YOU THINK?
HMM...

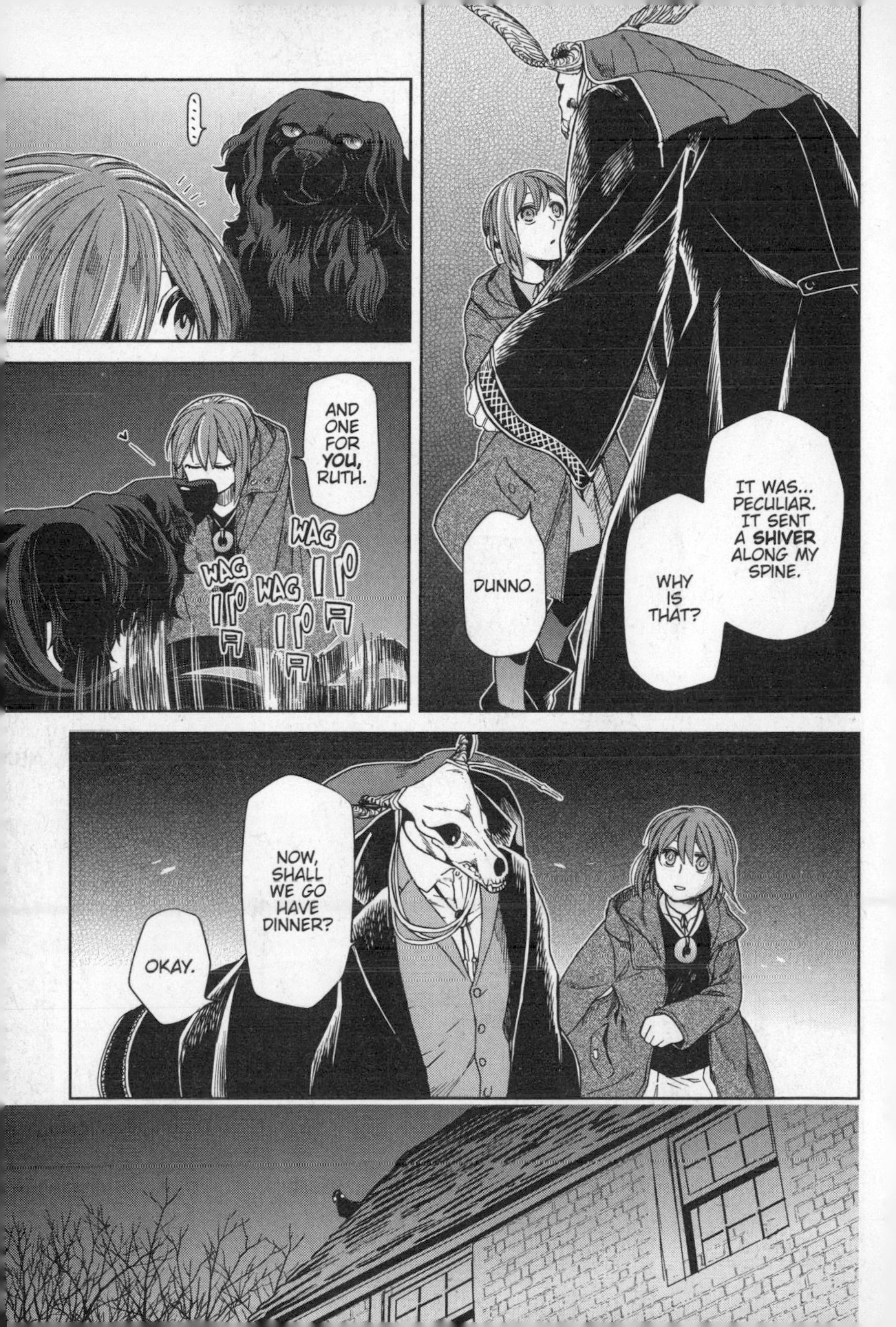
IT WAS... PECULIAR. IT SENT A SHIVER ALONG MY SPINE.
WHY IS THAT?
DUNNO.
...!
AND ONE FOR YOU, RUTH.
WAG
WAG
WAG
NOW, SHALL WE GO HAVE DINNER?
OKAY.

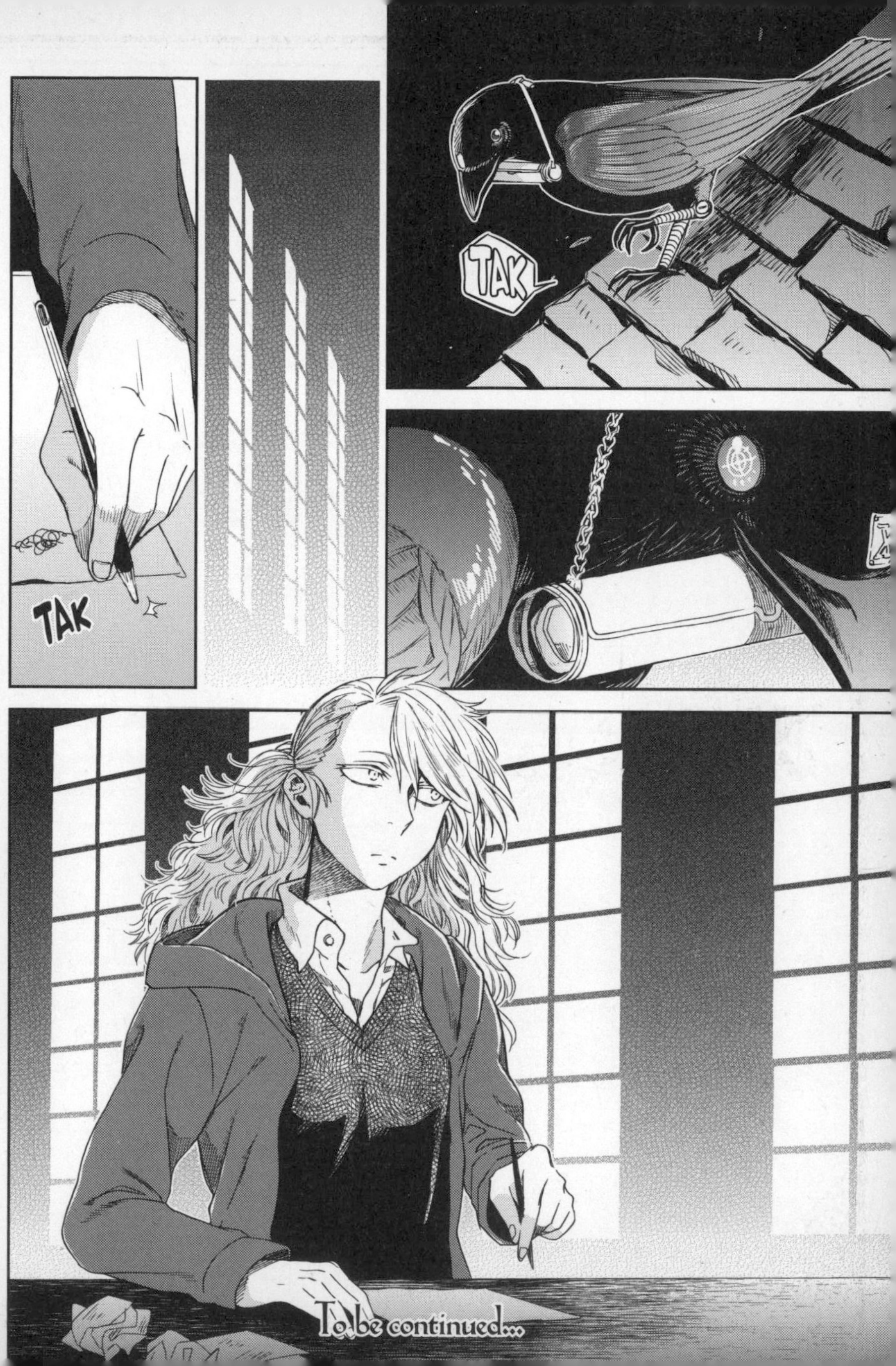
TAK
TAK
To be continued...

The Ancient Magus' Bride

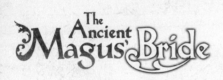

The Ancient Magus' Bride

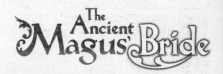

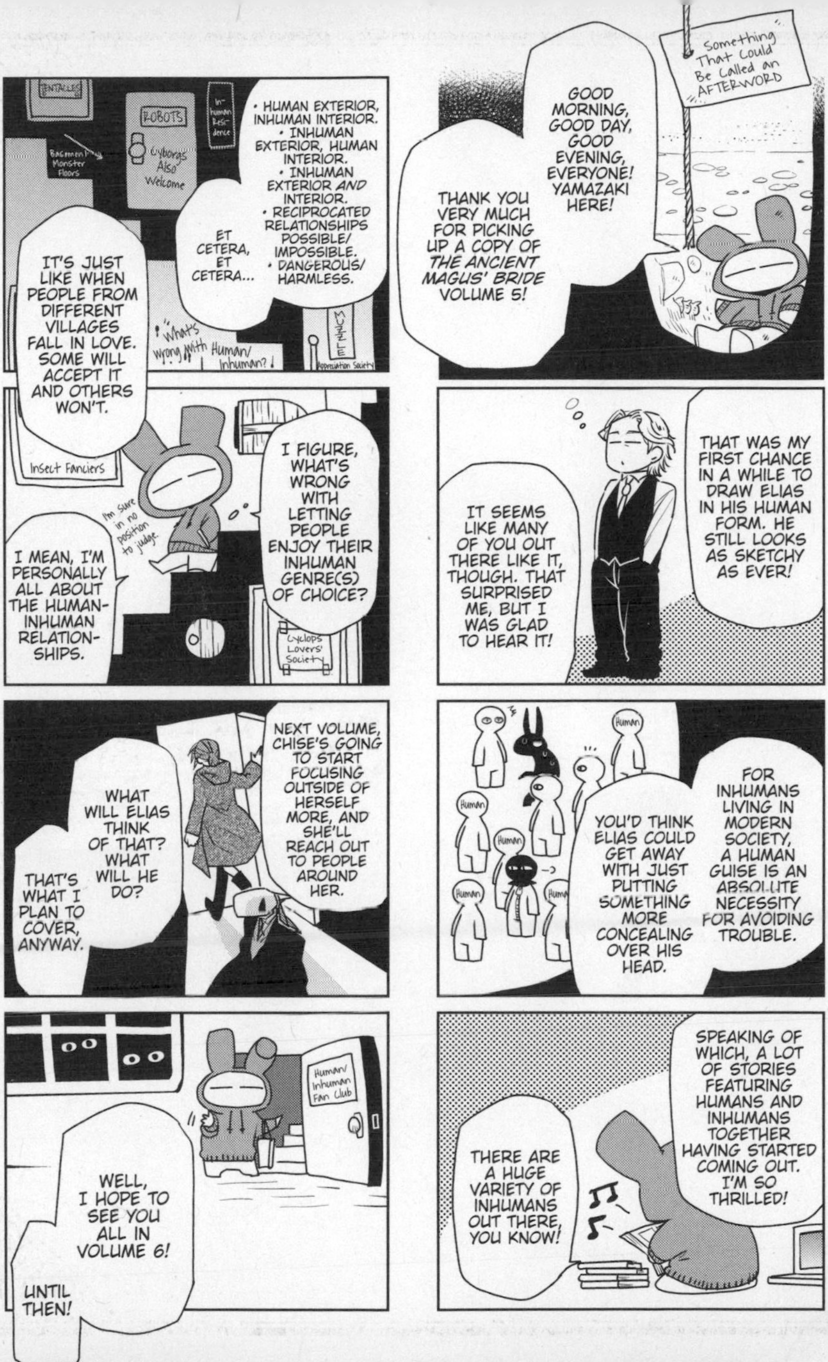
Something That Could Be Called an AFTERWORD
GOOD MORNING, GOOD DAY, GOOD EVENING, EVERYONE! YAMAZAKI HERE!
THANK YOU VERY MUCH FOR PICKING UP A COPY OF *THE ANCIENT MAGUS' BRIDE* VOLUME 5!
• HUMAN EXTERIOR, INHUMAN INTERIOR. • INHUMAN EXTERIOR, HUMAN INTERIOR. • INHUMAN EXTERIOR *AND* INTERIOR. • RECIPROCATED RELATIONSHIPS POSSIBLE/ IMPOSSIBLE. • DANGEROUS/ HARMLESS.
ET CETERA, ET CETERA...
IT'S JUST LIKE WHEN PEOPLE FROM DIFFERENT VILLAGES FALL IN LOVE. SOME WILL ACCEPT IT AND OTHERS WON'T.
TENTACLES
ROBOTS
Cyborgs Also Welcome
In-human Resi-dence
Basement Monster Floors
"What's wrong with Human/ Inhuman?"
MUZZLE Appreciation Society
THAT WAS MY FIRST CHANCE IN A WHILE TO DRAW ELIAS IN HIS HUMAN FORM. HE STILL LOOKS AS SKETCHY AS EVER!
IT SEEMS LIKE MANY OF YOU OUT THERE LIKE IT, THOUGH. THAT SURPRISED ME, BUT I WAS GLAD TO HEAR IT!
I FIGURE, WHAT'S WRONG WITH LETTING PEOPLE ENJOY THEIR INHUMAN GENRE(S) OF CHOICE?
I MEAN, I'M PERSONALLY ALL ABOUT THE HUMAN-INHUMAN RELATIONSHIPS.
I'm sure in no position to judge.
Insect Fanciers
Cyclops Lovers' Society
FOR INHUMANS LIVING IN MODERN SOCIETY, A HUMAN GUISE IS AN ABSOLUTE NECESSITY FOR AVOIDING TROUBLE.
YOU'D THINK ELIAS COULD GET AWAY WITH JUST PUTTING SOMETHING MORE CONCEALING OVER HIS HEAD.
Human
Human
Human
Human
NEXT VOLUME, CHISE'S GOING TO START FOCUSING OUTSIDE OF HERSELF MORE, AND SHE'LL REACH OUT TO PEOPLE AROUND HER.
WHAT WILL ELIAS THINK OF THAT? WHAT WILL HE DO?
THAT'S WHAT I PLAN TO COVER, ANYWAY.
SPEAKING OF WHICH, A LOT OF STORIES FEATURING HUMANS AND INHUMANS TOGETHER HAVING STARTED COMING OUT. I'M SO THRILLED!
THERE ARE A HUGE VARIETY OF INHUMANS OUT THERE, YOU KNOW!
Human/ Inhuman Fan Club
WELL, I HOPE TO SEE YOU ALL IN VOLUME 6!
UNTIL THEN!

Silky's Diary

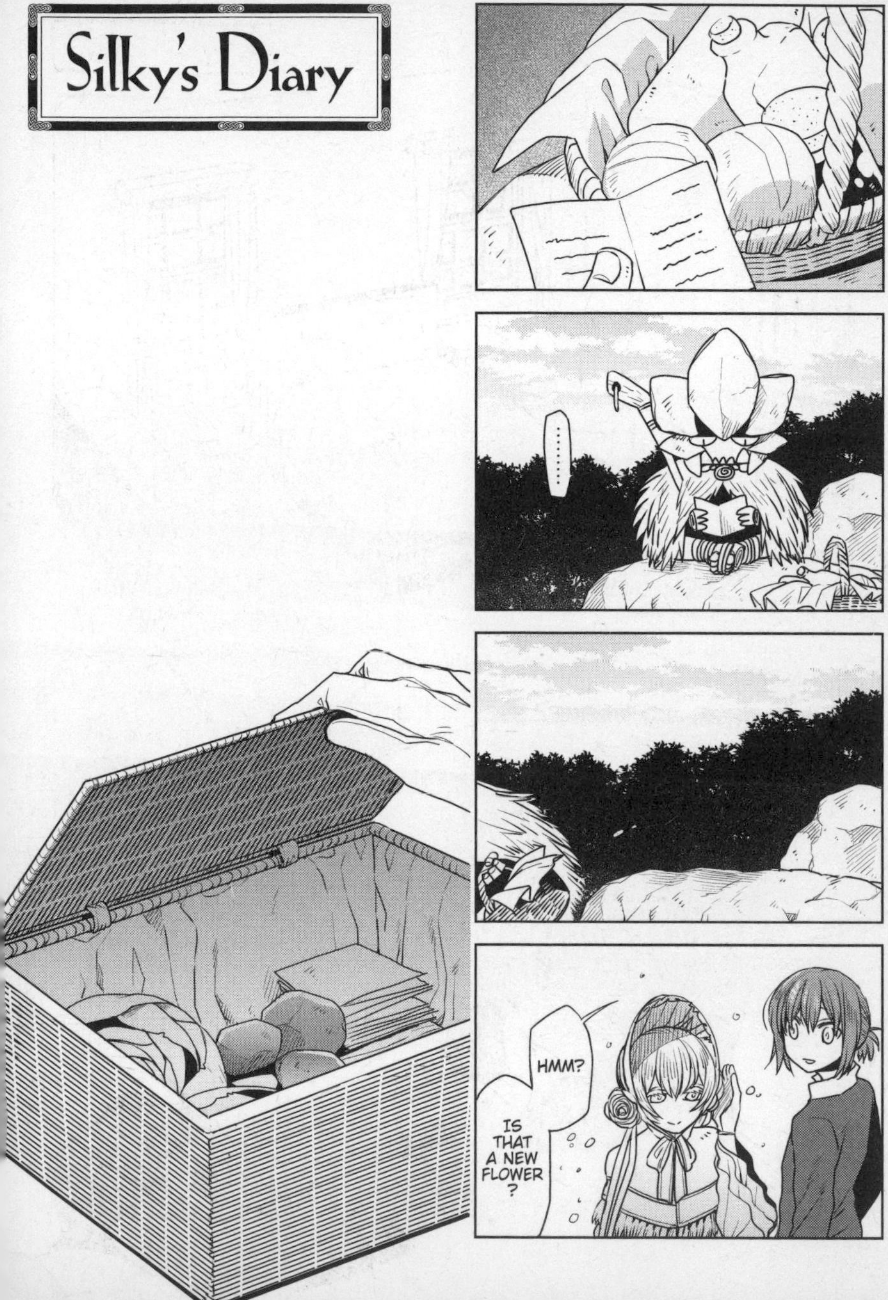

....
HMM?
IS THAT A NEW FLOWER?

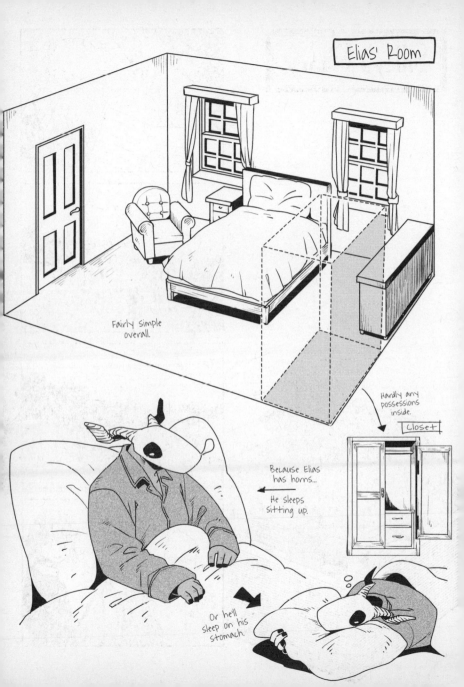

Elias' Room

Fairly simple overall.

Hardly any possessions inside.

Closet

Because Elias has horns...

He sleeps sitting up.

Or he'll sleep on his stomach.

The Ancient Magus' Bride

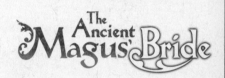

SEVEN SEAS ENTERTAINMENT

J

The Ancient Magus' Bride
VOLUME 5

story and art by KORE YAMAZAKI

TRANSLATION
Adrienne Beck

ADAPTATION
Ysabet Reinhardt MacFarlane

LETTERING AND LAYOUT
Lys Blakeslee

COVER DESIGN
Nicky Lim

PROOFREADER
Shanti Whitesides

PRODUCTION MANAGER
Lissa Pattillo

EDITOR-IN-CHIEF
Adam Arnold

PUBLISHER
Jason DeAngelis

THE ANCIENT MAGUS' BRIDE VOL. 5
© Kore Yamazaki 2016
Originally published in Japan in 2016 by MAG Garden Corporation, Tokyo.
English translation rights arranged through TOHAN CORPORATION, Tokyo.

Seven Seas books may be purchased in bulk for educational, business, or
promotional use. For information on bulk purchases, please contact Macmillan
Corporate & Premium Sales Department at 1-800-221-7945 (ext 5442)
or write specialmarkets@macmillan.com.

Seven Seas and the Seven Seas logo are trademarks of
Seven Seas Entertainment, LLC. All rights reserved.

ISBN: 978-1-626922-84-6

Printed in Canada

First Printing: July 2016

10 9 8 7 6 5 4 3 2 1

FOLLOW US ONLINE: www.gomanga.com

READING DIRECTIONS

This book reads from *right to left*, Japanese style. If
this is your first time reading manga, you start
reading from the top right panel on each page and
take it from there. If you get lost, just follow the
numbered diagram here. It may seem backwards at
first, but you'll get the hang of it! Have fun!

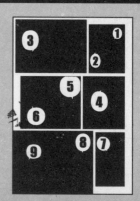